JOHN JULIUS NORWICH has kn[...]
he first visited it with his parents [...]
author of *A History of Venice*, a [...]
volumes but now available in o[...]
standard history of the Venetian Republic; and he has been
Chairman of the Venice in Peril Fund since its inception in
1970. He lectures regularly in Britain, Canada and the USA
on the art and architecture of Venice and the problems of its
preservation.

Lord Norwich has made two TV films on the protection
of Venice, and a five-part TV series, with Professor H. C.
Robbins Landon, on the history of music in Venice over the
past 500 years.

In recognition of his services to Venice he has been made
Commendatore of the Ordine al Merito della Repubblica
Italiana.

Praise for *Venice: A Traveller's Companion*

'A dazzling anthology of writings about the Queen of Cities,
from those who have travelled far to see her. Byron, Ruskin,
Browning, Jan Morris and many more give some explanation
of why Venice is a city without parallel.'   *Oxford Times*

'A book as entrancing as the place it describes.'
                                                  Catholic Herald

'Will enrich anyone's experience of the city . . .'   *The Times*

A TRAVELLER'S COMPANION TO

VENICE

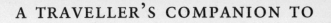

INTRODUCED AND EDITED BY

John Julius Norwich

Interlink Books
An imprint of Interlink Publishing Group, Inc.
New York • Northampton

This edition first published in 2002 by

INTERLINK BOOKS
An imprint of Interlink Publishing Group, Inc.
99 Seventh Avenue, Brooklyn, New York 11215 and
46 Crosby Street, Northampton, Massachusetts 01060
www.interlinkbooks.com

Published simultaneously in the UK by Constable & Robinson Ltd.

First published in the UK as *Venice: A Traveller's Companion*,
by Constable & Co. Ltd, 1990

ISBN 1-56656-465-4

Printed and bound in the EU

To Ashley and Frances Clarke
whose contribution to the survival of Venice
has been, and continues to be,
immeasurable

Contents

THE LAGOON AND THE ISLANDS

Illustrations

Between pp. 180 and 181

The Palazzo Barbaro

A regatta on the Grand Canal, by Canaletto *(by permission of the National Gallery)*

Canaletto's view of the Basin of St Mark on Ascension Day *(by permission of the National Gallery)*

SS Giovanni e Paolo

An aerial view of the Arsenal at the end of the seventeenth century

The entrance to the Arsenal *(by permission of the Trustees of the British Museum)*

Between pp. 300 and 301

The Grand Canal: detail from Jacopo de' Barbari's view of Venice, 1500

The Venetian gondola and gondolier, by Giacomo Franco, 1610

The railway bridge over the Venetian Lagoon

A Venetian theatre

Santa Fosca on the island of Torcello

The battle on the bridges

A ridotto in eighteenth-century Venice

A Carnival procession, *c.* 1700

The Bucintoro on Ascension Day 1619, engraved by Jan Sedeler after Stefano Scolari *(by permission of the National Maritime Museum)*

Carnival in St Mark's Square

Acknowledgments

I should like to thank my friend Michael Severne for permission to reproduce the letter from his uncle, Roland Burden-Muller; Julia Owen for many valuable suggestions; and Edward Chaney, co-author of *A Traveller's Companion to Florence*, for all his encouragement and help.

I am also grateful to the following for permission to quote from works in copyright: Doubleday, Weidenfeld & Nicolson and Susan Mary Alsop for *To Marietta from Paris 1945–1960*; to Penguin for *Aretino, Selected Letters* translated and introduced by George Bull, for Dorothy L. Sayers's translation of Dante's *Inferno*, and for A. J. A. Symons's *The Quest for Corvo*; to Faber & Faber and G. Keynes for *The Letters of Rupert Brooke* and to Faber, Harcourt Brace Jovanovich and Jan Morris for *Venice*; To Quadrangle/The New York Times Book Co. for *Elizabeth Barrett Browning's Letters to Mrs David Ogilvy* edited by Peter N. Heydon and Philip Kelley; to the University of Illinois Press for *Letters of the Brownings to George Barrett* edited by Paul Landis with the assistance of Ronald E. Freeman; to Yale University Press and J. C. Bradley for Ruskin's *Letters from Venice 1851–52*;

to Wayne State University Press for John Adington Symonds's *Letters* edited by H. M. Schneller and R. L. Peters; to Michael Meredith, Armstrong Browning Library of Baylor University and Wedgestone Press for *More than Friend: the Letters of Robert Browning to Katharine de Kay Bronson*; to Oxford University Press for *The Letters of Charles Dickens* edited by Kathleen Tillotson and for *The Letters of Horace Walpole* edited by W. S. Lewis *et al*; to Cambridge University Press for Richard Wagner's *My Life* translated by Andrew Gray and edited by Mary Whittall; to the Folio Society and George Bull for *Venice, the Most Triumphant City*; to John Murray and Leslie A. Marchand for *'The Flesh is Frail': Byron's Letters and Journals*, and to John Murray and Mary Lutyens for *Effie in Venice*; to Elizabeth David and Macdonald for *Italian Food*; to Mrs Janet Pollock for Arthur Machen's translation of *The Memoirs of Jacques Casanova de Seingalt*; to Cassell and J. E. Norton for *The Letters of Edward Gibbon*; to Macmillan and Leon Edel for *The Letters of Henry James*; to Rizzoli, New York and Lynne Lawner for *Lives of the Courtesans*; to Collins, W. H. Auden and Elizabeth Mayer for *Italian Journey 1786–1788* by J. W. Goethe; to Cecil Roth and the Jewish Publication Society of America for *Personalities and Events in Jewish History*; and to G. B. Parks for William Thomas's *The History of Italy* (1549).

My most heartfelt thanks of all, however, go to my wife Mollie, who has devoted countless hours to this book and whose name should, if there were any justice in this world, be on the title page with my own.

Introduction

No city ever had more undistinguished beginnings. Venice started life as a funk-hole – a refuge for frightened men. During the great days of the Roman Empire she simply did not exist: the ancestors of the first Venetians kept wisely to *terra firma*, where a whole chain of splendid imperial cities had grown up around the northern and north-western shores of the Adriatic and its neighbouring hinterland. After all, who in their right mind would build a village, far less a town or city, on a cluster of soggy shoals and sandbanks rising from a malarial, malodorous lagoon? A few fishermen and salt-gatherers may occasionally have erected a hut or two amid the couch-grass; but not many, and not for long. For the rest, desolation and silence.

Then, in the early years of the fifth century, the barbarians swept down. The Goths came first, under their leader Alaric – raping, burning and pillaging, laying waste everything in their path. In 402 they fell on Aquileia; eight years later they would ravage Rome. The local populations, meanwhile, had fled for their lives, seeking a refuge at once unenviable and inviolable, where their enemies would have neither the incentive nor the ability to follow them; and in the Venetian lagoon they found it. In those early days they probably contemplated an only temporary stay, expecting to return to their homes once the barbarians had passed. If so, they were disappointed. Those who attempted to do so soon discovered that they had no homes to return to; and as soon as they started to rebuild them another wave of barbarians would descend and the whole sad story would be repeated.

For the Goths were only the beginning. In 452 they were followed by the Huns under the brutal and dwarfish Attila, and the flow of refugees increased. By this time they had grouped themselves into a number of separate island communities, still technically part of the Roman Empire but for all practical purposes self-governing; and the fall of the Empire of the West, with the deposition in 476 of its last Emperor – a feckless youth named Romulus Augustulus, whose double diminutive must have prepared his subjects for the worst – gave still further strength to their effective independence. The famous letter[1] written to them by the Prefect Cassiodorus in 523 suggests that his master Theodoric, King of the Ostrogoths, who had assumed power in Italy (under the nominal overlordship of the Emperor in Constantinople) at the end of the previous century, was distinctly uncertain how far he could count on their loyalty and obedience; and this impression grows stronger still when we read their address of welcome[2] to the imperial general Longinus nearly half a century later.

Thus, even at this early stage in their history it seems clear that the peoples of the lagoon were determined to be their own men; but they were still only a loose federation of individual settlements, scattered over a relatively wide area and, as was probably inevitable in the circumstances, constantly squabbling with one another. A central focus was still lacking; indeed, the islands of Rialto which comprise the Venice we know today were still, in the sixth and seventh centuries, largely uninhabited. But then, in the eighth century and the beginning of the ninth, two things occurred which gave those early Venetians the cohesion they

[1] No. 2, p. 39.
[2] No. 3, p. 40.

needed. The first was the puritanical decree promulgated by the Byzantine Emperor Leo III in 726, ordering the destruction of all the Christian icons and holy pictures in the Empire. The people of the imperial Exarchate in Italy, which had its capital at Ravenna, rose – with the enthusiastic support of Pope Gregory II – in immediate revolt; the Exarch was assassinated, his officials fleeing for their lives; and the rebellious garrisons, all of whom had been recruited locally, chose their own commanders and proclaimed their independence. Thus it was that the communities of the Venetian lagoon placed a certain Orso from Heraclea at the head of the former provincial administration and honoured him with the title of *Dux* – a title which, transformed by the rough Venetian dialect into *Doge*, was to pass down for the next one thousand and seventy-one years till the Republic's end.

The second decisive event in the formation of Venice was the expedition of Charlemagne's son Pepin in 810. For the first time, the lagoon settlements presented a united front against a common enemy and were victorious. It was then, as they watched Pepin's ships disappearing over the horizon, that the people resolved to build themselves a true capital, one that would be situated not around the edge of the lagoon but in its very centre, protected by its surrounding girdle of shallow water – so much more effective a defence than deep – from any possibility of attack. And so, on that little group of islands known as Rialto, building at last began; and the city of Venice was born.

Not once in all their history did the Venetians have cause to regret that decision. For centuries to come, mainland Italy was to be torn apart by war. Sometimes it would be war against a foreign invader, but more usually – and far more tragically – the strife would be internal: city against city, Guelf against Ghibelline, Emperor against Pope. Again and again over those centuries, every great city of Lombardy and the Veneto – Milan and Verona, Bergamo and Brescia, Padua and Mantua – was to see its streets running red with blood. Only Venice remained inviolate, secure in her lagoon, never once in more than a millennium to be invaded, pillaged, put to fire or sword. And even when the end came at last, even when the old, exhausted Republic finally collapsed in the hurricane unleashed by the young Napoleon, few lives were lost and little lasting damage was done.

And the sea continued as the city's guardian. Just as in former centuries it saved Venice from foreign invaders, so in our own day it has proved an equally effective defence against that still more insidious invader, the motor car. In any other Italian town, the Piazza San Marco would long ago have been transformed into an enormous car-park; thanks to the lagoon, wheeled traffic can still approach no nearer than the Piazzale Roma and the cranes and derricks of Tronchetto, and we must pray that it never will. (Beware, however, of over-confidence: only twenty years ago a serious scheme was proposed to fill in the entire Grand Canal and transform it into a six-lane *autostrada*. The forces of darkness are never far away.)

Venice is thus unique, not only for her surpassing beauty nor for the fact that she seems to use water as other cities use concrete, but in another respect as well: as an astonishing document of history. No other city anywhere has changed less. A few of the smaller canals have been filled in, a few more acres reclaimed from the sea; but a Venetian of the fifteenth century, miraculously translated into the twentieth, would experience no difficulty in finding his way through the *campi* and the *calli*, most of which have survived virtually intact since he first saw them. And this applies not just to the more remote and forgotten parishes; it is equally true of the great ceremonial centre itself. Look at Gentile Bellini's glorious portrayal of the Piazza, painted in 1496 as one of the series representing *The Miracles of the Relic of the True Cross* in the Accademia. To the far right we see a corner of the Doge's Palace, the base of the Campanile, and the Porta della Carta, its details picked out in gold leaf; on the Basilica itself, the four horses are in position above the central door, where they have already been for two and a half centuries. Only the mosaics – four of the five – in the lunettes above the doors have been replaced, by the sad seventeenth-to-nineteenth-century travesties that we see today; but even these have not been entirely lost, since Gentile's painting is large and meticulous enough to reveal to us, in quite remarkable detail, their exact composition and the story they told.

It is one of the oldest stories of Venice, and one of the most important; for it concerns the bringing to the city of the body of St Mark, and his adoption as its patron saint. In the years immediately following the repulse of Pepin, when the lagoon people were just beginning to feel themselves a nation, it was vital for them to gain the respect and recognition of their neighbours; not surprisingly, however, the ancient cities of Italy and beyond found it difficult to give serious consideration to the pretensions of these upstart parvenus and tended to dismiss their claims out of hand. Now in those distant, God-fearing days, there was one way above all to acquire international prestige, and that was to be the possessor of a really good relic: not just a finger or a knucklebone but a complete body, and not just of any saint either, but of an apostle – or, better still, an evangelist.

As so often at crucial moments in their history, the Venetians were lucky: for there existed an old tradition (or, if there did not, it was quickly fabricated) that St Mark had been Bishop of Aquileia, and that one day, while sailing through the lagoon on his way to Rome, he had been visited by an angel bearing a message from the Almighty Himself: *Pax tibi, Marce, evangelista meus: hic requiescat corpus tuum.* More fortunate still, the saint's body was known to be in Alexandria, where he had spent the last years of his life and where he had been buried in a large and ornate tomb which still existed, despite the city's capture by the armies of Islam some 200 years before. The solution to Venice's problem was clear to see. In the year 828 two Venetian merchants sailed to Alexandria and returned with a body which they claimed to be that of the evangelist, stolen from his tomb and smuggled out of the city in a basket by the simple expedient of covering it with pork – a commodity rightly calculated to revolt the harbour customs officers who, pious Muslims to a man, had turned up their noses in disgust and given the merchants no trouble.

With the saint's body now safe in Venice in accordance with the ancient prophecy, one might have expected it to have been reburied in the recently completed cathedral, on the site of the present church of S. Pietro di Castello;[1] such a decision, however, would have associated it from the outset with the religious rather than the civil authorities of the State, a possibility which Doge Giustiniano Participazio refused to contemplate. Instead, a great new basilica was built expressly to house it, described as the Chiesa Ducale and actually adjoining the Doges' Palace; and the poor Cathedral of S. Pietro, now hopelessly overshadowed and impossibly remote in the eastern extremity of the city, embarked on long centuries of that near-oblivion from which, even today, it has not wholly emerged.

The day on which St Mark was carried, shoulder-high, into his new basilica – the scene is depicted, in full and fascinating detail, in the thirteenth-century mosaic occupying the lunette above the northernmost door of the west front – marked a watershed in Venice's history. Her ancient tutelary saint, the dragon-slaying Theodore, was relegated to the top of a column in the Piazzetta and forgotten. Henceforth she was a city and a republic worthy of universal respect, proud of her Evangelistic patronage and, in her ecclesiastical rank, second in Italy only to Rome herself. St Mark himself had taken her under his protection, and the world was never to be allowed to forget it: his lion, its wings outspread, its forepaw proudly holding open the book in which was inscribed the angelic utterance, was to be emblazoned for the next thousand years on banners and bastions, on poops and prows, wherever the Venetian writ was to run.

The mosaic of St Alipio (as it is invariably called) clearly portrays the existing church, of which it is the earliest known representation. In fact, the building first erected to receive the precious relic was a much simpler, wooden construction, which was burnt to the ground during a revolution in 976 and was temporarily replaced by what seems to have been a somewhat unworthy, makeshift affair. This second St Mark's was itself demolished by Doge Domenico Contarini (1043–71) to make way for the present basilica, the third on

[1] S. Pietro di Castello remained, technically speaking, the Cathedral Church of Venice throughout the lifetime of the Republic. It was only on the orders of Napoleon in 1807 that it yielded its primacy to St Mark's.

the site, which was finally consecrated in 1904. Interestingly enough, however, all three buildings were almost certainly based on the same model – Constantine the Great's Church of the Holy Apostles in Constantinople.

Here is further dramatic evidence that Venice, even at this comparatively early stage, was determined to pursue her own destiny. True, there had been a time when she, like the rest of Italy, had owed nominal allegiance to the Eastern Empire. But in the north at least the authority of the Emperors, having steadily diminished over the years, had been thrown offfor ever in 727; Lombard and Frankish influences had long since taken the place of Byzantine. Certainly no other North Italian city, planning its supreme religious monument towards the end of the eleventh century, would have dreamt of turning for inspiration to Constantinople. Venice, however, was not like other cities. Her encircling sea protected her not only from the armies of the West but from its cultural influences too. Where art and architecture were concerned, she remained loyal to the old regime. She could afford quite simply to turn her back on Italy, fixing her eyes instead upon the East, whence came her rapidly growing prosperity. And for her the East meant, first and foremost, Byzantium.

Thus, wherever the mainland towns and cities are Romanesque, Venice is Byzantine. Dotted about all over the city we may still find buildings whose huge, carved horseshoe arches proclaim beyond any possibility of doubt their oriental origins. There are half a dozen of them on the Grand Canal alone, including the Palazzi Loredan and Farsetti which together comprise the City Hall and, a little way beyond the Rialto, the Ca' da Mosto, parts of which may go back to the eleventh century. Older than any, however, and infinitely more beautiful, is the Basilica of St Mark itself – since the secularization of St Sophia in Istanbul more than half a century ago, far and away the greatest Byzantine building in the world still regularly used for religious worship.

The Byzantine architectural style, it need hardly be said, is not just a matter of horseshoe arches, or of a cross-in-square ground-plan. It reveals itself also in a wholly oriental love of colour, and consequently in the art of incrustation – two immensely important characteristics, of which Ruskin provides the most searching analysis and St Mark's the most outstanding example. And so strong were these strains in the city's psyche that they both survived even the eclipse of the style to which they fundamentally belonged; they are still in evidence in Venetian Gothic building and even in the early Renaissance, where such architects as the Lombardi (in the Palazzo Dario for example, or the church of the Miracoli) or Mauro Coducci (in the Clock Tower or S. Michele) used slabs of polychrome marble as integral parts of their designs – and to wondrous effect.

Of Venice's genuinely Byzantine buildings, most were already standing on 24 July 1177 when, for the first time, the city became the centre of the world stage; for it was there, immediately in front of the central doors of St Mark's and in the presence of most of the leading princes and bishops of Christendom, that the Emperor Frederick Barbarossa knelt at the feet of Pope Alexander III and kissed his slipper, thus putting an end to the eighteen-year hostilities that had existed between them.[1] (The little lozenge of porphyry set into the huge rounder of red Verona marble in the centre of the atrium of the basilica marks the spot where he did so.) This tremendous reconciliation, perhaps the most important event ever staged in the Piazza as we know it, was also one of the first; for its architect, Doge Sebastiano Ziani, had also been responsible a few years before for giving his city's superb ceremonial centre the appearance it still has today. He it was who pulled down the old church of S. Geminiano[2] which occupied what is now the centre of the Piazza, purchased from the nuns of S. Zaccaria the orchard which lay between it and the lagoon, filled in the old canal which ran from halfway along the present Procuratie Vecchie, across the front of the basilica and past the campanile to the Zecca, and paved the whole thing over in herring-bone brick. He also ordered that all the houses surrounding it should be built with arches

[1] No. 30, p. 90.
[2] The church was later re-erected in the centre of the far western end of the Piazza, where it stood until it was demolished by Napoleon in 1807 to make way for his new Ala Napoleonica.

and colonnades. The result was what, over six centuries later, Napoleon was to call *le plus beau salon de l'Europe*. He might well have said *du monde*; of all the great city squares I know, only one – the Campo in Siena – even runs it close.

With Pope and Emperor now firmly reconciled, the great nobles and prelates whose interminable retinues thronged Venice during the summer of 1177 might have been forgiven for believing that, after a generation of turmoil, all was once again well with Christendom. It was, however, barely a decade before news arrived from the East which filled Europe with anguish and dismay: Jerusalem, since 1099 a Christian kingdom, had been reconquered by the Saracens under their brilliant general Saladin. The result was the Third Crusade, led jointly by Richard Coeur-de-Lion and Philip Augustus of France – old Barbarossa having been drowned on his way to Palestine, in the icy waters of an Anatolian river. The Crusaders fought well, and managed to regain Acre; but the Holy City remained in the hands of the Infidel.

Venice never played much of a part in the first three Crusades. She was no good at fighting on terra firma; besides, that religious zeal which drove so much of Christian Europe to plant the banner of the Cross in pagan lands was totally foreign to her nature. As a merchant republic, her interest was always in peace – for the excellent reason that it was good for trade: she infinitely preferred doing business with the Saracens to killing them. On the other hand, she had no objection to cashing in on any military successes; and after the First Crusade (to which she had made only a minimal contribution, her promised fleet having arrived in the East well after Jerusalem had been taken) she had been astute enough to gain free trading rights throughout the Holy Land, a market in every Christian town and a third of any other town that she might help to take in the future. In return for an annual tribute, she also appropriated the entire City of Tripoli.

From that time on, her only real interest in any subsequent ventures of this kind was to preserve her new markets or to provide transportation, for which she invariably charged a high price; and it was doubtless for the latter reason that we find her in 1189 participating in the Third Crusade with an impressive war fleet, laden to the gunwales with soldiers from all over Italy. Some time afterwards, there are reports of Venetian merchants setting up business in their quarter of Acre within days of the city's recapture. And yet with regard to any actual fighting the chroniclers are strangely silent: we can only deduce that once the Venetian ships had disembarked their passengers and received due payment they returned to the Adriatic just as quickly as they could.

With Pope Innocent III, on the other hand, and with many of the Princes of Europe, the loss of Jerusalem continued to rankle; and it was this that in 1201 brought a party of six Frankish knights, led by Geoffrey de Villehardouin, Marshal of Champagne, to Venice. Geoffrey's account of the visit, of his formal request for yet another huge fleet to convey yet another army on yet another Crusade, and of the splendid scenes in St Mark's when the stone-blind octogenarian Doge Enrico Dandolo not only agreed – for a considerable price – to provide the transport but, a year later when the ships were ready, undertook to participate in the expedition himself, makes captivating reading;[1] sadly, however, it proves to be only a preface to the blackest chapter in the history of Venice.

The full story of the Fourth Crusade, ending not in the recapture of Jerusalem but in the pitiless sack by both Franks and Venetians of Christian Constantinople, the deposition of the Greek Emperor and the establishment of a fifty-year dynasty of Frankish thugs on the throne of Byzantium, falls – fortunately – outside the scope of this book. What concerns us here is the loot brought back by the Venetians for the adornment of their city – and above all its *pièce de résistance*, the four glorious bronze horses which, as much even as the Lion of St Mark himself, have become symbols of the city. They are a mystery, those horses. Their origins are unknown; the experts cannot even agree on whether they are Greek or Roman. If Greek, they may very likely have come from the studio of Lysippus, court sculptor to Alexander the Great; but we can never be sure. All that we know for certain is that they were brought by Constantine from Rome to Constantinople at the time of the city's foundation, that they were set

[1] No. 31, p. 92.

up above the Hippodrome and that there they remained for nearly 900 years before the Venetians carried them off. On their arrival they were at first consigned to the Arsenal where, we are told, they narrowly escaped being melted down for scrap; saved in the nick of time, they were then erected on the west gallery of St Mark's, from which they presided for more than seven further centuries over the whole life of the Piazza – admired by Dante and Goethe, painted by Canaletto and Guardi and Gentile Bellini, even set in mosaic by the nameless master of S. Alipio.

It is one of the great tragedies of Venice that those in charge of such matters should have decided a few years ago that atmospheric pollution was taking its toll and that the horses must be removed to an allegedly safe refuge within the basilica. Perhaps they are indeed deteriorating; so are we all. But unlike the rest of us – they have several centuries more life in them yet; moreover, even the most cursory examination shows that they have been patched before, and there is no reason why they should not be patched again. Surely they have not deserved their present incarceration in the darkness of the interior, their places on the gallery defiled by dull and lifeless facsimiles in fibreglass? We can only pray that the authorities will reconsider, and allow these god-horses – for such they are, collectively perhaps the greatest work of art in all Venice – to return to the façade of which they have so long been an integral part, and which they should never have left.

But the horses of St Mark's were not the only spoils from the Fourth Crusade. Blind old Dandolo – who had actually been the first to leap ashore when the attack on Constantinople began, astounding everyone by his energy and courage – proved an astute negotiator when the Empire fell. In the city itself he took possession of the whole district surrounding St Sophia and the Patriarchate, reaching right down to the shore of the Golden Horn; for the rest, he appropriated for Venice the western coast of the Greek mainland, the Ionian islands, the Peloponnese, Euboea, Naxos and Andros, Gallipoli, the Thracian seaboard, the inland city of Adrianople (now Edirne) and – after some hard bargaining – the all-important island of Crete. The Republic now controlled a whole chain of ports and harbours running from the lagoon to the Black Sea; at a single stroke, she had become mistress of the entire Eastern Mediterranean. As for her Doge, he had acquired a new and sonorous title which, unlike most of the empty honorifics which attached to his office, meant precisely what it said: *Lord of a Quarter and Half a Quarter of the Roman Empire.*

It was thus the thirteenth century that witnessed the emergence of Venice as a world power. For a good deal of it she was at war, fighting to defend her newly acquired possessions against Pisans and Genoese, Greeks and Saracens – to say nothing of pirates from every corner of the Middle Sea. At home, however, the expansion of her trade had brought ever-greater prosperity; in 1264 a new bridge was built at the Rialto, equipped with bascules[1] to allow the laden argosies to sail all the way up the Grand Canal and unload in the open loggias fronting the merchants' *palazzi*. This was also the time when the two huge churches of the Mendicant Orders – the Franciscan Frari and the Dominican SS. Giovanni e Paolo – were rising ever higher, dwarfing all the buildings around them. Meanwhile in the political sphere Venice was putting the finishing touches to her unique constitution, perhaps the most efficient ever devised by man, which was to survive virtually unchanged for the last five centuries of the Republic's life.

The word oligarchy, so often applied to the Venetian system, somehow suggests government by a small, privileged junta, dominating – and probably exploiting – the large bulk of the population. The truth, where Venice was concerned, was very different. She was indeed an oligarchy, technically speaking; true democracy in the middle ages did not exist. But though from the fourteenth century her Great Council, the *Maggior Consiglio*, was limited to the male members of her noble families – those listed in the so-called Golden Book – they usually numbered well over 1,000, and sometimes more than twice that figure. Thus, for most of her existence as an independent state her government was probably more

---

[1] A prototype of that portrayed in Carpaccio's contribution to the *Miracles of the True Cross* in the Accademia (see plate section).

broadly based than that of any other European country except Switzerland.

As for exploitation, the Venetians had watched with growing repugnance the seizure of power by political adventurers that had long been a feature of the Italian political scene; in the early days of the Republic they had thwarted attempts by several Doges to establish family dynasties; and by the time of which we are speaking they had developed an almost pathological mistrust of anything that might nowadays be described as the cult of personality. The Doge's own status had long been reduced to little more than a figure-head. On assuming office he was required to sign a *promissione*, a sort of coronation oath in which he swore to renounce all claims on the revenue of the state (apart from his salary, paid quarterly), to contribute to public loans, to respect government secrets, and to enter into no communication with Pope, Emperor or any foreign princes without prior permission. Nor could he accept any presents, except precisely stipulated quantities of food and wine. Once installed as Doge, he was attended at all times by his six counsellors of state – the seven forming what was known as the Signoria – and could take no action without their knowledge and approval. All these restrictions might have been thought enough; but the Venetians were taking no chances, and after the death of Doge Renier Zeno in 1268 they instituted a new system of election to the Dogeship which must surely be the most complicated ever devised by a civilized state. It may strike us as mildly ridiculous; but it is worth setting down in some detail, if only to demonstrate the lengths to which Venice was prepared to go to ensure that the supreme office should not fall into ambitious or unscrupulous hands.

On the day appointed, the youngest member of the Signoria was to pray in St Mark's; then, on leaving, he was to stop the first boy he met and take him to the Doges' Palace, where all those members of the Great Council over the age of thirty were in session. This boy would be the *ballotino*, responsible for picking the slips of paper from the urn during the drawing of lots. By the first of these, the Council chose thirty of their own number. By the second, the thirty were reduced to nine, who would then vote for forty, each of whom must receive at least seven nominations. The forty would then be reduced, again by lot, to twelve, who then had to vote for twenty-five, of whom each required nine votes. The twenty-five were in turn reduced to another nine; the nine voted for forty-five, with a minimum of seven votes each, from whom the *ballotino* picked out the names of eleven. The eleven now voted for forty-one – nine or more votes each. It was these, finally, whose task it was to elect the Doge.

After attending Mass and swearing individual oaths that they would act for the good of the Republic, the forty-one electors went into conclave, guarded by a special force of sailors and denied all contact or communication with the outside world till their work was done. Each elector then wrote the name of his candidate on a slip and dropped it into the urn, after which a list was drawn up of all the names proposed, regardless of the number of nominations for each. A single slip for each name was now placed in another urn, and one drawn. If the candidate named was present he would retire, together with any other elector who bore the same surname, while the remainder discussed his suitability. He was then called back to answer questions or to defend himself against any accusations. A ballot followed. If he obtained the required twenty-five votes, he was declared Doge; otherwise a second name was drawn, and so on.

There must, one feels, have been an easier way; but, as any Venetian would have been quick to point out, the system worked. Over on the mainland, dictators and ruling families rose and fell: the Sforza and Visconti in Milan, the Gonzaga in Mantua, the Scaligeri in Verona, the Este in Ferrara, the Carrara in Padua, the Medici in Florence. In Venice, such phenomena were unthinkable. Instead, Doge succeeded Doge in quiet succession. All the power, all the glory – and even most of the wealth – went to the State, the Serenissima.

There was, inevitably, the occasional hiccup. In 1310 a group of discontented young noblemen under a certain Bajamonte Tiepolo essayed an insurrection, which was foiled when an old woman tipped a heavy stone mortar out of a window on to the head of their standard-bearer, as they galloped down what is now the Merceria into the

Piazza.[1] The indirect result of this fiasco was the formation of the Council of Ten, at first a temporary but after 1334 a permanent body in charge of State security, the very mention of whose name – thanks to its formidable efficiency and apparent omniscience – would soon be enough to send a shudder through the nations of Europe. Twenty-one years later still, in 1355, there was another attempted *coup*, equally unsuccessful and still more bizarre in that it was originated by the Doge himself, a certain Marin Falier, already in his middle seventies. He seems to have developed, owing to a number of insults real and imagined, an obsessive hatred of the young nobility of Venice; his plan was to provoke violent disturbances in the Piazza in order to attract them there, and then to call out the workers from the Arsenal – who traditionally provided an unofficial bodyguard for the Doge – to kill as many of them as possible. He then proposed to proclaim himself Prince. In retrospect, it can hardly be doubted that the old man was suffering from a form of senile dementia; in any case his plot was discovered, and its ten ringleaders were hanged from the windows of the Doges' Palace overlooking the Piazzetta. Falier himself was arrested, pleaded guilty to all charges and on 18 April was beheaded at the top of the marble staircase within the Palace courtyard. It was Venice's only ducal execution, and we are reminded of it every time we raise our eyes up to the frieze of ducal portraits that runs around the upper walls of the Hall of the Maggior Consiglio: where we should expect to find the likeness of Falier we see only a painted black curtain and the legend HIC EST LOCUS MARINI FALEDRI DECAPITATI PRO CRIMINIBUS.[2]

Modern tourist guides love to point out the two columns of red Verona marble in the first-floor arcade of the Palace facing the Piazzetta as marking the spot where the conspirators were hanged, and may even suggest that the Doge himself met his death at the head of the great Scala dei

---

[1] A plaque, bearing in low relief a representation of the old woman and her mortar, can be seen just under the Clock Tower, on the building that now occupies the site of her house: see No. 65, p. 146.

[2] See also No. 20, p. 67.

Giganti within the courtyard. Alas, neither the arcade nor the staircase existed in 1355; and since the Palace was at that very moment undergoing the transformations that were ultimately to give it the appearance it has today, this may be as good a moment as any to retrace the course of its building history. There had been several palaces on the site since the first had been erected in the early eighth century, culminating in that left by Sebastiano Ziani in the late twelfth; since then, however, this in turn had become too small for the steadily developing Republic, and the addition of a new Council Chamber in 1300 had not really solved the problem. Thus in 1341 work started on a completely new design, the work of an architect of genius, Pietro Baseggio. It was to continue, on and off, for the next eighty-two years. The first stage was the construction of the new Chamber, involving most of the south side and the southern end of that facing the Piazzetta, as far as the seventh column; it took a quarter of a century, but must have been essentially complete by 1365 when Guariento was commissioned to cover the eastern wall with a vast fresco depicting the Coronation of the Virgin in Paradise. The central balcony facing the Molo was added, as its inscription proclaims, in 1404; even then, however, the interior must have been unfinished, since the Great Council did not in fact sit in its new Chamber until 1423. In that same year it was decided to extend the Piazzetta façade to its present length. Thus it was only in 1425 or thereabouts that the south and west sides of the building first appeared as we know them today.

John Ruskin called the Doges' Palace 'the central building of the world' – whatever that may mean; it is certainly, for many of us, the loveliest secular monument in the Gothic style to be found anywhere. But one of its most remarkable features becomes apparent only when we compare it with its counterpart in any other major city of Italy. We have first of all to remember that it was a great deal more than just the residence of the Doge: it was the seat of government, not only of the city of Venice but of the entire Republic and Empire – the Venetian equivalent, in fact, of Buckingham Palace, 10 Downing Street and the Palace of Westminster combined. Consider now the corresponding seats of power in other cities; nearly all are dark, gloomy, and forbidding, built primarily for defence – as, given the circumstances of life in medieval Italy, they had to be. Machiavelli was right when he claimed that in Florence the Palazzo della Signoria was built as a protection for the civic authorities; so, later, was John Addington Symonds when he wrote of Ferrara, 'where the Este's stronghold, moated, drawbridged and port-cullized, casting dense shadow over the water that protects the dungeons, still seems to threaten the public square and overawe the homes of men'. Venice, on the other hand, feared no attack from within or without, and the Doges' Palace proves it. That shimmering fantasy of colour, lightness and grace might have been designed expressly to be indefensible: it could not keep out a Pekingese. A more convincing proclamation of confidence and security could hardly be imagined.

It was fortunate indeed that the completion of the Piazzetta façade was put in hand when it was; for the Renaissance, at long last, was on the way. It came late to Venice: in Florence it had already been in existence for well over a century. Why the Venetians were so dilatory in coming to terms with it remains a mystery; perhaps they were so enchanted by their own version of Gothic – as well they might be – that they simply saw no reason to change. But even they could not indefinitely postpone the inevitable, and if you want to see the place in which Venice felt the very first breath of the Renaissance you must go to the church of S. Zaccaria. There, half-way along the south aisle, you will find a door leading indirectly to the chapel of S. Tarasio, where the frescoed saints by Andrea del Castagno and Francesco da Faenza in the apse ceiling are dated 1442. What makes them more interesting still is their immediate context: for only just below them is an exquisite altarpiece in purest Gothic, painted in the *following* year, 1443. It marks the end of an epoch. By mid-century the young Giovanni Bellini was at work, and the 150-year Golden Age of Venetian painting had begun.

In architecture, the moment of transition came slightly later – with Antonio Gambello's gateway to the Arsenal, of 1460, projecting like some great Roman triumphal arch from the crenellated brick walls to each side. Seven years later arrived Pietro Lombardo, breathing exhilaration after four years in Donatello's Padua and bringing with him his two equally brilliant sons, Antonio and Tullio; and, at about the same time, Mauro Coducci (or Codussi) from Bergamo who – quite apart from his superb Clock Tower – was to transform the whole north range of the Piazza with his rebuilding of the Procuratie Vecchie and to provide Venice with some of her best-loved monuments, including the churches of S. Giovanni Crisostomo, S. Maria Formosa and the finished façade of S. Zaccaria, the Scuola di S. Marco and the Palazzi Corner-Spinelli and Vendramin-Calergi (where Wagner died).

As for sculpture, the very first Renaissance examples are hard to identify; perhaps Pietro Lombardo's three statues on his own portal of S. Giobbe (1471) are as early as any. But they, and any rivals that they may have, are all overshadowed by the tremendous mounted figure of Bartolommeo Colleoni, which was begun just five years later. Its story is well known, but is worth briefly recounting here for the wonderfully revealing light it sheds on the Venetian mentality. Its subject was the greatest *condottiere* of his day, a mercenary general who, when he died in 1475, had commanded the land forces of the Republic for a quarter of a century and who left it a vast legacy – 216,000 ducats in gold and silver and more than twice that sum in land and property – on condition that they erected an equestrian statue in his memory in the Piazza of St Mark.

Here was a problem indeed. The idea of any statue in the Piazza was unthinkable: there was not even one of St Mark himself. As for Colleoni, having been born in Bergamo he was not even a citizen of the Republic; on occasion he had even fought against it. On the other hand a windfall of such magnificence was clearly not to be refused. After long discussion a solution was found at last – and a quintessentially Venetian solution at that. The statue would be erected not in the Piazza of St Mark but immediately in front of his *Scuola*, in the square of SS. Giovanni e Paolo. So monstrous a piece of casuistry must have had poor Colleoni positively spinning in his grave; if so, however, the fact that the completed monument – begun by Andrea Verocchio and finished, after his death in 1488, by Alessandro di Leopardi – proved to be the greatest equestrian statue ever cast or carved must have done much to reconcile him.

By this time Venice was the most powerful secular state in Italy. Verona and Vicenza had voluntarily been absorbed into the Republic at the start of the fifteenth century, with Padua following soon afterwards; since then, after twenty-five years of intermittent fighting – during which Venice was represented largely by mercenary forces under the command of *condottieri* – she had extended her western frontiers to the upper reaches of the river Adda, only a few miles short of Milan: a line which she was to hold, with only minor modifications, for the rest of her history as an independent nation. To the east, in addition to all that she had gained after the Fourth Crusade, she had established trading posts in the Levant, the Black Sea and even the Indies. Commercial links with China had been in existence since the days of Marco Polo, and as early as the 1380s there was a Venetian agent actually resident in Siam.

But the clouds were gathering; and the biggest and blackest of those clouds was that represented by the Turks. These warlike tribesmen from Central Asia were relative newcomers to the Mediterranean; the first wave of them, the Seljuks, had arrived only in the late eleventh century, while the great dynasty that was to strike such terror in the heart of Europe – the Ottoman – was unheard of before 1300 or so. A century later, however, they had mopped up the whole of Asia Minor, Bulgaria and Serbia, and controlled all the Eastern Balkans to within a few miles of Constantinople itself. After the Greek reconquest of the city from the Latins in 1261, the Byzantine Empire – though by now a shadow of what it had once been – was still roughly the size of the British Isles; by 1437 – when the Emperor John VIII Palaeologus travelled to the West to make a last desperate (and fruitless) appeal for European aid – it would have fitted comfortably into Lincolnshire.

Its destruction, it was clear, could only be a matter of time; and on Tuesday 29 May 1453 the cannon of the young Sultan Mehmet II – he was just twenty-one – finally smashed down the walls of Constantinople and brought the thousand-year Empire to an end. Venice had not responded to the Emperor's appeal. She was well aware that the cause of Byzantium was lost and that the Turks were there to stay, and as a trading nation her primary interest was to remain on as good terms with them as possible. Thus, if the Sultan had been content to call a halt and consolidate his conquest, she might well have continued her commercial activities in the East as successfully as she had in Byzantine days. But he was not content. A missionary as well as a conqueror, he believed it to be his divinely appointed duty to spread the word of the Prophet across all Europe and beyond. Twenty years after the fall of Constantinople, the whole continent was on the defensive; and Venice was in the front line.

The struggle was to continue for the next 200 years, becoming ever more desperate as time went on – especially after the accession in 1520 of Mehmet's great-grandson, Suleyman the Magnificent, under whom Ottoman power reached its apogee. Nine years later, having captured and sacked Budapest, Suleyman brought his massive army to the very gates of Vienna; but for the appalling weather conditions and the consequent difficulty of moving up his heavy artillery, he might well have taken the city – and the whole history of Europe might have been changed. Meanwhile, little by little, Venetian power in the Eastern Mediterranean was being whittled away. The all-important colony of Cyprus fell in 1571 – its commander, Marcantonio Bragadin, having been seized by the Turks after his surrender and publicly flayed alive. And in 1669, after 465 years of Venetian occupation and twenty-two of siege, the banner of St Mark was finally lowered on the island of Crete.

By this time, however, the Republic had long since ceased to be a considerable force in Europe. Her power had been founded on wealth, her wealth on trade; but her Mediterranean trade had been stifled by the Turks, and her commercial links with the Orient never really recovered from the two momentous events which had occurred almost simultaneously in the last years of the fifteenth century. The first of these was the discovery of the New World, in which Venice never gained a foothold: she was thus forced to watch impotently while Spain and Portugal – and, to a lesser extent, England and France – divided the spoils between them. The second was the opening up of the Cape route to the Indies, after which the pirate-infested Mediterranean was no longer a necessary – or even, after a while, a particularly convenient – highway to the East. No longer would oriental merchants be obliged to unload their cargoes of silks and spices at Suez or Hormouz, carry them overland to the Mediterranean shore and re-embark them at Alexandria, Antioch or Constantinople. Henceforth the same vessel that picked them up at their point of departure could deliver them at their destination. Almost overnight Venice had become a backwater.

She continued, however, to survive. Whatever disasters might befall her colonies, she herself remained safe, inviolate in her lagoon. In 1499 the Turks advanced so close that their watch-fires were clearly visible at night from the tops of the *campanili*. The Venetians may have felt for their fellow-citizens on terra firma, but they had no fear of meeting a similar fate. In 1509 the Republic faced, unflinching, all the principal powers of Europe – the Empire, the Papacy, France, Milan, Spain, Naples and Hungary – bound together by the League of Cambrai for the sole purpose of her destruction. Eight years later she had regained virtually all her former Italian possessions and became once again the leading secular state in the peninsula. The sixteenth century may have seen the beginning of her decline; but never in her history did she present a more magnificent face to the world. This was the age of Titian and Giorgione, of Carpaccio and Veronese, of Palma Vecchio and Lorenzo Lotto, of Sansovino and Palladio. Her power might be declining, her influence on the wane; but her beauty and opulence had never been more dazzling.

At sea, too, she remained a force to be reckoned with. In October 1571, just two months after the fall of Cyprus, the combined navies of Spain, Venice and the Papacy had smashed the Turkish fleet at Lepanto: the last major battle to be fought with oared galleys and – although it was to have little long-term political significance – one of the great naval engagements of history. Three years later, in the course of a State visit by the twenty-three-year-old King Henry III of

France – during which, incidentally, the Republic gave him a welcome which he was to remember all his life – his hosts took him early one morning to the Arsenal, where he saw the keel of a ship being laid. That same evening at sunset they took him back: there was the same vessel going down the slipway – fully rigged, armed, victualled and ready for action.

King Henry might be considered the first of the Grand Tourists. It was to be another century or so before the young English *milords* and their Continental counterparts were to come flocking to Venice in their hundreds to pick up their fashionable doses of culture, Canalettos and the clap; already, however, Venice had become something of a legend. That curious combination of scholar and buffoon Thomas Coryat walked there and back between May and October 1608 from his home at Odcombe, Somerset, hanging up his shoes in the parish church on his return as a votive offering; John Evelyn, paradigm of the seventeenth-century virtuoso, was there in 1645; and by the reign of William and Mary the flood-gates had opened. The beginning of the eighteenth century saw the Venetian transformation accomplished: Venice was no longer the point of departure from which travellers sailed; she was, more and more frequently, the object of their journey. Her people, formerly Europe's leading purveyors of silks and spices from China and the Indies, ivory and slaves from Africa, gold and furs from Russia, had now reduced their range of merchandise to a single item – their own city.

No other in the world could rival it in appeal. The beauty of course came first – the wealth and opulence of the churches and *palazzi*, the reflections of stone and polychrome marble in the unrippled canals, the unfailing miracle of the Piazza S. Marco and the great basilica behind it, the splendour of the ceremonies and processions, the luxury of the women. Underlying it all, an element of slightly sinister mystery provided an agreeable *frisson*: the *bocche di leoni*, their open mouths hungrily awaiting denunciations; the secret sessions of the Ten (or, worse still, the Three) with their vast networks of agents all over Europe; that most prominent of prisons, conveniently adjacent to the Doges' Palace and inviting speculations on the unhappy, if invisible, traffic over the Bridge of Sighs; even the blackness of the silent gondolas, each in those days with its *felze* or covered cabin, in which – or so it was rumoured – many a young man had lost his life and young woman her virtue.

And then came the pleasure. Here again, Venice stood supreme. Those countless young noblemen, all eager to make proof of their wealth and their virility, found on their arrival in Venice that the half had not been told them. Here at last were the 'balls and masques begun at midnight, burning ever till mid-day' of which Browning would write so wistfully. In the *ridotti*, the gambling was the most smoothly organized, the stakes the highest anywhere; there, too, the play would go on till the morning sun was high in the sky. As for the courtesans – in no way to be confused with the regiments of whores that are part and parcel of the life of any flourishing sea-port – they had been a speciality of Venice since the sixteenth century. Long celebrated for their loveliness and elegance, they were said to take a genuine pride in their work, catering for every taste and able to satisfy the most fastidious and exacting of clients. With a carnival that was the most protracted and abandoned anywhere – the mandatory masks providing all the anonymity that could be desired – it was no wonder that Venice became the eighteenth-century equivalent of Las Vegas. But she was a Las Vegas with a difference: for visitors of an intellectual turn of mind, there were books, pictures and sculptures to be bought, churches and palaces to be wondered at, and the music and opera for which the city was famous throughout the civilized world.

Life in the Serenissima must have been pleasant indeed; but man was not, alas, intended for too much pleasure. Slowly but ineluctably, it begins to sap his strength and eat away at his moral fibre. And so it was with Venice. Faced, in her centuries of greatness, with a threat comparable to that presented by the twenty-six-year-old Napoleon, she would have entered into some sharp diplomacy, set in motion a number of behind-the-scenes intrigues, formed suitable alliances, and generally made dispositions which, successful or not, she would at least known to have been the best possible in the circumstances. In 1796, she panicked. She allowed him to intimidate her, fell for all his bluffs, decided against re-arming or mobilizing her hopelessly rundown forces, and put all her faith in a policy of appeasement – with the inevitable results. On Friday May 1797 the Great Council agreed, by a majority of 512 to twenty with five abstentions, to accept unconditionally all Napoleon's terms. These included the occupation of the city by French troops and the dissolution of the Republic. Doge Lodovico Manin then returned to his private apartments, where he slowly removed his *corno* – the cap of State which had been worn by himself and his predecessors for the best part of a thousand years – and handed it to his valet. 'Take it,' he murmured, 'I shall not be needing it again.'

The French occupation of Venice did not last long – though long enough, alas, for the symbolic burning of a *corno* and other emblems of ducal dignity and a copy of the Golden Book, and for the ruthless sack of many of her finest works of art. (Some, like the Horses of St Mark, were later returned; others, including Veronese's tremendous *Marriage at Cana* from the refectory of S. Giorgio Maggiore, are still in the Louvre and likely to remain there.) In October of the same year, by the Treaty of Campo Formio, Napoleon handed over Venice, together with Istria and Dalmatia, to Austria. In 1805, after Austerlitz, he took it back again, to incorporate it in his new Kingdom of Italy; but ten years later the Congress of Vienna returned it once more, with the provinces of Venetia and Lombardy, to the Hapsburg Empire, and Austrian it remained – apart from seventeen heroic, hopeless months in 1848–9 during which the Venetians rose up in arms and declared a new independent republic – until 1866 and the destruction of the Imperial army by the Prussians at Sadowa. Then, and only then, was Venice finally allowed to take her place in Cavour's united Italy. No longer was she independent; but she was, at least, free.

It has seemed a good idea to devote the greater part of this introduction to a brief – and inevitably episodic – outline of the Republic's history in order to provide something of a background for the passages that follow; for the same reason, something must now be said of Venice today. If that fifteenth-century Venetian of whom we spoke earlier would find modern Venice not entirely unfamiliar, one born in the early twentieth who returned to the city of his birth for the first time in fifty years would be astonished at how little it had altered. There are, admittedly, a few unforgivable eyesores: the post-war extension to the Danieli, for example, or the elevation of the Bauer-Grunwald on S. Moisè, or the Teatro Goldoni, or that dreadful new bank on Campo Manin. But Venice's record in this respect still remains a good deal better than that of any other major city of Europe, and for that we must be duly grateful. What would cast a far darker shadow over the return of the native would be the people. Venice has been a tourist city for 300 years; indeed, since the decline of her commercial prosperity, foreign visitors have been her life's blood. But the explosion of air travel and group excursion touring now threatens to destroy her. During the summer months, over and above those staying in her bursting hotels some 30,000 tourists *a day* are poured into the city by whole fleets of motor coaches, filling the Piazza – which many of them never leave until the time comes to depart – to the point of impenetrability, threatening to sink the *vaporetti* by sheer weight of numbers and effectively depriving the resident population of any public transport for most of their working hours. Since these tourists usually bring packed lunches with them – leaving the packages in or around the hundred or more litter bins that already disfigure the Piazza and are invariably overflowing by noon – they spend virtually no money in the city except, perhaps, on a can or two of Coca-Cola and a few packets of bird-seed for the disgustingly overfed pigeons; inexorably, however, they are wearing it down.

Much has been written, in the twenty years that have passed since the great floods of 1966, about the dangers that Venice has nowadays to face: from the sea that floods, the land that sinks, the air that pollutes. Much, too, has been and is being done to avert them. Gradually, however, it is becoming clear that the tourist menace is greater and more immediate than any of these; and that, if decisive steps are not soon taken to stem the tide, it will engulf the city just as surely – and just as fatally – as her surrounding waters could ever have done. Any such steps, we all know, will be greeted by howls of protest: there will be the usual accusations of élitism, claims that the shopkeepers and restaurateurs are being victimized, and all the other complaints that invariably follow unpopular conservation measures. So be it. My own solution, were I in authority, would be first to require every tourist to provide proof of at least one night's hotel accommodation, and secondly to ban all tourist motor coaches from Venice. I should then proclaim that every visitor would be welcome to the city, provided only that he made his own way there by private or normal public transport: by car or bicycle, by train or regular scheduled bus service. Thus the sole sufferers would be those who were not prepared to take a modicum of trouble; and the influx would be limited to those who really wanted to be in Venice, rather than those who were there only because it was Tuesday.

Pending some action of this sort, I can only advise intending visitors, for their own sakes, to avoid the months of high summer – while consoling them, if they have no choice in the matter, with the assurance that even when the tourist tide is at its height, a walk of less than five minutes in any direction from the Piazza–Merceria–Rialto axis will bring them to some quiet church and *campo* in which the gondola tee-shirts and the flag-brandishing guides – though not, alas, the ubiquitous mask shops – are alike unknown. Finally, I would commend to them the delights of night walks through the city: walks in which they will find the silence broken only by the sound of their own footsteps and, occasionally, the gentle slap of water on stone. They will rejoice, too, in a new beauty; for the absence of motor cars permits a level of street lighting that beguiles the eye instead of assaulting it. Nor, finally, need they have any fear; Venice remains a safe, law-abiding community, with one of the lowest crime rates in Europe.

The authors represented in the following pages are not by any means all favourably disposed. They do, however, span a period of some fourteen centuries, each casting his own individual spotlight on the Serenissima in such a way as to cover virtually every stage of her development; and the composite – and often self-contradictory – portrait that emerges, whatever its shortcomings, consequently possesses an additional and relatively unfamiliar dimension – that of time. Here, in short, is Venice through the ages: from her misty, moisty beginnings among the scattered communities of the lagoon to her high zenith as the Queen of Cities All, and then down through the years of carnival and Casanova to the present day.

What is she now? A waterlogged and overcrowded museum? A condemned playground? The thinking man's Disneyland? Or a living, breathing, working city which has the fortune, and at the same time the misfortune, of being the loveliest in the world and all the nightmare responsibility that that entails? This book will not provide the answer; but it will, with any luck, help the reader to make up his mind.

John Julius Norwich
1989

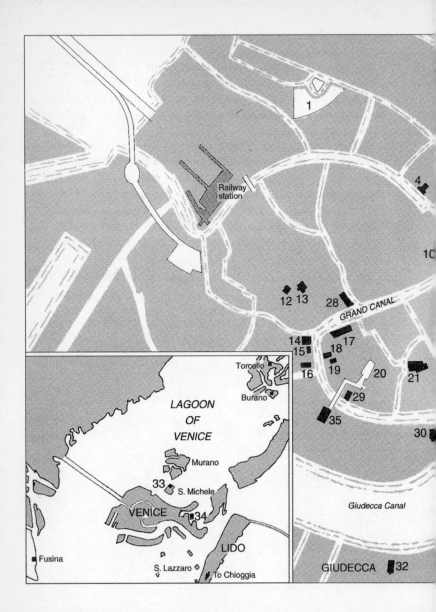

1

4

10

Railway
station

12 13

28

GRAND CANAL

14
15   18   17
16   19   20   21

29

35   30

Giudecca Canal

GIUDECCA   32

Torcello

Burano

*LAGOON
OF
VENICE*

Murano

33
S. Michele

VENICE   34

Fusina

LIDO

S. Lazzaro

To Chioggia

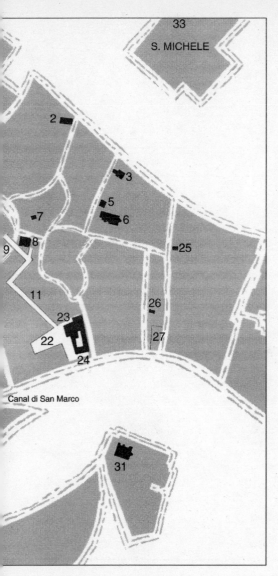

S. MICHELE

Canal di San Marco

Map of the city locating the places described

1 Ghetto
2 Gesuiti
3 S. Lazzaro dei Mendicanti
4 Ca d'Oro
5 Scuola di S. Marco
6 SS. Giovanni e Paolo
7 S. Giovanni Crisostomo
8 Fondaco dei Tedeschi
9 Rialto Bridge
10 Rialto Market
11 Merceria
12 Scuola di S. Rocco
13 Frari
14 Palazzo Foscari
15 Palazzo Giustinian
16 Ca Rezzonico
17 Palazzo Mocenigo
18 Palazzo Grassi
19 S. Samuele
20 Campo S. Stefano
21 Fenice Theatre
22 St. Mark's Square
23 Basilica of St. Mark
24 Doges' Palace
25 S. Giustina
26 S. Giorgio dei Greci
27 Pieta
28 Palazzo Barberigo
29 Palazzo Barbaro
30 Sta Maria della Salute
31 S. Giorgio Maggiore
32 Redentore
33 S. Michele
34 S. Pietro di Castello
35 Scuola della Carita
   (now Accademia)

VENICE

CHILDE HAROLD'S PILGRIMAGE

CANTO THE FOURTH

I

I stood in Venice, on the Bridge of Sighs;
A palace and a prison on each hand:
I saw from out the wave her structures rise
As from the stroke of the enchanter's wand:
A thousand years their cloudy wings expand
Around me, and a dying Glory smiles
O'er the far times, when many a subject land
Look'd to the winged Lion's marble piles,
Where Venice sate in state, throned on her hundred isles!

II

She looks a sea Cybele, fresh from ocean,
Rising with her tiara of proud towers
At airy distance, with majestic motion,
A ruler of the waters and their powers:
And such she was; – her daughters had their powers:
From spoils of nations, and the exhaustless East
Pour'd in her lap all gems in sparkling showers.
In purple was she robed, and of her feast
Monarchs partook, and deem'd their dignity increased.

III

In Venice Tasso's echoes are no more,
And silent rows the songless gondolier;
Her palaces are crumbling to the shore,
And music meets not always now the ear:
Those days are gone – but Beauty still is here.
States fall, arts fade – but Nature doth not die,
Nor yet forget how Venice once was dear,
The pleasant place of all festivity,
The revel of the earth, the masque of Italy!

IV

But unto us she hath a spell beyond
Her name in story, and her long array
Of mighty shadows, whose dim forms despond
Above the dogeless city's vanish'd sway;
Ours is a trophy which will not decay
With the Rialto; Shylock and the Moor,
And Pierre, can not be swept or worn away –
The keystones of the arch! though all were o'er,
For us repeopled were the solitary shore . . .

XI

The spouseless Adriatic mourns her lord
And annual marriage, now no more renew'd,
The Bucentaur lies rotting unrestored,
Neglected garment of her widowhood!
St Mark yet sees his lion where he stood,
Stand, but in mockery of his wither'd power,
Over the proud Place where an Emperor sued,
And monarchs gazed and envied in the hour
When Venice was a queen with an unequall'd dower.

XII

The Suabian sued, and now the Austrian reigns –
An Emperor tramples where an Emperor knelt;
Kingdoms are shrunk to provinces, and chains
Clank over sceptred cities; nations melt
From power's high pinnacle, when they have felt
The sunshine for a while, and downward go
Like lauwine loosen'd from the mountain's belt;
Oh for one hour of blind old Dandolo!
Th'octogenarian chief, Byzantium's conquering foe.

XIII

Before St Mark still glow his steeds of brass,
Their gilded collars glittering in the sun;
But is not Doria's menace come to pass?
Are they not *bridled*? – Venice, lost and won,

Her thirteen hundred years of freedom done,
Sinks, like a sea-weed, into whence she rose!
Better be whelm'd beneath the waves, and shun,
Even in destruction's depth, her foreign foes,
From whom submission wrings an infamous repose.

Byron

. . . you will find on the morrow that you are deeply attached to Venice. It is by living there from day to day that you feel the fulness of its charm; that you invite its exquisite influence to sink into your spirit. The place is as changeable as a nervous woman, and you know it only when you know all the aspects of its beauty. It has high spirits or low, it is pale or red, grey or pink, cold or warm, fresh or wan, according to the weather or the hour. It is always interesting and almost always sad; but it has a thousand occasional graces and is always liable to happy accidents. You become extraordinarily fond of these things; you count upon them; they make part of your life. Tenderly fond you become; there is something indefinable in those depths of personal acquaintance that gradually establish themselves. The place seems to personify itself, to become human and sentient and conscious of your affection. You desire to embrace it, to caress it, to possess it; and finally a soft sense of possession grows up and your visit becomes a perpetual love-affair.

From 'Portraits of Places' by Henry James

Landfall

[1] No one has described the first landfall better than James (now Jan) Morris; from *Venice*.

At 45° 14′N, 12° 18′E, the navigator, sailing up the Adriatic coast of Italy, discovers an opening in the long low line of the shore: and turning westward, with the race of the tide, he enters a lagoon. Instantly the boisterous sting of the sea is lost. The water around him is shallow but opaque, the atmosphere curiously translucent, the colours pallid, and over the whole wide bowl of mudbank and water there hangs a suggestion of melancholy. It is like an albino lagoon.

It is encircled with illusory reflections, like mirages in the desert – wavering trees and blurred hillocks, ships without hulls, imaginary marshes: and among these hallucinations the water reclines in a kind of trance. Along the eastern reef strings of straggling fishing villages lie empty and unkempt. Away in the wastes there stand the sails of fishing boats, orange, yellow and magenta, with cabalistic signs or heraldic symbols, a rampant red horse, an all-seeing eye. The shallows are littered with intricate shambling palisades of sticks and basket-work, and among them solitary men, knee-deep in sludge and water, prod in the mud for shellfish. A motor boat chugs by with a stench of fish or oil. A woman on the shore shouts to a friend, and her voice eddies away strangely, muffled and distorted across the flats.

Silent islands lie all about, lapped in marsh and mud-bank. Here is a glowering octagonal fort, here a gaunt abandoned lighthouse. A mesh of nets patterns the walls of a fishermen's islet, and a restless covey of boats nuzzles its water-gate. From the ramparts of an island barracks a listless soldier with his cap over his eyes waves half-heartedly out of his sentry-box. Two savage dogs bark and rage from a broken villa. There is a flicker of lizard on a wall. Sometimes a country smell steals across the water, of cows or hay or fertilizer: and sometimes there flutters in the wake of the boat, not an albatross, but a butterfly.

Presently this desolate place quickens, and smart white villas appear upon the reef. The hump of a great hotel protrudes above the trees, gay parasols ornament a café. A trim passenger steamer flurries southwards, loaded deep. A fishing flotilla streams workmanlike towards the open sea. To the west beneath a smudge of mountains, there is a thin silver gleam of oil drums, and a suggestion of smoke. A yellow barge, piled high with pop bottles, springs from a landing-stage like a cheerful dove from an ark. A white yacht sidles indolently by. Three small boys have grounded their boat on a sand-bank, and are throwing slobbery mud at each other. There is a flash of oxy-acetylene from a dark shed, and a barge stands on stilts outside a boat yard. A hooter sounds; a bell booms nobly; a big white sea-bird settles heavily upon a post; and thus the navigator, rounding a promontory, sees before him a city.

It is very old, and very grand, and bent-backed. Its towers survey the lagoon in crotchety splendour, some leaning one way, some another. Its skyline is elaborate with campaniles, domes, pinnacles, cranes, riggings, television aerials, crenellations, eccentric chimneys and a big red grain elevator. There are glimpses of flags and fretted rooftops, marble pillars, cavernous canals. An incessant bustle of boats passes before the quays of the place; a great white liner slips towards its port; a multitude of tottering palaces, brooding and monstrous, presses towards its waterfront like so many invalid aristocrats jostling for fresh air. It is a gnarled but gorgeous city: and as the boat approaches through the last church-crowned islands, and a jet fighter screams splendidly out of the sun, so the whole scene seems to shimmer – with pinkness, with age, with self-satisfaction, with sadness, with delight.

The navigator stows away his charts and puts on a gay straw hat: for he has reached that paragon among landfalls, Venice.

Early beginnings

[2] The first clear picture we have of the early Venetians is found in a letter from Cassiodorus, the Praetorian Prefect of King Theodoric the Ostrogoth. It is addressed from Theodoric's capital at Ravenna to 'the Maritime Tribunes', and is dated AD 523.

The Istrian harvests of wine and oil have this year been particularly abundant, and orders have been given for their safe transport to Ravenna. Pray show your devotion, therefore, by bringing them hither with all speed. For you possess many vessels in the region ... and you will be, in a sense, sailing through your native country. Besides your other blessings, there is open to you a way which is ever free of danger; for when the winds rage and the sea is closed against you, you may sail up the pleasantest of rivers. Your ships need fear no angry gusts, since they may continually hug the shore. Often, with their hulls invisible, they seem to be moving across the fields. Sometimes you pull them with ropes, at others men help them along with their feet ...

For you live like sea birds, with your homes dispersed, like the Cyclades, across the surface of the water. The solidity of the earth on which they rest is secured only by osier and wattle; yet you do not hesitate to oppose so frail a bulwark to the wildness of the sea. Your people have one great wealth – the fish which suffices for them all. Among you there is no difference between rich and poor; your food is the same, your houses are all alike. Envy, which rules the rest of the world, is unknown to you. All your energies are spent on your salt-fields; in them indeed lies your prosperity, and your power to purchase those things which you have not. For though there may be men who have little need of gold, yet none live who desire not salt.

Be diligent, therefore, to repair your boats – which, like horses, you keep tied up at the doors of your dwellings – and make haste to depart . . .

[3] Forty-two years later, after the death of the Emperor Justinian, his military commander Longinus paid an official visit to the lagoon. He was given an enthusiastic reception, 'with bells and flutes and cytherns and other instruments of music, loud enough to drown the very thunder of heaven'; but the Venetians' address of welcome hinted clearly enough that they were not to be trifled with.

The Lord, who is our help and protection, has preserved us that we may live in these watery marshes, in our huts of wood and wattle. For this new Venice which we have raised in the lagoons has become a mighty habitation for us, so that we fear no invasion or seizure by any of the Kings or Princes of this world, nor even by the Emperor himself . . . unless they come by sea, and therein lies our strength.

[4] The island of Torcello was, in the seventh and eighth centuries, one of the most important settlements in the Venetian lagoon, but in the ninth focus shifted to the islands known as Rialto, where it has remained ever since; from *The Stones of Venice* by John Ruskin.

(John Ruskin 1819–1900) was by far the most influential art historian and critic of the Victorian age. *The Stones of Venice* is perhaps the most important book ever written on Venetian art. It is long and enormously detailed – most readers will be better off with an abridgement – but it contains many passages of extraordinary beauty.)

Seven miles to the north of Venice, the banks of sand, which near the city rise little above low-water mark, attain by degrees a higher level, and knit themselves at last into fields of salt morass, raised here and there into shapeless mounds, and intercepted by narrow creeks of sea. One of the feeblest of these inlets, after winding for some time among buried fragments of masonry, and knots of sunburnt weeds whitened with webs of fucus, stays itself in an utterly stagnant pool beside a plot of greener grass covered with ground ivy and violets. On this mound is built a rude brick campanile, of the commonest Lombardic type, which if we ascend towards evening (and there are none to hinder us, the door of its ruinous staircase swinging idly on its hinges), we may command from it one of the most notable scenes in this wide world of ours. Far as the eye can reach, a waste of wild sea moor, of a lurid ashen grey; not like our northern moors with their jet-black pools and purple heath, but lifeless, the colour of sackcloth, with the corrupted sea-water soaking through the roots of its acrid weeds, and gleaming hither and thither through its snaky channels. No gathering of fantastic mists, nor coursing of clouds across it; but melancholy clearness of space in the warm sunset, oppressive, reaching to the horizon of its level gloom. To the very horizon, on the north-east; but, to the north and west, there is a blue line of higher land along the border of it, and above this, but farther back, a misty band of mountains, touched with snow. To the east, the paleness and roar of the Adriatic, louder at momentary intervals as the surf breaks on the bars of sand; to the south, the widening branches of the calm lagoon, alternately purple and pale green, as they reflect the evening clouds or twilight sky; and almost beneath our feet, on the same field which sustains the tower we gaze from, a group of four buildings, two of them little larger than cottages (though built of stone, and one adorned by a quaint belfry), the third an octagonal chapel, of which we can see but little more than the flat red roof with its rayed tiling, the fourth, a considerable church with nave and aisles, but of which, in like manner, we can see little but the long central ridge and lateral slopes of roof, which the sunlight separates in one glowing mass from the green field beneath and grey moor beyond. There are no living creatures near the buildings, nor any vestige of village or city round about them. They lie like a little company of ships becalmed on a far-away sea.

Then look farther to the south. Beyond the widening branches of the lagoon, and rising out of the bright lake into which they gather, there are a multitude of towers, dark, and scattered among square-set shapes of clustered palaces, a long and irregular line fretting the southern sky.

Mother and daughter, you behold them both in their widowhood – TORCELLO, and VENICE.

First impressions

[5] Before the middle of the sixteenth century, travellers' accounts of Venice are rare indeed. But Simon Fitz-Simon, an Irish friar, arrived there on 28 June 1323, on his way to the Holy Land, and found the centre of the city already very much as we find it today. From a manuscript in the library of Corpus Christi College, Cambridge.

... it is completely set in the sea, yet by the name of its beauty and the merit of its elegance it could be set between the star Arcturus and the shining Pleiades. It is two miles from terra firma, and its streets are one-third paved with brick and two-thirds made of navigable streams, through which the sea flows and ebbs continuously without respite. In the city lie the bodies of saints, which are whole and uncorrupted: Mark evangelist, Zacharias prophet and father of St John [the] Baptist, whose skeleton is revealed to this day, Gregory of Nazarenus, Theodore the martyr, and the holy virgins Lucy virgin and martyr, Marina virgin, and many more martyrs, confessors, and holy virgins. In honour of the aforesaid evangelist is a most sumptuous church, built incomparably of marble and other valuable stones, and excellently adorned and worked with Bible stories in mosaic. Opposite it is that public square which, all things considered, has no equal anywhere. To this church is joined almost continuously that famous palace of the Duke of Venice, in which are fed at all times live lions for the glory of the state and the magnificence of its citizens. And opposite this palace near the harbour are two round marble columns, large and high, on the top of one of which, for their magnificence, is the figure of a lion shining in gold like the moon or the sun; and at the west door of the church are two bronze horses likewise always shining.

[6] A seventeenth-century Scot describes the city to his sister, the Countess of Erroll, on 25 February 1695; from *Letters from James Drummond, Earl of Perth* . . .

(James Drummond (1648–1716), fourth Earl and first Duke of Perth, had had a chequered career before he left for Italy in 1693. Hated in Scotland for his cruelty (as Sheriff of Edinburgh he had introduced the thumbscrew for the first time in Great Britain) and for his apostasy (he had become a Roman Catholic on the accession of James II), he had been imprisoned after the Glorious Revolution and had subsequently fled the country.)

Here are rich churches, a city of pallaces, and instead of streets alleys of water; gondolas are our coaches, and, although they be all covered with only black cloth, yet no coach in Europe has finer glasses than they have, so that you go in a box of christall through the town. The canalls are generally very narrow, only the Canall Grande is like a river; it has only one bridge, that of Rialto, which is of white marble, and the widest arch in Europe; [the bridge over the] Don is a mere bauble compared with it. St Mark's is a building after the Greek mode; it has six cupolas. The church is low and dark; but the pictures in the roof, the floor, the front without, &c. are all mosaick, and so lovely that I never weary to look at them; the ground is gold, the figures all in their naturall colours, made of pieces of stone indented, and

so disposed that no pencill can outdo them. The place
[square], as you may see it in many pictures and books, is
thus:

The church is where the three strokes are; the water, (which
is very wide), is where the two points are; the two pillars, St
Theodore on one and St Mark's lion on the other; the Librarie
is next you, and St Mark's pallace, the Doge's residence, over
against it; the one point in the corner is St Mark's steeple.
The other place is the finest in Europe, and very large it is; a
gallery upon pillars goes quite round, where eight or ten may
walk abreast, and all is uniform. Here are pictures innumerable and inestimable, and some admirable churches and many
noble edifices. I have not yet seen the Arsenall. When I see it
I will tell you my thoughts of it.

[7] Edward Gibbon wrote in his memoirs that 'the
spectacle of Venice afforded some hours of astonishment
and some days of Disgust'; in short, he hated Venice.
But then, as author of *The Decline and Fall of the
Roman Empire*, he was a classicist through and through,
and such a reaction was, perhaps, only to be expected;
from a letter written 22 April 1765, in his *Letters*, edited
by J. E. Norton.

(Edward Gibbon (1739–1794) visited Venice on his way back
from his fateful pilgrimage to Rome.)

Of all the towns in Italy I am the least satisfied with Venice;
objects which are only singular without being pleasing, produce a momentary surprise which soon gives way to satiety
and disgust. Old and in general ill built houses, ruined
pictures, and stinking ditches dignified with the pompous
denomination of Canals; a fine bridge spoilt by two rows of
houses upon it, and a large square decorated with the worst

Architecture I ever yet saw, and wonderfull only in a place where there is more land than water: such are the colours I should employ in my portrait of Venice; a portrait certainly true in general, tho' perhaps you should attribute the very great darkness of the shades of my being out of humour with the place. Here are no English, and all communication with the natives of the place is strictly forbid.

[8] The twenty-one-year old Disraeli saw it very differently, as he wrote to his father in September 1826; from *Letters of Benjamin Disraeli, Earl of Beaconsfield.*

(Benjamin Disraeli (1804–1881) statesman and novelist, Prime Minister in 1868 and 1874–80 and later Earl of Beaconsfield, had an Italian grandfather who had come to England from Modena as an importer of Leghorn chip and straw hats.)

I entered Venice with a magnificent setting sun on a grand fete day. As we glided in a gondola up the great Lagune we passed St Mark's, the Campanile, the Palace of the Doges, the Bridge of Sighs, the Prison, before we reached our hotel, once the proud residence of the Bernardinis, a family which has given more than one Doge to the old Republic; the floors of our rooms were of marble, the hangings of satin, the ceilings painted by Tintoretto and his scholars full of Turkish triumphs and trophies, the chairs of satin and the gilding though of two hundred years' duration as brightly burnished as the new mosaic invention. After a hasty dinner we rushed to the mighty Place of St Mark. It was crowded, two Greek and one Turkish ship of war were from accidental circumstances in port, and their crews mingled with the other spectators with high foreheads and higher caps and elevated eyebrows; then there was the Austrian military band, and the bearded Jew with his black velvet cap was not wanting. Three gorgeous flags waved on the mighty staffs which are opposite the Church in all the old drawings and which once bore the standards of Candia, Crete, and the Morea. Tired with travelling we left the gay scene crowded, but the moon was so bright that a juggler was conjuring in a circle under

our window, and an itinerant Italian opera performing by
our bridge. Serenades were constant during the whole night;
indeed music is never silent in Venice. I wish I could give
you an idea of the moonlight there, but that is impossible.
Venice by moonlight is an enchanted city; the floods of silver
light upon the moresco architecture, the perfect absence of
all harsh sounds of carts and carriages, the never-ceasing
music on the waters produced an effect on the mind which
cannot be experienced, I am sure, in any other city in the
world . . .

Sailing down the Grand Canal the palaces of Foscari,
Grimani, Barbarigo, and other names which make the coldest
heart thrill rise rapidly before you . . . The Palace of the
Doges is still kept up for public offices, library, &c. Its walls
are painted by the greatest masters of the miraculous Venetian
school, and its roof is gilt and adorned in a manner which
leaves far behind all the magnificence of all the palaces in the
world. In every room you are reminded of the glory and the
triumphs of the Republic: the door of one chamber once
closed the Mosque of St Sophia, the pillars of another graced
a temple in the Morea, and even Solomon's Temple is not
forgotten, and two pillars of fantastic architecture were
carved from large columns of granite which were brought in
triumph by a noble Venetian from the ruins of Jerusalem. St
Mark's Church is a pile of precious stones, the walls are of
all kinds of the rarest marbles and even of jasper, lapis lazuli,
and the richest porphyry and Oriental agates, the interior is
cased with mosaics of gold, and in the front figure five
hundred pillars of all kinds of architecture and colours, some
of which are of verd antique. The four brazen horses amble,
not prance, as some have described, on the front, and five
cupolas, hooded cupolas, crown this Christian Mosque. It is
vain to write anything here of the pictures, the churches, the
palaces, with which this city abounds. According to the
common opinion I saw all that ought to be seen, but I never
felt less inclined to quit a place. It is in these spots that I wish
to stay, for it is in such places that the mind receives that
degree of wholesome excitation which is one of the great
benefits of travel. I mean an excitation which quickens the
feelings and the fancy, and which enables the mind to arrive

at results with greater facility and rapidity than we do at home, and in our studies

[9] To Charles Dickens, his first sight of Venice had the effect of a bombshell. He described it to his friend John Forster in a letter dated 12 November 1844; from *The Letters of Charles Dickens*, edited by Kathleen Tillotson.

(Charles Dickens (1812–1870) spent three and a half months travelling in Europe during the summer and autumn of 1844, after the publication of *Martin Chuzzlewit*. He passed five days in Venice in mid-November.)

My dear fellow, nothing in the world that ever you have heard of Venice, is equal to the magnificent and stupendous reality. The wildest visions of the Arabian Nights are nothing to the piazza of Saint Mark, and the first impression of the inside of the church. The gorgeous and wonderful reality of Venice is beyond the fancy of the wildest dreamer. Opium couldn't build such a place, and enchantment couldn't shadow it forth in a vision. All that I have heard of it, read of it in truth or fiction, fancied of it, is left thousands of miles behind. You know that I am liable to disappointment in such things from over-expectation, but Venice is above, beyond, out of all reach of coming near, the imagination of a man. It has never been rated high enough. It is a thing you would shed tears to see. When I came *on board* here last night (after a five miles' row in a gondola; which somehow or other, I wasn't at all prepared for); when, from seeing the city lying, one light, upon the distant water, like a ship, I came plashing through the silent and deserted streets; I felt as if the houses were reality – the water, fever-madness. But when, in the bright, cold, bracing day, I stood upon the piazza this morning, by Heaven the glory of the place was insupportable! And diving down from that into its wickedness and gloom – its awful prisons, deep below the water; its judgment chambers, secret doors, deadly nooks, where the torches you carry with you blink as if they couldn't bear the air in which the frightful scenes were acted; and coming out again into the radiant, unsubstantial Magic of the town; and diving in again, into

vast churches, and old tombs – a new sensation, a new
memory, a new mind came upon me. Venice is a bit of my
brain from this time. My dear Forster, if you could share my
transports (as you would if you were here) what would I not
give! I feel cruel not to have brought Kate and Georgy;
positively cruel and base. Canaletti and Stanny[1] miraculous
in their truth. Turner, very noble. But the reality itself, beyond
all pen or pencil. I never saw the thing before that I should be
afraid to describe. But to tell what Venice is, I feel to be an
impossibility. And here I sit alone, writing it: with nothing to
urge me on, or goad me to that estimate, which, speaking of
it to anyone I loved, and being spoken to in return, would
lead me to form. In the sober solitude of a famous inn; with
the great bell of Saint Mark ringing twelve at my elbow; with
three arched windows in my room (two stories high) looking
down upon the Grand Canal and away, beyond, to where the
sun went down to-night in a blaze; and thinking over again
those silent speaking faces of Titian and Tintoretto; I swear
(uncooled by any humbug I have seen) that Venice is *the*
wonder and the new sensation of the world! If you could be
set down in it, never having heard of it, it would still be so.
With your foot upon its stones, its pictures before you, and
its history in your mind, it is something past all writing of or
speaking of – almost past all thinking of. You couldn't talk
to me in this room, nor I to you, without shaking hands and
saying 'Good God my dear fellow, have we lived to see this!'

[10] Rupert Brooke, aged nineteen, writes to his friend
St John Lucas, from Padua in April 1906; from *Letters*,
chosen and edited by G. Keynes.

(Rupert Brooke (1887–1915) paid only one visit to Venice,
which was not a success. He found it hot, crowded and
malodorous, and confessed to his friend Geoffrey Keynes that
he hated it.)

Venice is a little disappointing in April. Germans and Americans rather obscure the view. Also I hate the brawling ugly

[1] Clarkson Stanfield R. A. (1794–1867).

steamers that disturb the Grand Canal. There were moments when the world seemed fine – when, after Mestre (although we came in by train) the lights of Venice started out of the sea: and again, when from the heat of the train and the bustle and noise of the station we rushed into a white silent city, and slid down the Grand Canal in a quiet gondola under a full Italian moon. To enter Venice at night is fit and proper. But it is disheartening to wake next morning to electric launches and cosmopolitan hotels and Americans and all the other evils that our civilized age gives. Some day when I have been driven away from Cambridge for being too young, I shall go and live in Venice in December or July, when the tourists have returned to their proper hells; till then I shall tell myself that I have never been to Venezia, only to Venice at Earl's Court.[1] Yet though the whole was a failure there were times when I was happy. Sometimes I sat in the vaporous gloom of St Mark and gazing on the mosaics, mused of all my religions, till everything became confused, the grand pulpit changed to an altar of Moloch, the figure of Mary grew like Isis, and the fair Byzantine Christ was lost in the delicate troubled form of Antinous. Also, when the ancient night made Venice ancient again, and the Teutons slept stertorously after their dinners, I escaped and stole in a gondola up lost little waterways till I forgot what the stars were like. But I was really miserable, being modern and decadent, in an ancient eternal city. And I hated almost all the Venetian painters, who are of the flesh and yet do not know that the most lovely flesh is that through which the soul shines. The stolid but respectable damsels of Bellini developed into the ponderous carnalities of Titian and Paolo – and I longed for my Botticellis. The Venetians were never purely young and never beautifully decadent, but always in a tawdry and sensual middle-age. But tomorrow I shall delight in the Giottos here; and they may prove a remedy. We spend Monday in Verona and then proceed to Paris, where I shall worship in

---

[1] Earl's Court entertainment ground (forerunner of the present Exhibition Hall) existed from 1887 to 1914. Its several permanent features were supplemented by annual exhibitions and 'spectaculars', for one of which an imaginary corner of Venice was recreated, complete with real gondolas and gondoliers.

turn the lovely classics at the Louvre and the wicked moderns in the Salons. And in a fortnight I return to taint the righteous atmosphere of Rugby School for one last purple term.

Yours

RUPERT BROOKE

The Doges' Palace

[11] A great fire destroys a large part of the Doges' Palace – fortunately the eastern side, on the Rio del Palazzo – in 1483; from *Annali Veneti* by Senator Domenico Malipiero. Translated by John Julius Norwich.

(Domenico Malipiero (1428–1515) was a Venetian nobleman, admiral and governor (*podestà*) of several mainland cities. His extremely informative diaries constitute one of the most important sources of Venetiari history from 1457 to the end of the century.)

On the night of 14 September, fire broke out in the upper part of the Palace of the Doge. A candle had been left burning in the chapel after mass, and during the night the flame caught the altar cloth. The first to arrive on the scene came from the house of Angelo Trevisan, opposite the Palace. The entire chapel was destroyed, together with the private rooms and the gilded hall with the paintings of the departure of Doge Moro for Ancona and his return. Also burnt was the *mappa mundi*, which included Italy, wrought by the hand of

Father Antonio di Leonardi – a most singular work. The Doge left his Palace and retired to the house of the Captain of the Prisons. But the gates of the Palace were closed, because all the Ducal furniture had been taken out into the courtyard; indeed, the fire might have done little damage had the people been able to gain entry earlier. And the building of the Cà Diedo close to the Palace was taken over for the habitation of the Doges and a wooden bridge was built to connect it with the part of the Palace in which the Signoria met. The majority of the Patricians decided to spend no more than 6,000 ducats to repair the Palace, owing to the straitened condition then prevailing ... but Nicolò Trevisan wished to buy all the neighbouring houses as far as the Calle delle Rasse, and to build there a new residence for the Doge with a large garden, and join it by a stone bridge to the Sala de Collegio in the old building, which was to be restored and used for administrative purposes. It was, however, finally decided to rebuild the original Palace in three storeys; and it was agreed to engage the sculptor Antonio Rizzo for 100 ducats a year. But by 1496 this Antonio Rizzo had spent 80,000 ducats and had not yet completed half of the work; and it was discovered that he had kept 12,000 for himself. So he fled and took refuge in the Romagna, and died soon after at Foligno.

[12] Pietro Casola, who was taken on a tour of the half-completed Palace in 1494, was unhappy about the decision not to adopt Nicolò Trevisan's plan; from *Canon Pietro Casola's Pilgrimage* by M. Margaret Newett.

(Pietro Casola (1427–1507) was a noble churchman from Milan, who made a pilgrimage to Jerusalem in 1494, and on the way there stopped briefly in Venice.)

I saw many beautiful palaces, beginning with the Palace of St Mark, which is always inhabited by the Doge and his family. The façade of the said palace has been renovated in part with a great display of gold; and a new flight of steps is being built there – a stupendous and costly work – by which to ascend to the said palace from the side of the Church of St Mark.

The lower portico on the ground floor is so well arranged that no more can be said; it is true, however, that it is spoiled by the prisons, which are not well placed there. The portico, which goes round above, looks partly over the piazza, partly over the Grand Canal, partly over a small canal, and one part towards the Church of St Mark, and all this portico has its columns of marble and other beautiful ornaments. In these porticos many Courts are established with their benches, and at every bench there are at least three assessors or hearers all together. At the time of the hearings many cries are heard there, as also happens at Milan at the Broletto at the time of the trials. Among the said tribunals there is that of the Lords of the Night, who employ in their hearings the torment, called in our tongue *the Curlo* [torture with the rope: *della corda*].

Besides the other notable things in the said palace, I saw a very long hall whose walls are painted very ornately. And there is painted the story how Frederick Barbarossa drove away Pope Alexander the Fourth,[1] who fled in disguise to Venice, and was recognized in a monastery called the Monastery della Carità. The whole story is represented with such richness and naturalness in the figures that I think little could be added. The ceiling of the said hall is decorated with great gilded pictures. Seats are placed around the said hall, and in addition there are three rows of double seats, in the body of the hall, placed back to back. There are two magnificent gilded seats, one at each end of the said hall; I was told they were for seating the Doge, one for the winter, and the other for the summer. In this hall the Great Council is held – that is, the Council of all the gentlemen, who, it is said, are two thousand five hundred in number.

The Council called the Council of the Pregadi is held in another hall. I will say little about it because it is not adorned like the others. The hall where the Doge and his Councillors hold audience constantly is not very large, but it is magnificently decorated, with its gilded ceiling and its painted and storied walls. The throne on which sits the Doge, also called by the Venetians the 'Prince,' is all gilded and much higher than the others.

[1] In fact Alexander III (see Introduction, p. 8).

With regard to the magnificence and decoration of the habitation of the aforesaid Doge – as I have seen many other princely palaces in this our time both in Italy and abroad, beginning at Rome – I venture to say that it is the most beautiful in Italy. It is so rich in carved work and everything gilded, that it is a marvel. One of the pages of the aforesaid Doge showed me everything, beginning with the bed in which he sleeps, and proceeding even to the kitchen, and in my opinion nothing could be added. The decorations are not movable, but fixed. There is no lack of marble and porphyry and woodwork subtly carved, and all is of such a nature that one is never weary of looking.

The said palace is being renovated, and in the new part the arms of the immediate predecessors of the present prince are to be seen. But after seeing the said palace several times, and especially after looking at the plan for the renovation, I hope the aforesaid Venetian gentlemen (who want to have the reputation of never sparing expense in carrying out their will), who have commenced the restoration of the said palace will pardon me if I say, that they have done ill in not enlarging it beyond the minor canal, for they will spend a great sum and nevertheless, because it is not extended on the side I name, they will never be able to build courtyards worthy of the said palace. And the only reason for this is that they have not wanted to spend enough. Several gentlemen with whom I discussed the matter as we stood on the balcony of the said palace agreed with me.

[13] A banquet given by the Doge in the Palace for King Henry III of France in 1574; from *Venice, its individual growth from the earliest beginnings to the fall of the Republic* by Pompeo Molmenti, translated by Horatio F. Brown.

(Pompeo Molmenti was a nineteenth-century Venetian social historian.)

Henry III also was given a banquet in the Hall of the Great Council, which was cleared for the purpose, and on the place where the ducal throne stood, was raised a huge sideboard

loaded with gold and silver plate to the value of two hundred
thousand crowns; facing this sideboard was the seat for the
king, under a canopy of crimson embroidered with golden
fleurs-de-lys. The guests numbered about three thousand, and
the banquet was served, to the sound of music, by a whole
army of carvers, waiters, and cupbearers. On another day a
collation was offered to the king in the same hall; the whole
dressing of the table – bread, plates, knives, forks, table-
cloths, napkins – were made of sugar so well imitated that it
startled the king when his napkin broke in his hand. The dish
set before the king represented a queen riding on two tigers
who bore on their breasts the arms of France and of Poland.[1]
On the right of the royal table were two lions with Pallas and
Justice; to the left were San Marco and David. The other
tables bore statuettes of popes, kings, doges, deities, figures
representing the planets, the arts, virtues, animals, fruit, flowers, and trees, all made in sugar from designs by Sansovino,
executed by the druggist Niccolò della Cavalliera, whose shop
was at the sign of the Pigna. There were one thousand two
hundred and sixty plates, and three hundred statuettes presented to the ladies. Two other tables were similarly adorned
in the Sala dello Scrutinio.

[14] An English traveller is amazed by the system of
electing Doges in 1618; from *Letters and Dispatches
from Sir Henry Wotton to James the First and his
Ministers in the years 1617–20*.

(Henry Wotton (1568–1639), diplomatist and poet, was
engaged in diplomatic duties in Venice over a period of nearly
twenty years. He was a close friend of John Donne, and later
an MP and the Provost of Eton College.)

The Election of the Duke of Venice is one of the most intricate
and curious form in the World; consisting of ten several
precedent Ballotations. Whereupon occurreth a pretty Question, what need there was of such a deal of solicitude in
choosing a Prince of such limited Authority? And it is the

---

[1] Henry had been crowned King of Poland the previous February.

stranger, for having been long in use, the ancient Forms being commonly the most simple. To which doubt, this Answer may serve the turn, That it was (as the tradition runneth) a Monk's Invention of the Benedictine Order. And in truth, the whole mysterious frame therein, doth much savour of the *Cloyster*. For first, a Boy must be snatched up below, and this Child must draw the Balls, and not themselves, as in all other Elections: then is it strangely intermingled, half with Chance and half with Choice. So as Fortune, as well as Judgment or Affection hath her part in it, and perhaps the greater. One point (as now and then hapneth, even in the most curious Webs of this nature) seemeth somewhat unequal. Namely, that the 41 (who are the last immediate Electors of the Duke) must be all of several Families, and of them twenty-five at least concur to his Nomination. For hereby the old names (which are but twenty-four) cannot make a Duke without help from some one of the new. And that is not easily gotten, through emulation between them, as strong perhaps as any public respect.

(Wotton goes on to describe the election of Antonio Priuli, in the same year.)

On Tuesday 8 May, Niccolo Donato died, about two hours of the night as near as the moment could be known, which his Nephews and Servants did conceal, and is never hastily published by the State. His Disease was an Apoplexy, where-with being surprised after a gentle fit or two of an Ague, he had no leisure, or no mind to alter a former Will, made while he was but a Senator, so miserably, as if he had meant to be frugal even after his Death: For therein he left but twenty-five Ducats to all his Servants, and only twenty to the Nuns of Sta Chiara at Murano, where he disposed his Body to be laid. The short time of his Princedom (having been but a Month and two days) did yield little matter of observation. One thing was notable, that entring with small applause of the common men, he suddenly got their favours upon a false conceit. For a Decree having passed in his Predecessor's time about the reformation of Bakers (who made scant Loaves) and being conceived to be his deed, the Plebyity (whose supream Object is Bread) cryed in all corners, Viva Donato. In his Nature there was a strange Conjunction of two things rarely seen together, Love of Learning, and Love of Money. And this is all that can be said of him.

Now being gone, the following Election was likely to be short, the same Concurrence appearing as before, and the affections having been so newly founded and prepared. Therefore (not to extend discourse) the Duke's Funeral Rites being performed the Monday after his death, the Thursday morning following Antonio Priuli was made Duke, with all Balls. For Giustiniano having but eight voices among the last One and forty Electors, and Nani (by strange and almost prodigious fortune) none, the foresaid eight friends of Giustiniano, unprofitable for him whom they loved best did immediately concur with Priuli's thirty-three voices. And so a solemn Ambassage is preparing out of the body of the Senate to determine his Commission in Friuli, and to recall him to the supream honour of his Country. When at the very same time, or little difference, one of the two Austrian Commissioners on the other wise, is dead in the midst of the Treaty. So various are human Fortunes and Conditions.

[15] Once elected, a new Doge proceeded immediately to his investiture, the ceremonies of which are described by Dr John Ray, FRS; from *Observations ... made on a journey through Part of the Low Countries, Germany, Italy and France, 1673.*

(The Revd Dr John Ray, FRS (1627–1705), son of a blacksmith, was lecturer in Greek, mathematics and the humanities at Trinity College, Cambridge, before becoming the greatest naturalist of his day. He produced an important classification of plants, while his zoological works have been described as the basis of all modern zoology. In Venice in 1663, he would not actually have witnessed the investiture he describes, Doge Domenico Contarini having occupied the ducal throne since 1659.)

The Duke being on this wise crealed, many ceremonies are wont to be performed. First of all the 41 by the great chancellor send word to the *Signoria* who it is that is created

Duke, who first of all go to congratulate him, and give him joy; and, if it be in the day time, cause all the bells to be rung. Then his kindred and friends come to visit him, and at the same time there is money coined with his name upon it. After which the 41 electors with the *Duke* go into St *Mark's* church, and having done reverence to God, all mount up a scaffold, and the ancientest of them tells the people (who by this time have filled the church) that they have chosen a Duke in the room of the deceased; and commending the election, shews him to the people, who in token of confirmation and joy give him loud acclamations. The Duke then speaks to the people, and encourages them to hope well of his government; which done, they go down the scaffold, and bring the Duke before the altar; where by the procurators of the church, an oath is tender'd him to observe the laws, and a standard put into his hand by the vicar of the *Primicerius* of St *Mark's*. After this, having made an offering at the altar, he comes to the door of the choir, where he is placed upon a little low moveable scaffold (*Pergoletta* they call it) accompanied by one that carries the standard, and by another of his near friends or relations, who carries a cup full of gold and silver money stamped with his name; and by the mariners of the arsenal he is drawn out of St *Mark's*, and carried round about the *Piazza*, he that carries the cup scattering money among the people as he goes along. When he hath rounded the *Piazza*, he enters in by the principal gate into the palace; where being arrived at the foot of the stairs he goes off the *Pergoletta* to go up. In the midst of the stairs he finds the counsellors and *Capi de Quaranta* who there wait for him. When he is got up to the top of the stairs, the eldest counsellor puts upon his head the ducal cap; and thence he is led into the *Sala de Pioveghi*,[1] 'and after he hath sitten a while there in a seat appointed for that purpose, he is conducted by them to his lodgings, and the palace being resign'd to him, they all go to their own homes. His habit much differing from the common renders him venerable. On his head he wears a ducal cap, called *il Corno*, because it hath an *Apex* or horn arising above

---

[1] To put him in mind of his mortality, because that is the place where the corps of the deceased Dukes lie in state.

the top of it on the hinder part, and under that a white coif, with little strings, which from the ears hang down backward upon his neck. On his back a loose vest or mantle without sleeves so long that it draws upon the ground, of velvet, damask, scarlet, or any other rich cloth. When he goes abroad the bells of St *Mark's* are rung: there are certain banners carried before him, and trumpets of an extraordinary greatness sounded: then follow the cushion or pillow, and the seat of gold, and after that the Duke himself under an *Umbrella*, between two of the principal foreign ambassadors or agents then in town, and the others behind him. After him follow about 30 couple of the chief gentlemen, all in cloth of scarlet; and he, that hath the right hand in the first couple, carries a sword upright in his hand.

[16] Not only the Doge but virtually all the senior offices of State were elective, and elections of one kind or another constituted the principal business of the Maggior Consiglio, or Great Council. The President de Brosses describes one such election in 1739; from *Selections from the Letters of de Brosses*, translated by Lord Ronald Sutherland Gower.

(Charles de Brosses (1709–1777) became President of the Parliament of Burgundy. He wrote on a wide variety of subjects, including archaeology, exploration, primitive religions, linguistics, as well as composing a history of the Roman Republic. His *Lettres Écrites d'Italie en 1739–40* were published in 1885.)

We were allowed to be present in the Great Council Chamber on the occasion of the election of the General of the Galleys, an important post. The Grand Council has its sittings in a vast and highly decorated hall. At the end of the hall is a raised platform, occupied by the Councillors of State and the Inquisitors, with the Doge's throne in the centre. This platform is in the form of a semicircle, and seats ranged in tiers fill the sides of the walls. All the nobles took their seats without any order. Those who wore red cloaks had their particular place, and others were scattered throughout the

Fire in the Doges' Palace, 1577

The arrival of Henry III, King of France and Poland, in Venice in 1574

The interior courtyard of the Doges' Palace, and the Giants' Staircase

The Doges' Palace: John Ruskin called it 'the central building of the world'

The columns in the Piazzetta, between which
gaming was allowed and criminals were executed

A Venetian torture chamber as imagined by French
propagandists of the eighteenth century

The Grand Canal as seen c. 1500 by Carpaccio,
with the old Rialto Bridge

The bend of the Grand Canal, by Samuel Prout

hall with the object of keeping order, but in this they were unsuccessful, for the noise was terrific. On the platform by the side of the Chancellor, stood an urn holding in it as many little balls as there were people present. Among these balls some were gilt; every person drew out one. Those who drew out the gilded balls were chosen as the electors of the general, but besides these there were many electors by right. After this ceremony was over we went into the balloting hall, ornamented in the same manner as the one we had left, but not so large and here the crowd was not so great. The other electors entered and saluted those present by bowing to the ground with the utmost gravity.

When these had all passed in the Chancellor appeared, preceded by his secretaries, and himself preceding the Vice-Doge; for the Doge being indisposed, the oldest of the councillors represented him. He does not take his seat on the throne, nor does he wear the *corno*, though he copied one as nearly as he could, having placed his biretta of black silk on his head, and bringing the front of it forward like a Phrygian cap, which made him look like a venerable Antenor. He was followed by the councillors in their red robes. As soon as he entered every one rose; and he bowed profoundly, without removing his 'biretta,' except to the Council of Forty of criminal justice when he passed before them. He alone remained covered; and, mounting the platform, he sat down, the others grouping themselves on either side of him. The whole scene was highly impressive. Then the Chancellor rose and announced that the following gentlemen requested to have the charge of the Galleys. These were the Signors Priuli, Badoer, Donato, and Vendramini. As soon as this announcement had been made their relations rose and left the room; then the three *avvogadori* took a little New Testament and passed down the room, each person touching the book with the point of his finger, as a mark that he intended to proceed to the election in good faith and without malice. When all these preambles were accomplished, a huge clerk, having begirt a monstrous nose with a colossal pair of spectacles, proclaimed, in a whining voice, 'l'eccellentissimo Signore Luca Priuli' had carried the election. In an instant a score of little boys dressed in red ran through the building shouting, like beings possessed, 'Priuli! Priuli!' Each carried in his hand a box in which were two compartments, one white for the nomination, the other green for pilling, the opening being shaped like a funnel. Outside this box was a pouch full of little balloting papers rolled up like buttons; they gave one of each of these to the nobles present, who placed it in one or other compartment. The children then brought the boxes to the Chancellor, who emptied the white ballots into a basin and threw away the others. The three other candidates were then balloted for in the same manner, and then the papers were counted. Donato was elected, and we departed. The whole ceremony was got through with the greatest rapidity, and in less time than it takes to describe. It was very comical, as we left the palace, to see Donato's profound bows, and the way in which he was kissed right and left; the kisses could be heard as far as the middle of the square.

[17] Richard Lassels was greatly struck in the mid-seventeenth century by the armoury in the Doges' Palace; from *The Voyage of Italy*.

(Richard Lassels (?1603–1668) was a Roman Catholic divine who made no fewer than five journeys to Italy as tutor and travelling companion to various members of the English aristocracy. *The Voyage of Italy* was published posthumously in 1670.)

From hence we were led into the Armory or little Arsenall in the Dukes pallace, where there are armes for a thousand or fifteen hundred men ready upon all sudden occasions of sedition or treason. The muskets are allwayes charged and discharged every three months; and they with the pikes and swords are so ordered, that by unbuckling a leather which holdeth them up, they fall in order into your hand without confusion: so that there a thousand or 500 men may be armed in lesse then half an houre. In the end of this great roome, farre from the charged muskets, stands a great round ball of Iron twice as big as a mans head, pierced thorough like a close basket hilt: within it there is a spring which being lett go with a corde, strikes fire into powder which lyeth round

about this great ball in a traine, and into which powder so
many several ends of match as there are muskets here, do
reach; half of these matches hanging out, and the other half
being within: so that (if need were) the first man that should
come in and pluck the foresayd corde, would light all those
matches, and every man catcheing one and a musket, the
Senators would presently leap out Soldiers. There is allso a
back dove which openeth from the Senate house or great
Chamber of the Councel into this armory; and the keys of
that dove are allwayes layd beside the Duke when he sitts in
Counsel. This is not so much an Italian jealousy, as a prudent
caution caused by past danger. For they shew us there the
armour (with one arme onely, to be worne under a Venetian
gowne) of bold Baiamante de Theopoli and his complices,
who intended to kille the Senate and make himself master of
Venise [in 1310]. But the plots could not scape four thousand
eyes, and Baiamante was taken and executed; and his house
turned into a Butchers-shambles, a fitt punishment or disgrace
for him who would have been the butcher of his Prince and
country. Here in this armory we saw:

1. The armes of brave Scanderbeg Prince of the Epirots;
and I was willing to handle his owne sword (which had done
such notable execution upon Turks) to see whether his arme
were stronger than ours are now a dayes. I found it a broad
thinn blade of a reasonable length; but of an excellent temper,
and light.

2. The several sutes of armour of the Dukes of Venise
anciently who had gone to warre in person. Brave sutes of
armour, and strewing those Dukes to the number of 40 or 50
(if I remember well) to have been allso brave men.

3. Then the sute of armour of Henry the fourth of France
with his pocket pistol: armour which cost the Venetians deare:
for the sayd king oweing them money sent them onely his
armour, but no money.

4. The armour of a little boy who was found dead in a
battle feighting for the Venetians, and not knowne who he
was. Poore child who being worthy never to have dyed, doth
not so much as live in memory and history! I did not thinck
till now, that Mars had his abortives too, dyeing before they
be named.

[18] Throughout most of its history, the government of the Most Serene Republic was as stable as any in Europe; by the mid-seventeenth century there had been no serious breach of the peace since the attempted *coup* of Marin Falier in 1355 (see p. 46). But the Venetians never took unnecessary chances – witness this account by F. N. Misson, who was in Venice in 1688; from *A New Voyage to Italy*.

(Francis Misson (?1650–1722) was a French Huguenot who fled to England after the Revocation of the Edict of Nantes and found a position as tutor to a young English *milord*, whom he accompanied on the Grand Tour.)

I shall only add two Remarks on the Palace of St *Mark*, which, in my Opinion, deserve to be taken notice of. The Rebellion of *Bajamonte*, the Story of which you know, was the occasion of the Erecting of a little Arsenal in the Palace, to which there is a Passage from the Hall of the Grand Council, by Gallery of Communication; that if the People should conspire against the Nobles, and make any Attempt against them while they are sitting, they might be furnish'd with Arms upon the Spot to defend themselves. And 'twas also for the same Reason that they built that little Tribunal called the *Loggietta*, which is at the foot of the Tower of St. *Mark*, in sight of the Palace, and of the Hall of the Grand Council. There are always some of the Procurators of St. *Mark* there, upon the Watch, while the Council is Assembled; making a shew of doing other Business. This Arsenal is furnished with a competent Number of Fusees and Musquets, which lie always ready Charged; and a great many other good Arms. There is a Machine, a little out of order, which is to light Five hundred Matches at once. Besides these, they keep, in the same Place, a considerable Number of curious ancient Arms, among which they preserve, the Sword of the Valiant *Scanderbeg*. I observ'd there the Bust of *Francis Carrara*,[1] the last Lord of *Padua*, so famous for his Cruelties. They shew a little Box for a *Toilette*, in which are six little Guns, which

---

[1] Strangled at Padua with his four children, by order of the Senate of Venice, in the year 1405.

are so order'd with Springs adjusted in such a manner, that upon the opening of the Trunk, the Guns fir'd, and kill'd the Lady[1] to whom *Carrara* sent it for a Present. They show also with this, some little Pocket Cross-Bows, and Arrows of Steel, with which he took Pleasure to kill those he met, so secretly that they cou'd hardly either perceive the Blow, or him that gave it. I must not forget the two little Statues of *Adam* and *Eve*, which *Albert Dürer* made in Prison, with the point of a Pen-knife, and for which he obtain'd his Liberty.

[19] On 3 October 1786 Goethe watched the administration of justice in the Doges' Palace; from J. W. Goethe's *Italian Journey*.

(Johann Wolfgang von Goethe (1749–1842) set out on his Italian journey on 3 September 1786, and reached Venice on 28th. He remained just over a fortnight, showing himself to be the serious sightseer one would expect.)

Today I saw a very different kind of comedy which I enjoyed much more. In the Palazzo Ducale I witnessed an important trial, which, luckily for me, had come on during the vacation. One of the advocates was everything an exaggerated buffo should be: short and fat but agile, a very prominent profile, a booming voice and an impassioned eloquence, as though everything he said came from the bottom of his heart.

I call it a comedy because everything has probably already been settled before the public performance takes place; the judges know what they have to say, and the contending parties what they have to expect. Nevertheless, I much prefer this kind of proceeding to our fussy and complicated bureaucratic system. Let me try to give some idea of the amusing, informal and natural way in which such things are conducted here.

In a large hall of the palazzo, the judges sit on one side in a semicircle. Opposite them, on a platform large enough to seat several persons side by side, sit the advocates of both

---

[1] The Countess Sacrati. In January 1696 there were no more than two guns in the box.

parties. On a bench facing them sit the plaintiff and the defendant. When I entered, the advocate for the plaintiff had left the platform, since today's session was not to be a legal duel. All the documents, pro and con, were to be read aloud, although they had already been printed. A scraggy clerk in a dingy black coat with a bulging file in his hands was preparing to perform his duties as reader. The hall was packed and it was obvious that the legal issue was as important to the Venetian public as it was to the parties involved.

Fideicommissums enjoy a high legal status in the Republic. Once an estate is stamped with this character, it keeps it permanently, even though, for some special reason or other, it may have been sold several centuries ago and passed through many hands. If the question of ownership is ever raised, the descendants of the original family can claim their rights and the estate must be restored to them.

On this occasion the litigation was of particular importance because the complaint was against the Doge himself, or rather against his spouse, who was sitting there, on the little bench, wrapped in her *zendale*, with only a small space between her and the plaintiff. She was a lady of a certain age with a noble stature, regular features, and a serious, even sour expression. The Venetians were very proud to see the princess appear before the court, in public and in her own palace.

The clerk started reading, and only then did I realize the significance of a little man sitting on a low stool behind a little table, not far from the advocates' platform, and of the hourglass he had in front of him. So long as the clerk is reading, the time is not counted, but if the advocate wishes to interrupt the reading, he is granted only a limited time. While the clerk reads, the hourglass lies on its side with the little man's hand touching it. As soon as the advocate opens his mouth, the hourglass is raised; as soon as he stops talking, it is laid down again.

Therefore, when the advocate wishes to attract the attention of the public or to challenge the evidence, it requires great skill on his part to do this effectively with brief comments. When he does, the little Saturn is completely nonplussed; he has to keep switching the hourglass from a horizontal to a vertical position and back every minute and

finds himself in a similar situation to that of the evil spirits in
the puppet play when the mischievous harlequin cries '*Berli-
cke! Berlocke!*' in such rapid succession that they never know
whether they should come or go.

Only someone who has heard the collating of documents
in a law court can have any idea of this method of reading –
rapid, monotonous, but quite articulate. A skilful advocate
knows how to relieve the general boredom with facetious
remarks, and the public responds to them with roars of
laughter. I remember one joke, the most amusing of those I
could understand.

The clerk was reciting a document in which the owner,
whose right was in doubt, disposed of the property in question. The advocate asked him to read slower, and when the
clerk came to the words 'I bestow, I bequeath' flew out at
him, shouting: 'And what do *you* want to bestow? What do
you want to bequeath? You poor starved devil, without a
penny to your name! However,' he continued, apparently
pulling himself together, 'the same could be said of our
illustrious proprietor. He also wanted to bestow and to
bequeath what belonged to him as little as it belongs to you.'
A burst of laughter ensued which went on for a long time,
but the hourglass was immediately returned to its horizontal
position, and the clerk went on droning and pulling faces at
the advocate. All this clowning, however, is arranged in
advance.

[20] Mark Twain, visiting the Doges' Palace in the
1860s, is less moved by the art and architecture than by
what he conceives, with wild exaggeration, as the machi-
nations of the most sinister of police states; from *The
Innocents Abroad* by Mark Twain.

(Mark Twain (Samuel Langhorne Clemens: 1835–1910) visited Venice twice. His first visit in 1868, as part of a longer
journey to the Mediterranean and the Holy Land, inspired his
most famous travel book, *The Innocents Abroad* (1869): his
second, ten years later, as part of a walking tour with a

friend, gave rise to a somewhat similar volume, *A Tramp Abroad*.)

What would one naturally wish to see first in Venice? The Bridge of Sighs, of course – and next the Church and the Great Square of St Mark, the Bronze Horses, and the famous Lion of St Mark.

We intended to go to the Bridge of Sighs, but happened into the Ducal Palace first – a building which necessarily figures largely in Venetian poetry and tradition. In the Senate Chamber of the ancient Republic we wearied our eyes with staring at acres of historical paintings by Tintoretto and Paul Veronese, but nothing struck us forcibly except the one thing that strikes *all* strangers forcibly – a black square in the midst of a gallery of portraits. In one long row, around the great hall, were painted the portraits of the Doges of Venice (venerable fellows, with flowing white beards, for of the three hundred Senators eligible to the office, the oldest was usually chosen Doge,) and each had its complimentary inscription attached – till you came to the place that should have had Marino Faliero's picture in it, and that was blank and black – blank, except that it bore a terse inscription, saying that the conspirator had died for his crime. It seemed cruel to keep that pitiless inscription still staring from the walls after the unhappy wretch had been in his grave five hundred years.

At the head of the Giant's Staircase, where Marino Faliero was beheaded, and where the Doges were crowned in ancient times, two small slits in the stone wall were pointed out – two harmless, insignificant orifices that would never attract a stranger's attention – yet these were the terrible Lions' Mouths! The heads were gone (knocked off by the French during their occupation of Venice,) but these were the throats, down which went the anonymous accusation, thrust in secretly at dead of night by an enemy, that doomed many an innocent man to walk the Bridge of Sighs and descend into the dungeon which none entered and hoped to see the sun again. This was in the old days when the Patricians alone governed Venice – the common herd had no vote and no voice. There were one thousand five hundred Patricians; from these, three hundred Senators were chosen; from the Senators a Doge and a Council of Ten were selected, and by secret ballot the Ten chose from their own number a Council of Three. All these were Government spies, then, and every spy was under surveillance himself – men spoke in whispers in Venice, and no man trusted his neighbor – not always his own brother. No man knew who the Council of Three were – not even the Senate, not even the Doge; the members of that dread tribunal met at night in a chamber to themselves, masked, and robed from head to foot in scarlet cloaks, and did not even know each other, unless by voice. It was their duty to judge heinous political crimes, and from their sentence there was no appeal. A nod to the executioner was sufficient. The doomed man was marched down a hall and out at a door-way into the covered Bridge of Sighs, through it and into the dungeon and unto his death. At no time in his transit was he visible to any save his conductor. If a man had an enemy in those old days, the cleverest thing he could do was to slip a note for the Council of Three into the Lion's mouth, saying 'This man is plotting against the Government.' If the awful Three found no proof, ten to one they would drown him anyhow, because he was a deep rascal, since his plots were unsolvable. Masked judges and masked executioners, with unlimited power, and no appeal from their judgments, in that hard, cruel age, were not likely to be lenient with men they suspected yet could not convict.

We walked through the hall of the Council of Ten, and presently entered the infernal den of the Council of Three.

The table around which they had sat was there still, and likewise the stations where the masked inquisitors and executioners formerly stood, frozen, upright and silent, till they received a bloody order, and then, without a word, moved off, like the inexorable machines they were, to carry it out. The frescoes on the walls were startlingly suited to the place. In all the other saloons, the halls, the great state chambers of the palace, the walls and ceilings were bright with gilding, rich with elaborate carving, and resplendent with gallant pictures of Venetian victories in war, and Venetian display in foreign courts, and hallowed with portraits of the Virgin, the Saviour of men, and the holy saints that preached the Gospel of Peace upon earth – but here, in dismal contrast, were none but pictures of death and dreadful suffering! – not a living figure but was writhing in torture, not a dead one but was smeared with blood, gashed with wounds, and distorted with the agonies that had taken away its life!

[21] The prisons of the Serenissima were connected to the Palace itself; and this proximity provided Venice with many legends and probably did much to increase her sinister reputation. A favourite story is that of the *condottiere*, or soldier of fortune, Francesco Bussone, better known as Carmagnola. In 1426 he was appointed Commander-in-Chief of the Venetian army on *terra firma*; but after a promising start he became more and more inactive, until by 1432 treachery was suspected. The story is told in *A History of Venice* by John Julius Norwich.

The noose was by now being prepared; and when, early in 1432, the war was resumed with the loss of four small towns in rapid succession – one of them apparently given up on the express order of Carmagnola himself – it began to tighten.

On 27 March the evidence against Carmagnola was considered by the Council of Ten, who resolved on immediate and decisive measures. First they requested a *zonta* – a supplementary addition of co-opted members – their normal practice in matters of extreme urgency or importance; next, they decreed the death penalty for anyone who should divulge any word of their present business; finally, on the 29th, they dispatched their Chief Secretary to Carmagnola in Brescia, with a message summoning him to come with all convenient speed to Venice.

From this moment on, the actions of the Ten were obviously dominated by a single overriding consideration: that Carmagnola should not be allowed to escape, to Milan or anywhere else. Until he was safely in Venice, everything possible must be done to avoid arousing his suspicions. The ostensible reason for the summons was to decide the overall strategy for the coming campaign, various possibilities for which were set out in detail in the Secretary's brief; he was to add, for example, that the Marquis of Mantua had also been invited to Venice to take part in the talks. Instructions were meanwhile dispatched to all Venetian governors and officials in the cities and towns between Venice and Brescia, enjoining them to provide armed escorts for Carmagnola on every stage of the way, showing him all possible courtesy as befitted his rank and distinction; if, however, he were to betray any reluctance to proceed, he was to be immediately arrested and imprisoned pending further orders.

In fact these precautions proved unnecessary. Carmagnola at once agreed to come to Venice, and at no point on the journey showed the slightest misgivings. Arriving on 7 April, he was welcomed at the Palace and politely requested to wait until Doge Foscari was ready to receive him. After some time one of the *Savii*, Leonardo Mocenigo, came to apologize for the delay. The Doge, it appeared, was indisposed; the meeting must be postponed till the following morning. Carmagnola rose to leave; but when he reached the foot of the stairs and was about to emerge on to the Riva, one of the nobles stepped in front of him and indicated an open door to the left – that which led to the prisons.

'That is not the way,' objected Carmagnola.

'Your pardon, my lord, but it is,' came the reply.

Then, and then only, did the *condottiere* understand the nature of the trap into which he had fallen. '*Son perduto*,' he is said to have murmured as the door closed behind him.

Two days later the trial began. Carmagnola himself was interrogated by what the state archives describe as 'a master torturer from Padua' and, not surprisingly, confessed at once; his wife, his secretary and his servants – to say nothing of a mysterious lady known simply as *la Bella* who was reported as being seen frequently at his house – were also interrogated, rather more humanely. All his letters and papers were brought from Brescia and submitted to minute examination. Unfortunately many of the official records, including the confession itself, have disappeared; but there seems to have been evidence enough to satisfy the tribunal that the charges should be upheld. On 5 May, after a ten-day suspension during Holy Week and Easter, Carmagnola was found guilty of treason, twenty-six of his judges voting in favour and one against. On

the sentence, opinion was more sharply divided. The proposal
for life imprisonment, put forward by the Doge and three of
his counsellors, received eight votes; nineteen, however, were
cast in favour of the death penalty. That same evening the
condottiere, dressed in crimson velvet, a gag in his mouth and
his hands tied behind his back, was led out to the customary
place of execution, in the Piazzetta between the two columns.
At the third blow of the axe, his head was severed from his
shoulders. The body was then carried off, escorted by twenty-
four torch-bearers, to S. Francesco della Vigna for burial; but
scarcely had the work begun when his confessor came to
report that his last wish had been to lie in the Frari. Thither
it was immediately transferred. Carmagnola's fortune was
confiscated, apart from 10,000 ducats for his widow and
5,000 for each of his two sons, provided that certain conditions of residence were met. In the circumstances, and
considering where most of the wealth had come from, this
was generous treatment indeed – a good deal more so,
perhaps, than they could have expected in any other city in
Italy.

[22] Antonio da Ponte's new prison building of 1589 –
though one might take exception to its location – is
architecturally the most distinguished of its kind in the
world. Thomas Coryat was much taken with it; from
Coryat's Crudities.

(Thomas Coryat (?1577–1617) was famous even during his
lifetime as a traveller. Between May and October 1608 he
walked the 2,000 miles to Venice and back. According to
Thomas Fuller, Coryat 'carried folly (which the charitable
called merriment) in his very face. The shape of his head had
no promising form, being like a sugar-loaf inverted, with the
little end before, as composed of fancy and memory without
any common-sense.')

There is near unto the Dukes Palace a very faire prison, the
fairest absolutely that ever I saw, being divided from the
Palace by a little channell of water, and againe joyned unto
it, by a marveilous faire little gallery that is inserted aloft into

the middest of the Palace wall Eastward. I think there is not a fairer prison in all Christendome: it is built with very faire white ashier stone having a little walke without the rooms of the prison, which is forty paces long and seven broad. For I meated it: which walke is fairly vaulted over head, and adorned with seven goodly arches, each whereof is supported with a great square stone pillar. The outside of these pillars is curiously wrought with pointed diamond worke. In the higher part of the front towards the water there are eight pretty pillars of freestone, betwixt which are seven iron windows for the prisoners above to look through: In the lower part of the prison where the prisoners do usually remaine, there are six windows, three on each side of the core, whereof each hath two rowes of great iron barres, one without and the other within: each row containing ten barres that ascend in heigth to the toppe of the window, and eighteene more that crosse those tenne. So that it is altogether impossible for the prisoners to get forth. Betwixt the first row of windows in the outside, and another within, there is a little space or an entry for people to stand in that will talke with the prisoners, who lie within the inner windowes that are but single barred. The West side of the prison which is neare to the Dukes Palace, is very curiously wrought with pointed diamond worke, with three rowes of crosse-barred iron windowes in it, whereof each row containeth eleven particulars: it is reported that this prison is so contrived, that there are a dozen roomes under the water, and that the water doth oftentimes distill into them from above, to the great annoyance of the prisoners that lodge there. Before this prison was built, which was not (as I heard in Venice) above ten years since, the towne prison was under the Dukes Palace, where it is thought certain prisoners being largely hired by the King of Spaine, conspired together to blow up the Palace with gun powder, as the Papists would have done the Parliament house in England. Whereupon the Senate thought good having executed those prisoners that were conspirators in that bloudy desseigne, to remove the rest to another place, and to build a prison in the place where this now standeth.

[23] Details of the prisons of the Serenissima; from *Venice, its individual growth from the earliest beginnings to the fall of the Republic* by Pompeo Molmenti, translated by Horatio Brown.

The state prisons were at the Terranova at Saint Mark's, close to the grain-stores, and also in the Ducal Palace. The prisons on the upper floor of the Palace were called *carceri superiori*, or *Torreselle*, 'dove si meteva li homeni de Conto, retenuti per el conseio dei X'; they dated from the construction of the Palace. The prisons called *inferiori* were built in 1321 and 1326. They ran along the quay, and bore the names of *Liona, Morosina, Mocenigo, Forte, Orba, Frescagioia, Vulcano*, and so on. Although called in decrees prisons *de subtus Palatium*, they were not subterranean. When that part of the Palace which looks on to the Canal was reconstructed, about the middle of the sixteenth century, other prisons were built along the rio, not below the level of the water, nor even on the level of the water, but at the height of the pavement of the Palace entrance. On to a narrow corridor with three turnings there open the doors of nine cells; then, descending a stair of sixteen steps, we find another nine. These cells, called *camerotti* or *Pozzi*, must have all been of one size and shape, like those which still remain in fairly good preservation. They were vaulted, 2.45 metres high, 2.55 metres wide, 5.48 metres long. At the end was a wooden plank bed, 2.05 metres long, and 0.74 wide. The light was dim, but not so scanty as to leave the prisoner in thick darkness; the prisoner was probably allowed a lamp or a light, for on the walls, either scratched or drawn in pencil, we can still read inscriptions.

> De chi me fido guardami Iddio
> De chi no me fido me guarderò io.[1]

writes one called Francesco, whose prudence here expressed in verse does not seem to have served him to escape the arm of the Inquisitors . . .

The prisoners in the *Pozzi* were in the dark and damp in

---

[1] 'God protect me from all those I trust
From those I trust not, I'll protect myself.'

the basements of the Palace; the prisoners in the *Piombi*, on the contrary, lived high up under the roof. The *Piombi* were opened in 1591, and took their name from the lead covering of the roof. There were only four cells, one to the west looking into the Court and three to the east looking over the Canal. They were from 1.85 to 2.57 metres high, and varied between 2.78 and 3.85 in length. The walls were made of larch balks. In 1589 the Republic built the prisons on the other side of the rio della Paglia, from designs by Antonio da Ponte. The Police Magistrates, the *Signori di Notte al Criminale*, had their office there. These new prisons received many who would otherwise have gone to the *Pozzi*, which, however, were not entirely abandoned even in the last years of the Republic. The Palace was joined to the Prisons by a clumsy bridge in the style of the Seicento, called by the suggestive name of Bridge of Sighs, over which the prisoners passed to their trial.

The prisons of Venice were not worse than the prisons of other countries at that time. Nor can they be justly described as horrible caves, a few hand-breadths wide, below the level of the water, where the prisoners were left to rot, buried alive and dying of hunger, anguish, and torment.

[24] Perhaps the most celebrated of all the prisoners of the Serenissima, and one of the very few who (if his account is to be believed) succeeded in escaping, was Casanova, who was, he tells us, astonished to be arrested on 26 July 1755, and dragged off to the *piombi*; from *The Memoirs of Jacques Casanova de Seingalt* translated by Arthur Machen.

(Giovanni Giacomo Casanova, Chevalier de Seingalt (1725–1798), adventurer, *abbé*, violinist, alchemist, spy and knight of the Papal Order of the Golden Spur, had once already been obliged to leave Venice by reason of his debaucheries. After his escape he wandered through Europe, visiting most of its capitals and meeting most leading figures of the day. His posthumously published memoirs have been described as 'unmatched as a self-revelation of scoundrelism'.)

In course of time the captain of the men-at-arms came to tell me that he was under orders to take me *under the Leads*. Without a word I followed him. We went by gondola, and after a thousand turnings among the small canals we got into the Grand Canal, and landed at the prison quay. After climbing several flights of stairs we crossed a closed bridge which forms the communication between the prisons and the Doge's palace, crossing the canal called Rio di Palazzo. On the other side of this bridge there is a gallery which we traversed. We then crossed one room, and entered another, where sat an individual in the dress of a noble, who, after looking fixedly at me, said, '*E quello, mettetelo in deposito.*'

This man was the secretary of the Inquisitors, the prudent Dominic Cavalli, who was apparently ashamed to speak Venetian in my presence as he pronounced my doom in the Tuscan language.

Messer-Grande then made me over to the warden of The Leads, who stood by with an enormous bunch of keys, and accompanied by two guards, made me climb two short flights of stairs, at the top of which followed a passage and then another gallery, at the end of which he opened a door, and I found myself in a dirty garret, thirty-six feet long by twelve broad, badly lighted by a window high up in the roof. I thought this garret was my prison, but I was mistaken; for, taking an enormous key, the gaoler opened a thick door lined with iron, three and a half feet high, with a round hole in the middle, eight inches in diameter, just as I was looking intently at an iron machine. This machine was like a horse shoe, an inch thick and about five inches across from one end to the other. I was thinking what could be the use to which this horrible instrument was put, when the gaoler said, with a smile, –

'I see, sir, that you wish to know what that is for, and as it happens I can satisfy your curiosity. When their excellencies give orders that anyone is to be strangled, he is made to sit down on a stool, the back turned to this collar, and his head is so placed that the collar goes round one half of the neck. A silk band, which goes round the other half, passes through this hole, and the two ends are connected with the axle of a wheel which is turned by someone until the prisoner gives up the ghost, for the confessor, God be thanked! never leaves him till he is dead.'

'All this sounds very ingenious, and I should think that it is you who have the honour of turning the wheel.'

He made no answer, and signing to me to enter, which I did by bending double, he shut me up.

Stunned with grief, I leant my elbows on the top of the grating. It was crossed by six iron bars an inch thick, which formed sixteen square holes. This opening would have lighted my cell, if a square beam supporting the roof which joined the wall below the window had not intercepted what little light came into that horrid garret. After making the tour of my sad abode, my head lowered, as the cell was not more than five and a half feet high, I found by groping along that it formed three-quarters of a square of twelve feet. The fourth quarter was a kind of recess, which would have held a bed; but there was neither bed, nor table, nor chair, nor any furniture whatever, except a bucket – the use of which may be guessed – and a bench fixed in the wall a foot wide and a four feet from the ground. On it I placed my cloak, my fine suit, and my hat trimmed with Spanish point and adorned with a beautiful white feather. The heat was great, and my instinct made me go mechanically to the grating, the only place where I could lean on my elbows. I could not see the window, but I saw the light in the garret, and rats of a fearful size, which walked unconcernedly about it; these horrible creatures coming close under my grating without shewing the slightest fear. At the sight of these I hastened to close up the round hole in the middle of the door with an inside shutter, for a visit from one of the rats would have frozen my blood. I passed eight hours in silence and without stirring, my arms all the time crossed on the top of the grating.

At last the clock roused me from my reverie, and I began to feel restless that no one came to give me anything to eat or to bring me a bed whereon to sleep. I thought they might at least let me have a chair and some bread and water. I had no appetite, certainly; but were my gaolers to guess as much? And never in my life had I been so thirsty. I was quite sure, however, that somebody would come before the close of the day; but when I heard eight o'clock strike I became furious, knocking at the door, stamping my feet, fretting and fuming, and accompanying this useless hubbub with loud cries. After more than an hour of this wild exercise, seeing no one, without the slightest reason to think I could be heard, and shrouded in darkness, I shut the grating for fear of the rats, and threw myself at full length upon the floor. So cruel a desertion seemed to me unnatural, and I came to the conclusion that the Inquisitors had sworn my death. My investigation as to what I had done to deserve such a fate was not a long one, for in the most scrupulous examination of my conduct I could find no crimes. I was, it is true, a profligate, a gambler, a bold talker, a man who thought of little besides enjoying this present life, but in all that there was no offence against the state. Nevertheless, finding myself treated as a criminal, rage and despair made me express myself against the horrible despotism which oppressed me in a manner which I will leave my readers to guess, but which I will not repeat here. But notwithstanding my grief and anxiety, the hunger which began to make itself felt, and the thirst which tormented me, and the hardness of the boards on which I lay, did not prevent exhausted nature from reasserting her rights; I fell asleep . . .

The clock striking midnight awoke me. How sad is the awaking when it makes one regret one's empty dreams. I could scarcely believe that I had spent three painless hours. As I lay on my left side, I stretched out my right hand to get my handkerchief, which I remembered putting on that side. I felt about for it, when – heavens! what was my surprise to feel another hand as cold as ice. The fright sent an electric shock through me, and my hair began to stand on end.

Never had I been so alarmed, nor should I have previously thought myself capable of experiencing such terror. I passed three or four minutes in a kind of swoon, not only motionless but incapable of thinking. As I got back my senses by degrees, I tried to make myself believe that the hand I fancied I had touched was a mere creature of my disordered imagination; and with this idea I stretched out my hand again, and again with the same result. Benumbed with fright, I uttered a piercing cry, and, dropping the hand I held, I drew back my arm, trembling all over.

Soon, as I got a little calmer and more capable of reasoning, I concluded that a corpse had been placed beside me whilst I slept, for I was certain it was not there when I lay down.

'This,' said I, 'is the body of some strangled wretch, and they would thus warn me of the fate which is in store for me.'

The thought maddened me; and my fear giving place to rage, for the third time I stretched my arm towards the icy hand, seizing it to make certain of the fact in all its atrocity, and wishing to get up, I rose upon my left elbow, and found that I had got hold of my other hand. Deadened by the weight of my body and the hardness of the boards, it had lost warmth, motion, and all sensation.

[25] Charles Dickens obviously swallowed the hoary old legends about Venetian prisons wholesale. He writes with horror from Verona to Douglas Jerrold on 16 October 1844; from *The Letters of Charles Dickens* edited by his sister-in-law and his eldest daughter.

Oh God! the cells below the water, underneath the Bridge of Sighs; the nook where the monk came at midnight to confess the political offender; the bench where he was strangled; the deadly little vault in which they tied him in a sack, and the stealthy crouching little door through which they hurried him into a boat, and bore him away to sink him where no fisherman dare cast his net – all shown by torches that blink and wink, as if they were ashamed to look upon the gloomy theatre of sad horrors; past and gone as they are, these things stir a man's blood, like a great wrong or passion of the instant. And with these in their minds, and with a museum there, having a chamber full of such frightful instruments of torture as the devil in a brain fever could scarcely invent, there are hundreds of parrots, who will declaim to you in speech and print, by the hour together, on the degeneracy of the times in which a railroad is building across the water at Venice; instead of going down on their knees, the drivellers, and thanking Heaven that they live in a time when iron makes roads, instead of prison bars and engines for driving screws into the skulls of innocent men. Before God, I could almost turn bloody-minded, and shoot the parrots of our island with as little compunction as Robinson Crusoe shot the parrots in his.

[26] The last days of the Republic in 1797; from *Venice: The Greatness and the Fall* by John Julius Norwich.

When the report of Donà and Giustinian[1] of their first meeting with Bonaparte reached Venice, Doge Manin and the Signoria already knew that the Republic was doomed. War was imminent; further negotiation was impossible; the *terra firma* was as good as lost; and the only hope of saving the city itself from destruction lay in capitulation to the conqueror's demands. These demands were terrible indeed – nothing less than the abdication of the entire oligarchy, the abandonment of a constitution that had lasted more than a thousand years, and its replacement by a democracy. A revolution, in fact: but a revolution initiated from above, by those who were to be its principal victims – the suicide of the State.

But how was this suicide to be accomplished? It could not come to pass constitutionally, through the Senate, where such a proposal would meet with violent opposition; the resulting debates would drag on for days, and long before they were resolved the French would be within the lagoon. In any case, what use was discussion when the issue was inevitable, and why respect a constitution in the very act of abolishing it? The Senate gathered on 29 April to conduct some formal business of no particular interest or importance. When that business was over it broke up as usual. It never met again.

The following day, towards evening, the Doge summoned a special meeting. Present, apart from himself and his six Councillors, were the three chiefs of the *Quarantia*, all the *Savii* including the three outgoing *Savii del Consiglio*, the three *Capi* of the Council of Ten and the three *Avogadori di Comun*. Although such a grouping was wholly unconstitutional, its forty-two members included representatives of all

---

[1] The two ambassadors sent by the Republic to Napoleon.

the principal executive organs in the government; its moral authority was therefore considerable. Robes of office were set aside. The members all wore informal black clothes, and the *Consulta Nera*, as it came to be called, was the only effective decision-making body in the Republic's last days.

The Great Council, however, was still in existence, its 1,169 members still constituting the fount of political authority in the Republic. It could not be cast aside as the Senate had been, and the first decision of the *Consulta Nera* was that it should be summoned to an extraordinary session the next morning, when the Doge in person should officially inform it of Bonaparte's ultimatum and seek its approval for the measures proposed. The *Consulta* was still discussing the precise terms of the resolution when there suddenly arrived a dispatch from Tommaso Condulmer, written from his flagship off Fusina, reporting that the first French soldiers had already arrived on the shores of the lagoon and were even now positioning their heavy guns well within range of the city. The effect of this news was electric. In the general consternation some members panicked, others broke down and wept. Francesco Pesaro – hitherto one of the most courageous and robust advocates of a strong line against the French – openly declared his intention of taking flight to Switzerland. The Doge himself set an example only slightly more edifying, walking up and down the room wringing his hands and repeating those words which, for the rest of his life, he was never able to live down: '*Sta notte no semo sicuri nè anche nel nostro letto*' ('Tonight there will be no safety for us, not even in our own beds').

But the night passed uneventfully enough, and the next morning, 1 May, the Great Council met as arranged, in a Doges' Palace now heavily guarded by *Arsenalotti* and Dalmatian troops. Doge Manin, 'his face deathly pale and with tears streaming down his cheeks',[1] took his place at the rostrum, warning his audience at the outset that his emotional

---

[1] '*Squallido in viso, e grondante di lagrime*': such at least is the description of the Abbate Tentori, who may not have been an eye-witness, but who has left the only reliable account of the dealings of the *Consulta Nera*, and of much else besides, during this chaotic time.

and physical state might prevent him from finishing even the short allocution he had prepared. Then, simply and sadly, he described the circumstances in which the Republic now found itself, and proposed a resolution instructing the two deputies, Donà and Giustinian, to inform Bonaparte that all political prisoners would be freed at once and all those who had taken up arms against Frenchmen punished. The deputies were also empowered to discuss and elucidate the constitutional changes the General required.

The Doge was not to know that, by the time this resolution was approved – by 598 to seven, with fourteen abstentions – the deputies were already on their way back to Venice; nor that on that very same day Bonaparte was issuing a manifesto adducing fifteen separate proofs of Venetian hostility – most of them travesties of the truth – and formally declaring war on the Republic. Simultaneously he sent instructions to his representative in Venice, Lallement, to leave the city forthwith – his sinister and intrigue-loving secretary, Villetard, remaining as *chargé d'affaires*. Other directives were sent to the French commanders in Italy, ordering them to treat all Venetians as enemies and to pull down or efface the Lion of St Mark wherever it appeared.

Henceforth the collapse was swift. On 9 May Villetard produced an ultimatum, spelling out Bonaparte's requirements in considerably greater detail than before. These were the following:

The Comte d'Antraigues – the self-styled Ambassador of Louis XVIII, but never recognized as such by Venice – to be arrested, and freed only after the seizure of all his papers and their transmission to the Directory in Paris.

The *pozzi* and *piombi* – respectively the cells on the ground floor (above the water level) of the *prigioni* and those immediately under the leads of the Doges' Palace roof – to be opened for inspection by the people, after the release of the last three political prisoners from the latter.

The cases of all other prisoners to be reviewed and the death penalty abolished.

The Dalmatian troops to be disbanded and discharged.

The policing of the city to be entrusted to patrols under the authority of a specially constituted committee headed by

General Salimbeni, the former Venetian commander-in-chief on *terra firma*, and others of known democratic sympathies.

A Tree of Liberty to be erected on the Piazza.

A provisional *Municipalità* to be established of twenty-four Venetians, later to be supplemented by delegates from the cities of *terra firma*, Istria, Dalmatia and the Levant.

A manifesto to be issued announcing the creation of a democracy, inviting the populace to choose its representatives.

The insignia of the former government to be burnt at the foot of the Tree of Liberty, a general amnesty to be proclaimed for all political offenders and the freedom of the press to be decreed, 'with the proviso that there should be no discussion about the past, either of personalities or government.'

Services of thanksgiving to be held in St Mark's.

Three thousand French troops to be invited into Venice, to take over the Arsenal, the fortress of S. Andrea, Chioggia and any other strategic points that the French general might designate.

The Doges' Palace, the *Zecca* and other important buildings to be entrusted to the Civic Guard for protection.

The Venetian fleet (such as it was) to be recalled to the lagoon and to be placed under the joint command of the French and of the Municipality, of which Manin and the democratic leader Andrea Spada were to be co-Presidents.

All Venetian ambassadors abroad to be replaced by 'democrats'.

The credit of the mint and the national bank to be guaranteed by the state.

To approve these demands – there was no longer any influential voice to advocate resistance, or even argument – the Great Council was called for Friday, 12 May. From soon after sunrise the people of Venice had been congregating in the Piazza and Piazzetta, just as they had done countless times before in the city's history. In the past, however, they had usually assembled for purposes of celebration or – on rare occasions – to express their dissatisfaction or concern. Never before had they gathered together out of fear. By now all were aware that the end had come; but none had any clear idea of what form that end would take. The atmosphere was an unfamiliar one in Venice – an atmosphere of uncertainty, bewilderment, and ill-defined apprehension. Among the working population there were many who, in contrast to their enfranchised superiors, believed that the Republic, doomed or not, could and should have fought for her survival; for them, there was anger mingled with their shame, and they were in no mood to conceal it. Bands of these rough loyalists were roaming the streets, crying '*Viva San Marco!*' and hurling abuse at any patricians they chanced to encounter on their path. Partly, perhaps, for this reason – though many of the nobles seemed already to have fled the city, or to have hurried to their mainland estates in an effort to save them from the French soldiery – the Council fell short, by sixty-three members, of its constitutional quorum of 600.

But the time for such niceties was past. The Doge called the meeting to order, apprised it of Bonaparte's terms and proposed a motion by which, 'with the most high object of preserving unharmed the Religion, life and property of all these most beloved inhabitants', the oligarchy surrendered all its powers to a provisional democratic government. When he had finished, one of the members mounted the rostrum to open the debate; even though the conclusion was foregone, the Council had to be given the chance to express its views. Scarcely had he begun to speak, however, when the sound of firing was heard just outside the Palace.

At once, all was confusion. To the terrified members of the Council, such sounds could mean one thing only: the popular uprising that they had so long dreaded had begun. Some saw themselves being torn to pieces by the mob as they left the Palace; others had visions of days and weeks in the *pozzi* or *piombi*, so recently vacated by their former occupants, while the guillotine was set up in the Piazza. All had one single object in view: to escape from the Palace, in disguise if necessary, while there was still time. Within minutes, the true source of the firing had been established: some of the Dalmatian troops, who were being removed from Venice on Bonaparte's orders, had simply discharged their muskets into the air as a parting salute to the city. But the panic had begun; reassurances were useless. To urgent cries of 'Vote! Vote!' the debate was abandoned and the remaining legislators of the

Venetian Republic rushed to the ballot boxes to perform their last hurried duty to the state they had claimed to govern. The final count was 512 in favour of the resolution, twenty against, and five abstentions; but few of those who voted remained to hear it. Leaving their all-too-distinctive robes of office behind them, they were already slipping discreetly away out of side entrances to the Palace when, to an almost empty chamber, the Doge declared the resolution adopted. The Republic of Venice was no more.

Lodovico Manin himself made no attempt to flee. Almost alone among his fellow-nobles, he had maintained a quiet calm amid the hubbub – a calm born, perhaps, of fatalism or even of despair, but a calm none the less that enabled him to keep his dignity, even while the last frail structure of the Republic crumbled about him. In the sudden stillness that followed the break-up of the meeting he slowly gathered up his papers and withdrew to his private apartments. There, having laid aside his ducal *corno*, he carefully untied the ribbons of the close-fitting cap of white linen worn beneath it, the *cuffietta*, and handed it to his valet, Bernardo Trevisan, with those sad words which, more than any others, seem to symbolize the fall of Venice: '*Tolè, questa no la doperò più*' ('Take it, I shall not be needing it again').

[27] By the nineteenth century the Doges' Palace had already become the tourist attraction it is today; from a letter to his brother William, in September 1869, in *The Letters of Henry James* edited by Leon Edel.

(Henry James (1843–1916) paid his first visit to Venice in 1869, and returned regularly for the rest of his life. It was there that he wrote *The Wings of the Dove*; it is also the setting for *The Aspern Papers*.)

But what has fascinated me most here after Tintoretto and Co. are the two great buildings – the Ducal Palace and St Mark's church. You have a general notion of what they amount to; it's all you can have, until you see them. St Marks, within, is a great hoary shadowy tabernacle of mosaic and marble, entrancing you with its remoteness, its picturesqueness and its chiaroscuro – an immense piece of Romanticism. But the Ducal Palace is as pure and perpetual as the façade of the Parthenon – and I think of all things in Venice, it's the one I should have been gladdest to achieve, the one most worthy of civic affection and gratitude. When you're heated and weary to death with Tintoretto and his feverish Bible Stories, you can come out on the great Piazetta, between the marble columns, and grow comparatively cool and comfortable with gazing on this work of art which has so little to do with *persons*!

(For James, certain of the pictures in the Palace seem to have been an integral part of the building; from his Italian Hours.*)*

This deeply original building is of course the loveliest thing in Venice, and a morning's stroll there is a wonderful illumination. Cunningly select your hour – half the enjoyment of Venice is a question of dodging – and enter at about one o'clock, when the tourists have flocked off to lunch and the echoes of the charming chambers have gone to sleep among the sunbeams. There is no brighter place in Venice – by which I mean that on the whole there is none half so bright. The reflected sunshine plays up through the great windows from the glittering lagoon and shimmers and twinkles over gilded walls and ceilings. All the history of Venice, all its splendid stately past, glows around you in a strong sea-light. Every one here is magnificent, but the great Veronese is the most magnificent of all. He swims before you in a silver cloud; he thrones in an eternal morning. The deep blue sky burns behind him, streaked across with milky bars; the white colonnades sustain the richest canopies, under which the first gentlemen and ladies in the world both render homage and receive it. Their glorious garments rustle in the air of the sea and their sun-lighted faces are the very complexion of Venice. The mixture of pride and piety, of politics and religion, of art and patriotism, gives a splendid dignity to every scene. Never was a painter more nobly joyous, never did an artist take a greater delight in life, seeing it all as a kind of breezy festival and feeling it through the medium of perpetual success. He revels in the gold-framed ovals of the ceilings, multiplies himself there with the fluttering movement of an embroidered banner that tosses itself into the blue. He was the happiest of painters and produced the happiest picture in the world. 'The Rape of Europa' surely deserves this title; it is impossible to look at it without aching with envy. Nowhere else in art is such a temperament revealed; never did inclination and opportunity combine to express such enjoyment. The mixture of flowers and gems and brocade, of blooming flesh and shining sea and waving groves, of youth, health, movement, desire – all this is the brightest vision that ever descended upon the soul of a painter. Happy the artist who could entertain such a vision; happy the artist who could paint it as the masterpiece I here recall is painted.

The Basilica of St Mark

[28] Perhaps the most momentous single event in the entire history of Venice was the theft of the body of St Mark from Alexandria in 828; the story is told by Martino da Canale, a thirteenth-century historian, translated by Horatio Brown in his *Venice, an historical sketch of the Republic.*

(Horatio F. Brown (1854–1926) settled in Venice in 1879, setting up house with his mother and a beloved gondolier. He lived there for the next forty-seven years until his death. He wrote several admirable books about Venice, and its history, the first of which, *Life on the Lagoons*, was published in 1884.)

In those days there was a ship of Venice in the port of Alexandria, and in that city was the precious body of Monsignore S. Mark, whom the infidels had slain. Now on board the ship of Venice were three brave men, Rustico of Torcello, Buono of Malamocco, and Stauraco. In these three men so strong was the hope and so great their desire to carry Monsignore S. Mark to Venice, that they went cunningly about him who was guardian of the body, and became friends to him. Then it came to pass that they said unto him, 'Sir, an you will with us to Venice, we will carry away with us the body of S. Mark, and we will make you very rich.' But when the good man – Theodore he was called – heard this he said, 'Silence, sirs, speak not such words. This thing can never be. For the pagans hold him above all price; and, should they suspect your desire, not all the riches of the world would save you from being cut to bits. So I beg you say not such words.' Then said one of them, 'Well, we will wait till the Evangelist himself shall bid you come with us!' And so they said no more that time. But presently it came to pass, that into the heart of that good man came the desire to take the body of S. Mark from thence, and to go with him to Venice; and he said to those brave men, 'Sirs, how shall we lift the holy body, and no one be the wiser?' And one replied, 'We will do it right cleverly.' Then they went to the tomb with all speed, and lifted the body of S. Mark from where it lay, and put it in a basket, and covered it with cabbages and pork. And they took another body and dressed it in the vesture they had stripped from the body of S. Mark, and laid it in the tomb, and sealed the tomb as it was sealed before. Then those brave men took S. Mark and carried him in the basket aboard their ship, and they placed the body between two quarters of pork, and hung them to the mast. Now at the very moment when they were opening the tomb, an odour spread through the city, so sweet that had all the spice shops of the world been in Alexandria it would not have been enough to scent it so. Then the pagans said, 'Mark is moving'; for once each year they were wont to smell this odour. All the same they went to the tomb, and opened it, and saw the body wrapped in the vesture of S. Mark, and were content. But some of the pagans came to the ship, and searched her through; for they thought that the Venetians were carrying off S. Mark. But when they saw the pork hanging from the mast they began to cry, 'hanzir, hanzir,' [pork! pork!] and fled from the vessel. The wind was fresh and fair. They set their canvas to the wind and passed out into the open sea. On the third day they came to Roumania. It was night. They were under full sail, and all asleep, so that they bore right down upon an island. But the

precious Evangelist roused the master and said, 'Lower your
sails, or we go on shore.' Then the master roused the crew
and lowered the sail; and so that ship came into Venice.

[29] The body of St Mark is miraculously discovered
after the destruction of the Basilica by fire in 976; the
story is told by the eighteenth-century Venetian historian
Flaminio Corner, and translated by John Ruskin in *The
Stones of Venice*.

After the repairs undertaken by the Doge Orseolo, the place
in which the body of the holy Evangelist rested had been
altogether forgotten; so that the Doge Vital Falier was entirely
ignorant of the place of the venerable deposit. This was no
light affliction, not only to the pious Doge, but to all the
citizens and people; so that at last, moved by confidence in
the Divine mercy, they determined to implore, with prayer
and fasting, the manifestation of so great a treasure, which
did not now depend upon any human effort. A general fast
being therefore proclaimed, and a solemn procession
appointed for the 25th day of June, while the people assembled in the church interceded with God in fervent prayers for
the desired boon, they beheld, with as much amazement as
joy, a slight shaking in the marbles of a pillar (near the place
where the altar of the Cross is now), which, presently falling
to the earth, exposed to the view of the rejoicing people the
chest of bronze in which the body of the Evangelist was laid.

[30] On 24 July 1177, Venice was the scene of the
formal reconciliation, after an eighteen-year schism,
between Pope Alexander III and the Holy Roman
Emperor, Frederick Barbarossa. The most vivid eye-
witness description of the ceremony is to be found in the
so-called *De Pace Veneta Relatio*, whose author seems
to have been a senior German churchman. Translated
by John Julius Norwich.

At daybreak, the attendants of the Lord Pope hastened to the
church of St Mark the Evangelist and closed the central doors

of the great portal in front of the church, and thither they brought much timber and deal planks and ladders, and so raised up a lofty and splendid throne. And they also erected two masts of pine wood of wondrous height on each side of the quay, from which hung the standards of St Mark, magnificently embroidered and so large that they touched the ground; for that quay, which is known as the *Marmoreum*, is but a stone's throw from the church. Thither the Pope arrived before the first hour of the day [6 a.m.] and, having heard Mass, soon afterwards ascended to the higher part of his throne to await the arrival of the Emperor. There he sat, with his patriarchs, cardinals, archbishops and bishops innumerable; on his right was the Patriarch of Venice, and on his left that of Aquileia.

And now there came a quarrel between the Archbishop of Milan and the Archbishop of Ravenna as to which should be seen to take precedence; and each strove to sit himself in the third place from that of the Pope, on his right side. But the Pope determined to put an end to their contention, and leaving his own exalted seat descended the steps and placed himself below them. Thus was there no third place to sit in, and neither could sit on his right. Then about the third hour there arrived the Doge's barge, in which was the Emperor, with the Doge and the cardinals that had been sent to him on the previous day; and he was led by seven archbishops and canons of the Church in solemn procession to the papal throne. And when he reached it, he threw off the red cloak he was wearing, and prostrated himself before the Pope, and kissed first his feet and then his knees. But the Pope rose, and taking the head of the Emperor in both his hands he embraced him and kissed him, and made him sit at his right hand, and at last spoke the words 'Son of the Church, be welcome.' Then he took him by the hand and led him into the Basilica. And the bells rang, and the *Te Deum Laudamus* was sung. When the ceremony was done, they both left the church together. The Pope mounted his horse, and the Emperor held his stirrup and then retired to the Doges' Palace. And all this happened on Sunday, the Eve of St James.

And on the same day the Pope sent the Emperor many gold and silver jars filled with food of various kinds. And he sent also a fatted calf, with the words 'It is meet that we should make merry and be glad, for my son was dead, and is alive again; and was lost, and is found.'

[31] As the thirteenth century opened, preparations began for a Fourth Crusade to recapture Jerusalem from the Saracens, but it was now clear that any new expedition would require an immense transport fleet such as only Venice was able to provide. Geoffrey de Villehardouin, Marshal of Champagne arrived with six French knights in 1201 and reports how Doge Enrico Dandolo, who was well into his eighties and almost stone blind, obtained the approval for this of his closest advisers; from Villehardouin's *La Conquête de Constantinople*, edited by Edmond Faral. Translated by John Julius Norwich.

(Geoffrey de Villehardouin was appointed Marshal of Champagne in 1185 and joined the loot-hungry band of Western warriors who enrolled in the Fourth Crusade and 'took the Cross'. Fortunately for posterity, he left a full record of his visit to Venice, as of the catastrophic Crusade that followed. He probably died around 1218 in Rumania, whose Marshal he had by then become. He never went home.)

Then [the Doge] assembled some ten thousand people in the church of St Mark, the most beautiful that there is, to hear the Mass and to pray God for his guidance . . . and after the Mass he summoned the envoys and besought them, that they themselves should ask of the people the services they required . . . Geoffrey de Villehardouin, Marshal of Champagne, spoke by consent for the others: 'Good people, the greatest and most puissant lords of France have sent us to you, that we should implore you to take pity on Jerusalem, which is in bondage to the Turks, and to join with them to avenge this humiliation of Jesus Christ.' . . .

And the six messengers knelt, weeping; and the Doge and people raised their hands and cried aloud, 'We grant it! We grant it!' And so great was the noise and tumult, that the very earth seemed to tremble underfoot.

(A year later, the Crusading army gathered on the Lido. Unfortunately it numbered less than one third of what had been expected, and it proved impossible to raise the 84,000 silver marks which Venice had demanded as a fee. At last, however, agreement was reached; and the Doge called another assembly in St Mark's. Geoffrey reports his speech.)

'Signors, you are joined with the worthiest people in the world, for the highest enterprise ever undertaken. I myself am old and feeble. I need rest; my body is infirm. But I know that no man can lead you and govern you as I, your Lord, can do. If therefore you will allow me to direct and defend you by taking the Cross, while my son remains in my place to guard the Republic, I am ready to live and die with you and the pilgrims.'

And when they heard him they cried with one voice, 'We pray God that you will do this thing, and come with us!'

So he came down from the pulpit and moved up to the altar, and knelt there, weeping; and he had the Cross sewn on to his great cotton hat, so determined was he that all men should see it.

[32] Pietro Casola witnesses the great procession in St Mark's church on the Feast of Corpus Christi, 1494; from *Canon Pietro Casola's Pilgrimage* by M. Margaret Newett.

I had heard from those who knew, that all the pilgrims were expected to assemble in the Church of St Mark to join the procession. In order therefore, not to neglect my duty, and fearing lest otherwise I might not find a place, I went early in the morning to the palace of St Mark, thinking to be among the first. There I found the royal and ducal ambassadors already congregated, and several bells were ringing continually in the bell-tower of St Mark's. About the eleventh hour the most illustrious Doge descended from the palace to go into the Church of St Mark. His name is the Lord Agostino Barbarigo. He is a handsome old man, with a fine white beard, and wore his tiara on his head and a mantle made in the ducal fashion, as he always does when he appears in public. He was accompanied by the Reverend Father, the Lord Nicolo Francho, Bishop of Treviso (said to be the Papal legate), by the magnificent ambassadors aforesaid, and by a great number of Venetian gentlemen. These were dressed, one better than the other, in cloth of gold – each more beautiful than the other – crimson velvet, damask and scarlet; and each had his stole over his shoulder. As they entered the Church of St Mark all the noises of the bells and every other noise ceased.

The aforesaid Doge was conducted to his seat, which seemed to me very much in the background; that is to say, it was behind the choir; however, it was draped with cloth of gold. He was accompanied by the Ambassadors only. I was told that that is not his usual place, but only for that day in order to see the whole of the procession. The other gentlemen were all seated in the choir.

The musical Mass began, and was chanted by the most Reverend Lord the Patriarch of Aquileia, named the Lord Nicolo Donato, because the Patriarch of Venice, whose name is the Lord Tommaso Donato and who belongs to the Order of the Preachers, was infirm. The aforesaid Lord of Aquileia was assisted by a large number of deacons and sub-deacons. A great silence was maintained – more than I have ever observed on similar occasions – even in seating so many Venetian gentlemen; every sound could be heard. One single person appeared to me to direct everything, and he was obeyed by every man without a protest. This filled me with astonishment, because I had never seen such perfect obedience at similar spectacles elsewhere. . . .

The Mass closed with the benediction, and after the declaration of the Indulgence, which was for forty-two days, the procession was set in movement by the organisers and directors in the following way: – It entered by the great door of the said church, and mounting upwards into the choir, went close to the high altar, on which the body of Christ was placed in a transparent pyx shaped like a golden throne. It stood upon a chalice, the largest I ever saw; they said it was of gold; it was very beautiful. Then the said procession turned to the right of the altar to leave the choir, and passed in front of the Doge and the Ambassadors, so that they saw it all without impediment.

The first to set out was the Scuola della Misericordia. The brethren were all dressed in long white over garments, which had a small red sign on one side containing the name of the Misericordia. Certain of them, to the number of fifty-six, went in front, each carrying a beautiful gilded wooden candlestick; I mean like the long ones commonly used by the friars when they go in procession at home. They were so beautiful that I do not think anything could be added. For every candlestick there was a *doppiero* of at least two pounds weight each, of green wax, and all lighted. Behind these walked a man who carried a very ornate cross – with a certain little painted banderole – on which the gold had not been spared to make it beautiful. Many boys followed after him, and I think there were some girls as well, to judge by their heads, arranged as they arrange the little angels. Each one of them carried in the hand a *conjectera* or bowl of silver or some other vase such as they could carry, full of flowers and of rose leaves, and when they came where the aforesaid Doge was seated with the Ambassadors and the other gentlemen, they scattered the flowers over all of them and there was a very sweet smell. After these children walked as many as five hundred brethren, all belonging to the said school, all dressed in white garments, as I said above, all in pairs, and each one of them carried a large lighted candle of green wax weighing six ounces. But before these brethren passed after their cross, there were certain singers who sang many praises by the way, and who – when they came to the altar opposite the Sacrament of the body of Christ – knelt down, and there they continued to sing praises until the said brethren had all passed; then they got up and followed the said school.

Next came the brethren of Our Lady of Charity, as they are called, in the order aforesaid, and wearing a similar dress, except that the red sign was different. In front, there were forty brethren with candlesticks as beautiful as the first. Their *doppieri* were of the same weight, but they were red. Behind them was their cross with its banner, and behind the cross many children arranged and adorned like the first; and they scattered flowers like the first. Then followed the singers, who did as was said of the first. After them walked five hundred brethren, each carrying a large candle, six ounces in weight, of green wax.

The Scuola di San Marco went next. All the brethren were dressed as has been said above – that is, in white garments – and the sign they wore on their breasts was a small St Mark in red. Before their cross walked at least thirty-six brethren with their candlesticks, made as was said above, and the *doppieri* they held were of the same weight, but they were of white wax. There followed a great company of children adorned as I said above, and throwing flowers in the manner above mentioned. Then came their singers, who observed the order observed by the first. Behind them, there were at least five hundred brethren, each with his big lighted candle of white wax weighing also six ounces.

Behind these walked the brethren of the Scuola di San Giovanni, preceded by twenty-eight of their number dressed, as is said, in white, and having a red mark different from the others. Their candlesticks were made like those above, and their *doppieri* were similar in weight, but of yellow wax, that is, the natural colour. Next to these came their cross with its banner, and behind the cross there was a great company of little angels, who threw flowers in the way described above. They were followed by at least two hundred brethren in white garments also, each carrying his great candle of six ounces, which was also of the natural colour. They were preceded by singers like the foregoing schools.

Finally, behind these walked the brethren of the Scuola di San Rocco, dressed like the others, though the red sign they wore was different from the others. Before their cross there were at least thirty-four of the brethren with magnificent candlesticks like the others, and as far as I could see their *doppieri* were grey, other people said they were black; be that as it may, they were of the same weight as the others. Then came their cross, as was said of the other schools; then many little boys dressed as little angels, who threw flowers as described above; then the singers, who did as the other singers did; and behind them at least two hundred brethren dressed as was said above, and each of them with his great candle of black or grey wax, also lighted.

After these schools there followed every kind of observant and conventual friars; from the Gesuati to those of the congregation of Santa Justina there was not one lacking. Their number was counted up to eight hundred; really there were a few more, but not many. All, or the greater part of them, carried white *doppieri* or at least lighted candles in their hands, and they all wore the most beautiful vestments they possess. So beautiful were they that we cannot come even after them. For I saw certain pluvials that between the border and the cape had so many and such large and beautiful pearls that they appeared to me worth all the vestments in our city. I cannot describe the abundance of the brocades of every kind, because there were so many that my eyes became confused, and I lost count. After the friars all the clergy followed in good order with their crosses well adorned, but their vestments were not rich; indeed, they seemed to me very old-fashioned and of small value. The only other observation I will make about the Venetian clergy is, that they are few in number compared with our clergy; for, comparing them with the clergy of Milan, even the *Stradioti* – who are those without benefices – are more numerous than all the clergy of Venice.

The clergy were followed by sixty men in togas – twelve for each of the above-named schools, which are five in number – and each one of them had in his hand a large and heavy *doppiero*. I think the weight of each must have been not less than thirty-six or forty pounds, and there were twelve of every colour used by the said schools, as I said above. When I asked what order they belonged to, I was told that they were twelve brethren of each of the said schools, and all Venetian gentlemen, and they went thus in procession two by two.

When all these had passed by, the aforenamed most Reverend Lord the Patriarch, who had chanted the Mass, took up the Sacrament of the body of Christ arranged as I said, and followed after them. He was accompanied only by those who had assisted him at Mass, and the canopy was carried by priests only. Thus he commenced to walk after the procession, which, proceeding as I said, went out by the door which led to the palace of St Mark, and passed through the court of the palace. Behind him, the aforesaid Doge took his place, together with the Ambassadors, and after them the Lord Councillors and the other gentlemen. The pilgrims who were there, being very courteously invited to do so, followed, and were paired with the aforesaid gentlemen as long as there were any pilgrims unaccompanied. At the said door of Saint Mark's, by which the procession went out, there were two priests, one on the right side and the other on the left, who offered a white lighted candle of six ounces and more to each person, beginning with the aforesaid Doge down to the end, and to the pilgrims as well as the others. And so they went in procession.

It must be noted that the said procession did not go further than out of the door of Saint Mark's, as I said, and all round the piazza, which was covered the whole way it went with white cloths. At the side of the course taken by the procession many oak trees – otherwise called *rovere* – and other kinds of trees were planted in such numbers that it would have sufficed if they had had all the woods of Bachano over the doors. And another magnificent thing; beside the said trees many large candlesticks of every kind stood, which contained lighted *doppieri*. Thus the procession returned to St Mark's Church.

[33] John Evelyn in 1645 found much to admire in the Basilica but was, one feels, ultimately unimpressed; from *The Diary of John Evelyn* edited by William Bray.

(John Evelyn (1620–1706) held several administrative posts in England and helped to found the Royal Society, but he is best remembered for his Diary, which covers the years 1641–1706. He travelled in Europe during the Civil War.)

The church is also Gothic: yet for the preciousnese of the materials being of severall rich marbles, aboundance of porphyrie, serpentine, &c. far exceeding any in Rome, St Peter's hardly excepted. I much admired the splendid historic of our B. Saviour compos'd all of Mosaic over the faciata, below which and over the cheife gate are four horses cast in coper as big as the life, the same that formerly were transported from Rome by Constantine to Byzantium, and thence by the

Venetians hither. They are supported by 8 porphyrie columns
of very great size and value. Being come into the Church, you
see nothing, and tread on nothing, but what is precious. The
floore is all inlayed with achats, lazuli's, calcedons, jaspers,
porphyries and other rich marbles, admirable also for the
work; the walls sumptuously incrusted and presenting to the
imagination the shapes of men, birds, houses, flowers, and a
thousand varieties. The roofe is of most excellent Mosaic; but
what most persons admire is the new work of the emblematic
tree at the other passage out of the Church. In the midst of
this rich volto rise five cupolas, the middle very large and
sustayn'd by 36 marble columns, eight of which are of
precious marbles: under these cupolas is the high altar, on
which is a reliquarie of severall sorts of jewells, engraven with
figures after the Greeke maner, and set together with plates
of pure gold. The altar is cover'd with a canopy of ophit, on
which is sculptur'd the storie of the Bible, and so on the
pillars, which are of Parian marble, that support it. Behind
these are four other columns of transparent and true Oriental
alabaster, brought hither out of the mines of Solomon's
Temple as they report. There are many chapells and notable
monuments of illustrious persons, Dukes, Cardinals, &c. as
Zeno, Jo. Soranzi, and others: there is likewise a vast baptis-
terie of coper. Among other venerable reliques is a stone on
which they say our Blessed Lord stood preaching to those of
Tyre and Sidon, and neere the dove is an image of Christ,
much ador'd, esteeming it very sacred, for that a rude fellow
striking it, they say, there gush'd out a torrent of blood. In
one of the corners lies the body of St Isidore, brought hither
500 years since from the island of Chios. A little farther they
shew the picture of St Dominic and Francis, affirm'd to have
been made by the Abbot Joachim (many yeares before any of
them were born.) Going out of the Church they shew'd us the
stone where Alexander III trod on the neck of the Emperor
Fred. Barbarossa, pronouncing that verse of the psalm, 'super
basiliscum,' &c. The dores of the Church are of massie coper.
There are neere 500 pillars in this building, most of them
porphyrie and serpentine, and brought cheifly from Athens
and other parts of Greece formerly in their power. At the
corner of the Church are inserted into the maine wall four

figures as big as life cut in porphyrie, which they say are the images of four brothers who poysoned one another, by which meanes there escheated to the Republiq that vast treasury of relicques now belonging to the Church. At the other entrance that looks towards the Sea, stands in a small chapell that statue of our Lady, made (as they affirme) of the same stone or rock out of which Moses brought water to the murmuring Israelites at Meriba.

After all that is said, this Church is in my opinion much too dark and dismal, and of heavy work; the fabric, as is much of Venice both for buildings and other fashions and circumstances, after the Greekes, their next neighboures.

[34] To Charles de Brosses, arch-classicist, the Gothic style was barbarous, the Byzantine even worse, as he wrote to his friend, Monsieur de Quintin, in 1739; from *Selections from the Letters of de Brosses* translated by Lord Ronald Sutherland Gower.

But we must hurry on to the Church of St Mark's. You probably imagine that this church is altogether admirable, but there you make a great mistake. It is of the Greek style, low in structure, very sombre, in miserable taste, both within and without, with seven domes lined with mosaics on a golden ground, which makes them look more like copper kettles than cupolas. Considering the immense wealth lavished on this building, it could not escape being interesting, in spite of the diabolical design of the structure. From floor to ceiling, externally and internally, the church is covered with pictures in mosaic on a golden background. You are aware that this mosaic is composed of small cubes of glass and of coloured marbles. These mosaics can never be very delicate or finished in execution, but they have the advantage of being imperishable, and this quality has made the first artists adopt them for their designs. As these date back to the year 1071, they may be regarded as among the earliest examples of painting in existence; they were executed by Greeks, who were imported especially for this work. With all respect to the Florentines, it is here, and not in Florence, that the art of painting was renewed. Cimabue, more than a century and a half after these mosaics were made, came here and got his ideas from them. Except for the colour, nothing can be more pitiable than these designs; and it is fortunate that the workmen took the wise precaution of writing on each, the name of the subject it is intended to represent. The later styles are better; but, although brilliant in colour, they are unsatisfactory as works of art. Exception may be made to the mosaics in the sacristy, where, instead of figures, they have had the good idea of making borders and arabesques of exceeding beauty; in that style only is mosaic work admirable. The pavement is also of mosaic, composed of millions of little morsels of marble, jasper, lapis, agate, serpentine, copper, &c., on which one cannot take a step without sliding. It is all so well put together that, although the pavement has sunk in places and risen in others, not a single morsel has fallen out or become detached; in short, it is an admirable place for spinning a top. A truly noble thought! A person of your good taste must approve of the idea. I will not detain you over the church relics, which Mission has fully described, neither with the treasure; the fact is I did not trouble to see these things, and was content to examine the famous Gospel of St Mark, which is kept with the greatest care, as being the oldest MSS in the world. It is an in-quarto, written on papyrus, and all one can see are some Greek capital letters here and there, and it is impossible to tell whether the book is a treatise on medicine or a Gospel.

Above the portal of the church are the four bronze horses of wonderful beauty, the work of Lysippus, the Greek bronze-founder, who, it is said, cast them for Nero. They are the only things throughout the whole building worthy of admiration.

[35] A visitor more enthusiastic about the Basilica's visual splendours was William Beckford in 1780; from his *Italy, with sketches of Spain and Portugal.*

(William Beckford (1760–1844) inherited a fortune as a child and spent it on art, building Fonthill Abbey and travelling extensively in Europe. He wrote a Gothic novel, Vathek, two travel books and a journal.)

Sometimes I go and pry about in the great church of Saint
Mark, and examine the variety of marbles, and mazes of
delicate sculpture with which it is covered. The cupola, glittering with gold, mosaics and paintings of half the wonders of
the Apocalypse, never fails transporting me to the period of
the Eastern Empire. I think myself in Constantinople, and
expect Michael Palaeologus with all his train. One circumstance alone prevents my observing half the treasures of the
place, and holds down my fancy, just springing into the air: I
mean the vile stench which exhales from every recess and
corner of the edifice and which all the altars cannot subdue.

[36] Another visitor from England, at about the same
time, was more interested in the contents of St Mark's
Treasury; from *A View of Society and Manners in Italy*
by John Moore MD.

(Dr John Moore (1729–1802), physician and man of letters,
was in Venice in 1777 as guardian and tutor to the young
Duke of Hamilton.)

The treasury of St Mark is very rich in jewels and relics; and
it was necessary to apply to one of the Procurators of St Mark
for leave to see it. I shall only mention a few of the most
valuable effects kept here. Eight pillars from Solomon's temple at Jerusalem; a piece of the Virgin Mary's veil, some of
her hair, and a small portion of her milk; the knife used by
our Saviour at his last supper; one of the nails of the cross,
and a few drops of his blood. After these it would be
impertinent to enumerate the bones, and other relics, of saints
and martyrs, of which there is a plentiful show in this church,
and still less need I take up your time with an inventory of
the temporal jewels kept here; it would be unpardonable,
however, to omit mentioning the picture of the Virgin, by St
Luke. From this, compared with his other works, it is plain,
that St Luke was a much better evangelist than painter: some
professions seem to be almost incompatible with each other.
I have known many very good painters who would have
made bad saints, and here is an instance of an excellent saint
who was but an indifferent painter.

[37] John Ruskin's dazzling description of the Basilica of St Mark begins, rightly, with the approach to the Piazza from the west; from *The Stones of Venice*.

[We] presently emerge on the bridge and Campo San Moisè, whence to the entrance into St Mark's Place, called the Bocca di Piazza (mouth of the square), the Venetian character is nearly destroyed, first by the frightful façade of San Moisè and then by the modernising of the shops as they near the piazza, and the mingling with the lower Venetian populace of lounging groups of English and Austrians. We will push fast through them into the shadow of the pillars at the end of the 'Bocca di Piazza', and then we forget them all; for between those pillars there opens a great light, and, in the midst of it, as we advance slowly, the vast tower of St Mark seems to lift itself visibly forth from the level field of chequered stones; and, on each side, the countless arches prolong themselves into ranged symmetry, as if the rugged and irregular houses that pressed together above us in the dark alley had been struck back into sudden obedience and lovely order, and all their rude casements and broken walls had been transformed into arches charged with goodly sculpture, and fluted shafts of delicate stone.

And well may they fall back, for beyond those troops of ordered arches there rises a vision out of the earth, and all the great square seems to have opened from it in a kind of awe, that we may see it far away; – a multitude of pillars and white domes, clustered into a long low pyramid of coloured light; a treasure-heap, it seems, partly of gold, and partly of opal and mother-of-pearl, hollowed beneath into five great vaulted porches, ceiled with fair mosaic, and beset with sculpture of alabaster, clear as amber and delicate as ivory, – sculpture fantastic and involved, of palm leaves and lilies, and grapes and pomegranates, and birds clinging and fluttering among the branches, all twined together into an endless network of buds and plumes; and in the midst of it, the solemn forms of angels, sceptred, and robed to the feet, and leaning to each other across the gates, their figures indistinct among the gleaming of the golden ground through the leaves beside them, interrupted and dim, like the morning light as it faded back among the branches of Eden, when first its gates were angel-guarded long ago. And round the walls of the porches there are set pillars of variegated stones, jasper and porphyry, and deep-green serpentine spotted with flakes of snow, and marbles, that half refuse and half yield to the sunshine, Cleopatra-like, 'their bluest veins to kiss' – the shadow, as it steals back from them, revealing line after line of azure undulation, as a receding tide leaves the waved sand; their capitals rich with interwoven tracery, rooted knots of herb-age, and drifting leaves of acanthus and vine, and mystical signs, all beginning and ending in the Cross; and above them, in the broad archivolts, a continuous chain of language and of life – angels, and the signs of heaven, and the labours of men, each in its appointed season upon the earth; and above these, another range of glittering pinnacles, mixed with white arches edged with scarlet flowers – a confusion of delight, amidst which the breasts of the Greek horses are seen blazing in their breadth of golden strength, and the St Mark's lion, lifted on a blue field covered with stars, until at last, as if in ecstasy, the crests of the arches break into a marble foam, and toss themselves far into the blue sky in flashes and wreaths of sculptured spray, as if the breakers on the Lido shore had been frost-bound before they fell, and the sea-nymphs had inlaid them with coral and amethyst . . .

Let us enter the church. It is lost in still deeper twilight, to which the eye must be accustomed for some moments before the form of the building can be traced; and then there opens before us a vast cave, hewn out into the form of a Cross, and divided into shadowy aisles by many pillars. Round the domes of its roof the light enters only through narrow apertures like large stars; and here and there a ray or two from some far-away casement wanders into the darkness, and casts a narrow phosphoric stream upon the waves of marble that heave and fall in a thousand colours along the floor. What else there is of light is from torches, or silver lamps, burning ceaselessly in the recesses of the chapels; the roof sheeted with gold, and the polished walls covered with alabaster, give back at every curve and angle some feeble gleaming to the flames; and the glories round the heads of the sculptured saints flash out upon us as we pass them, and sink again into the gloom. Under foot and over head, a continual succession of crowded imagery, one picture passing into another, as in a dream; forms beautiful and terrible mixed together; dragons and serpents, and ravening beasts of prey, and graceful birds that in the midst of them drink from running fountains and feed from vases of crystal; the passions and the pleasures of human life symbolized together, and the mystery of its redemption; for the mazes of interwoven lines and changeful pictures lead always at last to the Cross, lifted and carved in every place and upon every stone; sometimes with the serpent of eternity wrapt round it, sometimes with doves beneath its arms, and sweet herbage growing forth from its feet; but conspicuous most of all on the great road that crosses the church before the altar, raised in bright blazonry against the shadow of the apse.

[38] Henry James evokes the magic of St Mark's in 1881; from his *Italian Hours*.

It is surely the best-described building in the world. Open the *Stones of Venice*, open Théophile Gautier's *Italia*, and you will see. These writers take it very seriously, and it is only because there is another way of taking it that I venture to speak of it; the way that offers itself after you have been in Venice a couple of months, and the light is hot in the great Square, and you pass in under the pictured porticoes with a feeling of habit and friendliness and a desire for something cool and dark. There are moments, after all, when the church is comparatively quiet and empty, and when you may sit there with an easy consciousness of its beauty. From the moment, of course, that you go into any Italian church for any purpose but to say your prayers or look at the ladies, you rank yourself among the trooping barbarians I just spoke of; you treat the place as an orifice in the peep-show. Still, it is almost a spiritual function – or, at the worst, an amorous one – to feed one's eyes on the molten colour that drops from the hollow vaults and thickens the air with its richness. It is all so quiet and sad and faded and yet all so brilliant and living. The strange figures in the mosaic pictures, bending with the curve of niche and vault, stare down through the glowing dimness; the burnished gold that stands behind them catches the light on its little uneven cubes. St Mark's owes nothing of its character to the beauty of proportion or perspective; there is nothing grandly balanced or far-arching; there are no long lines nor triumphs of the perpendicular. The church arches indeed, but arches like a dusky cavern. Beauty of surface, of tone, of detail, of things near enough to touch and kneel upon and lean against – it is from this the effect proceeds. In this sort of beauty the place is incredibly rich, and you may go there every day and find afresh some lurking pictorial nook. It is a treasury of bits, as the painters say; and there are usually three or four of the fraternity with their easels set up in uncertain equilibrium on the undulating floor. It is not easy to catch the real complexion of St Mark's, and these laudable attempts at portraiture are apt to look either lurid or livid. But if you cannot paint the old loose-looking marble slabs, the great panels of basalt and jasper, the crucifixes of which the lonely anguish looks deeper in the vertical light, the tabernacles whose open doors disclose a dark Byzantine image spotted with dull, crooked gems – if you cannot paint these things you can at least grow fond of them. You grow fond even of the old benches of red marble, partly worn away by the breeches of many generations and attached to the base of those wide pilasters of which the precious plating, delightful in its faded brownness, with a faint grey bloom upon it, bulges and yawns a little with honourable age.

[39] At this time, however, James was deeply concerned about restoration work on the outside of the building, as he writes to Grace Norton on June 1881; from *The Letters of Henry James* edited by Leon Edel.

. . . Tell Charles, whom I salute *caramente*, that I can tell him little good of St Mark's. I know nothing of the necessities of what they are doing to the poor dear old beautiful building; but the effect produced is that of witnessing the forcible *maquillage* of one's grandmother! In a word, if it be a necessity, it is an abominable necessity, and the side of the church toward the Piazzetta where the *maquillage* is now complete, is a sight to make the angels howl . . .

[40] Over the centuries, writers have compared the basilica of St Mark to many things. No comparison, however, is more surprising than that drawn by Mark Twain; in *A Tramp Abroad* (1880).

. . . One lingers about the Cathedral a good deal, in Venice. There is a fascination about it – partly because it is so old, and partly because it is so ugly . . . Propped on its long row of thick-legged columns, its back knobbed with domes, it seemed like a vast, warty bug taking a meditative walk.

[41] In *Venice* – the best descriptive book on the city ever written – James (now Jan) Morris describes St Mark's.

The church in Venice, though, is something more than all things bright and beautiful. It is descended from Byzantium, by faith out of nationalism: and sometimes to its high ritual in the Basilica of St Mark there is a tremendous sense of an eastern past, marbled, hazed and silken. St Mark's itself is a barbaric building, like a great Mongolian pleasure pavilion, or a fortress in Turkestan: and sometimes there is a suggestion of rich barbarism to its services too, devout, reverent and beautiful though they are.

In Easter week each year the Patriarch and his clergy bring from the vaults of the church treasury all its most sacred relics, and display them ceremonially to the people. This ancient function is heavy with reminders of the Orient. It takes place in the evening, when the Piazza is dark, and the dim lights of the Basilica shine mysteriously on the gold mosaics of its roof. The congregation mills about the nave in the half-light, switching from side to side, not knowing which way to look. A beadle in a cocked hat, with a silver sword and the face of a hereditary retainer, stands in a peremptory eighteenth-century attitude beside a pillar. The organ plays quietly from its loft, and sometimes there is a chant of male voices, and sometimes a sudden hubbub from the square outside when the door of the church is opened. All is murmurous, brown and glinting.

A flash of gold and silver from an aisle, a swish of stiff vestments, the clink of a censer, and presently there advances through the crowd, clouded in incense, the patriarchal procession. Preceded by flurrying vergers, clearing a way through the congregation, it sweeps slowly and rheumatically up the church. A golden canopy of old tapestry sways and swings above the mitred Patriarch, and around it walk the priests, solemn and shuffling, clasping reverently the celebrated relics of St Mark's (enclosed in golden frames, jewelled caskets, crucifixes, mediaeval monstrances). You cannot see very well, for the crowd is constantly jostling, and the atmosphere is thick; but as the priests pass slowly by you catch a queer glimpse of copes and reliquaries, a cross set with some strange sacred souvenir, a fragment of bone in a crystal sphere, weird, ornate, elaborate objects, swaying and bobbling above the people as the old men carrying them stumble towards the altar.

It is an eastern ceremonial, a thing of misty and exotic splendour. When you turn to leave the great church, all those holy objects are placed on the rim of the pulpit, and all those grave priests are crowded together behind, like so many white-haired scholarly birds. Incense swirls around them; the church is full of slow shining movement; and in the Piazza outside, when you open the door, the holiday Venetians stroll from café to café in oblivion, like the men who sell Coca-Cola beneath the sneer of the Sphinx.

St Mark's Square and the Piazzetta

[42] Ducal processions in the piazza in the thirteenth century; the description is by Martino da Canale, translated by Horatio Brown in his *Venice, an historical sketch of the Republic.*

So long have I lived in beautiful Venice, that I have seen the processions which Monsignor the Doge makes upon high festivals, and which he would not, for all the world, omit to make each year. On Easter Day, then, the Doge descends from his palace; before him go eight men bearing eight silken banners blazoned with the image of S. Mark, and on each staff are the eagles of the Empire. After the standards come two lads who carry, one the faldstool the other the cushion of the Doge; then six trumpeters who blow through silver trumpets, followed by two with cymbals, also of silver. Comes next a clerk who holds a great cross all beautiful with gold, silver, and precious stones; a second clerk carries the Gospels, and a third a silver censer, and all three are dressed in damask of gold. Then follow the twenty-two canons of S. Mark in their robes, chaunting. Behind the canons walks Monsignor the Doge, under the umbrella which Monsignor the Apostle (the Pope) gave him; the umbrella is of cloth of gold, and a lad bears it in his hands By the Doge's side is the Primiciero of S. Mark's who wears a bishop's mitre; on his other side, the priest who shall chaunt the mass. Monsignor the Doge wears a crown of gold and precious stones, and is draped in cloth of gold. Hard by the Doge walks a gentleman who bears a sword of exquisite workmanship; then follow the gentlemen of Venice. In such order Monsignor the Doge comes into the Piazza of S. Mark, which is a stone's-throw long; he walks as far as the church of San Gimignano [to be demolished later by Napoleon], and returns thence in the same order. The Doge bears a white wax candle in his hands. They halt in the middle of the Piazza, and three of the ducal chaplains advance before the Doge and chaunt to him the beautiful versicles and responses. Then all enter the church of S. Mark; three chaplains move forward to the altar rails, and say in loud voice, 'Let Christ be victorious, let Christ rule, let Christ reign; to our Lord Renier Zeno, by the grace of God illustrious Doge of Venice, Dalmatia, and Croatia, conqueror of a fourth part and of half a fourth part of all the Roman Empire, salvation, honour, life and victory, let Christ be victorious, let Christ rule, let Christ reign.' Then the three chaplains say, 'Holy Mary,' and all respond, 'Help thou him.' The Primiciero removes his mitre and begins the mass. Then the Doge shows himself to the people from the loggia and afterwards enters his palace, where he finds the table spread; he dines there, and with him all the chaplains of S. Mark.

[43] Celebrations in the Piazza to mark the putting down of the Cretan Rebellion in 1364; described by Petrarch, from *The life of Petrarch* by Mrs Dobson.

(Francesco Petrarch (1304–1374), the poet, spent the years 1362 to 1367 in Venice, as the guest of the Republic.)

When religion had amply received its due, everyone turned to games and spectacles. It would be tiresome to enumerate all the different kinds of games, their forms, costs, solemnity, and decorum such that, remarkably enough, there was nowhere confusion and ill-feeling. Everything breathed joy, courtesy, concord, love. Such a lofty mood pervaded the city that modesty and sobriety, far from disappearing, ruled everywhere and prevented excesses in the celebrations. These continued in various forms through many festive days, and concluded with two great functions.

The first was a race; the second a contest, or joust. In the first the contestants dash down a straight course; in the second they dash against each other. In both the participants are mounted; in the first the riders do not clash but give a warlike note by brandishing spear and shield and carrying fluttering silk banners. The second is a sort of duel in armor. In the first reigns the utmost of elegance, with a minimum of peril. The second is a mock conflict; the French call it, not very properly, 'jeu de lance'; this would better fit the first game, for in that they play, and in the second they fight. In both I realized something I should hardly have accepted on others' testimony, but I must credit my own eyes: this people possesses a rare eminence, not only, as everyone is aware, in nautical and seafaring skills but in military exercises. They display the arts of horsemanship and of weapon-handling, *élan* and endurance, enough to rank them with the fiercest fighters on earth.

Both performances were held in that great square, which I doubt has any match in this world, in front of the marble and gold façade of the temple. No outsider took part in the first contest. Twenty-four noble youths, handsome and splendidly clad, were chosen for this part of the ceremony.

It was a marvellous sight to see all these gallant youths, dressed in purple and gold, checking and spurring their fleet-footed steeds adorned with glittering trappings so that they seemed hardly to touch the ground. They followed their captain's orders so exactly that at the moment one reached the goal another sprang from the mark, and another made ready. With this alternation of uniform riders there was a constant race. One man's finish was another man's starting point; when one stopped another began; so that, though many coursed in full view, you would have said at the end that just one man had ridden the whole way. Now you would see the spear-points flash through the air, now the purple banners fluttering in the breeze. The size of the multitude is hard to reckon and hard to believe; both sexes and every age and station were represented. The Doge himself with a great band of the leading men occupied the loggia above the church vestibule; at their feet, below this marble tribune, the crowd was massed. This is where the four gilded bronze horses stand, the work of some ancient unknown but illustrious sculptor. On their high place they look almost alive, whinnying and stamping. To avoid the heat and dazzle of the descending summer sun, the loggia was everywhere protected with varicolored awnings.

I was invited, as I had often been similarly honoured. I sat at the right of the Doge. Down below there was not a vacant inch; as the saying goes, a grain of millet could not have fallen to earth. The great square, the church itself, the towers, roofs, porches, windows were not so much filled as jammed with spectators. An inestimable, an incredible throng covered the face of the earth. Under our eyes the swarming, well-mannered offspring of the flourishing city augmented the joy of the festival. The general gaiety was reflected and redoubled by one's recognition of it in one's neighbour's face.

On the right a great wooden grandstand had been hastily erected for this purpose only. There sat four hundred young women of the flower of the nobility, very beautiful and splendidly dressed. They watched the daily spectacles, and early and late they adorned brilliant receptions for invited guests. Nor should I overlook the presence of certain high noblemen from Britain, kinsmen of the king, who had journeyed here by sea to celebrate our victory, and who were reposing after the hardships of life at sea . . .

A heavy crown of pure gold, sparkling with gems, was granted to the victor; a silver-mounted sword-belt of splendid workmanship went to solace him who merited the glory of second place. A challenge in military form and in italian, authenticated with the Doge's seal, had been sent to the provinces near and far, by which all those who were tempted by such glory were summoned to that tourney on horseback. Many indeed assembled not only of different cities but of different languages, who possessed military training, confidence in their own merit, and hope of distinction.

When the races were over, the jousts began on the fourth of August and lasted four successive days with such splendour that the memory of man records nothing comparable since the founding of the city. On the last day, by the decision of the Doge, of the senators, of the visiting military men, and noteworthily of our general, author (after God) of our victory and of all our joy, the first prize was awarded to one of our citizens, the second to a visitor from Ferrara. This was the end of our games, but not of our joy and of our successes. And let this be also the end of this letter, in which I have tried to present to your eyes and ears what illness deprived you of, in order that you may know the succession of affairs here and recognize that in a maritime people there may exist a soldierly spirit, and a sense of magnificent display, and mettlesome character, and contempt for lucre and a lust for glory.

[44] The Corpus Christi procession in the Piazza, as witnessed by Fra Felix Fabri; from *Felix Fabri* translated by Aubrey Stewart.

(Fra Felix Fabri was a learned Dominican friar from Ulm, whose *Evagatorium in Terrae Sanctae, Arabiae et Egypti* vividly records his pilgrimage to Jerusalem in 1483.)

On the 29th [May], which was the feast of the most holy 'Corpus Christi,' we went up to St Mark's and attended the solemn procession. Never had we seen such magnificence on that day as at Venice. The procession was marvellous, and contained a vast multitude of priests and religious of all orders, all of whom, wearing their sacred vestments, and carrying most precious reliquaries of every kind, walked in regular order all round the great square of St Mark, which was covered with linen cloths all round the great circuit along which the procession moved from one of the doors of the church of St Mark to another. The Patriarch bore the Host, and by his side walked the Doge in his costly ducal cap. After them came the Abbots, wearing their mitres, and the entire Venetian Senate. Besides the ecclesiastical display, which was magnificent, it was interesting to see the gravity of the lords senators, and their very becoming robes: after them came many guilds, and then the common people. The religious, both regular and secular, walked first, with singing and every kind of musical instruments, interludes and spectacles of all sorts. In this procession no college, no monastery, no guild appeared without some pageant of its own for the admiration and delight of the beholders. The Friars Preachers of St John and St Paul embellished the whole procession by their droll and beauteous pageants: we saw there so much gold and silver, so many precious stones and costly dresses, that no man could reckon their value. There is nothing but a confused crowding, running, and pushing multitude ... Among these holy solemnities how many vanities are to be seen, how much extravagant dress of women and dissolute behaviour of lay-men, and disorderly conduct of both regular and secular clergy, may be conceived by anyone who considers what an enormous multitude is there gathered together. Whether the honour thus profanely bestowed on the most holy and divine sacrament is acceptable, God, who knoweth all things, alone can tell.

[45] A description of St Mark's Square at the end of the sixteenth century, by one of the earliest of true travel writers; from *An Itinerary* . . . by Fynes Moryson, Gent.

(Fynes Moryson (1566–1630) wrote that 'from my tender youth I had a great desire to see forraine Countries.' Leaving England in 1591, he spent the next six years wandering through Europe and the Near East. After diplomatic service in Ireland, he settled in London where he wrote his *Itinerary*.)

It remaines to adde something of the magnificall building of this City. And in the first place, the market place of Saint Marke is paved with bricke, and it consists of foure market places, joined in one; whereof two may rather be called the market places of the Dukes Pallace (joining to the Church of Saint Marke) the one being on the furthest side from Saint Marke, betweene the pallace and the great channell, the other right before the pallace towards the channell, foure hundred foot in length, and some one hundred and thirty in breath. The third is before the Church doore of Saint Mark, and lies in length five hundred and twenty foot towards the Church of Saint Geminiano, and hath one hundred and thirty foot in

breath, which may more properly be called the market place
of Saint Marke. The fourth is on the other side of the Church,
towards the Church of Saint Basso. In this market place of
foure joined in one, are solemne spectacles or shewes, and all
processions made, and there on Ascension day, is the Faire
held, and the markets on wednesday and saterday: there they
use to muster souldiers; and there the gentlemen and strangers
daily meet and walke. Before the doore of Saint Markes
Church, are three peeces of brasse carved, and for bignesse
like the bodies of trees, upon which at festivall daies three
rich banners are hung in signe of liberty, or as others say, for
the three Dominions of Venice, Cypro, and Candia.

Under the tower of the Clocke, fifty foot distant from Saint
Markes Church, is a passage to and from this market place;
and this tower all covered with marble, beares a remarkeable
Clocke, which sheweth the course of the Sunne and the
Moone daily, and the degrees they passe, and when they enter
into a new signe of the Zodiacke, and above that the guilded
Image of our Lady shineth, placed betweene two doores, out
of one of which doores, onely at solemne Feasts, an Angell
with a Trumpet, and the three Wise Men of the East following, passe before our Ladies Image, and adore her, and so goe
in at the other doore. Above that, there is a carved Image of
a Lyon with wings, and upon the very top, two brasen Images,
called the Mores, which by turnes striking with a hammer
upon a great bell, sound the houres.

The houses opposite to the Pallaces of the Procurators of
Saint Marke, are called the houses of the State, and they
belong to the Church of Saint Marke, and having some fifty
shops under the Arches of the upper roofes (where men may
walke dry when it raines) they yeeld great rents to the Church.
Opposite to these are the Pallaces of the said Procurators,
which are also in the said market place, which I said to be
more properly called the market place of Saint Marke, and
these being stately built, sixty sixe foot high, and the stones
curiously carved, doe not onely adorne the market place, but
in summer give a pleasant shade to passengers, besides that
under the Arches of them, men may walke drie in the greatest
raine, and the shops under these Arches yeeld great rents, and
under these Pallaces out of foure little streetes there be so

many passages to and from the market place. These Pallaces
are built at the charge of the State, the nine Procurators being
to have nine Pallaces: for as yet they were not all built; but in
the meane time any pallace falling voide, it was given to the
eldest of them that had none, yet not according to their age,
but according to their election.

The steeple or belfrey of Saint Marke, distant some eighty
foote from the Church, and set over against it, is to be
admired, not onely for the foundation, strangely laid under
the earth; but also for many other causes. It is built foure
square, each square containing forty foot, and it is three
hundred thirty three foot high, of which feet the pinacle
containes ninety sixe, and the woodden Image of an Angell
above the pinacle covered with brasse and guilded, and
turning with the wind, containes sixteene feete. It is adorned
with high pillars of marble, and with a gallery at the bottome
of the pinacle, made with many pillars of brasse, and upon
the pinacle with great marble Images of Lyons, and from the
top in a cleere day, men may see a hundred miles off the ships
under sayles; and it beares foure great bels, whereof the
greater called La Trottiera, is rung every day at noone, and
when the Gentlemen meet in Senate with like occasions: but
when a new Pope or Duke is made, all the bels are rung, and
the steeple is set round about with waxe candles burning. I
went to the top of this steeple, which hath thirty seven
ascents, whereof each hath foureteene lesse ascents, by which
the going up as is as easie, as if a man walked on plaine
ground, at the contriving whereof I much wondered. In the
lodge of this steeple, the foure brasen Images of Pallas,
Apollo, Mercury, and of Peace, and above them, the figure of
Venice, with the Dominion by sea and land, and the Image of
Venus the Goddesse of Cyprus, and of Jupiter the King of
Candia, present themselves, and neere the great gate the
Images of the blessed Virgin and of Saint John Baptist, are
highly valued.

[46] Thomas Coryat, in Venice in 1608, fourteen years
after Fynes Moryson, describes – with more enthusiasm
than accuracy – many of the details of St Mark's Square,

particularly Sansovino's *loggetta* at the base of the Campanile, with which he was much taken; from *Coryat's Crudities*.

At the South corner of St *Markes* Church as you go into the Dukes Palace there is a very remarkable thing to be observed. A certaine Porphyrie stone of some yard and halfe or almost two yards high, and of a pretty large compasse, even as much as a man can claspe at twice with both his armes. On this stone are laide for the space of three days and three nights, the heads of all such as being enemies or traitors to the State, or some notorious offenders, have been apprehended out of the citie, and beheaded by those that have beene bountifully hired by the Senate for the same purpose. In that place do their heads remain so long, though the smell of them doth breede a very offensive and contagious annoyance. For it hath beene an aunciant custome of the Venetians whensoever any notorious malefactor hath for any enormous crime escaped out of the City for his security to propose a great reward to him that shal bring his head to that stone. Yea, I have heard that there have beene twenty thousand duckats given to a man for bringing a traytors head to that place.

Near to this stone is another memorable thing to be observed. A marvailous faire paire of gallowes made of alabaster, the pillars being wrought with many curious borders and workes, which served for no other purpose but to hang the Duke whensoever he shall happen to commit any treason against the State. And for that cause it is erected before the very gate of his Palace to the end to put him in minde to be faithfull and true to his country, if not, he seeth the place of punishment at hand. But this is not a perfect gallowes, because there are only two pillars without a transverse beame, which, beame (they say) is to be erected when there is any execution, not else. Betwixt this gallowes malefactors and condemned men (that are to goe to be executed upon a scaffold betwixt the two famous pillars before mentioned at the South end of St *Marks* street, near the Adriaticque Sea) are wont to say their prayers to the Image of the Virgin Mary, standing on a part of St *Marks* Church right opposite unto them . . .

There is adjoyned unto this tower a most glorious little roome that is very worthy to be spoken of, namely the Logetto, which is a place where some of the Procurators of Saint *Markes* doe use to sit in judgement, and discusse matters of controversies. This place is indeed but little, yet of that singular and incomparable beauty being made all of Corinthian worke, that I never saw the like before for the quantity thereof. The front of it looking towards the Dukes Palace is garnished with eight curious pillars *versicoloris marmoris*, that is, of marble that hath sundry colours; wherof foure are placed at one side of the core, aud four at another. The steppes of the staires which are in number four, are made of red marble. Two faire benches without it of red marble. The walke a little without paved with Diamond pavier contrived partly with free stone and partly with red marble: all the front of red marble, except the images which are made of most pure alabaster: over the tribunal where the Procurators sit, the image of the Virgin *Mary* is placed bearing Christ in her armes, made of alabaster, and two pretty pillars of changeable-coloured marble on both sides of her, under whom this is written in a little white stone: *Opus Iacobi Sansovini*. The sides of the dore are made of alabaster, and the top rayled with a curious tarrasse of alabaster. On both sides of the dore are foure very goodly faire statues made in brasse, two on one side, and two on the other; each betwixt a paire of those curious pillars that I have spoken of. On the right hand as you enter the core, there are these two, the statue of Mercury with a dead mans skull under his feete: The other, the statue of peace with a burning torch in her hand, wherwith she burneth an helmet (a strange thing to burn steele with fire) and a Target. On the left hand these two; *Pallas* very exquisitely made with an helmet and a feather in the crest, a shield in one hand, and a trunchin in another, a mantle about her and a Souldiers coat of maile: the other the Statue of *Apollo* like a stripling without a beard, with an horne in one hand, and a quiver full of arrowes in another hanging downe about his neck. All these statues were made by *Iacobus Sansovinus* a Florentine . . .

[The Piazzetta] is worthy to be celebrated for that famous concourse and meeting of so many distinct and sundry nations twice a day, betwixt sixe and eleven of the clocke in the morning, and betwixt five in the afternoone and eight, as I have before mentioned, where also the Venetian long gowned gentlemen doe meete together in great troupes. For you shall not see as much as one Venetian there of the Patrician ranke without his blacke gowne and tippet. There you may see many Polonians, Slavonians, Persians, Grecians, Turks, Iewes, Christians of all the famousest regions of Christendome, and each nation distinguished from another by their proper and peculiar habits. A singular shew, and by many degrees the worthiest of all the Europaean Countries . . .

At the farther end of this second part of the Piazza of S. *Marke* there stand two marvellous lofty pillars of marble, which I have before mentioned, of equall heigth and thicknesse very neare to the shore of the Adriatique gulfe, the fairest certainely for heigth and greatnesse that ever I saw till then. For the compasse of them is so great, that I was not able to claspe them with both mine armes at thrice, their Diameter in thicknesse containing very neare foure foote (as I conjecture). Besides they are of such an exceeding heigth, that I thought a good while there were scarce the like to be found in any place of Christendome, till at length I called to my remembrance that wondrous high pillar in a certain market place of Rome, on whose top the ashes of the Emperour *Traian* were once kept. For that pillar was about one hundred and forty foot high, but this I thinke is scarce above thirty. They are said to be made of Phrygian marble, being solid and all one peece. They were brought by Sea from Constantinople for more then foure hundred years since. Upon the top of one of them are advanced the armes of Venice, the winged Lyon made all of brasse; on the other the statue of S. *Theodorus* gilt, and standing upon a brasen Crocodile with a spectre in one hand and a shield in another. This S. *Theodorus* was a valiant warriour, and the generall Captaine of the Venetian armies, whom by reason of his invincible courage, and fortunate successe in martiall affaires that he atchieved for the good of this citie, the Venetians caused to be canonized for a saint, and do with many ceremonious solemnities celebrate his feast every year. There was a third pillar also brought from Constantinople at the same time that these were: which through the exceeding force of the weight when they were drawing of it out of the ship into the land, fell down into the water, by reason that the tackling and instruments that those men used which were set a worke about it, brake asunder. That same pillar is yet to be felt within some ten paces of the shore: those two that doe now stand hard by the sea shore were erected about some eighteene paces asunder, by one *Nicolas Beratterius* a Longobard, and a very cunning architect. It is reported that this man craved no other reward of the Senate for his labour, then that it might be lawfull for any man to play at dice at all times betwixt those pillars without any contradiction, which was granted, and is continually performed. In this distance betwixt the pillars condemned men and malefactors are put to death. For whensoever there is to be any execution, upon a sudden they erect a scaffold there, and after they have beheaded the offendors (for that is most commonly their death) they take it away againe.

[47] The execution of Antonio Foscarini in St Mark's Square in 1622 was one of the great scandals of Venetian history; as reported in *Reliquiae Wottonianae* . . . by the Curious Pencil of the Ever Memorable Sir Henry Wotton Kt, Late Provost of Eton College.

For that the Case of the late Cavalier Antonio Foscarini hath been diversly misreported, and perhaps not the least, even by those that were his Judges, to cover their own disgrace, I have thought a little curiousity not ill spent in research of the whole Proceeding, that his Majesty (to whom he was so well known) may have a more due information of this rare and unfortunate example. There is among the partitions of this Government a very awful Magistracy under Title of Inquisitori di Stato; to which are commonly deputed three Gentlemen of the gravest and severest natures, who receive all secret Delations in matter of practice against the Republick, and then refer the same, as they shall judge the consequence thereof, to the Decemviral Council, being the supremest Tribunal in Criminal Enquiries; of which Body they are usually themselves.

To these Inquisitors, about the beginning of April last, came two Fellows of mean condition, born about the Lago di Garda, but inhabitants in Venice, by name Girolamo and Domenico Vani; as some say, Uncle and Nephew; certainly near of kindred, which in this report is a weighty circumstance; for thereby they were the likelier to conspire, and consequently their united Testimonies of the less validity. These persons capitulate with the inquisitors of that time (whose names may be civilly spared) about a reward (which is usual) for the discovery of some gentlemen, which at undue times, and in disguised forms, did haunt the houses of Foreign Ministers, and in particular, of the Spanish Agent: who being the most obnoxious to public jealousie, these Accusers were likeliest upon that subject to gain a favourable hearing. In the head of their secret list, they nominate Anthonio Foscarini, then an actual Senator, and thereby upon pain of Death restrained from all conference in this ombragious State with publick instruments, unless by special permission. To verifie their discovery, besides their own Testimonies, they alledge one Giovan Battista, who served the foresaid Spanish agent and had, as they said, acquainted them with the Accesses of such and such Gentlemen unto him. But first they wished, or so the Inquisitors thought fit, to proceed against Foscarini, upon this double attestation, without examining the foresaid Giovan Battista; because that would stir some noise, and then perhaps those other, whom they meant to delate, might take fear and escape. Hereupon Foscarini, coming from the next Senate at night down the Palace, was by order of the Inquisitors suddenly muffled, and so put in close Prison, and after usual Examinations, his own single denyal being not receivable against two agreeing Informers, he was by sentence at the councel of Ten, some fifteen days after his retention, strangled in Prison, and on the 21 of the foresaid April, was hanged by one Leg on a Gallows in the publick Piazza, from break of day till sun-set with all imaginable circumstances of infamy: his very face having been bruised by dragging on the ground, though some did construe that for a kind of favour, that he might be the less known.

After this the same Artificers pursue their occupation, now animated with success; and next they name Marco Miani. But one of the Inquisitors, either by Nature more advised than the rest or intenerated with that which was already done, would by no means proceed any farther, without a pre-examination of the foresaid Giovan Battista. Which now might the more conveniently, and the more silently be taken, because he had left the house of the Spanish Agent, and was married in the town to a Goldsmiths daughter. To make short, they draw this man to a secret account; where he doth not only disavow the having ever seen any Gentleman in the Spanish Agents house, but likewise all such interest as the accusers did pretend to have in his acquaintance, having never spoken with any of them but only three words by chance with the elder, namely Girolamo, upon the Piazza di St Stephano. Hereupon the Inquisitors confronted him with the Accusers; they confess without any torture their malicous Plot, and had sentence to be hanged, as was afterwards done. But now the voice running of this detection, the nephews of the executed Cavalier, namely Nicolo and Girolamo Foscarini, make haste to present a Petition (in all opinion most equitable) to the Decemviral Tribunal, that the false Accusers of the abovesaid Marco Miani, might be reexamined likewise about their Uncle. The Counsel of Ten, upon this Petition, did assemble early in the morning, which had not been done in long time before; and there they put to voices, whether the Nephews should be satisfied?

In the first Ballotation, the Balls were equal: in the second there was one Ball more (as they say) in the negative Box. Either because the false Witnesses, being now condemned men, were disabled by course of Law to give any further Testimony, or for that the Councel of Ten thought it wisdom to smother an irrevocable error. The Petition being denied, no possible way remained for the Nephews to clear the defamation of their Uncle (which in the rigour of this Government, had been likewise a stop to their own Fortunes) but by means of the Confessor, to whom the Delinquents should disburthen their souls before their death; and by him, at importunity of the said Nephews, the matter was revealed. Whereupon did ensue a solemn Declaration of the Councel of Ten, touching the Innocency of the foresaid Anthonio Foscarini, eight months and twenty five days after his death.

Whether in this case there were any mixture of private passion, or that perhaps some light humours, to which the Part was subject, together with the taint of his former Imprisonment, might precipitate the credulity of the Judges, I dare not dispute. But sure in 312 years that the Decemviral Tribunal hath stood, there was never cast upon it a greater blemish; which being so high a piece, and on the reputation of whose grave and indubitable proceedings the regiment of manners hath most depended, is likely to breed no good consequence upon the whole. Since the foresaid Declaration, the Nephews have removed the body of their Uncle from a place where condemned Persons are of custom interred, to the Monument of their Ancestors in another Temple, and would have given it a solemn Burial. But having been kept (though rather by disswasion than prohibition) from increasing thereby the publick Scandal, they now determine to repair his fame with an Epitaph, the last of miserable remedies. It is said, that at the removing of his Body, the Heart was found whole: which kind of conceits are easily entertained in this Country, and scant any notable case without some superstitious adjunct. It is said likewise, that by Testament he did appoint a great summ for him that should discover his Innocency: which receiving from credible Authors, I was not willing to omit; because it argueth, that notwithstand some outward lightness, he was composed of generous Elements. Certain it is that he left divers Legacies to the best Patriots, as now appeareth not artifically. But here I may breed a question, with which I will end this report. How a man in his case could dispose of his Fortune? I must answer, That in the composition of this State Confiscations are rare, be the Crime never so high, unless in case of interventing the public Money; which the Delinquent is commonly condemned to repair, not so much in the quality of a Traytor, as of Debtor. Whereof searching the reason, I find this to be the most immediate; that if in a Dominion meerly managed by their own Gentry, they should punish them as much in their means, as in their persons, it would in conclusion prove a punishment, not of particulars, but of the general. For it is a rule here, that the poorest families are the loosest.

[48] The Scottish traveller William Lithgow arrives in Venice in 1609 or 1610, and disembarks at the Piazzetta in somewhat dramatic circumstances; from his *Rare Adventures and Painefull Peregrinations*.

(William Lithgow (c. 1582-post 1645) was a Scotsman who claimed that 'his paynefull feet traced over ... thirty-six thousand and odde miles' between 1609 and 1629. He travelled in Europe, Asia and Africa, being arrested as a spy in Malaga and tortured on the rack by the Inquisition. His *Rare Adventures and Painefull Peregrinations*, published in 1632, is one of the most entertaining, and at the same time one of the least known, of seventeenth-century travel books.)

After three dayes sayling (having passed by Malamucko, which is the Haven of the great Venetian shippes) we arrived at St Marks place in Venice.

Mine associate and I, were no sooner landed, and perceiving a great throng of people, and in the midst of them a great smoke; but we begun to demaund a Venetian what the matter was? who replied, there was a grey Frier burning quicke at S. Markes pillar, of the reformed order of S. Francis, for begetting fifteene young Noble Nunnes with child, and all within one yeare; he being also their Father confessor. Whereat, I sprung forward through the throng, and my friend followed me, and came just to the pillar as the halfe of his body and right arme fell flatlings in the fire; The Frier was forty sixe yeares old, and had bene Confessor of that Nunnery of Sancta Lucia five yeares: Most of these young Nunnes were Senators daughters; and two of them were onely come in to learne vertue, and yet fell in the midst of vice.

These fifteene with child, were all re-cald home to their fathers Pallaces; the Lady Prioresse, and the rest of her voluptuous crew, were banished for ever from the precincts of Venice. The Monastery was razed to the ground, their rents were allowed to be bestowed upon poore families, and distressed age, and their Church to be converted to an Hospitall. Most part of all which M. Arthur and I saw, before ever we either eate, drunke, or tooke our lodging in Venice: And I cannot forget, how after all this, we being inhungred, and also overjoyed tumbled in by chance, Alla capello Ruosso, the greatest ordinary in all Venice, neare to which the Friars bones were yet a burning: And calling for a Chamber, we were nobly & richly served.

[49] John Evelyn visited Venice in 1646, and began his sightseeing at once: it was to include an execution by guillotine – preceding the French Revolution by nearly a century and a half; from *The Diary of John Evelyn* edited by William Bray.

. . . to the sea-side, where stand those two columns of ophite stone in the intire piece, of a greate height, one bearing St. Mark's Lion, the other St Theodorus; these pillars were brought from Greece, and set up by Nic. Baraterius the architect; betweene them publique executions are performed.

Having fed our eyes with the noble prospect of the Island St George, the gallies, gondolas, and other vessels passing to and fro, we walked under the Cloyster on the other side of this goodly Piazza, being a most magnificent building, the design of Sansovino. Here we went into the Zecca, or Mint; at the entrance stand two prodigious Giants or Hercules of white marble: we saw them melt, beate, and coyne silver, gold, and coper. We then went up into the Procuratorie, and a Library of excellent MSS and books belonging to it and the Publiq. After this we climb'd up the Toure of St Mark, which we might have don on horseback, as 'tis said one of the French Kings did, there being no stayres or steps, but returnes that take up an entire square on the arches 40 foote, broad enough for a coach. This Steeple stands by itselfe without any Church neere it, and is rather a watch toure in the corner of the greate Piazza, 230 foote in height, the foundation exceeding deepe; on the top is an Angel that turns with the wind, and from hence is a prospect down the Adriatic as far as Istria and the Dalmatian side, with the surprizing sight of this miraculous Citty, which lies in the bosome of the sea, in the shape of a lute, the numberless Islands tacked together by no fewer than 450 bridges. At the foote of this Toure is a public Tribunal of excellent work in white marble polish'd, adorn'd with several brasse statues and figures of stone in mezzo relievo, the worke of some rare artist.

The next day I saw a wretch executed who had murther'd his master, for which he had his head chop'd off by an axe that slid down a frame of timber, between the two tall columns in St Mark's Piazza at the sea brink; the executioner striking on the axe with a beatle, and so the head fell off the block.

[50] There was, however, a less splendid aspect of the Piazza; from *Letters from Italy . . . in the years 1765 and 1766* by Samuel Sharp.

(Samuel Sharp (1700–1778) was a distinguished surgeon rather than a traveller or writer; but his single journey to Italy in the winter of 1765–6 enabled him to write his *Letters from Italy*, of which Dr Johnson wrote approvingly that there was 'a great deal of matter in them'.)

The common people flatter themselves they are the freest state in *Europe*; and the nasty fellows esteem it a proof they are so, that they can let down their breeches wherever, and before whomsoever they please; accordingly all *St Mark's-Place*, and many parts of that sumptuous marble building, the Doge's palace, are dedicated to *Cloacina*, and you may see the votaries at their devotions every hour of the day, as much whilst the Nobles are going in, and coming out, as at any other time.

[51] The situation had clearly not improved when Mrs Hester Piozzi – formerly Thrale, and bosom friend of Dr Johnson – visited Italy in 1784–5 with her new husband; from her *Glimpses of Italian Society*.

St Mark's Place is all covered over in a morning with chicken-coops, which stink one to death, as nobody, I believe, thinks of changing their baskets; and all about the ducal palace is made so very offensive by the resort of human creatures for every purpose most unworthy of so charming a place, that all enjoyment of its beauties is rendered difficult to a person of any delicacy, and poisoned so provokingly, that I do never cease to wonder that so little police and proper regulation are established in a city so particularly lovely to render her sweet and wholesome.

[52] An eighteenth-century visitor finds St Mark's Square full of crowds and cafés; from *Letters from Italy . . . in the Years 1770 and 1771* by Anna, Lady Miller.

(Anna, Lady Miller (1741–1781) is described in the *Dictionary of National Biography* as a 'verse-writer'; she was best known in her lifetime for the mildly ridiculous literary salon which she started in Bath in 1778. *The Letters from Italy* enjoyed a better reputation, though Horace Walpole maintained that she 'does not spell one word of French or Italian right through her three volumes of travel.')

The first orders we gave to our gondoliers, were to conduct us to the *Place St. Mark*, which is the only spot one can call *terra firma* in this city. We were soon there, and found it answer all its descriptions. This is the center of Venetian amusement; here you see every body; hear all the news of the day, and every point discussed: here are the senators, nobles, merchants, fine ladies, and the meanest of the people: Jews, Turks, puppets, Greeks, mountebanks, all sorts of jugglers and sights. Although such a heterogeneous mixture of people throng this place during the day, and often pass great part of the night here, yet there is no riot or disturbance: the Venetians are so accustomed to see strangers, as not to be the least surprised at their being dressed in a fashion different from themselves; nor inclined to esteem them objects of ridicule, on account of their not speaking the Venetian language: in short, from the moment you enter the Place St Mark, the advantage a free government has over a despotic is obvious in the easy and liberal manners of the people; the same air extends to their faces, and it is rare to meet any body at Venice with a dark suspicious countenance. Here are arcades or *piazzas*, extremely convenient for shelter from the sun, wind, or rain; under some of them are coffee-houses and shops: in the former, the women enter as freely as the men, make their parties, are served with all kinds of refreshments, and converse with as much ease as if they were in their own houses. The two columns of granite, which terminate this Place St Mark on the side of the sea, were brought hither from Greece, and give the entrance a noble air.

The portico or piazza which is under the palace of St Mark, is called the *Broglio*, and is destined to the noble Venetians, who repair to this walk in the morning to converse at their ease about the business of the state; the people and others are careful not to mix with them on these occasions, nor even by walking too near the *Broglio* hazard the interrupting them. There is an universal politeness here in every rank; the people expect a civil deportment from their nobles towards them, and they return it with much respect and veneration; but should a *noble* assume an insolent arrogant manner towards his inferior, it would not be born with.

[53] Foreign visitors mingle in St Mark's Square in 1780; from William Beckford's *Italy, with sketches of Spain and Portugal.*

I passed the gates of the palace into the great square, which received a faint gleam from its casinos and palaces, just beginning to be lighted up, and to become the resort of pleasure and dissipation. Numbers were walking in parties upon the pavement; some sought the convenient gloom of the porticos with their favourites; others were earnestly engaged in conversation, and filled the gay illuminated apartments, where they resorted to drink coffee and sorbet, with laughter and merriment. A thoughtless giddy transport prevailed; for, at this hour, anything like restraint seems perfectly out of the question; and however solemn a magistrate or senator may appear in the day, at night he lays up wig and robe and gravity to sleep together, runs intriguing about in his gondola, takes the reigning sultana under his arm, and so rambles half over the town, which grows gayer and gayer as the day declines . . .

Whilst the higher ranks were solacing themselves in their casinos, the rabble were gathered in knots round the strollers

and mountebanks, singing and scaramouching in the middle
of the square. I observed a great number of Orientals amongst
the crowd, and heard Turkish and Arabic muttering in every
corner. Here the Sclavonian dialect predominated; there some
Grecian jargon, almost unintelligible. Had Saint Mark's
church been the wondrous tower, and its piazza the chief
square, of the city of Babylon, there could scarcely have been
a greater confusion of languages.

The novelty of the scene afforded me no small share of
amusement, and I wandered about from group to group, and
from one strange exotic to another, asking and being asked
innumerable ridiculous questions, and settling the politics of
London and Constantinople, almost in the same breath. This
instant I found myself in a circle of grave Armenian priests
and jewellers; the next amongst Greeks and Dalmatians, who
accosted me with the smoothest compliments, and gave proof
that their reputation for pliability and address was not ill-
founded.

[54] The Piazza witnesses the day of Venice's deepest
humiliation; from *A History of Venice* by John Julius
Norwich.

It was Sunday, 4 June – Whit Sunday, a day which in former
years the Venetians had been accustomed to celebrate with all
the pomp and parade appropriate to one of the great feasts of
the Church. But this year, 1797, was different. Shocked and
stunned to find their city occupied by foreign troops for the
first time in its thousand years of history, the people were in
no mood for rejoicing. Nevertheless, General Louis Baraguey
d'Hilliers, the French commander, had decided that some
form of celebration would be desirable, if only to give a
much-needed boost to local morale. He had discussed the
form it should take with the leaders of the Provisional Municipality, in whom, under his own watchful eye, the supreme
political power of the new Republic was now entrusted; and
plans had been accordingly drawn up for a *Festa Nazionale*,
at which the citizens were to be given their first full-scale
public opportunity to salute their 'Democracy' and the reso-
nant revolutionary principles that inspired it.

Those who, prompted more by curiosity than by enthusiasm, made their way to the Piazza that Sunday morning had grown accustomed to the 'Tree of Liberty' – that huge wooden pole, surmounted by the symbolic scarlet Phrygian cap which bore a more than passing resemblance to the ducal corno – rising incongruously from its centre. This they now found to have been supplemented by three large tribunes, ranged along the north, south and west sides. The western one, which was intended for the sixty members of the Municipality, carried the inscription LIBERTY IS PRESERVED BY OBEDIENCE TO THE LAW; the other two, destined for the French and other less distinguished Italian authorities, respectively proclaimed that DAWNING LIBERTY IS PROTECTED BY FORCE OF ARMS and ESTABLISHED LIBERTY LEADS TO UNIVERSAL PEACE. The Piazzetta was similarly bedecked, with a banner in praise of Bonaparte stretched between the two columns by the Molo, one of which was draped in black in memory of those brave Frenchmen who had perished victims of the Venetian aristocracy. . . .

After Baraguey d'Hilliers and the Municipality had taken their places, the bands began to play – there were four of them, disposed at intervals around the Piazza, comprising a total of well over 300 musicians – and the procession began. First came a group of Italian soldiers, followed by two small children carrying lighted torches and another banner with the words GROW UP, HOPE OF THE FATHERLAND. Behind them marched a betrothed couple (DEMOCRATIC FECUNDITY) and finally an aged pair staggering under the weight of agricultural implements, bearing words 'referring to their advanced age, at which time liberty was instituted'.

The procession over, the President of the Municipality advanced to the Tree of Liberty, where, after a brief ceremony in the Basilica, he proceeded to the most dramatic business of the day: the symbolic burning of a *corno* and other emblems of ducal dignity (all obligingly provided for the purpose by Lodovico Manin himself) and a copy of the Golden Book. He and his fellow-*municipalisti*, together with the General and the senior members of his staff, then led off the dancing round the Liberty Tree, while the guns fired repeated salutes, the church bells rang and the bands played '*La Carmagnole*'. The celebrations ended with a gala performance of opera at the Fenice Theatre, completed less than five years before.

This was the level to which Venice had sunk within a month of the Republic's end – the level of tasteless allegory and those empty, flatulent slogans so beloved of totalitarian governments of today: a demoralization so complete as to allow her citizens, many of whom had been crying *'Viva San Marco!'* beneath the windows of the Great Council as it met for the last time, to stand by and applaud while all their proud past was symbolically consigned to the flames. Not long afterwards one Giacomo Gallini, head of the stone-masons' guild, signed a contract to remove or efface every winged lion in the city, as had already been done by the French, with horrible thoroughness, throughout the *terra firma*. We can only be thankful that he proved less conscientious: though he accepted his pay – 982 ducats – relatively few lions were touched. But the fact that such an action was even contemplated is indication enough of the mentality of French and Venetians alike through that nightmare summer.

[55] Richard Wagner praises the 'unique and quite unparalleled splendour' of St Mark's Square in a letter to his wife dated 28 September 1858; from *Richard to Minna Wagner: letters to his first wife* translated by William Ashton Ellis.

(Richard Wagner (1813–1883) stayed for six months in Venice in 1859. For most of the time he occupied the Palazzo Giustinian on the Grand Canal, where he completed the second act of *Tristan und Isolde*. He and his family were to return in September 1882 and to remain there until his death on 13 February 1883 in the Palazzo Vendramin-Calergi.)

My manner of life is as follows: The whole day till 4 I work – at whatever there has been to do yet – then I get ferried across the Canal, walk up S. Mark's piazza, meet Karl there at 5 in the restaurant, where I dine *à la carte*, well, but dear (I can never get off under 4 to 5 francs! – without wine, too); after dinner, so long as the fine season permits, out in a gondola to the Public Garden, promenade there, and return either afloat or on foot through the town; then another promenade on shore for the length of the Molo, a glass of ice at the pavilion there, and then home, where the lamp stands lit for me at 8; a book picked up, and finally to bed. So I have been living for 4 whole weeks now, and am not tired of it yet, even without real absorbing work. What affords the never-flagging charm, is the strange contrast of my dwelling with the part that serves me for a promenade: here all still, supremely tranquil, a broad track of lapping water from the sea, with ebb and flow; instead of carts and horses, gondolas moored to the houses' very doors; wonderful palaces in front and everywhere, all lofty, silent, melancholy. Then of a sudden, on one's stepping forth, mean alleys of the strangest twists and crossings, often scarcely wide enough for two to pass, all flanked with open shops and stalls in which one feels as if upon the pavement; continually flooded with a stream of people one only needs to join, when without the smallest notion of topography one either arrives at the Rialto – the business quarter – or the Square of S. Mark, where nobody does anything but promenade.

The amazing, unique and quite unparalleled splendour of this Square, and everything connected with it down to the water's brink, is not to be described; each time I reach it from my house, the whole thing staggers me afresh. By all means I must send you some good pictures of it soon. One would never believe one was in the street, if only since it all – there being no horse traffic – is paved with slabs of marble just like some great prince's court. (I've a bad foot, and for many days have been going out in my slippers.) Everything strikes one as a marvellous piece of stage-scenery. Here it is one continual surging up and down, everyone doing nothing but stroll and amuse himself. This peculiar gaiety never fails of its effect on the newcomer; one feels at ease, and the eye is perpetually entertained. For myself the chief charm consists in its all remaining as detached from me as if I were in an actual theatre; I avoid making any acquaintances, and therefore still retain the feeling. The gondola trip out to sea always has an extremely soothing and beneficial effect: the battle in the sky twixt day and night is glorious; ever new isles in the distance to keep the fancy alert with their gardens, churches, palaces.

In brief, I believe the choice of Venice was the happiest I could have made; for there was everything to fear for me if I had not lit on such an element, if I had felt uncomfortable, not come to rest, lost patience, roved about, and never got to work – which in fine is the one and only thing to enthral me sustainedly. Now that is overcome, and hope thereby won for a turn in our fortunes.

[56] Wagner discovers also that the Piazza has a 'superb acoustic', especially for performances of his own music; from *My Life* by Richard Wagner, translated by Andrew Gray.

Beyond this there was little to attract my attention in the very oppressed and degenerate life of the Venetian populace, for as far as human activity in the glorious ruins of this wonderful city was concerned, the only impression I was able to form was that it was maintained as a bathing resort for tourists. Strangely enough, it was the thoroughly German element of good military music, so well represented in the Austrian army, that brought me here into a certain contact with public life. The bandmasters of the two Austrian regiments stationed in Venice got the idea of playing overtures of mine, such as those to *Tanahäuser* and *Rienzi*, and invited me to attend rehearsals at the barracks. Here I found the whole officer corps assembled, which on this occasion treated me very respectfully. The two bands took turns playing in the evening in the middle of a brilliantly illuminated St Mark's Square, which offered a truly superb acoustical setting for such music. Several times at the end of dinner I was surprised to hear my overtures all of a sudden; when I sat at the restaurant window abandoning myself to the impressions of the music, I did not know which dazzled me most – the incomparable square in its magnificent illumination filled with countless numbers of moving people, or the music which seemed to be wafting all these phenomena aloft in a resounding transfiguration. But there was one thing utterly lacking here which one would otherwise have certainly expected from an Italian audience: thousands of people grouped themselves around the band and listened to the music with intense concentration; but no two hands ever forgot themselves to the extent of applauding, for any sign of approbation for an Austrian military band would have been looked upon as treason to the motherland. All public life in Venice suffered from this strange tension between the populace and the authorities, and this was particularly obvious in the behavior of the people toward the Austrian officers, who floated about in public life in Venice like oil on water. The populace also behaved with equal reserve, and even hostility, to the clergy, whose members were in fact mostly of Italian descent. I once saw a procession of clerics crossing St Mark's Square in full ceremonial vestments to the accompaniment of unconcealed derision on the part of the people.

[57] Coffee and pigeons in St Mark's Square in 1851; from *Elizabeth Barrett Browning's Letters to Mrs David Ogilvy, 1849–1861* edited by Peter N. Heydon and Philip Kelley.

(Elizabeth Barrett Browning (1806–1861) with her husband Robert and their two-year-old son Wiedemann (later to be universally known as Pen) visited Venice from their home in Florence in May 1851. They stayed a month; Venice, she wrote, sent her into 'a sort of rapture'.)

Robert & I were sitting outside the caffè in the piazza of St Mark last night at nearly ten, taking our coffee & listening to music, & watching the soundless crowd drift backwards & forwards through that grand square, as if swept by the airs they were listening to. I say 'soundless' – for the absence of carriage or horse removed all ordinary noises. You heard nothing but the music. It was a phantom-sight altogether.

We go to the traiteur to dine – even Wiedeman [sic] does. By which you may judge what a good *adaptable* child he really is. He has made friends with the 'holy pigeons,' & they were surrounding him like a cloud today for the sake of his piece of bread, . . . he stamping & crying out for rapture in the grand piazza. You have read perhaps about these pigeons, & remember how the whole people of Venice protect them,

& how to kill one of them is a crime against the nations. In consequence of which, they are so tame that they mix with the crowd, having no fear of man. You may fancy that Wiedeman is enchanted with the holy pigeons.

[58] Social life in the Piazza during the Austrian occupation; from *Venetian Life* by William Dean Howells.

(William Dean Howells (1837–1920) was United States consul in Venice from 1861 to 1865 – a post offered him as a reward for writing an extremely successful campaign biography of Abraham Lincoln.)

As the social life of Italy, and especially of Venice, was in great part to be once enjoyed at the theatres, at the caffè, and at the other places of public resort, so is its absence now to be chiefly noted in those places. No lady of perfect standing among her people goes to the opera, and the men never go in the boxes, but if they frequent the theatre at all, they take places in the pit, in order that the house may wear as empty and dispirited a look as possible. Occasionally a bomb is exploded in the theatre, as a note of reminder, and as means of keeping away such of the nobles as are not enemies of the government. As it is less easy for the Austrians to participate in the diversion of comedy, it is a less offence to attend the comedy, though even this is not good Italianissimism. In regard to the caffè, there is a perfectly understood system by which the Austrians go to one, and the Italians to another; and Florian's, in the Piazza, seems to be the only common ground in the city on which the hostile forces consent to meet. This is because it is thronged with foreigners of all nations, and to go there is not thought a demonstration of any kind. But the other caffè in the Piazza do not enjoy Florian's cosmopolitan immunity, and nothing would create more wonder in Venice than to see an Austrian officer at the Specchi, unless, indeed, it were the presence of a good Italian at the Quadri.

It is in the Piazza that the tacit demonstration of hatred and discontent chiefly takes place. Here, thrice a week, in winter and summer, the military band plays that exquisite music for which the Austrians are famous. The selections are usually from Italian operas, and the attraction is the hardest of all others for the music-loving Italian to resist. But he does resist it. There are some noble ladies who have not entered the Piazza while the band was playing there, since the fall of the Republic of 1849; and none of good standing for patriotism has attended the concerts since the treaty of Villafranca in '59. Until very lately, the promenaders in the Piazza were exclusively foreigners, or else the families of such government officials as were obliged to show themselves there. Last summer, however, before the Franco-Italian convention for the evacuation of Rome revived the drooping hopes of the Venetians, they had begun visibly to falter in their long endurance. But this was, after all, only a slight and transient weakness. As a general thing, now, they pass from the Piazza when the music begins, and walk upon the long quay at the sea-side of the Ducal Palace; or if they remain in the Piazza they pace up and down under the arcades on either side; for Venetian patriotism makes a delicate distinction between listening to the Austrian band in the Piazza and hearing it under the Procuratie, forbidding the first and permitting the last. As soon as the music ceases the Austrians disappear, and the Italians return to the Piazza.

But since the catalogue of demonstrations cannot be made full, it need not be made any longer. The political feeling in Venice affects her prosperity in a far greater degree than may appear to those who do not understand how large an income the city formerly derived from making merry. The poor have to lament not merely the loss of their holidays, but also of the fat employments and bountiful largess which these occasions threw into their hands. With the exile or the seclusion of the richer families, and the reluctance of foreigners to make a residence of the gloomy and dejected city, the trade of the shop keepers has fallen off; the larger commerce of the place has also languished and dwindled year by year; while the cost of living has constantly increased, and heavier burdens of taxation have been laid upon the impoverished and despondent people. And in all this, Venice is but a type of the whole province of Venetia.

[59] The collapse of the Campanile in St Mark's Square in 1902; from *Venice* by James (now Jan) Morris.

Nothing on earth seemed stronger and stabler than the Campanile of St Mark's. It had, so one eighteenth-century guide book observed, 'never given the slightest sign of leaning, shaking or giving way'. It was so much a part of Venice, had supervised so many years of changing fortune, that it seemed eternal, and the people regarded it with an almost patronizing affection, and called it 'the Landlord'. According to popular rumour, the foundations of the tower ran deep beneath the pavement of the Piazza, extending star-wise in all directions; and every visitor to Venice made the ascent of the Campanile, whether he was an emperor inspecting the lagoon defences, or a renegade priest from the mainland, hung from the belfry in his wooden cage. All through the years, though, like a game but rocky old uncle, the Campanile was secretly weakening. It had been repeatedly struck by lightning, its gilded summit positively inviting calamity – as early as 1793 it was fitted with a lightning conductor, one of the earliest in Europe. It had been injudiciously restored and enlarged, and some rash structural alterations had been made inside the tower. Its bricks had been half-pulverized by centuries of salt wind and air. Its foundations, though strong, were not nearly as invulnerable as legend made them: though the tower was 320 feet high, the piles that supported it were driven less than sixty feet deep.

Thus, early that July morning, this famous tower gave a gentle shudder, shook itself, and slowly, gently, almost silently collapsed. The catastrophe had been foreseen a few days before: the firing of the midday cannon had been cancelled, in case it shook the structure, and even the bands in the Piazza were forbidden to play. Soon after dawn on the 14th the Piazza had been closed, and the anxious Venetians gathered around the perimeter of the square, waiting for the end. When it came, '*Il Campanile*', it was said, '*se stato galantuomo*' – 'the Campanile has shown himself a gentleman'. Not a soul was hurt. A hillock of rubble filled the corner of the Piazza, and a cloud of dust rose high above the city, like a pillar of guidance, or a shroud: but the only casualty was a

tabby cat, said to have been called Mélampyge after Casanova's dog, which had been removed to safety from the
custodian's lodge, but imprudently returned to finish its victuals. The weather-vane angel, pitched into the Piazza, landed
at the door of the Basilica, and this was regarded as a
miraculous token that the great church would not be dam-
aged: nor was it, much of the debris being kept from its fabric
by the stumpy pillar in the south Piazzetta from which the
laws of the Republic used to be proclaimed. When the dust
had cleared, and the loose masonry had subsided, there was
seen to be lying unbroken on the debris the Marangona, the
senior bell of Venice, which had called the people to their
duties for six centuries. Even half a dozen shirts, which the
custodian's wife had been ironing the day before, were found
as good as new under the wreckage.

In a matter of moments it was all over, and only a pyramid
of bricks and broken stones was left like an eruption in the
square. (The remains were later taken away in barges and
dumped, with a mourning wreath of laurel, in the Adriatic.) I
once met a man who was present at this melancholy occasion,
and who still seemed a little numbed by the shock of it.
'Weren't you astonished that such a thing could happen?' I
asked him. 'Well,' he replied heavily, 'yes, it *was* a surprise.
I had known the Campanile all my life, like a friend, and I
never really expected it to fall down.'

The news of this old great-heart's death rang sadly around
the world. The silhouette of Venice, one of the most universally familiar scenes on earth, was dramatically altered, and
the skyline was left looking oddly flat and featureless, like a
ship without masts. The city council met that same evening
under the chairmanship of an old Venetian patrician, Count
Grimani, who was mayor of the city for more than thirty
years: and grandly aristocratic was its decision. There were
some Venetians who thought the rebuilding of the tower
would cost more than it was worth. There were many others
who thought the Piazza looked better without it. The council,
however, did not agree. The Campanile would be rebuilt,
they decided, 'as it was and where it was', and the phrase has
become famous in Venetian lore – '*Com' erà, dov' erà*'.

Money poured in from many countries; the greatest experts

came from Rome; in nine years the Campanile was built again, modernized in structural design, 600 tons lighter, but looking almost identical. The shattered bells were recast at a foundry on the island of Sant' Elena, and paid for by the Pope himself – that same Pius X whom we saw returning so triumphantly to Venice half a century later. The foundations were reinforced with 1,000 extra piles. The broken little loggia at the foot of the tower was put together again, piece by piece, and so were the lions and figures at the top. The angel's cracked wings were splinted. On 25th April 1912, a millennium to the day after the foundation of the old Campanile, the new one was inaugurated. Thousands of pigeons were released to carry the news to every city in Italy: and at the celebratory banquet six of the guests wore those rescued shirts, whose ironing had been so abruptly interrupted nine years before.

The Rialto

[60] In the Museum of the Cà d'Oro can still be seen a few remains of the frescoes with which Giorgione and Titian, the two greatest painters of their age, adorned the newly rebuilt Fondaco dei Tedeschi in 1505. (The building still survives, and now serves as Venice's central post office.) Sadly, the two artists worked on their separate commissions not as partners but as rivals: their relationship never recovered; from *Lives of the Most Eminent Painters, Sculptors and Architects* by Giorgio Vasari translated by Gaston du C. de Vere.

(Giorgio Vasari (1511–1574) was a highly successful painter, working mostly for the Medici in Florence. It was during a tour of Italy when his patron had been assassinated that he conceived the idea of the *Lives*, which was published in 1550 and enthusiastically received.)

There broke out at Venice, in the year 1504, in the Fondaco de' Tedeschi by the Ponte del Rialto, a most terrible fire, which consumed the whole building and all the merchandise, to the very great loss of the merchants; wherefore the Signoria of Venice ordained that it should be rebuilt anew, and it was speedily finished with more accommodation in the way of living-rooms, and with greater magnificence, adornment, and beauty. Thereupon, the fame of Giorgione having grown great, it was ordained after deliberation by those who had charge of the matter, that Giorgione should paint it in fresco with colours according to his own fancy, provided only that he gave proof of his genius and executed an excellent work, since it would be in the most beautiful place and most conspicuous site in the city. And so Giorgione put his hand to the work, but thought of nothing save of making figures according to his own fancy, in order to display his art, so that, in truth, there are no scenes to be found there with any order, or representing the deeds of any distinguished person, either ancient or modern; and I, for my part, have never understood them, nor have I found, for all the inquiries that I have made, anyone who understands them, for in one place there is a woman, in another a man, in diverse attitudes, while one has the head of a lion near him, and another an angel in the guise of a Cupid, nor can one tell what it may all mean. There is, indeed, over the principal door, which opens into the Merceria, a woman seated who has at her feet the severed head of a giant, almost in the form of a Judith; she is raising the head with her sword, and speaking with a German, who is below her; but I have not been able to determine for what he intended her to stand, unless, indeed, he may have meant her to represent Germany. However, it may be seen that his figures are well grouped, and that he was ever making progress; and there are in it heads and parts of figures very well painted, and most vivacious in colouring. In all that he did there he aimed at being faithful to nature, without any imitation of another's manner; and the work is celebrated and famous in Venice, no less for what he painted therein than through its convenience for commerce and its utility to the commonwealth.

However, although Giorgione had himself painted the principal façade over the Fondaco de' Tedeschi, Tiziano had, through Barberigo, been commissioned to paint some scenes for the same building, where it faced the Merceria . . .

Concerning which façade, many gentlemen, not knowing

that Giorgione was not working there any more and that
Tiziano was doing it, who had uncovered one part, meeting
with Giorgione congratulated him in friendly fashion, saying
that he was acquitting himself better in the façade towards
the Merceria than he had done in that which is over the
Grand Canal. At which circumstance Giorgione felt such
disdain, that until Tiziano had completely finished the work
and it had become well known that the same had done that
part, he would scarcely let himself be seen; and from that
time onward he would never allow Tiziano to associate with
him or be his friend.

[61] The Rialto and its bridge in 1594; from *An Itinerary* ... by Fynes Moryson, Gent.

The foure square market place of Rialto, is compassed with
publike houses, under the arches whereof, and in the middle
part lying open, the Merchants meet. And there is also a
peculiar place where the Gentlemen meet before noone, as
they meet in the place of Saint Marke towards evening; and
here to nourish acquaintance, they spend an houre in dis-
courses, and because they use not to make feasts one to
another, they keepe this meeting as strictly as Merchants, lest
their frinship should decay. The Gold-smiths shoppes lie
thereby, and over against them the shoppes of Jewellers, in
which Art the Venetians are excellent. There is the Pallace of
a Gentleman, who proving a Traytor, the State (for his
reproch) turned the same into a shambles, and some upper
chambers to places of judgement. The fish market lies by this
shambles, a great length along the banke of the great channell,
and in the same shambles and fish market, as also in the like
of Saint Marke, great plenty of victuals, especially of fish, is
daily to be sold. A publike Pallace stately built lieth neere the
bridge of Rialto.

This bridge in the judgement of the Venetians, deserves to
be reputed the eighth miracle of the world. The old being
pulled downe, this new bridge began to bee built in the yeere
1588, and was scarce finished in three yeeres, and is said to
have cost two hundred fifty thousand Duckets. It is built of

the stone of Istria, upon one arch over the great channell, and the ascent to the toppe hath thirty five staires on each side, and upon each side of these staires, are twelve little shoppes covered with lead: not to speake of the carved Images, of the blessed Virgin, the Angell Gabriel, and the two protecting Saints of the City, namely Saint Marke, and Saint Theodore.

[62] In the mid-eighteenth century, as today, the time to go to the Rialto market was early in the morning: Casanova explains why; from *The Memoirs of Jacques Casanova de Seingalt* translated by Arthur Machen.

Three or four days before the Feast of St James, my patron saint, M—— M—— made me a present of several ells of silver lace to trim a sarcenet dress which I was going to wear on the eve of the feast. I went to see her, dressed in my fine suit, and I told her that I should come again on the day following to ask her to lend me some money, as I did not know where to turn to find some. She was still in possession of the five hundred sequins which she had put aside when I had sold her diamonds.

As I was sure of getting the money in the morning I passed the night at play, and I lost the five hundred sequins in advance. At day-break, being in need of a little quiet, I went to the Erberia, a space of ground on the quay of the Grand Canal. Here is held the herb, fruit, and flower market.

People in good society who come to walk in the Erberia at a rather early hour usually say that they come to see the hundreds of boats laden with vegetables, fruit and flowers, which hail from the numerous islands near the town; but everyone knows that they are men and women who have been spending the night in the excesses of Venus or Bacchus, or who have lost all hope at the gaming-table, and come here to breath a purer air and to calm their minds. The fashion of walking in this place shews how the character of a nation changes. The Venetians of old time who made as great a mystery of love as of state affairs, have been replaced by the modern Venetians, whose most prominent characteristic is to make a mystery of nothing. Those who come to the Erberia

with women wish to excite the envy of their friends by thus
publishing their good fortune. Those who come alone are on
the watch for discoveries, or on the look-out for materials to
make wives or husbands jealous, the women only come to be
seen, glad to let everybody know that they are without any
restraint upon their actions. There was certainly no question
of smartness there, considering the disordered style of dress
worn. The women seemed to have agreed to shew all the
signs of disorder imaginable, to give those who saw them
something to talk about. As for the men, on whose arms they
leaned, their careless and lounging airs were intended to give
the idea of a surfeit of pleasure, and to make one think that
the disordered appearance of their companions was a sure
triumph they had enjoyed. In short it was the correct thing to
look tired out, and as if one stood in need for sleep.

[63] Those who are to be seen at the early-morning
market today tend to be the larks rather than the night-
owls, but the rewards are great, and are eloquently
described by Elizabeth David; from her *Italian Food*.

Of all the spectacular food markets in Italy the one near the
Rialto in Venice must be the most remarkable. The light of a
Venetian dawn in early summer – you must be about at four
o'clock in the morning to see the market coming to life – is
so limpid and so still that it makes every separate vegetable
and fruit and fish luminous with a life of its own, with
unnaturally heightened colours and clear stencilled outlines.
Here the cabbages are cobalt blue, the beetroots deep rose,
the lettuces clear pure green, sharp as glass. Bunches of gaudy
gold marrow-flowers show off the elegance of pink and white
marbled bean pods, primrose potatoes, green plums, green
peas. The colours of the peaches, cherries and apricots,
packed in boxes lined with sugar-bag blue paper matching
the blue canvas trousers worn by the men unloading the
gondolas, are reflected in the rose-red mullet and the orange
vongole and *canestrelle* which have been prised out of their
shells and heaped into baskets. In other markets, on other
shores, the unfamiliar fishes may be vivid, mysterious, repel-

lent, fascinating, and bright with splendid colour; only in Venice do they look good enough to eat. In Venice even ordinary sole and ugly great skate are striped with delicate lilac lights, the sardines shine like newly-minted silver coins, pink Venetian *scampi* are fat and fresh, infinitely enticing in the early dawn.

The gentle swaying of the laden gondolas, the movements of the market men as they unload, swinging the boxes and baskets ashore, the robust life and rattling noise contrasted with the fragile taffeta colours and the opal sky of Venice – the whole scene is out of some marvellous unheard-of ballet.

[64] The Gobbo di Rialto, and the fish market; from *Venice* by James (now Jan) Morris.

Above the [vegetable market] stalls stands the old church of San Giacomo, a poky but friendly little place, which is known to the Venetians familiarly as San Giacometto, and stands among the vegetables precisely as the church of St Paul's stands in Covent Garden, only awaiting an Eliza. Its big blue twenty-four-hour clock appears in a famous painting by Canaletto, but has had a dismal mechanical history. It went wrong several times in the fourteenth century, and had to be renewed 'for the honour and consolation of the city'. It stopped again in the eighteenth century, apparently at four o'clock. In 1914 a traveller reported that it always showed the time as three in the afternoon, and today it is permanently stuck at midnight precisely.

Beneath this unreliable piece, hidden away among a clutter of sheds and packing cases, you will find the Gobbo di Rialto, one of the best-known images of mediaeval Venice. He stands now, abandoned and neglected, among a mass of boxes and old vegetables: a small hobbled granite figure of a man, supporting a flight of steps and a squat marble column. He used to be called a hunchback, but he is really only bent with burdens, for in the hey-day of the Rialto his responsibilities were great. Upon his pedestal the decrees of the Republic were promulgated, in the days when Venetian law was written in blood and enforced with fire: and to his steps men

convicted of petty crimes were forced to run naked from St
Mark's, hastened by a rain of blows, until at last, breathless,
bleeding and humiliated, they fell chastened at his knobbly
feet and embraced him in blind relief.

And around the corner, beside the Grand Canal, there lies
the incomparable fish market of Venice, a glorious, wet,
colourful, high-smelling concourse of the sea, to which in the
dawn hours fleets of barges bring the day's supply of sea-
foods. Its stalls are lined deliciously with green fronds, damp
and cool: and upon them are laid, in a delicately-tinted,
slobbering, writhing, glistening mass, the sea-creatures of the
lagoon. There are sleek wriggling eels, green or spotted, still
pugnaciously alive; beautiful little red fish packed in boxes
like shampoos, heads upwards; strange tube-like molluscs,
oozing at the orifice; fine red mullet, cruel pseudo-sharks,
undefeated crabs and mounds of gem-like shell-fish; skates,
and shoals of small flat-fish, and things like water-tarantula,
and pools of soft bulbous octopus, furiously ejecting ink; huge
slabs of tunny, fish-rumps and fish-steaks, joints of fish, fish
kidneys, innards and guts and roes of fish: a multitude of sea-
matter, pink, white, red, green, multilimbed, beady-eyed,
sliding, sensuous, shimmering, flabby, spongy, crisp – all lying
aghast upon their fresh green biers, dead, doomed or panting,
like a grove of brilliant foliage among the tundra of Venetian
stone.

[65] The delights of the Merceria in 1608; and two
fatal accidents at the Clock Tower; from *Coryat's Crudities* by Thomas Coryat.

The fairest streete of all Venice saving Saint *Markes*, which I
have already described, is that adjoyning to St *Markes* place
which is called the Merceria, which name it hath because
many Mercers dwell there, as also many Stationers, and
sundry other artificers. This streete reacheth from almost the
hither side of the Rialto bridge to Saint *Markes*, being of a
goodly length, but not altogether of the broadest, yet of
breadth convenient enough in some place for five or six
persons to walke together side by side; it is paved with bricke,

and adorned with many faire buildings of a competent height on both sides; there is a very faire gate at one end of this street even as you enter into St *Markes* place, when you come from the Rialto bridge, which is decked with a great deal of faire marble, in which gate are two pretty conceits to be observed, the one at the very top, which is a clocke with the images of two wilde men by it made in brasse, a witty device and very exactly done. At which clocke there fell out a very tragicall and rufull accident on the twenty fifth day of July being munday about nine of the clocke in the morning, which was this. A certaine fellow that had the charge to looke to the clocke, was very busie about the bell, according to his usuall custome every day, to the end to amend something in it that was amisse. But in the mean time one of those wild men that at the quarters of the howers doe use to strike the bell, strooke the man in the head with his brazen hammer, giving him such a violent blow, that therewith he fel down dead presently in the place, and never spake more. Surely I will not justifie this for an undoubted truth, because I saw it not. For I was at that time in the Dukes Palace observing of matters: but as soone as I came forth some of my country-men that tolde me they saw the matter with there owne eies, reported it unto me, and advised me to mention it in my journall for a most lamentable chance.

(Coryat tells how another accident at the Clock Tower saved the Senate from Bajamonte Tiepolo's insurrection in 1310.)

A Gentleman of the Patrician rank that was a man of an ambitious spirit, intending to depose him that was Duke, and to place himselfe in the Dukedom, spake privately to every particular Senator and Patrician of the whole citie to lend him an armed man, to the end to assist him in a certaine businesse that he undertook, and to send him to his house which was neare to the Rialto . . . After he had thus agreed, there came to his house a great multitude well armed at a certayne houre, with whom he himselfe being likewise well appointed, marched as their Captaine over the Rialto bridge towards Saint Markes, not communicating to any one of them his secret intent. Having thus marched with his followers through the street called the Merceria, all the people much wondering at him by the way what he meant by assembling so great a multitude of armed men; as he was upon entering into St Markes place through the sumptuous gate where the clocke standeth, of which I have before spoken, there hapned a very disastrous accident that confounded and frustrated his whole designement. For a certaine maide that looked out of the window hard by the gate to see the company, had by chance a pestell of a mortar in her hand, with which she was pownding in the said mortar at the very instant that they passed by; and whereas she looked out of the window with other, to see what was doing, her pestell which she then held in her hand, not intending any hurt with it, fell casually much against her will upon the head of the Ring-leader of this company, which strooke out his braines, and so by that dismall chance hee died in the place, being defeated of the effect of his project, for the execution whereof he assembled so many armed men; otherwise by force of armes hee had entred with his whole troupe of men into the Sala, where the Duke sat about the publicke affairs with the other Senators; and had surprized and massacred them al, and placed himselfe in the Dukedome. The window through the which the maide looked when her pestell fell on the Captaines head is yet shewed for a monument neare to the gate, at the entring of Saint Markes. After that time his Palace which was near to the Rialto, was alienated from his posterity, and converted to a shambles which I saw.

[66] The Merceria in 1646 sounds a good deal more attractive than it is today; from *The Diary of John Evelyn* edited by William Bray.

Next day I went to their Exchange, a place like ours frequented by merchants, but nothing so magnificent: from thence my guide led me to the Fondigo di Todeschi, which is their magazine, and here many of the merchants, especialy Germans, have their lodging and diet as in a college. The outside of this stately fabric is painted by Giorgione da Castelfranco, and Titian himselfe.

Hence I pass'd thro' the Merceria, which is one of the most

delicious streetes in the world for the sweetnesse of it, and is all the way on both sides tapistred as it were with cloth of gold, rich damasks and other silks, which the shops expose and hang before their houses from the first floore, and with that variety that for neere halfe the yeare spent cheifly in this Citty I hardly remember to have seene the same piece twice expos'd; to this add the perfumes, apothecaries shops, and the innumerable cages of nightingales which they keepe, that entertain you with their melody from shop to shop, so that shutting your eyes you would imagine yourselfe in the country, when indeede you are in the middle of the Sea. It is almost as silent as the middle of a field, there being neither rattling of coaches nor trampling of horses. This streete, pav'd with brick and exceedingly cleane, brought us thro' an arch into the famous Piazza of St Marc.

[67] And in 1771 it still excited the admiration of visitors; from Anna, Lady Miller's *Letters from Italy . . . in the Years 1770 and 1771.*

The little streets leading from this *Place*, are well furnished with elegant shops, which make the most brilliant appearance, from the curious arangement of their articles; and strike me, as far exceeding the *coup d'œil* of the *foire St Germain* at Paris. The street of the silversmiths makes a splendid show, there being no other sort of shops in it. That of the milliners and mercers is like a *parterre* of flowers, the goods, of the most glowing colours, being ingeniously mixed in such a manner in the windows, as to produce a striking effect.

Palaces and hotels

[68] A fifteenth-century Frenchman admires the buildings of Venice; from *The Memoirs of Philip de Commines* edited by Andrew R. Scoble.

(Philip de Commines (1445–1509) Seigneur d'Argenton, was a statesman and historian, who was sent to Venice in 1494 as the Ambassador of Charles VIII of France.)

I was extremely surprised at the situation of this city, to see so many churches, monasteries, and houses, and all in the water; and the people have no other passage up and down the streets but in boats, of which, I believe, they have near thirty thousand, but they are very small. About the city, within less than the compass of half a French league, there are seventy religious houses both of men and women, all situated in little islands, very beautiful and magnificent both in building and furniture, with fair gardens belonging to them; without reckoning those in the city, where there are the four orders of mendicants, and seventy-two parishes, besides several fraternities; and, indeed, it is most strange to behold so many stately churches in the sea ... I was conducted through the principal street, which they call the

Grand Canal, and it is so wide that galleys frequently cross one another; indeed I have seen vessels of four hundred tons or more ride at anchor just by the houses . . . Their buildings are high and stately, and all of fine stone. The ancient houses be all painted, but the rest that have been built within these hundred years, have their front all of white marble, brought thither out of *Istria* an hundred miles thence and are beautified with many great pieces of Porphire and Serpentine. In the most part of them are at the least two chambers, the ceiling whereof is guilded, the mantletrees of the chimnies very rich, to wit, of graven marble, the bedsteds guilded, the presses painted and vermiled with gold, and marvellous well furnished with stuff. To be short, it is the most triumphant City that ever I saw.

[69] The delights of living in a house on the Grand Canal in 1537: Pietro Aretino writes to his friend Messer Domenico Bollani, the owner of the house, which stood on the corner of the Grand Canal and the Rio di S. Giovanni Crisostomo; from *Aretino, Selected Letters* translated with an introduction by George Bull.

(Pietro Aretino (1492–1556) was born in Arezzo but lived in Venice for much of his life, and died there. He was intimate with many of the best-known figures of the time, and was in particular a friend and enthusiastic promoter of Titian. His *Letters* were published in six books between 1537 and 1557, and give an excellent picture of Venice at the time.)

It would seem to me, most honoured sir, a great sin of ingratitude were I not to repay at least a part of my great indebtedness by praising the divine beauty of the site where your house stands, and where, to the daily delight of my life, I have my lodging. For the house is in a spot that is completely without blemish either above or below, this side or that. So I am as shy of speaking of its merits as one would be of discussing those of the Emperor. For sure, he who built it did so on the noblest side of the Grand Canal. And as the Grand Canal is the patriarch of all waterways and Venice is the feminine Pope of all cities, I can truly say that I enjoy the finest highway and the loveliest view in all the world.

Never do I lean out of the windows but that I see at market time a thousand persons and as many gondolas. In my field of vision to the right stand the Fish Market and the Meat Market; in the space to the left, the Bridge and the Fondaco dei Tedeschi; where both views meet I see the Rialto, packed with merchants. I have grapes in the barges, game and game birds in the shops, vegetables on the pavement. I do not hanker after meadows irrigated by streams when at dawn I admire the water covered with every kind of produce in season. And it's a real joy to watch those who have brought vast loads of fruits and green vegetables distribute them to others for carrying to their various destinations.

It is all fascinating, including the spectacle of the twenty or twenty-five sailboats, choked with melons, which are lashed together to make a kind of island where people run and assess the quality of the melons by snuffing them and weighing them. In order not to detract from their famous pomp and splendour, I won't say a word about those beautiful ladies of the town, shimmering in silk and gold and jewels, and seated so proudly in their boats. But let me tell you I split my sides laughing when the hoots, whistles and shouts of the boatmen explode behind those who are rowed along by servants who aren't wearing scarlet breeches. And who wouldn't have pissed himself on seeing capsize in the bittermost cold a boat packed with Germans just escaped from the tavern, as did I and the famous Giulio Camillo?

And so that nothing may be lacking to delight the eyes, on one side I am charmed by the orange trees which gild the foot of the Palazzo dei Camerlinghi, and on the other by the water and bridge of San Giovan Crisostomo. Nor does the winter sun ever dare to rise without first sending word to my bedside, to my study, to my kitchen, my living-rooms and my hall.

I swell with tremendous pride when I see the *Bucentaur* going to and fro; and the regattas and the festivals which are always so resplendent on the Canal which I oversee like a lord.

But what of the lights which after nightfall seem like scattered stars, shining on the place where we buy what is needed for our supper-parties and dinners? And then the music, whose strains thrill my ears during the night with the harmony of their melodies? One would sooner explain the profound judgement you possess in letters and state affairs, before I could come to the end of the delights that I experience from what is displayed before me. And so, if I am inspired by any spirit of genius in the trifles I write down on paper, it comes from the benefit I derive not from the light, or the shade, or the violet, or the verdant, but from the graces received by me through the airy enchantment of your dwelling-place, in which may God grant that I shall spend in health and vigour all the years that a good man deserves to live.

[70] The history of the Palazzo Foscari, at the first bend of the Grand Canal, during the fifteenth and sixteenth centuries; from *Venice, its individual growth from the earliest beginnings to the fall of the Republic* by Pompeo Molmenti, translated by Horatio F. Brown.

The house was bought by the Republic, in 1429, for sixty-five hundred ducats, equal to ten thousand pounds, and given to the treacherous Duke of Mantua; but ten years later it was taken from him and given to Francesco Sforza, who in his turn forfeited it on account of his dubious conduct. It was then put up at auction, and was bought by the Doge Francesco Foscari, about 1447; he remodelled it, and added a story. It was gradually adorned with paintings by Giambellino, Titian, Paris Bordon, Tintoretto, and Veronese, who painted an *Aurora* on the ceiling of one of the rooms and designed the mosaic floor of another. When it was redecorated for the reception of Henry III, the vestibule was hung with tapestry, and a blue cloth sown with stars formed the ceiling. Upstairs, on the first floor, the three bedrooms reserved for the king give us some idea of the length to which sumptuous elegance was carried. The first had a great chimney-piece in precious marbles, and a table of black marble with a green velvet table-cloth; the hangings were of cloth of gold and crimson silk, relieved by stripes of cloth of silver wrought in gold with figures and monograms; the carpet was of crimson velvet with cloth of gold border; a gilded armchair under a cloth of gold canopy stood by the bed, whose sheets were embroidered on the hem and round the outside with gold thread and crimson silk. The furniture of the second chamber was similar, only the hangings were of blue satin semé of fleur-de-lys, relieved with strips of yellow satin. The third chamber, the one selected by the king, was hung with gold and green brocade, the gilded bed had curtains of crimson silk, the chair and canopy were in cloth of gold, and the table was of alabaster.

[71] Charles de Brosses in 1739 is not overly impressed by the comfort of private *palazzi*; from *Selections from the Letters of de Brosses* translated by Lord Ronald Sutherland Gower.

The interiors of the palaces are very gorgeous without showing much taste. In the Foscarini Palace alone there are two hundred rooms, all richly furnished, but everything is overdone, and there is not a chair or a stool on which one can sit with comfort, on account of the delicacy of the carving. The Labia Palace, recently fitted up, is the only one that appeared to me well arranged and comfortable. The lady of the house, once a beauty, and very fond of the French, and consequently of us, showed us all her jewels, probably the finest owned by any private individual in Europe. She has five complete sets of emeralds, sapphires, pearls and diamonds, all kept in cases, but she is not allowed to wear them, for the ladies of the Venetian nobility are only allowed to wear jewels and coloured dresses during the first year of their married life. I offered to take her with me to France as well as her jewels.

[72] Lady Miller, in 1771, can for once find little to complain about in her accommodation – would that her hotel were still in existence today; from her *Letters from Italy . . . in the Years 1770 and 1771*.

We are lodged in a large palace, now converted into an *hotel* for strangers; it is called the *Palazzo Contarini*. We have the

same apartment our acquaintance lord L – lately occupied; it
is much too large, but there is not a smaller that is commodi-
ous; judge of the size, when our anti-chamber, or outer
saloon, is an hundred and twenty feet long, and wide in
proportion; our sitting-room within is a cube of forty; our
bed-chamber and dressing-rooms exceedingly good and convenient; the saloon is stuccoed, but the rest of the apartments
richly furnished, and hung with crimson damask. The saloon
opens into a large balcony, from which is a beautiful view of
the *Rialto* and the grand canal, to appearance about a quarter
of a mile broad, bordered with several fine palaces and well
built houses; some of which are painted in fresco on the
outside . . .

The palaces at Venice are much in the same taste; having
seen one or two, you have in a manner seen all. The Venetians
cover their walls with pictures, and never think their apartments properly furnished, until they have such as shall fill all
the spaces from top to bottom, so as completely to hide the
hanging. This being their object, there are in all the collections
many more bad pictures than good; and on entering a room,
the number of paintings are such, that it is not till after some
recollection you can discriminate those pictures that merit
attention, from amongst a chaos of glowing colours that
surround them; and which are frequently so ill classed, that a
picture which requires to be hung high, is perhaps the lowest
in the room, whilst another that cannot be seen too close,
touches the cornice: this is occasioned by their great object of
covering the walls, never considering what light, *&c.* may suit
their pictures.

The palaces in general are furnished with velvet and damask, fringed or laced with gold. The floors are of a composition which imitates various marbles, and has an excellent
effect; but what I admire very much, and is universally found
in all the houses as well as palaces, is the elegant manner in
which they paint the doors, architraves, skirting boards, and
all their wainscotting: it is smooth as ivory, of very pale tints
for the ground, and prettily ornamented with various devices,
festoons, fruits, *&c.* They also paint in fresco on the walls
with a great deal of facility and taste, having an exceeding
good idea of perspective: this is to be met with in the poorest

houses, and where they do not go to the expence of painting the walls, their white-wash is of an uncommon neatness; it is glossy, of a soft colour, and never comes off. I shall write again before we leave this city, and must break off now, the time being come for our engagements to two Cassinos this evening. Adieu, &c.

PS I live almost the whole of the day when at home in the balcony, which is to me the most agreeable part of this great hotel, I should say *Pallazzo*. The people are so musical here, that all day long the houses send forth the most melodious sounds, which die off charmingly along the water; till they again awake the strings, and at the same time draw off my attention so much from what I am about, that I believe were I to reside here for any time, I should do nothing but listen to music the whole day.

[73] Thomas Moore tells of his first arrival in Venice in 1819 and of the warm welcome given him by Byron, who brings him to the Palazzo Mocenigo; from *Letters and Journals of Lord Byron, with Notices of his Life* by Thomas Moore.

(Thomas Moore (1779–1852) was obliged to flee to Europe in 1819 when his deputy as Admiralty Registrar in Bermuda (a post he had technically held since 1803) was found guilty of misappropriation of funds, rendering him liable for £6,000. Meeting Lord John Russell in Paris, he set off with him on a tour of Italy. In Venice he met Byron. His debt finally settled, he returned to England in 1822.)

The exuberant gaiety of my companion, and the recollections, – any thing but romantic, – into which our conversation wandered, put at once completely to flight all poetical and historical associations; and our course was, I am almost ashamed to say, one of uninterrupted merriment and laughter till we found ourselves at the steps of my friend's palazzo on the Grand Canal . . .

He had all along expressed his determination that I should not go to any hotel, but fix my quarters at his house during the period of my stay; and, had he been residing there himself, such an arrangement would have been all that I most desired. But, this not being the case, a common hotel was, I thought, a far readier resource; and I therefore entreated that he would allow me to order an apartment at the Gran Bretagna, which had the reputation, I understood, of being a comfortable hotel. This, however, he would not hear of; and, as an inducement for me to agree to his plan, said that, as long as I chose to stay, though he should be obliged to return to La Mira in the evenings, he would make it a point to come to Venice every day and dine with me. As we now turned into the dismal canal, and stopped before his damp-looking mansion, my predilection for the Gran Bretagna returned in full force; and I again ventured to hint that it would save an abundance of trouble to let me proceed thither. But 'No – no,' he answered – 'I see you think you'll be very uncomfortable here; but you'll find that it is not quite so bad as you expect.'

As I groped my way after him through the dark hall, he cried out, 'Keep clear of the dog;' and before we had proceeded many paces farther, 'Take care, or that monkey will fly at you;' – a curious proof, among many others, of his fidelity to all the tastes of his youth, as it agrees perfectly with the description of his life at Newstead, in 1809, and of the sort of menagerie which his visiters had then to encounter in their progress through his hall. Having escaped these dangers, I followed him up the staircase to the apartment destined for me. All this time he had been despatching servants in various directions – one, to procure me a *laquais de place*; another to go in quest of Mr Alexander Scott, to whom he wished to give me in charge; while a third was sent to order his Segretario to come to him. 'So, then, you keep a Secretary?' I said. 'Yes,' he answered, 'a fellow who *can't write* – but such are the names these pompous people give to things.'

When we had reached the door of the apartment, it was discovered to be locked, and, to all appearance, had been so for some time, as the key could not be found – a circumstance which, to my English apprehension, naturally connected itself with notions of damp and desolation, and I again sighed inwardly for the Gran Bretagna. Impatient at the delay of the key, my noble host, with one of his humorous maledictions, gave a vigorous kick to the door and burst it open; on which we at once entered into an apartment not only spacious and elegant, but wearing an aspect of comfort and habitableness which to a traveller's eye is as welcome as it is rare. 'Here,' he said, in a voice whose every tone spoke kindness and hospitality, – 'these are the rooms I use myself, and here I mean to establish you.'

He had ordered dinner from some Tratteria, and while waiting its arrival – as well as that of Mr Alexander Scott, whom he had invited to join us – we stood out on the balcony, in order that, before the daylight was quite gone, I might have some glimpses of the scene which the Canal presented. Happening to remark, in looking up at the clouds, which were still bright in the west, that 'what had struck me in Italian sunsets was that peculiar rosy hue –' I had hardly pronounced the word 'rosy', when Lord Byron, clapping his hand on my mouth said, with a laugh, 'Come, d——n it, Tom, *don't* be poetical.' Among the few gondolas passing at the time, there was one at some distance, in which sat two gentlemen, who had the appearance of being English; and observing them to look our way, Lord Byron putting his arms a-kimbo, said, with a sort of comic swagger, 'Ah! if you, John Bulls, knew who the two fellows are, now standing up here, I think you *would* stare!' – I risk mentioning these things, though aware how they may be turned against myself, for the sake of the otherwise indescribable traits of manner and character which they convey.

[74] The palaces of Venice in general, and the Barberigo Palace in particular, seen in 1824; from *Notes of a Journey Through France and Italy* by William Hazlitt.

(William Hazlitt (1778–1830), the British critic and essayist, travelled to Venice in 1824. The *Notes* were originally printed as articles in the *Morning Chronicle*.)

I never saw palaces anywhere but at Venice. Those at Rome are dungeons compared to them. They generally come down to the water's edge, and as there are canals on each side of them, you see them *four-square*. The views by Canaletti are

very like, both for the effect of the buildings and the hue of
the water. The principal are by Palladio, Longhena, and
Sansovino. They are messy, elegant, well-proportioned, costly
in materials, profuse of ornament. Perhaps if they were raised
above the water's edge on low terraces (as some of them are),
the appearance of comfort and security would be greater,
though the architectural daring, the poetical miracle would
appear less. As it is, they seem literally to be suspended in the
water. – The richest in interior decoration that I saw, was the
Grimani Palace, which answered to all the imaginary conditions of this sort of thing. Aladdin might have exchanged
his for it, and given his lamp into the bargain. The floors are
of marble, the tables of precious stones, the chairs and
curtains of rich silk, the walls covered with looking-glasses,
and it contains a cabinet of invaluable antique sculpture, and
some of Titian's finest portraits. I never knew the practical
amount to the poetical, or furniture seem to grow eloquent
but in this instance. The rooms were not too large for comfort
neither; for space is a consideration at Venice. All that it
wanted of an Eastern Palace was light and air, with distant
vistas of hill and grove. A genealogical tree of the family was
hung up in one of the rooms, beginning with the founder in
the ninth century, and ending with the present representative
of it; and one of the portraits, by Titian, was of a Doge of the
family, looking just like an ugly, spiteful old woman; but with
a truth of nature, and a force of character that no one ever
gave but he. I saw no other mansion equal to this. The Pisani
is the next to it for elegance and splendour; and from its
situation on the Grand Canal, it admits a flood of bright day
through glittering curtains of pea-green silk, into a noble
saloon, enriched with an admirable family-picture by Paul
Veronese, with heads equal to Titian for all but the character
of thought.

Close to this is the Barberigo Palace, in which Titian lived,
and in which he died, with his painting-room just in the state
in which he left it. It is hung round with pictures, some of his
latest works, such as the Magdalen and the Salvator Mundi
(which are common in prints), and with an unfinished sketch
of St Sebastian, on which he was employed at the time of his
death. Titian was ninety-nine when he died, and was at last

carried off by the plague. My guide who was enthusiastic on the subject of Venetian art, would not allow any falling-off in these latest efforts of his mighty pencil, but represented him as prematurely cut off in the height of his career. He knew, he said, an old man, who had died a year ago, at one hundred and twenty.

[75] The aura of melancholy decay that surrounds Venice's *palazzi* has always pleased visitors with a romantic turn of mind; from Lady Blessington's *The Idler in Italy*.

(Marguerite, Countess of Blessington (1789–1849) set out on a long Continental tour with her husband in 1822; in that year she also met Count d'Orsay, with whom she was to live until her death. Apart from *The Idler in France*, *The Idler in Italy* and *Conversations with Lord Byron*, she wrote a dozen worthless but highly successful novels.)

How strange, yet how beautiful was the first view of Venice! It seemed in the distance like a floating city, its domes, spires, cupolas, and towers, glittering in the sunbeams, and looked so glorious, that I could have fancied it one of those optical illusions presented by a mirage. As we entered the grand canal, the reality of the scene became impressed on my mind, and the grandeur of the houses, with the rich and solid architectural decorations lavished on them, formed so striking and melancholy a contrast to the ruin into which they are fast falling, that the scene awakened feelings of deep sadness in my breast. The palaces looked as if the touch of some envious wizard had caused them to decay, long ere Time the destroyer would have scathed them; and this premature ruin has in it something much more mournful than that gradually effected by the lapse of years. Windows whose architraves are supported by caryatides of exquisite sculpture, are blocked up in the rudest manner; and out of them protrude the iron pipes of German stoves, sending forth their murky vapours to the blue and cloudless sky whose purity they profane. Over balustrades of marble, where once beauty loved to lean, float the unseemly nether garments suspended to be dried, of the Teutonic inhabitants who now fill those sculptured dwellings with the mingled odours of cigars and garlick; and mutter the guttural sounds of their language, where once the dulcet ones of the softest of all the Italian dialects, were wont to be heard.

[76] Effie Ruskin writes to her mother in 1850 of a visit to the Palazzo Mocenigo, to see Donna Lucia, the Countess Mocenigo, who had been born in 1770; from *Effie in Venice* by Mary Lutyens.

(Euphemia Chalmers Gray Ruskin (1829–1897) arrived in Venice in November 1849 with her husband John and stayed for five months at the Danieli, paying 16s a night for their rooms – which included one for her friend Charlotte Ker and one for John's servant, George Hobbs. While John worked all day, studying the architecture and gathering material for *The Stones of Venice*, Effie had plenty of time for sight-seeing.)

The other day Mr [Rawdon] Brown came to take me to the Palazzo Mocenigo. I went with him because when I go to pay visits Charlotte never goes because for one thing she cannot speak a word and John prefers my going alone & she likes better not to go. Well, we went and as my visit had been advertised both the Dama Lurietta, the senior Countess, and Mde Clementine, La Sposa, or The Bride, although she is not very young, to distinguish her from the old Lady, were at home. They live in separate Palaces but joined together. The family is still a powerful one and is one of the most illustrious in Venetian History. The walls of the rooms are covered with full length pictures of Doges of the family in their Ducal robes, Admirals and Statesmen. It was also in this Palace that Byron lived when in Venice, and as the Count was not then married he lived with his mother in the adjoining Palace which he now occupys with his wife.

We were received by some well dressed servants and conducted through a number of cold, grand, marble & frescoed appartments, to some nice warm well furnished ones where sat the Lady on a small couch. She received us very kindly and considering her age, 80 years, she was extremely well looking and upright. She considers herself a sort of Queen in Venice as she is the last of the great Venetian Dames, and as she can no longer go out she receives visitors all day, or relations. Her manners were quite beautiful and took away from your first impressions caused by the absurdity of her dress which though excessively rich was not becoming for her age, and I could not help feeling thankful that in Britain old Ladies did not disfigure themselves. Generally speaking her features were marked and fine and still sparkling black eyes, her hair grey but false curls of jet black at each side of her face, the hair surmounted by a blonde cap with blue artificial flowers, a brown loose satin Polka cloak lined with white, hanging open and showing her neck very bare, pale yellow kid gloves and exquisite point lace collar and handkerchief, a fan and dress of purple & green silk. A little table stood beside her covered with Jars of flowers & two little antique bells, one she rang when she wanted her women attendants and the other the men. After we were seated she rang for the men servants and they entered instantly bearing on massive silver, plate & cups, black coffee, cake, & iced Lemonade in Tumblers. The latter I took & found delicious. She was very affectionate to me and kissed me on both cheeks, speaking French, and presented me with a work written I suppose a century ago by her Father, the Marquis Memmo. Whilst we were sitting, two young Ladies with their governess entered of the illustrious family of Lynar, the eldest not yet 14 but could speak already three Languages perfectly and a little English.

We took leave of the old Lady and walked through her sleeping apartment by her permission. Here I was much astonished by the toilette table; I had never seen anything like it before; there was the Mirror frame, two little other mirrors, essence pots, rouge pots, perfume bottles and boxes of various kinds, everything in wrought silver. It was very beautiful. Passing through some other apartments we found ourselves in the Luxurious boudoir of La Sposa. We chatted and laughed with her for half an hour. She is pleasant & plain but fashionable looking. She is daughter of Count Spaur, the last Governor of Venice, an Austrian. Her house and servants were in very good order, and you may believe I was much obliged to Mr Brown for taking me to see so much that was new and interesting, and all that I have yet seen of the Italians makes me come to this opinion that whatever their private morals may be, they respect those who are well conducted, and are themselves extremely goodnatured, amiable and well-bred and when they find English who sympathize with their tastes and understand them, they will do anything for them.

(But Effie Ruskin also complained of the general discomfort of palazzi *during the Venetian winters.)*

We went today and looked over several Palaces but although the outsides are splendid Venetian Gothic I cannot fancy how the Italians live, for the insides although perfectly clean have such a want of comfort about them, and the people in them never appear to be doing anything and no fire places, even in this cold weather. Each member of the family carries about on their arm an earthen basket or pot with hot charcoal in it and this remains hot for a considerable time. Charlotte and I had it one day but I cannot fancy it healthy for we both got headaches while we used it. The people seem to be in great distress for money and wish to sell their houses immediately. We could get one cheap, as in Italy you give always considerably less than is asked, but there is a heavy tax to the Austrian Government and they do not know whether the war is ended or not, but they hope so. Another expense would be putting it in habitable order for us, for we could not live the way they do. The tesselated floors, although very smooth and glittering, are extremely cold and all their arrangements seem made for heat & not cold.

[77] The Palazzo Grassi, and other *palazzi*, in 1852; from *The Journals and Correspondence of Lady East-lake* edited by Charles Eastlake Smith.

(Elizabeth, Lady Eastlake (1809–1893) visited Venice in 1852, just three years after she had married Sir Charles Eastlake, President of the Royal Academy.)

Our hotel – the Palazzo Grassi – is a grand edifice. We enter by splendid circular steps (sometimes by one high up, sometimes by one low down, for the tide rises and falls about four feet) into a gorgeous hall, supported on stupendous pillars, which extends round a court filled with oleanders, &c., and with no less than four wells forming a square, and finely sculptured. The great stairs are magnificent, and there are about ten other little ones. The salon on the first floor is fabulously big, with a gallery running round it, and chandeliers suspended by ropes which are invisible for the distance. The *remains* of the salon form an immense space, for our two rooms, as well as many others, are divided off from it, but not above one-third in height, though our rooms are at least forty feet high. The walls are painted in late Venetian style, and much of the old furniture remains, huge carved armoires and clumsy gilt chairs, in which I sit down with suspicion. Opposite to us is a gorgeous mass now belonging to a Spanish Infanta – the Palazzo Rezzonico, and next to it the proud edifice of the 'Foscari'. We hear only the splash of the gondolas, or the strange cries of the gondoliers; otherwise there is no sound in these watery streets. Music, however, we have had. At about ten o'clock one evening a gondola band of singers came nearer and nearer, singing enchantingly – a perfect fleet of gondolas, almost invisible in their black shapes in the dark, following noiselessly. There was not a sign of a creature listening; yet, when the chorus on the waters ceased, a mysterious clapping began, with sundry 'brai', which is what the lazy Venetians say for 'bravi'. The chorusgondola passed and repassed down the Grand Canal till midnight, when I heard its last faint sounds dying away in the distance.

To-day Lady Sorrell took me to some palaces to show me how the Venetian nobility still live. The two first, Mme Albrizzi, and Mlle Morosini, still keep up their grand old mansions respectably though not comfortably, being wealthy; but the third, old Mme Mocenigo, with whom Lord Byron lodged when here, presented a very melancholy picture. The glory was all departed from her vast pile, and the old lady, while surrounded by a few treasured relics of better days – a picture by Tintoretto, &c. – was only intent, like any old innkeeper, on recommending her lodgings to me . . .

[78] Richard Wagner settles comfortably into the Palazzo Giustinian in the summer of 1858; from *My Life* by Richard Wagner translated by Andrew Gray.

Starting out the next day from the Hotel Danieli, where we had found only some dark quarters in rooms overlooking narrow and tiny canals, I first hunted for a suitable place to live for my longer stay. I heard that one of the three Giustini-ani palaces, not far from the Palazzo Foscari, was at present almost free of lodgers as a result of a location deemed not very suitable for the winter season: I found some exception-ally big and imposing rooms there, being told that they would all remain unoccupied; thus I rented a large and stately room, with a spacious adjoining bedroom, had my bags brought there quickly, and could tell myself by that evening of August 30th that I was now residing in Venice. The desire to be able to work here unmolested governed me in everything. I at once wrote to Zürich, requesting that my Erard piano and my bed be sent on after me, for as to the latter I had a feeling I would learn in Venice what it is to freeze. Furthermore, I soon found the greyish walls of my main room distasteful, as they were ill-suited to the ceiling, which was painted with what I considered a rather tasteful fresco. I decided to have the large room completely hung with an admittedly very cheap dark red wallpaper: this caused a lot of commotion at first; yet it seemed worth the effort to go through with it, as I could gaze down from my balcony at the wonderful canal with a gradu-ally increasing sense of well-being and tell myself that here was the place I would complete my *Tristan*. I did some further decorating; I arranged to have dark red curtains, though of the cheapest calico, to cover the unworthy doors the Hungar-ian landlord had caused to be installed in the utterly dilapi-dated palace in place of the valuable originals, which had probably been stolen. Apart from that, the landlord had managed to get some showy furniture: there were some gilt chairs, though covered with cheap cotton plush, but above all a finely carved gilt table base, upon which a common deal top had been placed; this I now had to cover with a drape of a tolerable red. At last the Erard came; it was placed in the center of the large room, and now it was time to storm this wonderful Venice with music.

[79] On 28 September of the same year, Wagner describes his apartments to his wife Minna; from *Richard to Minna Wagner: letters to his first wife* translated by William Ashton Ellis.

Like all such apartments, it is in a big ancient palace, with wide halls and spaces. For my living room I have an enormous saloon looking on to the Grand Canal; then a very roomy bedchamber, with a little cabinet beside it for a wardrobe. Fine old ceiling-paintings, splendid floors inlaid with magnificent mosaic; badly distempered walls (once richly tapestried, no doubt), antique furniture, very elegant in appearance, covered with red cotton-velvet, but very rickety and miserably stuffed; nothing quite in working order, doors not shutting properly, all somewhat the worse for wear. I had a big state-bed removed at once, and replaced by a smaller iron bedstead with spring mattress. Linen so-so; pillows stuffed with wool; for the colder season a foot-quilt weighing 3 hundredweight. The landlord, an Austrian, is delighted to have me in his house, and does all he can to satisfy me; I have contrived a few conveniences myself, arranged a passable divan, fauteuil, etc. Things now will do quite well, and the piano is sure to sound glorious in my big saloon. The want of air-tightness in windows and doors is said to be no serious drawback even in winter here. The climate and the air are really heavenly; a regard in which Venice is said to be one of the most favoured of places, far more so than Florence, Rome, or even Naples. An agreeably refreshing East wind constantly blows from the sea, moderating any excessive heat, keeping the sky always clear, and furnishing beautiful air. For a whole month we've only had two rainy days, and only one at a time. Of course, one never sees a trace of drought, as the sea keeps the air always moist. I still go about in full summer clothing, and that of an evening; not until then do I make my promenade.

[80] The fifteenth-century Palazzo Barbaro is occupied in 1892 by Henry James; from *The Letters of Henry James* edited by Leon Edel.

(In 1882 Mr and Mrs Daniel Curtis bought the two principal floors of the Palazzo Barbaro; their descendants still own it today. For several years it was regularly taken by Mrs John (Jack) Lowell Gardner, better known as Isabella Stewart Gardner, who used it as a model for her house in Boston, which is now the Fenway Museum. Henry James and John Singer Sargent were both *habitués*.)

Dear Mrs Curtis.

J'y suis – would that I could add *j'y reste*! – till you return. Many thanks for your kind London note. I rejoice in everything that may be comfortable in your situation or interesting in your adventures. I came hither two days ago and Mrs J.L.G. has kindly put a bed for me in this divine old library – where I am fain to pass the livelong day. Have you ever *lived* here? – if you haven't, if you haven't gazed upward from your couch, in the rosy dawn, or during the postprandial (that is after-luncheon) siesta, at the medallions and arabesques of the ceiling, permit me to tell you that you don't *know* the Barbaro. Let me add that I am not here in wantonness or disorder – but simply because the little lady's other boarders are located elsewhere. I am so far from complaining that I wish I could stay here forever. I don't – I go out with the little lady, and even with the boarders. It is scorching scirocco, but I don't much care; it is the essence of midsummer, but I buy five-franc alpaca jackets and feel so Venetian that you might almost own me. I believe I am to go to Asolo for a day or two next week – and I confess that I have a dread of exchanging this marble hall for the top of a stable.

[81] Henry James made the Palazzo Barbaro the setting for part of his novel, *The Wings of the Dove*, where it appears as the Palazzo Leporelli.

Not yet so much as this morning had she felt herself sink into possession; gratefully glad that the warmth of the Southern summer was still in the high florid rooms, palatial chambers where hard cool pavements took reflexions in their lifelong polish, and where the sun on the stirred sea-water, flickering up through open windows, played over the painted 'subjects' in the splendid ceilings – medallions of purple and brown, of brave old melancholy colour, medals as of old reddened gold, embossed and beribboned, all toned with time and all flourished and scolloped and gilded about, set in their great moulded and figured concavity (a nest of white cherubs, friendly creatures of the air) and appreciated by the aid of that second tier of smaller lights, straight openings to the front, which did everything, even with the Baedekers and photographs of Milly's party dreadfully meeting the eye, to make of the place an apartment of state . . . Palazzo Leporelli held its history still in its great lap, even like a painted idol, a solemn puppet hung about with decorations. Hung about with pictures and relics, the rich Venetian past, the ineffaceable character, was here the presence revered and served: which brings us back to our truth of a moment ago – the fact that, more than ever, this October morning, awkward novice though she might be, Milly moved slowly to and fro as the priestess of the worship.

[82] Henry James expatiates on the advantages of the Palazzo Barbaro over anything smaller; from *The Letters of Henry James* edited by Leon Edel.

June 23, 1907

Dear Laura Wagnière,

I have waited since getting your good note to have the right moment and right light for casting the right sort of longing lingering look on the little house with the '*Giardinetto*' on the Canal Grande, to the right of Guggenheim as you face Guggenheim. I hung about it yesterday afternoon in the gondola with Mrs Curtis, and we both thought it very charming and desirable, only that she has (perhaps a little vaguely) heard it spoken of as 'damp', which I confess it looks to me just a trifle. However, this may be the vainest of calumnies. It does look expensive and also a trifle contracted, and is at present clearly occupied and with no outward trace of being to let about it at all. For myself, in this paradise of great household spaces (I mean Venice generally), I kind of feel that even the bribe of the Canal Grande and a *giardinetto* together wouldn't quite reconcile me to the purgatory of a very small, really (and not merely relatively) small house ... Mrs Curtis is eloquent on the sacrifices one must make (to a high rent here) if one *must* have, for 'smartness,' the 'Canal Grande' at any price. She makes me feel afresh what I've always felt, that what I should probably do with my own available ninepence would be to put up with some large marble halls in some comparatively modest or remote locality, especially *della parse di fondamenta nuova*, etc.; that is, so I got there air and breeze and light and *pulizia* and a dozen other conveniences! In fine, the place you covet is no doubt a dear little 'fancy' place; but as to the question of 'coming to Venice' if one can, I have but a single passionate emotion, a thousand times Yes! It would be for me, I feel, in certain circumstances (were I free, with a hundred other facts of my life different,) the solution of all my questions, and the consolation of my declining years. Never has the whole place seemed to me sweeter, dearer, *diviner*. It leaves everything else out in the cold. I wish I could dream of coming to *me mettre dans mes meubles* (except that my *meubles* would look so awful here!) beside you. I presume to enter into it with a yearning sympathy. Happy you to be able even to discuss it ...

This place and this large cool upper floor of the Barbaro, with all the space practically to myself, and draughts and scirocco airs playing over me indecently undressed, is more than ever delicious and unique ... The breath of the lagoon still plays up, but I mingle too much of another fluid with my ink, and I have no more clothes to take off ... I greet affectionately, yes affectionately, kind Henry, and the exquisite gold-haired maiden, and I am, dear Laura Wagnière, your very faithful old friend,

HENRY JAMES

[83] The Cà Rezzonico, one of the most magnificent Renaissance palaces on the Grand Canal, was bought in 1888 by Robert Browning's son Pen, who had married an American heiress: Robert Browning, overjoyed, wrote to a friend about the purchase; from *Letters of the Brownings to George Barrett* edited by Paul Landis with the assistance of Ronald E. Freeman.

(Robert Browning (1812–1889) first visited Italy in 1838.
When he eloped with Elizabeth Barrett in 1846, he took her
to Pisa and Florence where they lived for 15 years until her
death. Though he then returned to England, he continued to
visit Italy, and Venice, where in 1885 he had tried unsuccess-
fully to buy the Palazzo Manzoni.)

I don't think I have told you what an advantageous bargain
Pen has made in acquiring his huge Rezzonico Palace – the
finest now obtainable in Venice. He was most efficiently
helped by his kind and clever friend Mr Malcolm, a thoroughly business man – and he possesses a magnificent property worth more than double what was paid for it. he could
sell the mere adornments of the building – its statues, pillars
(internal decorations) and painted cielings [sic] (two by Tiepolo) for the full prize of the palazzo itself. He is full of
energy, and superintends all the restoration work, (all that is
requisite, and not much of even that and may safely be
considered 'the right man in the right place.' Far from neglect-
ing his art, he has every motive for devoting himself to it: and
there seems only one circumstance likely to overcloud the
sunshine of his life – the uncertain health of his wife. The two
would otherwise really seem perfectly happy in every condition of their fortunes here below . . .
    It is long since we met. And why not run over, in the
spring, to Venice – when Pen and his wife will be installed
in their palazzo and not let you get out of it, once inside.
He intends to fit up 'some Bachelor rooms': he himself will
occupy the Pope's old apartment – the snuggest: and quietly
wait till, bit by bit, he 'furnishes' the whole of his domain –
which he does not find at all too vast. He reminds me of
the mouse (in a poem of Donne's) who got into the trunk
of an elephant – 'wherein, as in a gallery, this mouse
walked and surveyed the rooms of this vast house.' But in
reality there was only two or three 'vast' rooms – those
habitable and not for mere passage or receptions, are quite
moderate in size. Good bye, dear George – my sister (at my
side) sends her best love with that of yours affectionately
ever

                                                    RB.

(Two months later, on 24 February 1889, Browning wrote again.)

I hear from the couple at Venice constantly – from Pen yesterday. They are, within the last few days, lodged in their fine Palazzo: they gave two modest entertainments there by way of house-warming, and were congratulated by everybody on what they had done for Pope Clement XIII – whose apartment they occupy: and it is pleasant to hear how grateful the old Venetian families are at the palace having fallen into such reverent hands (I will get a photograph of it for you when I can) – not being destined to vile uses, turned into an hotel, or the like. It is really, on the whole, the best palace in Venice, and has never been modified in the least – except in the trifling business of blocking up windows &c. – all which Pen has carefully restored. I am particularly happy to know that his wife – a woman of whom I can imagine no greater praise than I imply when I say Pen's Mother would have thoroughly loved and esteemed her – *she* is as satisfied with her new conditions as Pen's self. And now it will be for Pen to show he is worthy of his belongings. He is sending over his very striking Portrait for exhibition here, and will make a considerable show at the Paris grand affair. There is a funny circumstance connected with the 'Rezzonico.' There is – was – a family down in the Golden Book of the old Republic – that of 'Widmann' – very wealthy, owning many palaces still bearing the name, but now (lately however) extinct. The last of the Rezzonico family was one Widmann Rezzonico, nephew of the Pope: he died at the beginning of the present century. Now, my mother's maiden name was 'Wiedemann' – and Pen was named after her – Robert W. B. B. – which name he mispronounced as 'Pennini' – hence his old and customary appellation. He was not aware of the last of the Rs being so called till after we had bought the property: and the Venetians account for his getting such a bargain by thinking there was someting more than natural in his ability to do so!

[84] Browning was staying in the Cà Rezzonico when he died, as his son Pen wrote to his friend Katharine Bronson; from *More than Friend, the letters of Robert Browning to Katharine de Kay Bronson* edited by Michael Meredith.

(The reviews mentioned in the letter were of *Asolando*, published the day Browning died.)

Palazzo Rezzonico.
10.30 [p.m.] [12 December 1889]

Dearest Friend,
    Our beloved breathed his last as St Marks struck ten – without pain – unconsciously – I was able to make him happy a little before he became unconscious by a telegram from Smith saying 'reviews in all this day's papers most favourable. Edition nearly exhausted –' He just murmured 'How gratifying.' Those were the last intelligible words.

Yr Pen

[85] This letter from Rowland Burden-Muller (kindly made available by his nephew, Mr Michael Severne) is undated, but appears to have been written some time in the 1960s, when he was looking back over half a century. It gives the most vivid picture I know of life among the English colony in Venice in Edwardian days.

In those days I saw more of Venice where Aunt Enid [Lady Layard] lived at the Palazzo Cà Castello mourning, in widow's weeds à la Maria Stuart, a husband who had died some ten years before, after a useful life discovering the Ruins of Nineveh and later as ambassador to the Porte. However, her mourning did not preclude an active social life with receptions every evening during the month of April: her own on Thursday evenings, the Brandolins' on Friday, with remaining evenings taken by the Noces, della Grazias, Morosinis and others. To these, at 14, I was taken so that I should learn to conduct myself appropriately in polite society. On returning home at 1.30 a.m. I was made to stand beneath Carpaccio's 'Visit of the 3 Magi', now in the National Gallery, and recite the names, in full with correct titles and in proper precedence, of all the persons to whom I had been introduced that evening. Meanwhile Aunt Enid sipped her barley water before going to bed. The mornings started with most of us assembling in the dining room for breakfast, a meal usually interrupted for me since I had to go into the gallery and draw a faded green silk curtain over Gentile Bellini's portrait of Sultan Mohammed in order to protect it from the depredations of the parrot while taking its morning bath. I could never understand why the parrot's cage had to keep company with the Sultan.

On several mornings each week I was sent with Signor Malagola, Keeper of the Archives, 'to see the sights', occasionally accompanied by the vastly dull Princess Stephanie, widow of Crown Prince Rudolph of Austria, a lady-in-waiting and two dachshunds. My mother, fearful of my growing state, insisted on my wearing my Eton suit so as all possible use should be extracted from its cost and, being very Scotch, she insisted that I should top it with a Scotch bonnet with flowing ribbons. Thus garbed, I was taught to row the gondola, surreptitiously, by Ricardo and Giovanni, Aunt Enid's two charming gondoliers. One might have thought that such a sight upon the Grand Canal would have attracted some attention; but the spirit of the nineteenth century still hovered over the twentieth and individuality was rampant. Also I was a Victorian child, obedient and passive and quite devoid of self-consciousness. I suppose a modern child would have rebelled or had to be sent to a psychiatrist.

In those days the campanile had just collapsed and there were only three motor boats in the city and no hotels on the Lido which can hardly have changed since Byron rowed there. Aunt Enid owned a rush hut, a forerunner of today's cabanas; and sometimes we went there for a picnic. Gondolas were sent ahead with the chef and a couple of 'garçons de cuisine', and a butler and a pair of footmen who placed in position three easels for Aunt Enid, Princess Stephanie and Susie Duchess of Somerset who enjoyed painting in water colour, thus creating a scene in the manner of Boudin. Being under 15 years of age I was permitted to bathe, and later we were served a six-course collation in the rush hut by the butler and footmen with cotton gloves, returning to Venice by sunset.

The three motor launches belonged to the Spanish Pretender, who also owned an aged white parrot reputedly over 120 years old; to Val Prinsep, the artist son of Watts' patron from Little Holland House, and to a newly arrived American couple, not yet acknowledged by Venetian society. Often we had tea with old Mr and Mrs Eden in their garden on the Giudecca, the largest in Venice, and nearby was the small nursing home founded by Aunt Enid for British sailors. Sometimes I went out with Val Prinsep or the immensely fat and delightful Clara Montalba when they went sketching, for painting in water colour was a fashionable vocation. The Prinsep boys were at Eton with me and, occasionally, I got away to [them], although Aunt Enid disapproved of the family as being 'very bohemian', and Mrs Prinsep's father, Mr Leland, had made a scandal with Mr Whistler over the decoration of his dining room. On Sundays I sang in the choir of the English church, conducted with her fan by Helen Lady Radnor who took her pet gondolier home to Longford Castle in Wiltshire where he rowed her on the lake as part of his duties. The organ was played by Sir Hubert Miller, and was blown by his pet gondolier who was very handsome. Then there were luncheons with Mrs Browning, Pen's wife, who, as a disciple of Dr Fletcher, chewed her food 40 times before swallowing, a method my mother made me adopt at once. Also we were taken on an inspection of the ancient island lunatic asylum, where Mrs Cavendish Bentinck, arrayed in chiffon and pearls, prodded a female lunatic in the buttocks with her parasol exclaiming, 'Do tell me, what is wrong with that one?' Aunt Enid had a 'penchant' for minor royalty, a social pest now fortunately extinct, and they were a cause for much entertaining. I remember a beautiful reception for mother's friend, Princess Charlotte of Saxe Meiningen, given by the Duca della Grazia at the Palazzo Vendramin – the deathplace of Wagner – where there were two footmen in 18th-century costume outside every door and an orchestra brought from Vienna for the occasion; but I can also remember the trouble I encountered from my mother because of the difficulty I had in saying easily 'grossherzoglicher Hochheit' when talking to an archduke. For a boy of 14 it was quite a mouthful. It was a period of personalities, of parties, and of palazzos still inhabited by Venetians. Receptions had replaced the Ridotto but pleasure, if sedate, was in the air. Venice was gaily international, whereas Florence was intellectually international yet somewhat provincial. Of the Italians, the della Grazias, Brandolins, Noces and Countess Morosini entertained frequently, and Aunt Enid, Lady Radnor, Lady Helen Vincent and Sir Hubert Miller of the English. America was represented by the Ralph Curtis' of the Palazzo Barbaro whose father was said to have had to leave Boston after losing his temper and pulling a neighbour's nose on the train. The Countess Morosini and Lady Helen Vincent were famous beauties, one dark and the other fair. The former was greatly admired by the German Emperor who sent her his portrait after visiting Venice in his yacht. Many of these figures were caricatured by 'Baron Corvo' in his book 'The Pursuit of the Whole and the Past' [In fact, 'The Desire and Pursuit of the Whole']. It was the period of the English occupation and before the real American invasion when Venice became a fashionable summer resort. In those days the season closed in May.

Churches

[86] Fra Felix Fabri visits the church of SS Giovanni e Paolo in 1480; from *Felix Fabri* translated by Aubrey Stewart.

On the 29th, which is the feast of St Peter Martyr, of the Order of Preaching Friars, I took my lords to the church of St John and St Paul, where there is a great and exceeding stately convent of Preaching Friars, and there we heard service, which was performed with great solemnity. There is an exceeding great rush of people on that day to the church of these friars, because there is a festival there, and people are crowded together even up to the horns of the altar. The people run thither from the whole city to hear service, to kiss the relics of the holy martyr, and to drink the water of St Peter, which water, after being blessed in the name of God, and touched by the relics of the holy martyr, is believed to be of value as well for the body as for the soul. Wherefore in most parts of the world the faithful take this water of St Peter, and give it to women in their time of peril to drink, and they are saved from their peril. It is likewise given to those sick of a fever, that they may be made whole. Mariners also carry it to their ships and pour a little of it into the vessels wherein water is kept, and by its virtue the other water is preserved from becoming foul, and however old the water may be, it does not stink or become corrupt if some of this be poured upon it. This mariners learn by daily experience to be true. So after we had heard service, and kissed the relics of the saint, and tasted a draught of his life-giving water, we returned to our inn for a meal.

[87] Four hundred years later, John Ruskin examines the monuments in SS Giovanni e Paolo; from *The Stones of Venice.*

(The two Friars' churches of Venice, the Frari and SS Giovanni e Paolo, are by far the richest in funerary sculpture, and Ruskin examined the collections in both, more thoroughly than they had ever been inspected before. He was wrong, however, in attributing the Vendramin monument to Antonio Rizzo, if only by implication: it is almost certainly the work of Pietro and Tullio Lombardo.)

In the choir of the same church, SS Giovanni e Paoloj is another tomb, that of the *Doge Andrea Vendramin.* This doge died in 1478, after a short reign of two years, the most disastrous in the annals of Venice. He died of a pestilence which followed the ravage of the Turks, carried to the shores of the lagoons. He died, leaving Venice disgraced by sea and land, with the smoke of hostile devastation rising in the blue distances of Friuli; and there was raised to him the most costly tomb ever bestowed on her monarchs . . .

It is unanimously declared the chef d'œuvre of Renaissance sepulchral work, and pronounced by Cicognara (also quoted by Selvatico): 'Il vertice a cui l' arti Veneziane si spinsero col ministero del scalpello' – 'The very culminating point to which the Venetian arts attained by ministry of the chisel'.

To this culminating point, therefore, covered with dust and cobwebs, I attained, as I did to every tomb of importance in Venice, by the ministry of such ancient ladders as were to be found in the sacristan's keeping. I was struck at first by the excessive awkwardness and want of feeling in the fall of the hand towards the spectator, for it is thrown off the middle of the body in order to show its fine cutting. Now the Mocenigo hand, severe and even stiff in its articulations, has its veins finely drawn, its sculptor having justly felt that the delicacy of the veining expresses alike dignity and age and birth. The Vendramin hand is far more laboriously cut, but its blunt and clumsy contour at once makes us feel that all the care has been thrown away, and well it may be, for it has been entirely bestowed in cutting gouty wrinkles about the joints. Such as the hand is, I looked for its fellow. At first I thought it had been broken off, but on clearing away the dust, I saw the wretched effigy had only *one* hand, and was a mere block on the inner side. The face, heavy and disagreeable in its features, is made monstrous by its semi-sculpture. One side of the forehead is wrinkled elaborately, the other left smooth; one side only of the doge's cap is chased; one cheek only is finished, and the other blocked out and distorted besides; finally, the ermine robe, which is elaborately imitated to its utmost lock of hair and of ground hair on the one side, is blocked out only on the other: it having been supposed throughout the work that the effigy was only to be seen from below, and from one side.

It was indeed to be so seen by nearly every one; and I do not blame – I should, on the contrary, have praised – the sculptor for regulating his treatment of it by its position; if that treatment had not involved, first, dishonesty, in giving only half a face, a monstrous mask, when we demanded true portraiture of the dead; and, secondly, such utter coldness of feeling, as could only consist with an extreme of intellectual and moral degradation: Who, with a heart in his breast, could have stayed his hand as he drew the dim lines of the old man's countenance – unmajestic once, indeed, but at least sanctified by the solemnities of death – could have stayed his hand, as he reached the bend of the grey forehead and measured out the last veins of it at so much the zecchin?

I do not think the reader, if he has feeling, will expect that much talent should be shown in the rest of his work, by the sculptor of this base and senseless lie. The whole monument is one wearisome aggregation of that species of ornamental flourish, which, when it is done with a pen, is called penmanship, and when done with a chisel, should be called chisel-manship; the subject of it being chiefly fat-limbed boys sprawling on dolphins, dolphins incapable of swimming, and dragged along the sea by expanded pocket-handkerchiefs.

But now, reader, comes the very gist and point of the whole matter. This lying monument to a dishonoured doge, this culminating pride of the Renaissance art of Venice, is at least veracious, if in nothing else, in its testimony to the character of its sculptor. *He was banished from Venice for forgery* in 1487.

[88] A rare description of the Church of S. Giorgio dei Greci, in 1654. It continues to this day to serve the spiritual needs of the small Greek Catholic (i.e. Uniat) community in Venice; from *The Voyage of Italy* by Richard Lassels.

Upon S. Georges day we went to the Greek Church, belonging to the Greek schismaticks. Their Church being dedicated to God in honour of S. George they kept that day solemnly. There having heard the sermon in Greek, we heard the high Masse in Greeke after the manner of the Greek Church. I got an understanding Grecian to tell me in particular all the Ceremonies and their meaning; and in conclusion I found them saying of masse perfectly, that is, offering, consecrating, adoring Christs body in the Sacrament, and receiving it. I found that he that sung the Masse was a Bishop clad in his Pontificalibus with his miter upon his head, and his crosier staff in his hand; whiles the Deacon that sung the ghospel, and the subdeacon that sung the Epistle were clad in Tunicks as the Roman fashion is. I found them allso praying to Saints, praying for the dead, holding furth the consecrated hoast to be adored by the people who after Masse kissed the picture of S. George their patron after Masse, received holy bread, kissed the other pictures and relicks with as great Veneration as the Roman Catholicks do; and used divers other Ceremonies farre more in number then in the Roman Masse: whiles the very women had beads in their hands, and stores of candles were lighted up, both upon the altar, and els where.

[89] An early-morning tour of Venetian churches in 1780; from *Italy, with sketches of Spain and Portugal* by William Beckford.

It was not five o'clock before I was aroused by a loud din of voices and splashing of water under my balcony. Looking out, I beheld the grand canal so entirely covered with fruits and vegetables, on rafts and in barges, that I could scarcely distinguish a wave. Loads of grapes, peaches and melons arrived, and disappeared in an instant, for every vessel was in motion; and the crowds of purchasers hurrying from boat to boat, formed a very lively picture. Amongst the multitudes, I remarked a good many whose dress and carriage announced something above the common rank; and upon enquiry I found they were noble Venetians, just come from their casinos, and met to refresh themselves with fruit, before they retired to sleep for the day.

Whilst I was observing them, the sun began to colour the balustrades of the palaces, and the pure exhilarating air of the morning drawing me abroad, I procured a gondola, laid in my provision of bread and grapes, and was rowed under the Rialto, down the grand canal to the marble steps of *S. Maria della Salute*, erected by the Senate in performance of vow to the Holy Virgin, who begged off a terrible pestilence in 1630. The great bronze portal opened whilst I was standing on the steps which lead to it, and discovered the interior of the dome, where I expatiated in solitude; no mortal appearing except an old priest who trimmed the lamps and muttered a prayer before the high altar, still wrapt in shadows. The sunbeams began to strike against the windows of the cupola, just as I left the church and was wafted across the waves to the specious platform in front of *St Giorgio Maggiore*, one of the most celebrated works of Palladio.

When my first transport was a little subsided, and I had examined the graceful design of each particular ornament, and united the just proportion and grand effect of the whole in my mind, I planted my umbrella on the margin of the sea, and viewed at my leisure the vast range of palaces, of porticos, of towers, opening on every side and extending out of sight. The Doge's palace and the tall columns at the entrance of the

The Palazzo Barbaro, where Henry James lived in Venice

A regatta on the Grand Canal, by Canaletto

SS Giovanni e Paolo with the equestrian statue of Bartolommeo Colleoni

An aerial view of the Arsenal at the end of the seventeenth century

The entrance to the Arsenal

place of St Mark, form, together with the arcades of the
public library, the lofty Campanile and the cupolas of the
ducal church, one of the most striking groups of buildings
that art can boast of. To behold at one glance these stately
fabrics, so illustrious in the records of former ages, before
which, in the flourishing times of the republic, so many valiant
chiefs and princes have landed, loaded with oriental spoils,
was a spectacle I had long and ardently desired . . .

I contemplated the busy scene from my peaceful platform,
where nothing stirred but aged devotees creeping to their
devotions, and, whilst I remained thus calm and tranquil,
heard the distant buzz of the town. Fortunately some length
of waves rolled between me and its tumults; so that I ate my
grapes, and read Metastasio, undisturbed by officiousness or
curiosity. When the sun became too powerful, I entered the
nave.

After I had admired the masterly structure of the roof and
the lightness of its arches, my eyes naturally directed themselves to the pavement of white and ruddy marble, polished,
and reflecting like a mirror the columns which rise from it.
Over this I walked to a door that admitted me into the
principal quadrangle of the convent, surrounded by a cloister
supported on Ionic pillars, beautifully proportioned. A flight
of stairs opens into the court, adorned with balustrades and
pedestals, sculptured with elegance truly Grecian. This
brought me to the refectory, where the chef-d'œuvre of Paul
Veronese, representing the marriage of Cana in Galilee, was
the first object that presented itself. I never beheld so gorgeous
a group of wedding-garments before; there is every variety of
fold and plait that can possibly be imagined. The attitudes
and countenances are more uniform, and the guests appear a
very genteel, decent sort of people, well used to the mode of
their times and accustomed to miracles.

Having examined this fictitious repast, I cast a look on a
long range of tables covered with very excellent realities,
which the monks were coming to devour with energy, if one
might judge from their appearance. These sons of penitence
and mortification possess one of the most spacious islands of
the whole cluster, a princely habitation, with gardens and
open porticos, that engross every breath of air; and, what

adds not a little to the charms of their abode, is the facility of making excursions from it, whenever they have a mind . . .

Full of prophecies and bodings, I moved slowly out of the cloisters; and, gaining my gondola, arrived, I know not how, at the flights of steps which lead to the *Redentore*, a structure so simple and elegant, that I thought myself entering an antique temple, and looked about for the statue of the God of Delphi, or some other graceful divinity. A huge crucifix of bronze soon brought me to times present.

The charm being thus dissolved, I began to perceive the shapes of rueful martyrs peeping out of the niches around, and the bushy beards of capuchin friars wagging before the altars. These good fathers had decorated the nave with orange and citron trees, placed between the pilasters of the arcades; and on grand festivals, it seems, they turn the whole church into a bower, strew the pavement with leaves, and festoon the dome with flowers.

[90] Mrs Piozzi misses an opportunity at S. Giorgio Maggiore in April 1785; from her *Glimpses of Italian Society*.

The view of Venice from the Zueca – a word contracted from Giudecca, as I am told – would invite one never more to stray from it – farther, at least, than to St George's Church, on another little opposite island, whence the prospect is surely wonderful. It was to this church I was sent for the purpose of seeing a famous picture, painted by Paul Veronese, of the marriage at Cana in Galilee. When we arrived, the picture was kept in a refectory belonging to friars (of what order I have forgotten), and no woman could be admitted. My disappointment was so great that I was deprived even of the powers of solicitation by the extreme ill-humour it occasioned, and my few entreaties for admission were completely disregarded by the good old monk, who remained outside with me, while the gentlemen visited the convent without molestation. At my return to Venice I met little comfort, as everybody told me it was my own fault, for I might put on men's clothes and see it whenever I pleased, as nobody then would stop, though perhaps all of them would know me.

[91] The effect of colour on S. Giorgio Maggiore, seen in the nineteenth century; from Henry James's *Italian Hours*.

Straight across, before my windows, rose the great pink mass of San Giorgio Maggiore, which has for an ugly Palladian church a success beyond all reason. It is a success of position, of colour, of the immense detached Campanile, tipped with a tall gold angel. I know not whether it is because San Giorgio is so grandly conspicuous, with a great deal of worn, faded-looking brickwork; but for many persons the whole place has a kind of suffusion of rosiness. Asked what may be the leading colour in the Venetian concert, we should inveterately say Pink, and yet without remembering after all that this elegant hue occurs very often. It is a faint, shimmering, airy, watery pink; the bright sea-light seems to flush with it and the pale whiteish-green of lagoon and canal to drink it in. There is indeed a great deal of very evident brickwork, which is never fresh or loud in colour, but always burnt out, as it were, always exquisitely mild.

[92] John Ruskin compares the two plague churches, Palladio's Redentore and Longhena's Salute; from *The Stones of Venice*.

'Santa Maria della Salute', Our Lady of Health, or of Safety, would be a more literal translation, yet not perhaps fully expressing the force of the Italian word in this case. The church was built between 1630 and 1680, in acknowledgement of the cessation of the plague; – of course to the Virgin, to whom the modern Italian has recourse in all his principal distresses, and who receives his gratitude for all principal deliverances.

The hasty traveller is usually enthusiastic in his admiration of this building; but there is a notable lesson to be derived from it, which is not often read. On the opposite side of the broad canal of the Giudecca is a small church, celebrated among Renaissance architects as of Palladian design, but which would hardly attract the notice of the general observer, unless on account of the pictures by John Bellini which it contains, in order to see which the traveller may perhaps remember having been taken across the Giudecca to the church of the 'Redentore'.

But he ought carefully to compare these two buildings with each other, the one built 'to the Virgin', the other 'to the Redeemer' (also a votive offering after the cessation of the plague on 1576): the one, the most conspicuous church in Venice, its dome, the principal one by which she is first discerned, rising out of the distant sea; the other, small and contemptible, on a suburban island, and only becoming an object of interest because it contains three small pictures! For in the relative magnitude and conspicuousness of these two buildings, we have an accurate index of the relative import-ance of the ideas of the Madonna and of Christ, in the modern Italian mind.

[93] Mendelssohn is more impressed with the art than the music in the Frari, as he writes to his old teacher of composition, Professor Zelter, in 1830; from *Letters from Italy and Switzerland* by Felix Mendelssohn-Bartholdy.

(Felix Mendelssohn-Bartholdy (1809–1847) set off, with Goe-the's encouragement, on his Grand Tour of Italy in 1830, having already spent eleven years as a composer and per-former. He was to pay no fewer than ten visits to England, where he played regularly for Queen Victoria.)

My family have no doubt told you of the exhilarating impression made on me by the first sight of the plains of Italy. I hurry from one enjoyment to another hour by hour, and constantly see something novel and fresh; but immediately on my arrival I discovered some masterpieces of art, which I study with deep attention, and contemplate daily for a couple of hours at least. These are three pictures by Titian. The 'Presentation of Mary as a Child in the Temple;' the 'Assump-tion of the Virgin;' and the 'Entombment of Christ.' There is also a portrait by Giorgione, representing a girl with a cithern in her hand, plunged in thought, and looking forth from the picture in serious meditation (she is apparently about to begin a song, and you feel as if you must do the same): besides many others.

To see these alone would be worth a journey to Venice; for the fruitfulness, genius, and devotion of the great men who painted these pictures, seem to emanate from them afresh as often as you gaze at their works, and I do not much regret that I have scarcely heard any music here; for I suppose I must not venture to include the music of the angels, in the 'Assumption,' encircling Mary with joyous shouts of welcome; one gaily beating the tambourine, a couple of others blowing away on strange crooked flutes, while another charming group are singing – or the music floating in the thoughts of the cithern player. I have only once heard anything on the organ, and miserable it was. I was gazing at Titian's 'Martyrdom of St Peter' in the Franciscan Church. Divine service was going on, and nothing inspires me with more solemn awe than when on the very spot for which they were originally created and painted, those ancient pictures in all their grandeur, gradually steal forth out of the darkness in which the long lapse of time has veiled them.

As I was earnestly contemplating the enchanting evening landscape with its trees, and angels among the boughs, the organ commenced. The first sound was quite in harmony with my feelings; but the second, third, and in fact all the rest, quickly roused me from my reveries, and sent me straight home, for the man was playing in church and during divine service, and in the presence of respectable people, thus:

with the 'Martyrdom of St Peter' actually close beside him! I
was therefore in no great hurry to make the acquaintance of
the organist. There is no regular Opera here at this moment,
and the gondoliers no longer sing Tasso's stanzas; moreover,
what I have hitherto seen of modern Venetian art, consists of
poems framed and glazed on the subject of Titian's pictures,
or Rinaldo and Armida, by a new Venetian painter, or a St
Cecilia by a ditto, besides various specimens of architecture
in no style at all; as all these are totally insignificant, I cling
to the ancient masters, and study how they worked. Often,
after doing so, I feel a musical inspiration, and since I came
here I have been busily engaged in composition.

[94] In the Frari, Ruskin saves his most withering scorn
for the tomb of Doge Giovanni Pesaro, dating from
1669; from *The Stones of Venice*.

We are now in the latter half of the seventeenth century; the
progress of corruption has in the meantime been incessant,
and sculpture has here lost its taste and learning as well as its
feeling. The monument is a huge accumulation of theatrical
scenery in marble: four colossal negro caryatides, grinning
and horrible, with faces of black marble and white eyes,
sustain the first story of it; above this, two monsters, long-
necked, half dog and half dragon, sustain an ornamental
sarcophagus, on the top of which the full-length statue of the
Doge in robes of state stands forward with its arms expanded,
like an actor courting applause, under a huge canopy of
metal, like the roof of a bed, painted crimson and gold; on
each side of him are sitting figures of genii, unintelligible
personifications gesticulating in Roman armour; below,
between the negro caryatides, are two ghastly figures in
bronze, half corpse, half skeleton, carrying tablets on which
is written the eulogium: but in large letters, graven in gold,
the following words are the first and last that strike the eye;
the first two phrases, one on each side, on tablets in the lower
story, the last under the portrait statue above:

VIXIT ANNOS LXX   DEVIXIT ANNO MDCLIX
'HIC REVIXIT ANNO MDCLXIX'

We have here, at last, the horrible images of death in violent contrast with the defiant monument, which pretends to bring the resurrection down to earth, 'Hic revixit'; and it seems impossible for false taste and base feeling to sink lower.

Besides these tombs, the traveller ought to notice carefully that of Pietro Bernardo, a first-rate example of Renaissance work; nothing can be more detestable or mindless in general design, or more beautiful in execution. Examine especially the griffins, fixed in admiration of bouquets at the bottom. The fruit and flowers which arrest the attention of the griffins may well arrest the traveller's also; nothing can be finer of their kind. The tomb of Canova, *by* Canova, cannot be missed; consummate in science, intolerable in affectation, ridiculous in conception, null and void to the uttermost in invention and feeling.

[95] The church of S. Giustina, on the Rio dei Mendi-canti a little to the north of SS. Giovanni e Paolo, is now deconsecrated: during the last two centuries of the Republic, however, it was the scene of an annual visit by the Doge on 7 October, the Saint's day, which was also the anniversary of the Battle of Lepanto. Goethe was there in 1786; from his *Italian Journey*.

(The Doge of whom Goethe writes was Venice's penultimate, Paolo Renier. Despite the impression he made on Goethe, he was in fact unpopular in the city, and notoriously corrupt.)

This morning I attended High Mass at the Church of Santa Giustina, where, on this day of the year, the Doge has always to be present to commemorate an old victory over the Turks. The gilded barges, carrying the Prince and some of the nobility, and at the little square; oddly-liveried boatmen ply their red-painted oars; on shore the clergy and religious orders, holding lighted candles on poles and silver candelabra, jostle each other and stand around waiting; gangways covered with carpets are laid across from the vessels to the shore; first come the Savii in their long violet robes, then the Senators in their red ones, and, last, the old Doge, in his long golden gown and ermine cape and wearing his golden Phrygian cap, leaves the barge while three servants bear the train of his robe.

To watch all this happening in a little square before the doors of a church on which Turkish standards were displayed was like seeing an old tapestry of beautiful colour and design, and to me, as a fugitive from the north, it gave keen pleasure. At home, where short coats are *de rigueur* for all festive occasions and the finest ceremony we can imagine is a parade of shouldered muskets, an affair like this might look out of place, but here these trailing robes and unmilitary ceremonies are perfectly in keeping.

The Doge is a good-looking, imposing man. Although, apparently, in ill health, he holds himself, for the sake of dignity, erect under his heavy gown. He looks like the grand-papa of the whole race and his manner is gracious and courteous. His garments were very becoming and the little transparent bonnet he wore under his cap did not offend the eye, for it rested upon the most lovely snow-white hair.

He was accompanied by about fifty noblemen, most of them very good-looking. I did not see a single ugly one. Some were tall and had big heads, framed in blond curly wigs. As for their faces, the features were prominent and the flesh, though soft and white, had nothing repellently flabby about it. They looked rather intelligent, self-assured, unaffected and cheerful.

When they had all taken their places in the church and High Mass had begun, the religious orders entered in pairs by the west door, were blessed with holy water, bowed to the high altar, to the Doge and to the nobility, and then left by a side door to the right.

[96] The church of the Gesuiti – many of us, I suspect, would share the opinion of William Dean Howells in the 1860s; from his *Venetian Life*.

But by all means the coldest church in the city is that of the Jesuits, which those who have seen it will remember for its famous marble drapery. This base, mechanical surprise (for it is a trick and not art) is effected by inlaying the white marble of columns and pulpits and altars with a certain pattern of verd-antique. The workmanship is marvelously skillful, and the material costly, but it only gives the church the effect of being draped in damask linen; and even where the marble is carven in vast and heavy folds over a pulpit to simulate a curtain, or wrought in figures on the steps of the high-altar to represent a carpet, it has no richness of effect, but a poverty, a coldness, a harshness indescribably table-clothy. I think all this has tended to chill the soul of the sacristan, who is the feeblest and thinnest sacristan conceivable, with a frost of white hair on his temples quite incapable of thawing. In this dreary sanctuary is one of Titian's great paintings, The Martyrdom of St Lawrence, to which (though it is so cunningly disposed as to light that no one ever yet saw the whole picture at once) you turn involuntarily, envious of the Saint toasting so comfortably on his gridiron amid all that frigidity.

[97] The glorious Tintorettos – more than sixty of them – in the Scuola di S. Rocco have recently been magnificently restored; they are infinitely easier to enjoy nowadays than when Henry James wrote the following description in 1880. The impact of the great upper room, however, and of the vast *Crucifixion*, could never have been anything but overwhelming. From his *Italian Hours*.

It may be said as a general thing that you never see the Tintoret. You admire him, you adore him, you think him the greatest of painters, but in the great majority of cases your eyes fail to deal with him. This is partly his own fault; so many of his works have turned to blackness and are positively rotting in their frames. At the Scuola di San Rocco, where there are acres of him, there is scarcely anything at all adequately visible save the immense 'Crucifixion' in the upper story. It is true that in looking at this huge composition you look at many pictures; it has not only a multitude of figures but a wealth of episodes; and you pass from one of these to the other as if you were 'doing' a gallery. Surely no single picture in the world contains more of human life; there is everything in it, including the most exquisite beauty. It is one of the greatest things of art; it is always interesting. There are works of the artist which contain touches more exquisite, revelations of beauty more radiant, but there is no other vision of so intense a reality, an execution so splendid. The interest, the impressiveness, of that whole corner of Venice, however melancholy the effect of its gorgeous and ill-lighted chambers, gives a strange importance to a visit to the Scuola. Nothing that all travellers go to see appears to suffer less from the incursions of travellers. It is one of the loneliest booths of the bazaar, and the author of these lines has always had the good fortune, which he wishes to every other traveller, of having it to himself. I think most visitors find the place rather alarming and wicked-looking. They walk about a while among the fitful figures that gleam here and there out of the great tapestry (as it were) with which the painter has hung all the walls, and then, depressed and bewildered by the portentous solemnity of these objects, by strange glimpses of unnatural scenes, by the echo of their lonely footsteps on the vast stone floors, they take a hasty departure, finding themselves again, with a sense of release from danger, a sense that the *genius loci* was a sort of mad white-washer who worked with a bad mixture, in the bright light of the *campo*, among the beggars, the orange-vendors and the passing gondolas. Solemn indeed is the place, solemn and strangely suggestive, for the simple reason that we shall scarcely find four walls elsewhere that inclose within a like area an equal quantity of genius. The air is thick with it and dense and difficult to breathe; for it was genius that was not happy, inasmuch as it lacked the art to fix itself for ever. It is not immortality that we breathe at the Scuola di San Rocco, but conscious, reluctant mortality.

[98] Two pictures in S. Giovanni Crisostomo appeal to Henry James; from *Italian Hours*.

There is another noble John Bellini, one of the very few in which there is no Virgin, at San Giovanni Crisostomo – a St Jerome, in a red dress, sitting aloft upon the rocks and with a

landscape of extraordinary purity behind him. The absence of
the peculiarly erect Madonna makes it an interesting surprise
among the works of the painter and gives it a somewhat less
strenuous air. But it has brilliant beauty and the St Jerome is
a delightful old personage.

The same church contains another great picture for which
the haunter of these places must find a shrine apart in his
memory; one of the most interesting things he will have seen,
if not the most brilliant. Nothing appeals more to him than
three figures of Venetian ladies which occupy the foreground
of a smallish canvas of Sebastian del Piombo, placed above
the high altar of San Giovanni Crisostomo. Sebastian was a
Venetian by birth, but few of his productions are to be seen
in his native place; few indeed are to be seen anywhere. The
picture represents the patron-saint of the church, accompanied by other saints and by the worldly votaries I have
mentioned. These ladies stand together on the left, holding in
their hands little white caskets; two of them are in profile, but
the foremost turns her face to the spectator. This face and
figure are almost unique among the beautiful things of Venice,
and they leave the susceptible observer with the impression of
having made, or rather having missed, a strange, a dangerous,
but a most valuable, acquaintance. The lady, who is superbly
handsome, is the typical Venetian of the sixteenth century,
and she remains for the mind the perfect flower of that
society. Never was there a greater air of breeding, a deeper
expression of tranquil superiority. She walks a goddess – as if
she trod without sinking the waves of the Adriatic. It is
impossible to conceive a more perfect expression of the
aristocratic spirit either in its pride or in its benignity. This
magnificent creature is so strong and secure that she is gentle,
and so quiet that in comparison all minor assumptions of
calmness suggest only a vulgar alarm. But for all this there
are depths of possible disorder in her light-coloured eye.

The Riva

[99] Petrarch describes the triumphant return of the Venetian fleet after it had put down the Cretan Rebellion in 1364, as he saw it from his house on the Riva, just beyond the Ponte del Sepolcro (a plaque marks the spot today); from Petrarch's *Epistolae de rerum familiaribus et variae*. Translated by John Julius Norwich.

It was the fourth of June – perhaps the sixth hour of the day. I was standing at my window, looking out to sea ... when one of those long ships that they call galleys entered the harbour, all garlanded with green boughs, its oars thrusting through the water, its sails swollen by the wind. So swift was its advance that we could soon see the joyful faces of the sailors and a group of laughing young men, crowned with leaves and waving banners above their heads in greeting to their native city, victorious but still unaware of her triumph. By now the lookouts on the highest tower had signalled the arrival and, all unbidden but in universal excitement and curiosity, the citizens came flocking to the shore. As the ship came in we could see the enemy standards draped over her stern, and no shred of doubt remained in our minds that she brought news of victory ... And when he heard it Doge Lorenzo wished with all his people to give thanks and praises to God with splendid ceremonies throughout the city, but especially at the Basilica of St Mark the Evangelist than which there is nothing, I believe, on earth more beautiful.

[100] The story of the bequest of Petrarch's library to the Republic, in return for the house on the Riva which the Republic presented to him; from *The Life of Petrarch* by Mrs Dobson.

(The mystery of Petrarch's library, which disappeared shortly after his death, has long puzzled scholars.)

Petrarch always took his books when he went any long journey, which rendered travelling incommodious and expensive to him, as he required for their conveyance such a number of horses. When he had been some time at Venice, it came into his mind not to offer these books to a religious order, as he once proposed, but to place this treasure in the care of the republic, to whom he wrote as follows:

'Francis Petrarch desires to have the blessed evangelist Mark for the heir of those books he has, and may have, on condition that they shall neither be sold or separated; and that they shall all be placed in safety, sheltered from fire and water, and preserved with care for ever for his honour, and the use and amusement of the noble and learned persons of this city. If he makes this deposit, it is not because he has a great idea of his books, or believes he has formed a fine library; but he hopes by this means, the illustrious city of Venice will acquire other trusts of the same kind from the public; that the citizens who love their country, the nobles above all, and even some strangers, will follow his example, and leave their books to this church at their death, which may one day become a great library, and equal those of the ancients. Every one must see how honourable this will be to the republic. Petrarch will be much flattered with having been the original source of so great a good. If his design succeeds, he will explain himself more minutely hereafter upon this subject; in the mean time, he offers to execute this his promise.'

This proposal having been examined and approved, and the procurators of the church of St Mark having offered to be at the necessary expenses for the placing and preserving these books, the republic made the following decree:

'Considering the offer that messire Francis Petrarch has made us, whose reputation is so great, that we do not remember to have met in the Christian world, with a moral philosopher and poet united who can compare with him; persuaded that this offer may contribute to the glory of God and of St Mark, and do much honour to our city, we will accept it on the conditions he has made; and we order such a sum to be taken from our revenue as will purchase him a house for his life, according to the advice of the governor, counsellors, and chiefs.'

In compliance with this decree, Petrarch had assigned for his dwelling, and that of his books, a large mansion called the Palace of the Two Towers, belonging to the family of Molina. It is at present the monastery of the monks of St Sepulchre.

This house was of an immense size, and had two very high towers. It was delightfully situated fronting the port. Petrarch was delighted to see the vessels come in and go out. 'These vessels,' says he, 'resemble a mountain swimming on the sea, and go into all parts of the world amidst a thousand perils, to carry our wines to the English, our honey to the Scythians; our saffron, our oils, our linen, to the Syrians, to the Armenians, to the Persians, and the Arabians; and, which is more incredible, they carry our woods to the Achaians and Egyptians. From all these countries they bring merchandises which they carry all over Europe. They go even to the Tanais: the navigation of our sea extends no farther than that towards the north; but when they are there, they quit their ships, and go to trade in the Indies and to China, and, after having passed the Ganges and the Caucasus, they go by land as far as the Eastern Ocean. Behold what men will do for the thirst of gold!'

Petrarch's view toward the republic was fulfilled; several cardinals left their libraries to it after his example, and it appeared the best and fastest perpetuation of many valuable authors; but by the humidity of the place, they were almost all destroyed, together with a precious manuscript written by the evangelist St Mark.

[101] Stendhal, in a gondola off the Riva in 1817, deplores the Austrian occupation of Venice; from *Rome, Naples and Florence* by Stendhal, translated by Richard N. Coe.

(Marie-Henri Beyle ('Stendhal') (1783–1842) settled for some years in Milan after service in the disastrous Russian campaign of 1812. Returning to Paris, he quickly gained fame as a novelist (*Le Rouge et le Noir; La Chartreuse de Parme*).)

One o'clock in the morning, in the garden pavilion built by the Viceroy. I haven't the heart to write. I contemplate that quiet sea and, in the distance, that tongue of land known as the Lido, that separates the lagoon from the Adriatic and against which the sea breaks with a muffled roar; a line of gold marks the crest of each wave; a beautiful moon casts her peaceful light over the tranquil scene; the air is so clear that I can make out the masts of the ships at Malamocco, in the open sea – and this most romantic of views can be enjoyed from the most civilized of cities. How I loathe Bonaparte for having sacrificed all this to Austria! In twelve minutes, my gondola carried me the whole length of the Riva degli Schiavoni and deposited me at the Piazzetta, at the foot of the lion of St Mark. Venice was more in the path of civilization than London and Paris. Today, there are fifty thousand poor. The Palazzo Vendramin on the Grand Canal, is on sale for a thousand *louis*. It cost twenty-five thousand to build, and was still worth ten thousand in 1794.

The Arsenal

[102] The earliest description of the Venetian Arsenal is found in the twenty-first canto of Dante's *Inferno*; the translation is by Dorothy L. Sayers.

Quale ne l'arzana de' Viniziani
  Bolle l'inverno la tenace pece
  A rimpalmar li legni lor non sani,
Che navicar non ponno; e 'n quelle vece
  Chi fa suo legno novo e chi ristoppa
  Le coste a quel che più viaggi fece;
Chi ribatte da proda e chi da poppa;
  Altri fa remi e altri volge sarte;
  Chi terzeraolo e artimon rintoppa;
Tal, non per foco, ma per divin' arte,
  Bollia là giuso una pegola spessa,
  Che 'nviscava la ripa d'ogni parte.

For as at Venice, in the Arsenal
  In winter-time, they boil the gummy pitch
  To caulk such ships as need an overhaul,
Now that they cannot sail – instead of which
  One builds him a new boat, one toils to plug

Seams strained by many a voyage, others stitch
Canvas to patch a tattered jib or lug,
    Hammer at the prow, hammer at the stern, or twine
    Ropes, or shave oars, refit and make all snug –
So, not by fire, but by the art divine,
    A thick pitch boiled down there, spattering the brink
    With viscous glue . . .

[103] A well-to-do Spanish visitor in 1438 is particularly impressed by the Arsenal; from *Pero Tafur, travels and adventures 1435-1439* translated by Malcolm Letts.

(Pero Tafur (?1410–?1484) was born in Cordoba, and as a young man made his five-year journey through Europe to the Levant. His *Travels* were first published only in 1874, in Madrid.)

There is an arsenal at Venice which is the finest in the world, as well for artillery as for things necessary for navigation. The sea flows into it, and the ships enter the water there after they pass the castles. They told me that, including the war galleys and merchant vessels, and others which were in the water and on the stocks, there were altogether eighty galleys, besides other ships. One day, coming from hearing Mass in St Mark's, I saw about twenty men enter the square, some carrying benches and others tables and others chairs, and others large bags of money; thereupon a trumpet was blown, and the great bell, which they call the Council Bell, was rung, and in an hour the square was full of men who received pay and went into the arsenal. And as one enters the gate there is a great street on either hand with the sea in the middle, and on one side are windows opening out of the houses of the arsenal, and the same on the other side, and out came a galley towed by a boat, and from the windows they handed out to them, from one the cordage, from another the bread, from another the arms, and from another the balistas and mortars, and so from all sides everything which was required, and when the galley had reached the end of the street all the men required were on board, together with the complement of oars, and she was equipped from end to end. In this manner

there came out ten galleys, fully armed, between the hours of
three and nine. I know not how to describe what I saw there,
whether in the manner of its construction or in the management of the workpeople, and I do not think there is anything
finer in the world. If the Venetians desired to show their
strength, the enemies of the Faith in those parts would not, in
my opinion, have a single ship at sea, still less on the coast,
nor would they dare to match themselves against such a
powerful enemy.

[104] A sixteenth-century Englishman is amazed by the
scale of operations in the Arsenal – though he was
wrong about the number of workers in the Arsenal.
There were, in fact, 16,000 of them; from *The History
of Italy* by William Thomas.

(William Thomas, the date of whose birth is unknown, was
in 1544 'constrained by misfortune' (probably his religious
opinions) 'to abandon the place of his nativity' and travelled
to Italy. He returned in 1549 and the following year was
made Clerk of the Council to Edward VI; but he fell foul of
Bloody Mary and in 1554 was hanged, drawn and quartered
at Tyburn.)

Finally, the Arsenale in mine eyes exceedeth all the rest. For
they have well near 200 galleys in such order that upon a
very small warning they may be furnished out unto the sea.
Besides that, for every day in the year (when they would go
to the coast) they should be able to make a new galley,
having such a staple of timber (which in the water within
the Arsenal hath lien a-seasoning, some twenty year, some
forty, some an hundred, and some I wot not how long) that
it is a wonder to see it. And every one of these galleys hath
his covering or house by himself on the dry land so that the
long lying unoccupied cannot hurt them. Their masts, cables,
sails, anchors, rudders, oars and every other thing are ready
in houses of offices by themselves, that, unseen, it is almost
incredible, with such a quantity of artillery, both for sea and
land, as made me wonder, besides the harness and weapons
that suffice (as they say) to arm an 100,000 men. Finally, the

number of workmen waged for term of life about these exercises is wonderful. For by all that I could learn, their ordinary is never less than 600 working in the Arsenale, be it peace or war. And because they have such a number of boatmen that continually live by gain upon the water within the city, they need not to seek further for mariners to furnish their galleys withal. For it was credibly told me that there are no less than 12,000 boats daily serving in those their channels, and almost no boat rowed but of a sufficient mariner.

[105] By the beginning of the seventeenth century the Arsenal was one of the principal tourist sights of the city. Thomas Coryat, despite some shaky etymology – the word actually comes from the Arabic *Dar Sena'a*, 'house of industry' – perfectly captures the wide-eyed wonder that was the reaction of most visitors; from *Coryat's Crudities*.

I was at the Arsenall which is so called, *quasi ars navalis*, because there is exercised the Art of making tackling, and all other necessary things for shipping. Certainly I take it to be the richest and best furnished storehouse for all manner of munition both by Sea and Land not only of all Christendome, but also of all the world, in so much that all strangers whatsoever are moved with great admiration when they contemplate the situation, the greatness, the strength, and incredible store of provision thereof; yea I have often read that when as in the time of *Charles* the fifth a certaine great Prince that hapned to lie in Venice, one *Albertus Marquesse* of Guasto the Emperours Generall of his forces in Italy, came into this Arsenall: he was so desirous to survey all the particular furnitures and tacklings thereof, that hee spent a whole day in viewing the same, and in the evening when he went forth, being rapt with admiration, he called it the eighth miracle of the world, and said, that were he put to his choice to be lord either of foure of the strongest cities of Italy or of the Arsenall, he would preferre the Arsenall, before them. It is situate at the East end of the citie, in compasse two miles, and fortified with a strong wall that goeth round about it, in which are built many faire towers for the better ornament thereof. There are continually one thousand five hundred men working in it, unto whom there is paid every weeke two thousand crownes which doe amount to six hundred pound sterling, in the whole yeare twenty eight thousand and six hundred pound. Also those workemen that have wrought so long in the Arsenall that they are become decrepit and unable to worke any longer, are maintained in the same at the charge of the citie during their lives. Here are alwaies kept two hundred and fifty gallies, each having a severall roome fairely roofed over to cover and defend it from the injury of the weather, and fifty more are alwaies at Sea. The fairest gally of all is the Bucentoro, the upper parts whereof in the outside are richly gilt. It is a thing of marvailous worth, the richest gallie of all the world; for it cost one hundred thousand crownes which is thirty thousand pound sterling. A worke so exceeding glorious, that I never heard or read of the like in any place of the world, these onely excepted, viz: that of Cleopatra, which she so exceeding sumptuously adorned with cables of silke and other passing beautiful ornaments; and those that the Emperour *Caligula* built with timber of Ceder and poupes and sternes of ivory . . .

It is said that the Arsenall is able to furnish of all men both by sea and land about a hundred and fifty thousand. I was in one of their armouries which containeth three severall roomes, whereof the first armour onely for sea men, so much as would arme men enough to furnish fifty Galleys: the second for sixe hundred footemen: there I saw abundance of helmets, shields, breastplates, swords &c. Their swordes were pretily placed upon some cores opposite to each other, where some were set compasse-wise, some athwart and a crosse, some one way and some another, with such witty and pretty invention, that a man could not but commend the deviser thereof. I went to their places where they make their Anchors, and saw some making: also I saw great peeces of Ordinance making, whereof they have in the whole Arsenall at the least sixe thousand, which is more then twelve of the richest armouries of al Christendome have. Also I was in other roomes where was much canvasse and thred, and many other necessaries to make sailes. In one large room whereof there is prettily painted in a wall the History of the warres betwixt the Venetians under the conduct of their Generall Captaine *Barthelmew Coleon* of Bergomo, and the Emperor at Padua, where I saw their armies couragiously confronting each other, and the Imperialists by certaine witty stratagems that *Barthelmew Coleon* devised, were shamefully put to flight. Also I saw their roome wherein they make nothing but ropes and cables, others wherein they make onely Oares, and others also wherein they make their Anchors. Many other notable things were to be scene here, as many spoiles taken from the Turkes at the battell of *Lepanto, Anno* 1571, &c. which by reason of a certaine sinister accident that hapned unto mee when I was in the Arsenall, I could not see.

I have read that the Arsenall was extremely wasted with fire in the time of their Duke *Peter Lauredanus*, which was about the yeare 1568, much of their munition being utterly consumed to nothing, and that the noyse of the fire was so hideous that it was heard at the least forty miles from Venice. But since that time it hath been so well repaired that I think it was never so faire as at this present.

[106] John Evelyn in 1645 is, as one might expect, somewhat less breathless; from *The Diary of John Evelyn* edited by William Bray.

The Arsenal is thought to be one of the best furnish'd in the world. We entred by a strong port always guarded, and ascending a spacious gallery saw armes of back, breast, and head, for many thousands: in another were saddles, over them ensignes taken from the Turks. Another Hall is for the meeting of the Senat; passing a graff are the smiths forges, where they are continualy at work on ankers and iron work. Neere it is a well of fresh water, which they impute to two rhinoceros's horns which they say lie in it and will preserve it from ever being empoison'd. Then we came to where the carpenters were building their magazines of oares, masts, &c. for an hundred gallys and ships, which have all their aparell and furniture neere them. Then the founderie, where they cast ordinance; the forge is 450 paces long, and one of them has thirteen furnaces. There is one cannon weighing 16,573 lbs cast whilst Henry the Third dined, and put into a gally built, rigg'd, and fitted for launching within that time. They have also armes for 12 galeasses, which are vessels to rowe, of almost 150 foote long and 30 wide, not counting prow or poop, and contain 28 banks of oares, each 7 men, and to carry 300 men, with 3 masts. In another a magazin for 50 gallys, and place for some hundreds more. Here stands the Bucentaur, with a most ample deck, and so contriv'd that the slaves are not seene, having on the poop a throne for the Doge to sit, when he gos in triumph to espouse the Adriatic. Here is also a gallery of 200 yards long for cables, and over that a magazine of hemp. Over against these are their saltpetre houses, and a large row of cells or houses to protect their gallies from the weather. Over the gate as we go out, is a roome full of greate and small guns, some of which discharge six times at once. Then there is a court full of can'on, bullets, chaines, grapples, granados, &c. and over that arms for 800,000 men and by themselves armes for 400 taken from some that were in a plot against the State; together with weapons of offence and defence for 62 ships; 32 pieces of ordnance on carriages taken from the Turks, and one prodigious mortarpiece. In a word, 'tis not to be reckoned up what this large place containes of this sort. There were now 23 gallys, and 4 gally-grossi of 100 oares of a side. The whole Arsenal is wall'd about and may be in compasse about 3 miles, with towres for the watch, besides that the sea invirons it. The workmen, who are ordinarily 500, march out in military order, and every evening receive their pay thro' a small hole in the gate where the Governor lives.

[107] Dr John Moore, in the Arsenal in 1777 with the young Duke of Hamilton, judges the Bucintoro to be unseaworthy, though much admired by landsmen; from *A View of Society and Manners in Italy* by John Moore MD.

A few days after our arrival at Venice, we met the Archduke and Duchess, at the house of the Imperial Ambassador . . .

Next day the Duke of Hamilton accompanied the Archduke and Duchess to the arsenal. They were attended by a deputation from the Senate . . .

The arsenal at Venice is a fortification of between two and three miles in compass. On the ramparts are many little watchtowers, where sentinels are stationed. Like the arsenal at Toulon, it is at once a dockyard, and repository for naval and military stores. Here the Venetians build their ships, cast their cannon, make their cables, sails, anchors, &c. The arms are arranged here as in other places of the same kind, in large rooms divided into narrow walks by long walls of muskets, pikes, and halberts. Every thing having been prepared before the Archduke and Duchess arrived, a cannon was cast in their presence. After this the company were conducted on board the Bucentaur, or vessel in which the Doge is carried to espouse the Adriatic. Here they were regaled with wine and sweetmeats, the Venetian nobles doing the honours of the entertainment.

The Bucentaur is kept under cover, and never taken out but for the espousals. It is formed for containing a very numerous company, is finely gilt and ornamented within, and loaded on the outside with emblematical figures in sculpture. This vessel may possibly be admired by landsmen, but will not much charm a seaman's eye, being a heavy broad-bottomed machine, which draws little water, and consequently may be easily overset in a gale of wind. Of this, however, there is no great danger, as two precautions are taken to prevent such an accident; one of which seems calculated to quiet the minds of believers, and the other to give confidence to the most incredulous. The first is used by the Patriarch, who, as soon as the vessel is afloat, takes care to pour into the sea some holy water, which is believed to have the virtue of preventing or allaying storms. The second is entrusted to the Admiral, who has the discretionary power of postponing the marriage ceremony, when the bride seems in the smallest degree boisterous. One of the virtues of the holy water, that of allaying storms, is by this means rendered superfluous.

But when the weather is quite favourable the ceremony is

performed every Ascension Day. The solemnity is announced in the morning by the ringing of bells and firing of cannon. About mid-day the Doge, attended by a numerous party of the Senate and clergy, goes on board the Bucentaur; the vessel is rowed a little way into the sea, accompanied by the splendid yachts of the foreign Ambassadors, the gondolas of the Venetian nobility, and an incredible number of barks and gallies of every kind. Hymns are sung, and a band of music performs, while the Bucentaur and her attendants slowly move towards St Lido [*sic*], a small island, two miles from Venice. Prayers are then said; after which the Doge drops a ring of no great value into the sea, pronouncing these words – 'Desponsamus te, Mare, in signum veri perpetuique dominii.' The sea, like a modest bride, assents by her silence, and the marriage is deemed valid and secure to all intents and purposes.

Certain it is, the time has been, when the Doge had entire possession of, and dominion over, his spouse; but, for a considerable time past, her favours have been shared by several other lovers; or, according to that violent metaphor of Otway's,

> – now
> Their Great Duke shrinks, trembling in his palace,
> And sees his wife, the Adriatic, plough'd,
> Like a lewd whore, by bolder prows than his.

After viewing every thing in the arsenal, the Archduke and Duchess, with all the company, were invited on board some boats, which had been prepared for their reception. They were directly rowed to that part of the lake from whence there was the most advantageous view of Venice, a band of music performing all the time; while the sailors, in two or three small boats, were employed in fishing oysters, which they opened and presented to the company.

[108] In fact, the Bucintoro was by no means invariably admired by landsmen either, as Lady Miller had already written, six years earlier; from *Letters from Italy . . . in the years 1770 and 1771* by Anna, Lady Miller.

M– has been to see the Arsenal and the *Bucentaure*: as to the first, he says, it agrees with the description the writers of travels have given of it, but does not think it contains any thing that might compensate to me for the trouble of visiting it this hot weather. He thinks the *Bucentaure* the ugliest, most tawdry, worst contrived vessel he ever saw; loaded with ornaments and gilding, and totally void of grace.

The Ghetto

---

[109] It was in 1516 that the Venetian government decided that the Jews should henceforth be segregated in the area of the New Foundry, popularly known as the Ghetto, as the diarist Marin Sanudo records on 26 March of that year; from his *Diarii*. Translated by John Julius Norwich.

(Marin Sanudo (1466–1536), the Venetian scholar and diarist, kept a detailed diary in the Venetian dialect from January 1496 to March 1533. It was published in 58 volumes in the late nineteenth century.)

This morning, the Councillor Zaccaria Dolfin proposed in the *Collegio* that the Jews, who were an evil influence in the Republic and were responsible for much corruption in the State, contriving as they did to go against the laws through the operation of their synagogues, should all be sent to live in the New Ghetto, which is like a fortress and could be sealed off with a wall and drawbridges . . .

And then there was summoned the Jew Anselm and two other leaders of the Jews, and the Doge proposed to them that they should go and dwell in the New Ghetto, for they were holding their synagogues in the city contrary to the law. And Anselmo protested that the proposal was unjust in many respects: first, because if they did not live among the Christians and gentlemen they would be liable to robberies and victimization; they must live near the guard at the Rialto, not far away from any assistance. Moreover it had been promised by the Council of Ten that no further changes would be made to their condition, so that this would be a breach of trust, and that those who had paid so much money for their counters and offices on the Rialto would now be ruined . . .

(Alas, Anselm's pleas were ignored. To the Ghetto the Jews went, and there they were obliged to remain until Napoleon demolished the walls in 1797. But by then they had grown fond of the place; few of them left it, and a considerable number continue to live there today.)

[110] Thomas Coryat, visiting the Ghetto in 1608, sees a Jewish community for the first time – the Jews having been expelled from England by Edward I in 1290, not to be readmitted until the days of the Commonwealth; from *Coryat's Crudities*.

I was at a place where the whole fraternity of the Iews dwelleth together, which is called the Ghetto, being an Iland: for it is inclosed round about with water. It is thought there are of them in all betwixt five and sixe thousand. They are distinguished and discerned from the Christians by their habites on their heads; for some of them doe weare hats and those redde, only those Iewes that are borne in the Westerne parts of the world, as in Italy, &c. but the easterne Iewes being otherwise called the Levantine Iewes, which are borne in Hierusalem, Alexandria, Constantinople, &c. weare Turbents upon their heads as the Turkes do: but the difference is this: the Turkes weare white, the Iewes yellow. By that word Turbent I understand a rowle of fine linnen wrapped together upon their heads, which serveth them instead of hats, whereof many have bin often worne by the Turkes in London. They have divers Synagogues in their Ghetto, at the least seven, where all of them, both men, women and children doe meete together upon their Sabboth, which is Saturday, to the end to doe their devotion, and serve God in their kinde, each company having a several Synagogue. In the midst of the Synagogue they have a round seat made of Wainscot, having eight open spaces therein, at two whereof which are at the sides, they enter into the seate as by dores. The Levite that readeth the law to them, hath before him at the time of divine service an exceeding long piece of parchment, rowled up upon two woodden handles: in which is written the whole summe and contents of *Moyses* law in Hebrew: that doth he (being discerned from the lay people onely by wearing of a redde cap, whereas the others doe weare redde hats) pronounce before the congregation not by a sober, distinct, and orderly reading, but by an exceeding loud yaling, undecent roaring, and as it were a beastly bellowing of it forth. And that after such a confused and hudling manner, that I thinke the hearers can very hardly understand him: sometimes he cries out alone, and sometimes againe some others serving as it were his Clerkes hard without his seate, and within, do roare with him, but so that his voyce (which he straineth so high as if he sung for a wager) drowneth all the rest. Amongst others that are within the roome with him, one is he that cometh purposely thither from his seat, to the end to reade the law, and pronounce some part of it with him, who when he is gone, another riseth from his seat, and commeth thither to supply his roome. This order they keepe from the beginning of service to the end. One custome I observed amongst them very irreverent and prophane, that none of them, eyther when they enter the Synagogue, or when they sit downe in their places, or when they goe forth againe, doe any reverence or obeysance, answerable to such a place of the worship of God, eyther by uncovering their heads, kneeling, or any other externall gesture, but boldly dash into the roome with their Hebrew bookes in their handes, and presently sit in their places, without any more adoe; every one of them whatsoever he be, man or childe, weareth a kinde of light yellowish vaile, made of Linse Woolsie (as I take it) over his shoulders, something worse then our courser Holland, which reacheth a little beneath the middle of their backes. They have a great company of candlestickes in each Synagogue made partly of glasse, and partly of brasse and pewter, which hang square about their Synagogue. For in that forme is their Synagogue built: of their candlestickes I told above sixty in the same Synagogue.

I observed some fewe of those Iewes especially some of the Levantines to bee such goodly and proper men, that then I said to my selfe our English proverbe: To looke like a Iewe (whereby is meant sometimes a weather beaten warp-faced fellow, sometimes a phrenticke and lunaticke person, sometimes one discontented) is not true. For indeed I noted some of them to be most elegant and sweet featured persons, which gave me occasion the more to lament their religion. For if they were Christians, then could I better apply unto them that excellent verse of the Poet, then I can now.

Gratior est pulchro veniens è corpore virtue. In the roome wherin they celebrate their divine service, no women sit, but have a loft or gallery proper to themselves only, where I saw many Iewish women, whereof some were as beautiful as ever I saw, and so gorgeous in their apparel, jewels, chaines of gold, and rings adorned with precious stones, that some of our English Countesses do scarce exceede them, having marvailous long trainee like Princesses that are borne up by waiting women serving for the same purpose. An argument to prove that many of the Iewes are very rich. One thing they observe in their service which is utterly condemned by our Saviour Christ, Battologia, that is a very tedious babling, and an often repetition of one thing, which cloied mine eares so much that I could not endure them any longer, having heard them at least an houre; for their service is almost three hours long. They are very religious in two things only, and no more, in that they worship no images, and that they keep their sabboth so strictly, that upon that day they will neither buy nor sell, nor do any secular, prophane, or irreligious exercise; (I would to God our Christians would imitate the Iewes herein) no not so much as dresse their victuals, which is alwaies done the day before, but dedicate and consecrate themselves wholy to the strict worship of God. Their circumcision they observe as duely as they did any time betwixt *Abraham* (in whose time it was first instituted) and the incarnation of Christ. For they use to circumcise euery male childe when he is eight dayes old, with a stony knife. But I had not the opportunitie to see it. Likewise they keepe many of those ancient feastes that were instituted by *Moyses*. Amongst the rest the feast of tabernacles is very ceremoniously observed by them. From swines flesh they abstaine as their ancient forefathers were wont to do, in which the Turkes do imitate them at this day.

Truely it is a most lamentable case for a Christian to consider the damnable estate of these miserable Iewes, in that they reject the true Messias and Saviour of their soules, hoping to be saved rather by the observation of those Mosaicall ceremonies, (the date whereof was fully expired at Christ's incarnation) then by the merits of the Saviour of the world, without whom all mankind shall perish. And as pitifull it is to see that fewe of them living in Italy are converted to the Christian religion. For this I understand is the maine impediment to their conversion: all their goodes are confiscated as soone as they embrace Christianity: and this I heard is the reason, because whereas many of them doe raise their fortunes by usury, in so much that they doe not only sheare, but also flea many a poore Christians estate by their griping extortion; it is therefore decreed by the Pope, and other free Princes in whose territories they live, that they shall make a restitution of all their ill gotten goods, and so disclogge their soules and consciences, when they are admitted by holy baptisme into the bosome of Christs Church. Seing then when their goods are taken from them at their conversion, they are left even naked, and destitute of their meanes of maintenance, there are fewer Iewes converted to Christianity in Italy, than in any country of Christendome. Whereas in Germany, Poland, and other places the Iewes that are converted (which doth often happen, as *Emanuel Tremellius* was converted in Germany) do enjoy their estates as they did before.

[111] A scene in a Venetian synagogue in the first half of the seventeenth century – the celebration of the Rejoicing of the Law – recalled by the apostate Giulio

Morosini; from *Personalities and Events in Jewish History* by Cecil Roth.

(Morosini, formerly Samuel Nahmias, lived in Venice and wrote a scurrilous polemic entitled *Via della Fede*.)

In the cities in which the Jews have a ghetto, the synagogues are kept open all day and all night ... Similarly in many places, and in particular at Venice, a sort of half-carnival is held on this evening: for many maidens and brides mask themselves, so as not to be recognized, and go to visit all the synagogues. The synagogues are similarly thronged at this period by Christian ladies and gentlemen, out of curiosity, more than at any other feast, to see the preparations ... There are present all nations: Spaniards, Levantines, Portuguese, Germans, Greeks, Italians and others, and each sings according to his own usage. Since they do not use instruments, some clap their hands above the head, some smite their thighs, some imitate the castanets with their fingers, some pretend to play the guitar by scraping their doublets. In short, they so act with these noises, jumpings and dancings, with strange contortions of their faces, their mouths, their arms and all their other members, that it appears to be Carnival mimicry ...

(Another, happier memory from the same source.)

I well remember what happened at Venice in my times, about 1628, if I am not mistaken, when many of the Jews fled from Mantua through the war and came to Venice. Since every sort of study then flourished at Mantua, the Jews had similarly applied themselves to music and to playing. When these arrived at Venice, there was formed in the ghetto of that city a Musical Academy, which met generally twice a week, in the evenings. It was frequented only by some of the principal and richest members of the community, who supported it, of whom I was one: and my master, Leo da Modena, was *maestro di cappella*. That year there served as Bridegrooms in this feast (the Rejoicing in the Law), as described above, two wealthy and splendid persons, one of whom was a member of this same Academy. They accordingly introduced into the

Spanish *Scuola* (very richly prepared, and adorned with a great quantity of silver and precious stones) two choirs with music, after our custom. The two evenings, that is, on the Eighth Day of the Feast and on the Rejoicing in the Law, part of the evening service was chanted according to a musical setting in Hebrew, as well as different Psalms: and the *Minha*, that is, Vespers, on the last day similarly with solemn music, which lasted for some hours into the night. There were present many members of the nobility, both gentlemen and ladies, who greatly applauded; so that it was necessary to station at the door many captains and officers, so that it could pass off quietly. Among the instruments an organ was also taken into the synagogue, but the rabbis would not allow it to be played, it being an instrument which is ordinarily played in our churches. But what! All this was a blaze of straw. The Academy lasted little, and the Music returned to its former state . . .

[112] John Evelyn attends a Jewish wedding in the Ghetto in 1646; from *The Diary of John Evelyn* edited by William Bray.

The next day I was conducted to the Ghetta, where the Jews dwell together as in a tribe or ward, where I was present at a marriage. The bride was clad in white, sitting in a lofty chaire, and cover'd with a white vaile; then two old Rabbies joyned them together, one of them holding a glasse of wine in his hand, which in the midst of the ceremony, pretending to deliver to the woman, he let fall, the breaking whereof was to signify the frailty of our nature, and that we must expect disasters and crosses amidst all enjoyments. This don, we had a fine banquet, and were brought into the bride-chamber, where the bed was dress'd up with flowers, and the counterpart strewed in workes. At this ceremony we saw divers very beautifull Portuguez Jewesses with whom we had some conversation.

[113] Richard Lassels in 1654 is unimpressed by a Venetian rabbi; from *The Voyage of Italy*.

Then we went to the Jews Synagogue, and there heard a
Rabbi make a homely homilie. He looked iust like a Puritan
Lecturer, without surplis, without cap; but with his hatt on,
and snaffeling devoutly thorough the nose. He preached in
Italian, but pittifully ill.

[114] The American Consul, William Dean Howells,
visits the Ghetto in the 1860s; from *Venetian Life* by W.
D. Howells.

It was a warm, sunny day in the fall, as I said; yet as we drew
near the Ghetto, we noticed in the air many white, floating
particles, like lazy, straggling flakes of snow. These we afterward found to be the down of multitudes of geese, which are
forever plucked by the whole apparent force of the populace,
– the fat of the devoted birds being substituted for lard in the
kitchens of the Ghetto, and their flesh for pork. As we
approached the obscure little riva at which we landed, a
blond young Israelite, lavishly adorned with feathers, came
running to know if we wished to see the church – by which
name he put the synagogue to the Gentile comprehension.
The street through which we passed had shops on either
hand, and at the doors groups of jocular Hebrew youth sat
plucking geese; while within, long files of all that was mortal
of geese hung from the rafters and the walls. The ground was
webbed with the feet of geese, and certain loutish boys, who
paused to look at us, had each a goose dragging at his heels,
in the forlorn and elongated manner peculiar to dead poultry.
The ground was stained with the blood of geese, and the
smell of roasting geese came out of the windows of the grim
and lofty houses.

Our guide was picturesque, but the most helpless and
inconclusive cicerone I ever knew; and while his long, hooked
Hebrew nose caught my idle fancy, and his soft blue eyes
excused a great deal of inefficiency, the aimless fashion in
which he mounted dirty staircases for the keys of the synagogue, and came down without them, and the manner in
which he shouted to the heads of unctuous Jessicas thrust out
of windows, and never gained the slightest information by his

efforts, were imbecilities that we presently found insupportable, and we gladly cast him off for a dark-faced Hebrew boy who brought us at once to the door of the Spanish synagogue.

Of seven synagogues in the Ghetto, the principal was built in 1655, by the Spanish Jews who had fled to Venice from the terrors of the Holy Office. Its exterior has nothing to distinguish it as a place of worship, and we reached the interior of the temple by means of some dark and narrow stairs. In the floor and on the walls of the passage-way were set tablets to the memory of rich and pious Israelites who had bequeathed their substance for the behoof of the sanctuary; and the sacristan informed us that the synagogue was also endowed with a fund by rich descendants of Spanish Jews in Amsterdam. These moneys are kept to furnish indigent Israelitish couples with the means of marrying, and any who claim the benefit of the fund are entitled to it. The sacristan – a little wiry man, with bead-black eyes, and of a shoemakerish presence – told us with evident pride that he was himself a descendant of the Spanish Jews. Howbeit, he was now many centuries from speaking the Castilian, which, I had read, was still used in the families of the Jewish fugitives from Spain to the Levant. He spoke, instead, the abominable Venetian of Cannaregio, with that Jewish thickness which distinguishes the race's utterance, no matter what language its children are born to. It is a curious philological fact, which I have heard repeatedly alleged by Venetians, and which is perhaps worth noting here, that Jews speaking their dialect, have not only this thickness of accent, but also a peculiarity of construction which marks them at once.

We found the contracted interior of the synagogue hardly worth looking at. Instead of having any thing oriental or peculiar in its architecture, it was in a bad spirit of Renaissance art. A gallery encircled the inside, and here the women, during worship, sat apart from the men, who had seats below, running back from either side of the altar. I had no right, coming from a Protestant land of pews, to indulge in that sentimentality; but I could not help being offended to see that each of these seats might be lifted up and locked into the upright back and thus placed beyond question at the disposal of the owner: I like the freedom and equality in the Catholic churches much better. The sacristan brought a ponderous silver key, and unlocking the door behind the pulpit, showed us the Hebrew Scriptures used during the service by the Rabbi. They formed an immense parchment volume, and were rolled in silk upon a wooden staff. This was the sole object of interest in the synagogue, and its inspection concluded our visit.

We descended the narrow stairs and emerged upon the piazza which we had left. It was only partly paved with brick, and was very dirty. The houses which surrounded it were on the outside old and shabby, and, even in this Venice of lofty edifices, remarkably high. A wooden bridge crossed a vile canal to another open space, where once congregated the merchants who sell antique furniture, old pictures, and objects of vertu. They are now, however, found everywhere in the city, and most of them are on the Grand Canal, where they heap together marvelous collections, and establish authenticities beyond cavil. 'Is it an original?' asked a young lady who was visiting one of their shops, as she paused before an attributive Veronese, or – what know I? – perhaps a Titian. '*Sì, signora, originalissimo!*'

The Grand Canal, canals and gondolas

[115] Pietro Aretino describes his view of the Grand Canal in a letter addressed to his friend Titian in May 1544; from *Aretino, Selected Letters* translated and introduced by George Bull.

My revered friend, having despite my usual custom eaten dinner alone, or rather in company with the torments provided by the fever which now stops me enjoying the taste of any food at all, I rose from table overcome by despair. And then, resting my arms on the window-sill, and letting my chest and almost my whole body sink onto it, I fell to gazing at the marvellous spectacle presented by the countless number of barges, crammed by no fewer strangers than townspeople, which were delighting not only the onlookers but the Grand Canal itself, the delight of all who navigate her.

And after enjoying the sight of two gondolas, rowed in competition by as many brave oarsmen, I was beguiled by the crowd of people who to see the regatta had flocked to the Rialto bridge, the Riva dei Camerlinghi, the fish market, the ferry at Santa Sofia and the Casa da Mosto.

And after all these various streams of humanity applauded

happily and went their way, you would have seen me, like a man sick of himself and not knowing what to do with his thoughts and fancies, turn my eyes up to the sky; and, ever since God created it, never had it been so embellished by such a lovely picture of light and shades. Thus the air was such that those who envy you because they cannot be like you would have longed to show it.

As I am describing it, see first the buildings which appeared to be artificial though made of real stone. And then look at the air itself, which I perceived to be pure and lively in some places, and in others turbid and dull. Also consider my wonder at the clouds made up of condensed moisture; in the principal vista they were partly near the roofs of the buildings, and partly on the horizon, while to the right all was in a confused shading of greyish black. I was awestruck by the variety of colours they displayed: the nearest glowed with the flames of the sun's fire; the furthest were blushing with the brightness of partially burnt vermilion. Oh, how beautiful were the strokes with which Nature's brushes pushed the air back at this point, separating it from the palaces in the way that Titian does when painting his landscapes!

In some places the colours were green-blue, and in others they appeared blue-green, finely mixed by the whims of Nature, who is the teacher of teachers. With light and shades, she gave deep perspective and high relief to what she wished to bring forward and set back, and so I, who know how your brush breathes with her spirit, cried out three or four times: 'Oh, Titian, where are you?'

By heavens, if you had painted what I am telling you, you would have reduced people to the same stupor that so confounded me; and as I contemplated what I have now placed before you, I was filled with regret that the marvel of such a picture did not last longer.

[116] Fynes Moryson marvels at the canals of Venice in 1594; from *An Itinerary . . .* by Fynes Moryson, Gent.

Channels of water passe through this City (consisting of many Ilands joyned with Bridges) as the bloud passeth through the veines of mans body; so that a man may passe to what place he will both by land and water. The great channell is in length about one thousand three hundred paces, and in breadth forty paces, and hath onely one bridge called Rialto, and the passage is very pleasant by this channell; being adorned on both sides with stately Pallaces. And that men may passe speedily, besides this bridge, there be thirteene places called Traghetti, where boats attend called Gondole; which being of incredible number give ready passage to all men. The rest of the channels running through lesse streets, are more narrow, and in them many bridges are to be passed under. The aforesaid boats are very neat, and covered all save the ends with black cloth, so as the passengers may goe unseene and unknowne, and not bee annoyed at all with the sunne, winde, or raine. And these boats are ready at call any minute of the day or night. And if a stranger know not the way, hee shall not need to aske it, for if hee will follow the presse of people, hee shall be sure to bee brought to the market place of Saint Marke, or that of Rialto; the streets being very narrow (which they pave with bricke,) and besides if hee onely know his Hosts name, taking a boat, he shall be safely brought thither at any time of the night. Almost all the houses have two gates, one towards the street, the other towards the water; or at least the bankes of the channels are so neere, as the passage by water is as easie as by land. The publike boats, with the private of Gentlemen and Citizens, are some eight hundred, or as others say, a thousand. Though the flood or ebbe of the salt water bee small, yet with that motion it carrieth away the filth of the City, besides that, by the multitude of fiers, and the situation open to all windes, the ayre is made very wholesome, whereof the Venetians bragge, that it agrees with all strangers complexions, by a secret vertue, whether they be brought up in a good or ill ayre, and preserveth them in their former health.

[117] By the 1730s, however, the air of Venice strikes a German visitor as considerably less 'wholesome' than Fynes Moryson found it; from *Travels through*

Germany, Bohemia, Hungary, Switzerland, Italy and Lorrain by Johann Georg Keysler.

(Johann Georg Keysler (1693–1743) was a German antiquarian and a travelling tutor. His *De Dea Nehelennia numine veterum Walachorum topico* earned him Fellowship of the Royal Society, and his travel book was translated into many languages.)

Il canale maggiore, or the great canal, is indeed remarkable for its breadth, and has some very superb houses on its banks; but the other canals are crooked and narrow, and in summertime emit a very disagreeable smell, occasioned by the great quantity of filth of all kinds which runs into them. The tide flows here about six hours, and in spring-tides generally rises four or five feet; but this is not sufficient for cleansing the small canals. I have more than once observed a small wisp of straw, or any other light substance, floating on the water for two or three days, being hardly carried thirty or forty paces from the place where it was first thrown in. The sea-water is also generally thick and foul here . . .

The whole city is divided by a great number of canals; but by means of small bridges, of which there are above five hundred, one may go a great way by land. Most of the houses which front the water have back-doors to the streets, by which they have a communication with each other by land and the bridges. These streets are very narrow, and, after rain, something dangerous to walk on, the smooth and broad white stones with which they are paved being slippery in wet weather; but particular care is required in crossing the bridges, the steps and pavement of them being of the same smooth free-stone; besides very few of them have any fence on either side.

In allusion to this, there is a proverb, which advises to beware of the four P's at Venice, namely *Pietra bianca*, *Putana*, *Prete*, and *Pantalone*; i.e. 'A white stone, a whore, a priest and the last P may denote either mountebanks and jugglers, or the nobility themselves; that being a nickname given them by the vulgar.' To these inconveniencies may be added the great number of persons who share in the government; the violent tempests of thunder and lightning, frequent there in summer; and the diversions and public festivals. The three last inconveniences are specified in a common saying, viz. *Troppo teste, troppo feste, troppo tempeste.*

[118] The President de Brosses is enraptured by the gondolas in 1739; from *Selections from the Letters of de Brosses* translated by Lord Ronald Sutherland Gower.

We are lodged in what I may call the Fort of the street of St Honoré, and we can sleep the clock round without being disturbed by a sound. Everything passes by us silently on the water, and I think one could snore undisturbedly in the vegetable market. No carriage in the world can equal a gondola in comfort. It reminds me in its shape of a shark; there is room for two people at the end of the boat, and for others on either side, and you can open or shut the little cabin in the centre as you please. The prow is armed with a large bit of iron shaped like the neck of a stork, garnished with six large teeth – this helps to steady the boat. The entire boat is painted black and is varnished, and is furnished with black velvet and cloth, and with leather cushions of the same hue. Not even the greatest nobles are allowed any other decorations, nor are theirs different from those of the humblest individual; so that one cannot guess who is inside a closed gondola. One sits within as in one's own room, in which one can read, write, talk, make love, eat, drink, &c., while making a round of visits in the town. Two men of proved fidelity are in front; another behind conducts the vessel, without being able to see you if you do not wish to be seen. I do not expect to feel comfortable again in a carriage after having tried this mode of progression. I was told that there was never the crush with gondolas that one has with one's carriage in Paris; on the contrary, nothing is more frequent, especially in the narrow canals and under the bridges; but they certainly do not last long. Besides this, our water coachmen are so nimble, and glide along one cannot understand how, and turn these long machines in a twinkling on what appears to be no more than the point of a needle. It is necessary to be careful in putting your head outside your gondola windows, or the iron prow of some other gondola might cut it off in a moment.

The number of these gondolas is immense, and sixty thousand souls are said to make a living in Venice by their oars, either as gondoliers or sailors. One is also told that the town has annually thirty thousand visitors in it. It may be so during the days of the Carnival, which lasts six months, but except at that season I think that this number is greatly exaggerated.

[119] The gondoliers, or 'Barcaroles', of Venice in the mid-eighteenth century; from *Letters from Italy . . . in the years 1765 and 1766* by Samuel Sharp.

The number as well as the character of this people renders their body very respectable: When one considers, that in all the great families, every Gentleman keeps a distinct gondola, rowed by two men, except some few who have but one rower, it will be readily conceived that the number of Barcaroles must be very considerable. They are exceedingly proud of their station, and with some reason; for their profession leads them into the company of the greatest men of the state, and it is the fashion to converse with them, to hear their wit and humour, and applaud all they say; besides, the pay of a Barcarole is about eighteen pence a day, with liveries and little perquisites, which, in so cheap a country, is a plentiful income to a sober man: accordingly, it is notorious, that all of them can afford to marry, and do marry.

The manner of rowing a gondola, standing and looking forward, may be seen in every view of *Venice*, and this manner is absolutely necessary for the guidance of a boat in these narrow canals; but it is curious to observe how dexterous they are by use; for it is very rare that they touch, much less endanger over-setting, though they are every instant within half an inch of each other. One cannot be an hour on these canals without seeing several of the Barcaroles shifting themselves; for it is a custom amongst them to have always a dry shirt ready to put on, the moment after they have landed their fare; and they would expect to die, if by any accident

they were under the necessity of suffering a damp shirt to dry
on their bodies. On the other hand, it is curious to observe
how careless they are of damp sheets through all *Italy*, and
the people at inns are so little apprised of an objection to
damp sheets, that when you begin to beg they would hang
them before the fire, they desire you will feel how wet they
are, being preposessed that you mean they have not been
washed: In fact, unless you have servants who will dry them
for you, it is in vain to expect it should be done.

[120] The traditional singing of the Venetian gondoliers, which seems to have been something of an art
form in itself; from Goethe's *Italian Journey* (7 October
1786).

For this evening I had made arrangements to hear the famous
singing of the boatmen, who chant verses by Tasso and
Ariosto to their own melodies. This performance has to be
ordered in advance, for it is now rarely done and belongs,
rather, to the half-forgotten legends of the past. The moon
had risen when I took my seat in a gondola and the two
singers, one in the prow, the other in the stern, began chanting
verse after verse in turns. The melody, which we know from
Rousseau, is something between chorale and recitative. It
always moves at the same tempo without any definite beat.
The modulation is of the same character; the singers change
pitch according to the content of the verse in a kind of
declamation.

I shall not go into the question of how the melody evolved.
It is enough to say that it is ideal for someone idly singing to
himself and adapting the tune to poems he knows by heart.

The singer sits on the shore of an island, on the bank of a
canal or in a gondola, and sings at the top of his voice – the
people here appreciate volume more than anything else. His
aim is to make his voice carry as far as possible over the still
mirror of water. Far away another singer hears it. He knows
the melody and the words and answers with the next verse.
The first singer answers again, and so on. Each is the echo of
the other. They keep this up night after night without ever

getting tired. If the listener has chosen the right spot, which is halfway between them, the further apart they are, the more enchanting the singing will sound.

To demonstrate this, my boatmen tied up the gondola on the shore of the Giudecca and walked along the canal in opposite directions. I walked back and forth, leaving the one, who was just about to sing, and walking towards the other, who had just stopped.

For the first time I felt the full effect of this singing. The sound of their voices far away was extraordinary, a lament without sadness, and I was moved to tears. I put this down to my mood at the moment, but my old manservant said: '*è singolare, come quel canto intenerisce, a molto più, quando è più ben cantato.*' ['It is extraordinary how that song touches the heart – and much more when it is better sung.'] He wanted me to hear the women on the Lido, especially those from Malamocco and Pellestrina. They too, he told me, sing verses by Tasso to the same or a similar melody, and added: 'It is their custom to sit on the seashore while their husbands are out sea-fishing, and sing these songs in penetrating tones until, from far out over the sea, their men reply, and in this way they converse with each other.' Is this not a beautiful custom? I dare say that, to someone standing close by, the sound of such voices, competing with the thunder of the waves, might not be very agreeable. But the motive behind such singing is so human and genuine that it makes the mere notes of the melody, over which scholars have racked their brains in vain, come to life. It is the cry of some lonely human being sent out into the wide world till it reaches the ears of another lonely human being who is moved to answer it.

[121] Mrs Piozzi comments on a different skill practised by gondoliers, in 1785; from her *Glimpses of Italian Society*.

I have asked several friends about the truth of what one has been always hearing of in England – that the Venetian gondoliers sing Tasso's and Ariosto's verses in the streets at night, sometimes quarrelling with each other concerning the merits of their favourite poets; but what I have been told since I came here of their attachment to their respective masters, and secrecy when trusted by them in love affairs, seems far more probable, as they are proud to excess when they serve a nobleman of high birth, and will tell you with an air of importance that the house of Memmo, Monsenigo, or Gratterola has been served by their ancestors for these eighty or perhaps a hundred years, transmitting family pride thus from generation to generation, even when that pride is but reflected only like the mock rainbow of a summer sky. But hark! while I am writing this peevish reflection in my room, I hear some voices under my window answering each other upon the Grand Canal. It is – it *is* the gondolier) sure enough; they are at this moment singing to an odd sort of tune, but in no unmusical manner, the flight of Erminia from Tasso's 'Jerusalem.'

[122] An English traveller in 1789 pays his lodgings on the Grand Canal what he clearly considers the highest of compliments; from *Travels in France and Italy* by Arthur Young.

(Arthur Young (1741–1829), agriculturalist, traveller and writer, visited France in 1789 – enabling him, incidentally, to write a fascinating account of the outbreak of the Revolution – and continued into Italy.)

On entering the Adriatic a party of us quitted the bark, and to save time hired a large boat which conveyed us to this equally celebrated and singular place; it was nearly dark when we entered the grand canal. My attention was alive, all expectancy: there was light enough to show the objects around me to be among the most interesting I had ever seen, and they struck me more than the first entrance of any other place I had been at. To Signore Petrillo's inn. My companions, before the gondola came to the steps, told me that as soon as Petrillo found me to be a Signore Inglesi, there would be three torches lighted to receive me: – it was just so: I was not too much flattered at these three torches, which struck me at once as three pick-pockets. I was conducted to an apartment that looked on to the grand canal, so neat, and everything in it so clean and good, that I almost thought myself in England.

[123] The hazards of living on the canals; from a letter of Byron's to John Murray (1819, May 18) in *'The Flesh is Frail'; Byron's Letters and Journals* edited by Leslie A. Marchand.

I wrote to you in haste and at past two in the morning having besides had an accident. In going, about an hour and a half ago, to a rendezvous with a Venetian girl (unmarried and the daughter of one of their nobles), I tumbled into the Grand Canal, and, not choosing to miss my appointment by the delays of changing, I have been perched in a balcony with my wet clothes on ever since, till this minute that on my return I have slipped into my dressing-gown. My foot slipped in getting into my Gondola to set out (owing to the cursed slippery steps of their palaces), and in I flounced like a Carp, and went dripping like a Triton to my Sea nymph and had to scramble up to a grated window: –

> Fenced with iron within and without
> Lest the lover get in or the Lady get out.

[124] On 25 September 1869 Henry James wrote to his brother William about gondolas and the canals; from *The Letters of Henry James* edited by Leon Edel.

Gondolas spoil you for a return to common life. To begin with, in themselves they afford the perfection of indolent pleasure. The seat is so soft and deep and slumberous and the motion so mild elastic and unbroken that even if they bore you through miles of stupid darkness you'd think it the most delectable fun. But when they lift you thro' this rosy air, along these liquid paths, beneath the balconies of palaces as lovely in design and fancy as they are pathetic in their loneliness and decay – you may imagine that it's better than walking down Broadway. I should never have forgiven myself had I come to Venice any later in the season. The mosquitoes are perfectly infernal – and you can't say more for Venice

than that you are willing, at this moment, for the sake of the
days she bestows to endure the nights she inflicts. But, bating
this, all else is in perfection – the weather, the temperature
and the aspect of the canals. The Venetian population, on the
water, is immensely picturesque. In the narrow streets, the
people are far too squalid and offensive to the nostrils, but
with a good breadth of canals to set them off and a heavy
stream of sunshine to light them up as they go pushing and
paddling and screaming – bare-chested, bare-legged, magnificently tanned and muscular – the men at least are a very
effective lot. Besides lolling in my gondola I have spent a
good deal of time in poking thro' the alleys which serve as
streets and staring about in the Campos – the little squares
formed about every church – some of them most sunnily
desolate, the most grass-grown, the most cheerfully sad little
reliquaries of a splendid past that you can imagine. Every one
knows that the Grand Canal is a wonder; but really to feel in
your heart the ancient wealth of Venice, you must have
frequented these canalettos and campos and seen the number
and splendor of the palaces that stand rotting and crumbling
and abandoned to paupers.

[125] In his *Italian Hours*, Henry James pursues the
matter further.

There is something strange and fascinating in this mysterious
impersonality of the gondola. It has an identity when you are
in it, but, thanks to their all being of the same size, shape and
colour, and of the same deportment and gait, it has none, or
as little as possible, as you see it pass before you. From my
windows on the Riva there was always the same silhouette –
the long, black, slender skiff, lifting its head and throwing it
back a little, moving yet seeming not to move, with the
grotesquelygraceful figure on the poop. This figure inclines,
as may be, more to the graceful or to the grotesque – standing
in the 'second position' of the dancing-master, but indulging
from the waist upward in a freedom of movement which that
functionary would deprecate. One may say as a general thing
that there is something rather awkward in the movement even

of the most graceful gondolier, and something graceful in the movement of the most awkward. In the graceful men of course the grace predominates, and nothing can be finer than the large, firm way in which, from their point of vantage, they throw themselves over their tremendous oar. It has the boldness of a plunging bird and the regularity of a pendulum. Sometimes, as you see this movement in profile, in a gondola that passes you – see, as you recline on your own low cushions, the arching body of the gondolier lifted up against the sky – it has a kind of nobleness which suggest an image on a Greek frieze. The gondolier at Venice is your very good friend – if you choose him happily – and on the quality of the personage depends a good deal that of your impressions. He is a part of your daily life, your double, your shadow, your complement. Most people, I think, either like their gondolier or hate him; and if they like him, like him very much. In this case they take an interest in him after his departure; wish him to be sure of employment, speak of him as the gem of gondoliers and tell their friends to be certain to 'secure' him. There is usually no difficulty in securing him; there is nothing elusive or reluctant about a gondolier. Nothing would induce me not to believe them for the most part excellent fellows, and the sentimental tourist must always have a kindness for them. More than the rest of the population, of course, they are the children of Venice; they are associated with its idiosyncrasy, with its essence, with its silence, with its melancholy.

When I say they are associated with its silence I should immediately add that they are associated also with its sound. Among themselves they are an extraordinarily talkative company. They chatter at the *traghetti*, where they always have some sharp point under discussion; they bawl across the canals; they bespeak your commands as you approach; they defy each other from afar. If you happen to have a *traghetto* under your window, you are well aware that they are a vocal race. I should go even further than I went just now, and say that the voice of the gondolier is in fact for audibility the dominant or rather the only note of Venice. There is scarcely another heard sound, and that indeed is part of the interest of the place. There is no noise there save distinctly human noise; no rumbling, no vague uproar, nor rattle of wheels and hoofs.

It is all articulate and vocal and personal. One may say indeed that Venice is emphatically the city of conversation; people talk all over the place because there is nothing to interfere with its being caught by the ear. Among the populace it is a general family party. The still water carries the voice, and good Venetians exchange confidences at a distance of half a mile. It saves a world of trouble, and they don't like trouble. Their delightful garrulous language helps them to make Venetian life a long *conversazione*. This language, with its soft elisions, its odd transpositions, its kindly contempt for consonants and other disagreeables, has in it something peculiarly human and accommodating. If your gondolier had no other merit he would have the merit that he speaks Venetian. This may rank as a merit even – some people perhaps would say especially – when you don't understand what he says. But he adds to it other graces which make him an agreeable feature in your life. The price he sets on his services is touchingly small, and he has a happy art of being obsequious without being, or at least without seeming, abject. For occasional liberalities he evinces an almost lyrical gratitude. In short he has delightfully good manners, a merit which he shares for the most part with the Venetians at large.

[126] Many first-time visitors found the long journey from Fusina in a covered gondola deeply depressing: among them was Richard Wagner; from *My Life*, translated by Andrew Gray.

At sundown on August 29th, when we were looking down from the causeway at the image of Venice rising reflected from the waters beneath, Karl suddenly lost his hat out the railway car window when leaning out in delight. I thought I should follow suit and threw my hat out as well: thus we both arrived bare-headed in Venice and immediately got into a gondola, to proceed along the entire Canale Grande to the Piazzetta beside San Marco. The weather had suddenly turned somewhat unpleasant, and the sight of the gondola itself had shocked me a bit; for despite all I had heard of these conveyances, painted black on black, the actual sight of one was still a rude surprise: when I had to go under the black awning, my first thought was a revival of a fear of cholera that I had previously mastered; it decidedly seemed to me as if I were taking part in a funeral procession during an epidemic. Karl assured me that this was how most people felt, but that one got used to it very quickly. Now came an extremely long trip round the many bends of the Canale Grande: the impressions made by all this were not sufficient to dispel my anxious mood. Whereas Karl had eyes only for a Ca d'oro belonging to Fanny Elssler or some other famous palace between the deteriorating walls, my melancholy glance fell solely on the crumbling ruins between these interesting buildings. At length I fell silent and offered no objection to getting out at the world-famous Piazzetta to be shown the Palace of the Doges, though I reserved the right to admire it until such time as I had freed myself of the melancholy mood which my arrival in Venice had produced.

[127] But he was greatly impressed, and perhaps even influenced, by the folksongs of the gondoliers; from *My Life*, translated by Andrew Gray.

My principal recreation lay in the gondola trips to the Lido. Above all it was the homeward journey at sundown which invariably overwhelmed me by its incomparable impact. Right at the outset of our stay in September of that year we saw on such occasions the magical appearance of the great comet, which was at that time at its highest brilliance, and was generally held to be a portent of imminent catastrophe in war. Then there was the singing of a popular choral society, formed and directed by an official of the Venetian Arsenal, which sounded truly idyllic in the lagoon. These singers generally sang only three-part folksongs with simple harmonies. It was new to me to hear the top part not rising above the alto range, thus not touching the soprano at all and thereby imparting to the sound a quality of masculine youthfulness I had not known until then. On fine evenings they went along the Canale Grande singing in a big, illuminated gondola, stopping to serenade in front of certain palaces, no

doubt prearranged and for pay, and usually attracting countless other gondolas as a retinue. On a sleepless night that
drove me out on the balcony of my apartment at about three
o'clock in the morning, I heard for the first time the famous
old folksong of the gondolier). I thought the first call, piercing
the stillness of the night like a harsh lament, emanated from
the Rialto, barely a quarter hour's distance away, or thereabouts; from a similar distance this would be answered from
another quarter in the same way. This strange melancholy
dialogue, which was repeated frequently at longish intervals,
moved me too much for me to be able to fix its musical
components in my mind. Yet on another occasion I learned
that this folksong had an indisputably poetic interest. When I
was riding back late one evening along the dark canal, the
moon came out and illuminated, together with the indescribable palaces, the tall silhouette of my gondolier towering
above the stern of his gondola, while he slowly turned his
mighty oar. Suddenly from his breast came a mournful sound
not unlike the howl of an animal, swelling up from a deep,
low note, and after a long-sustained 'Oh', it culminated in the
simple musical phrase 'Venezia'. This was followed by some
words I could not retain in my memory, being so greatly
shaken by the emotion of the moment. Such were the
impressions that seemed most characteristic of Venice to me
during my stay, and they remained with me until the completion of the second act of *Tristan*, and perhaps even helped
to inspire the long-drawn-out lament for the shepherd's horn
at the beginning of the third act.

[128] Mark Twain, arriving in Venice in 1868, also put
up a stiff resistance to gondolas – but was seduced in
the end; from *The Innocents Abroad*.

We reached Venice at eight in the evening, and entered a
hearse belonging to the Grand Hotel d'Europe. At any rate, it
was more like a hearse than anything else, though to speak
by the card, it was a gondola. And this was the storied
gondola of Venice! – the fairy boat in which the princely
cavaliers of the olden times were wont to cleave the waters of

the moonlit canals and look the eloquence of love into the soft eyes of patrician beauties, while the gay gondolier in silken doublet touched his guitar and sang as only gondoliers can sing! This the famed gondola and this the gorgeous gondolier! the one an inky, rusty old canoe with a sable hearse-body clapped on to the middle of it, and the other a mangy, barefooted guttersnipe with a portion of his raiment on exhibition which should have been sacred from public scrutiny. Presently, as he turned a corner and shot his hearse into a dismal ditch between two long rows of towering, untenanted buildings, the gay gondolier began to sing, true to the tradition of his race . . .

I began to feel that the old Venice of song and story had departed for ever. But I was too hasty. In a few minutes we swept gracefully out into the Grand Canal, and under the mellow moonlight the Venice of poetry and romance stood revealed. Right from the water's edge rose long lines of stately palaces of marble; gondolas were gliding swiftly hither and thither and disappearing suddenly through unsuspected gates and alleys; ponderous stone bridges threw their shadows athwart the glittering waves. There was life and motion everywhere, and yet everywhere there was a hush, a stealthy sort of stillness, that was suggestive of secret enterprises of bravoes and of lovers; and clad half in moonbeams and half in mysterious shadows, the grim old mansions of the Republic seemed to have an expression about them of having an eye out for just such enterprises as these at the same moment. Music came floating over the waters – Venice was complete.

[129] The old art of sail-painting in Venice was declining by the late nineteenth century, as Horatio Brown laments; from his *Life on the Lagoon*.

The gondola is made for solitude or for company – the best company, the company of two – as the fancy may dispose. The rower is out of sight, behind. Nothing indicates movement but the ripple and the lap of water under the bows, the slow swaying of the steel ferro from side to side, and the slower gliding by of palace fronts. There is no jolt of springs, no rattle and bang of wheels, no noise of horses' hoofs upon the road, above all no dust; sea and sky are in your sole possession, and the breeze just born of the gondola's progress; there is an infinite liberty of contemplation secured by space and solitude. Or, in company, what lounge more admirably arranged than the cushions of the gondola? You are near your companion, but not too near; you may speak without raising your voice. Would you lean nearer, or lean away? You have only to wait the sway of the boat, yield to it, and the thing is done, naturally, not by you, without any *brusquerie*, almost unconsciously. The gondola lends itself to its master's mood. It is the boat for leisure, however, and not for business; the carriage of a leisured people; there is no hurry in its movement; all is quiet and deliberate. Life was not meant to be bustled through and done with, by the men who developed the gondola; and it would be difficult to discover any greater provocative to utter idling than this boat of Venice. That was surely a work of supererogation which the Venetian doctor undertook when he addressed a treatise to his English friend, upon the art of sitting in a gondola. The art is all too easy to learn; it consists in yielding yourself to the cushions and the boat. The gondola itself will teach it you without the help of any learned discourse.

The patterns on the Venetian sails are one of the most charming and peculiar features of the place; though it is to be feared that they are fast falling from their ancient splendour. The decay of the religious sentiment is fatal to the art of sail-painting, as it has been to so many other arts. But Saint George slaying an ink-black dragon, or Saint Anthony or Titian's Madonna in *The Assumption* are still displayed to the winds of the lagoon. Some of the most beautiful effects are obtained by simple colour without any design; there is one bragozzo which carries a large red sail with a canton painted in deep blue, pale sea-green, and white; in the distance it looks like the colouring on a drake's head and neck. The ragged and patched sails are no less picturesque, with here and there a splash of clear sky blue which you discover, on near approach only, to be a rent in the canvas and the real sky glowing through it. But the majority of sails that are not content with mere geometrical patterns – and these are by far the larger number – bear some symbolic design. Fortunes, lighthouses, the globe surmounted by a cross, even a huge yellow polenta on a red background. These are easy to interpret, and the significance of the last is not to be missed by a hungry seafaring people with a voracious appetite for their favourite food. Some designs, however, are not so easy to decipher. What is one to make of a cock with a star on its beak, for instance? or a star with a flash of lightning striking across the sail? and a heart split open by a wedge looks almost as though the maladie du siècle had reached these fishing folk; it is a device for Leopardi or De Musset, but hardly for a sailor of the Venetian lagoons. The only sail I have ever seen with an historical significance in its design, is one which carries the arms of Cyprus, Jerusalem, and Armenia, a cross with four crosslets in the cantons, recalling the time when a Venetian lady bore these titles and the Republic stole her kingdom from her.

[130] Aschenbach, like Horatio Brown, finds the gondola's armchair the most comfortable seat in the world; from *Death in Venice* by Thomas Mann, translated by H. T. Lowe-Porter.

Is there anyone but must repress a secret thrill, on arriving in Venice for the first time – or returning thither after a long absence – and stepping into a Venetian gondola? That singular conveyance, come down unchanged from ballad times, black as nothing else on earth except a coffin – what pictures it calls up of lawless, silent adventures in the plashing night; or even more, what visions of death itself, the bier and solemn rites and last soundless voyage! And has anyone remarked that the seat in such a bark, the armchair lacquered in coffin-black, and dully black-upholstered, is the softest, most luxurious, most relaxing seat in the world? Aschenbach realised it when he had let himself down at the gondolier's feet, opposite his luggage, which lay neatly composed on the vessel's beak. The rowers still gestured fiercely; he heard their harsh, incoherent tones. But the strange stillness of the water-city seemed to take up their voices gently, to disembody them and scatter them over the sea. It was warm here in the harbour. The lukewarm air of the sirocco breathed upon him, he leaned back among his cushions and gave himself to the yielding element, closing his eyes for very pleasure in an indolence as unaccustomed as sweet. 'The trip will be short', he thought, and wished it might last forever.

[131] The twentieth-century gondoliers of Venice; from *Venice* by James (now Jan) Morris.

And among them all, the very image of Venice, straight-descended from Carpaccio, moves the gondolier. He is not a popular figure among the tourists, who think his prices high and his manner sometimes overbearing: and indeed he is frequently a Communist, and no respecter of persons, and he often shamelessly pumps the innocent foreigner with inaccurate information, and sometimes unfairly induces him to disregard the tariff ('Ah, but today is the feast of San Marcuola, *signor*, and it is *traditional* to charge double fares on this holy day'). I have grown to like and admire him, though, and I can forgive a few peccadillos among men who live on a four-months' tourist season, and scrape the winter through as part-time fishermen and oddjob workers. The gondoliers are usually highly intelligent: they are also tolerant, sardonic, and, with some grumpy and usually elderly exceptions, humorous. They are often very good-looking, too, fair and loose-limbed – many of their forebears came from the Slav coasts of Istria and Dalmatia – and they sometimes have a cultivated, worldly look to them, like undergraduates punting on the Cherwell, naval officers amusing themselves, or perhaps fashionable ski instructors.

The Lagoon and the islands

[132] Anna, Lady Miller journeys to Venice by boat from a village near Ferrara, via the Po and the Lagoon; from *Letters from Italy . . . in the Years 1770 and 1771* by Lady Miller.

Two o'clock. We are now within two miles of Venice; but the wind is risen, and being rather against us, are obliged to take the assistance of another boat, come out to us for that purpose, being no longer towed by horses. I think my letter would make an admirable supplement to the *Voiageur de St Cloud tant par mere* [sic] *que par terre*. Venice has appeared before us for three miles past: but now, on our nearer approach, I believe the world cannot produce a more surprising, or more beautiful view; a city rising out of the bosom of the waves, crowned with glittering spires. This sea we are now upon is called the *Lagunes*, because of its calm property, being in a manner like a lake of sea-water; it is shallow, and not subject to agitation by storms. Adieu for the present, having just gained the great canal of Venice.

[133] Casanova, disguised as a pierrot, narrowly escapes shipwreck in the Lagoon in 1755; from *The Memoirs of Jacques Casanova de Seingalt* translated by Arthur Machen.

The weather was fearful. The wind was blowing fiercely, and it was bitterly cold. When I reached the shore, I looked for a gondola, I called the gondoliers, but, in contravention to the police regulations, there was neither gondola nor gondolier. What was I to do? Dressed in light linen, I was hardly in a fit state to walk along the wharf for an hour in such weather. I should most likely have gone back to the casino if I had had the key, but I was paying the penalty of the foolish spite which had made me give it up. The wind almost carried me offmy feet, and there was no house that I could enter to get a shelter.

I had in my pockets three hundred philippes that I had won in the evening, and a purse full of gold. I had therefore every reason to fear the thieves of Muran – a very dangerous class of cutthroats, determined murderers who enjoyed and abused a certain impunity, because they had some privileges granted to them by the Government on account of the services they rendered in the manufactories of looking-glasses and in the glass works which are numerous on the island. In order to prevent their emigration, the Government had granted them the freedom of Venice. I dreaded meeting a pair of them, who would have stripped me of everything, at least. I had not, by chance, with me the knife which all honest men must carry to defend their lives in my dear country. I was truly in an unpleasant predicament.

I was thus painfully situated when I thought I could see a light through the crevices of a small house. I knocked modestly against the shutter. A voice called out –

'Who is knocking?'

And at the same moment the shutter was pushed open.

'What do you want?' asked a man, rather astonished at my costume.

I explained my predicament in a few words, and giving him one sequin I begged his permission to shelter myself under his roof. Convinced by my sequin rather than my words, he opened the door, I went in, and promising him another sequin for his trouble I requested him to get me a gondola to take me to Venice. He dressed himself hurriedly, thanking God for that piece of good fortune, and went out assuring me that he would soon get me a gondola. I remained alone in a miserable room in which all his family, sleeping together in a large, ill-looking bed, were staring at me in consequence of my extraordinary costume. In half an hour the good man returned to announce that the gondoliers were at the wharf, but that they wanted to be paid in advance. I raised no objection, gave a sequin to the man for his trouble, and went to the wharf.

The sight of two strong gondoliers made me get into the gondola without anxiety, and we left the shore without being much disturbed by the wind, but when we had gone beyond the island, the storm attacked us with such fury that I thought myself lost, for, although a good swimmer, I was not sure I had strength enough to resist the violence of the waves and swim to the shore. I ordered the men to go back to the island, but they answered that I had not to deal with a couple of cowards, and that I had no occasion to be afraid. I knew the disposition of our gondoliers, and I made up my mind to say no more.

But the wind increased in violence, the foaming waves rushed into the gondola, and my two rowers, in spite of their vigour and of their courage, could no longer guide it. We were only within one hundred yards of the mouth of the Jesuits' Canal, when a terrible gust of wind threw one of the *barcarols* into the sea; most fortunately he contrived to hold by the gondola and to get in again, but he had lost his oar, and while he was securing another the gondola had tacked, and had already gone a considerable distance abreast. The position called for immediate decision, and I had no wish to take my supper with Neptune. I threw a handful of philippes into the gondola, and ordered the gondoliers to throw over-board the *felce* which covered the boat. The ringing of money, as much as the imminent danger, ensured instant obedience, and then, the wind having less hold upon us, my brave boatmen shewed Æolus that their efforts could conquer him, for in less than five minutes we shot into the Beggars' Canal, and I reached the Bragadin Palace. I went to bed at once, covering myself heavily in order to regain my natural heat, but sleep, which alone could have restored me to health, would not visit me.

Five or six hours afterwards, M. de Bragadin and his two inseparable friends paid me a visit, and found me raving with fever. That did not prevent my respectable protector from laughing at the sight of the costume of Pierrot lying on the sofa. After congratulating me upon having escaped with my life out of such a bad predicament, they left me alone. In the evening I perspired so profusely that my bed had to be changed. The next day my fever and delirium increased, and two days after, the fever having abated, I found myself almost crippled and suffering fearfully with lumbago. I felt that nothing could relieve me but a strict regimen, and I bore the evil patiently.

[134] Few of us today could emulate Byron's feat of swimming from the Lido to the Salute and thence the whole length of the Grand Canal; and fewer still would want to; from *The Flesh is Frail*, *Byron's Letters and Journals* edited by Leslie A. Marchand.

[TO JOHN CAM HOBHOUSE]   *Venice. June 25th. 1818*
Dear Hobhouse – I have received yrs. of the 5th. – & have had no letters from any one else – nor desire any – but *letters of Credit*. – Since my last I have had another *Swim* against Mingaldo – whom both Scott & I beat hollow – leaving him breathless & five hundred yards behind hand before we got from Lido to the entrance of the Grand Canal. – Scott went from Lido as far as the Rialto – & was then taken into his Gondola – I swam from Lido right to the end of the Grand Canal – including it's whole length – besides that space from Lido to the Canal's entrance (or exit) by the statue of Fortune – near the Palace – and coming out finally at the end opposite Fusina and Maestri – staying in half an hour & – I know not what distance more than the other two – & swimming easy – the whole distance computed by the Venetians at four and a half of Italian miles. – I was in the sea from half past 4 – till

a quarter past 8 – without touching or resting. – I could not be much fatigued having had a *piece* in the forenoon – & taking another in the evening at ten of the Clock – The Scott I mention is not the vice-Consul – but a traveller – who lives much at Venice – like My*sen*. – He got as far as the Rialto swimming well – the Italian – miles behind & knocked up – hallooing for the boat. – Pray – make Murray *pay* – & Spooney pay – & send the Messenger – & with the other things the enclosed *Corn rubbers*. – As you are full of politics I say nothing – except that I wish you more pleasure than such trash could give to me.

yrs. very truly & affectly.

B

P.S. – *The wind & tide were both with me. Corn rubbers two dozen – recollect they are light & may come in letters. –*

[135] Arriving in Venice before the building of the causeway; from *The Stones of Venice* by John Ruskin.

We have but walked some two hundred yards when we come to a low wharf or quay at the extremity of a canal, with long steps on each side down to the water, which latter we fancy for an instant has become black with stagnation; another glance undeceives us, – it is covered with the black boats of Venice. We enter one of them, rather to try if they be real boats or not, than with any definite purpose, and glide away; at first feeling as if the water were yielding continually beneath the boat and letting her sink into soft vacancy. It is something clearer than any water we have seen lately, and of a pale green; the banks only two or three feet above it, of mud and rank grass, with here and there a stunted tree; gliding swiftly past the small casement of the gondola, as if they were dragged by upon a painted scene.

Stroke by stroke, we count the plunges of the oar, each heaving up the side of the boat slightly as her silver beak shoots forward. We lose patience, and extricate ourselves from the cushions: the sea air blows keenly by, as we stand leaning on the roof of the floating cell. In front, nothing to be seen but long canal and level bank; to the west, the tower of

Mestre is lowering fast, and behind it there have risen purple shades, of the colour of dead rose-leaves, all round the horizon, feebly defined against the afternoon sky, – the Alps of Bassano. Forward still: the endless canal bends at last, and then breaks into intricate angles about some low bastions, now torn to pieces and staggering in ugly rents towards the water, – the bastions of the fort of Malghera. Another turn, and another perspective of canal; but not interminable. The silver beak cleaves it fast, – it widens: the rank grass of the banks sinks lower, and lower, and at last dies in tawny knots along an expanse of weedy shore. Over it, on the right, but a few years back, we might have seen the lagoon stretching to the horizon, and the warm southern sky bending over Malamocco to the sea. Now we can see nothing but what seems a low and monotonous dockyard wall, with flat arches to let the tide through it; – this is the railroad bridge, conspicuous above all things. But at the end of those dismal arches there rises, out of the wide water, a struggling line of low and confused brick buildings, which, but for the many towers which are mingled among them, might be the suburbs of an English manufacturing town. Four or five domes, pale, and apparently at a greater distance, rise over the centre of the line; but the object which first catches the eye is a sullen cloud of black smoke brooding over the northern half of it, and which issues from the belfry of a church.

It is VENICE.

[136] The Lagoon and its islands in the late nineteenth century; from *Italian Hours* by Henry James.

May in Venice is better than April, but June is best of all . . . Then the gondola is your sole habitation, and you spend days between sea and sky. You go to the Lido, though the Lido has been spoiled. When I first saw it, in 1869, it was a very natural place, and there was but a rough lane across the little island from the landing-place to the beach. There was a bathing-place in those days, and a restaurant, which was very bad, but where in the warm evenings your dinner didn't much matter as you sat letting it cool on the wooden terrace that stretched out into the sea. To-day the Lido is a part of united Italy and has been made the victim of villainous improvements. A little cockney village has sprung up on its rural bosom and a third-rate boulevard leads from Santa Elisabetta to the Adriatic. There are bitumen walks and gas-lamps, lodging-houses, shops and a *teatro diurno*. The bathing-establishment is bigger than before, and the restaurant as well; but it is a compensation perhaps that the cuisine is no better. Such as it is, however, you won't scorn occasionally to partake of it on the breezy platform under which bathers dart and splash, and which looks out to where the fishing-boats, with sails of orange and crimson, wander along the darkening horizon. The beach at the Lido is still lonely and beautiful, and you can easily walk away from the cockney village. The return to Venice in the sunset is classical and indispensable, and those who at that glowing hour have floated toward the towers that rise out of the lagoon will not easily part with the impression. But you indulge in larger excursions – you go to Burano and Torcello, to Malamocco and Chioggia. Torcello, like the Lido, has been improved; the deeply interesting little cathedral of the eighth century, which stood there on the edge of the sea, as touching in its ruin, with its grassy threshold and its primitive mosaics, as the bleached bones of a human skeleton washed ashore by the tide, has now been restored and made cheerful, and the charm of the place, its strange and suggestive desolation, has well-nigh departed.

It will still serve you as a pretext, however, for a day on the lagoon, especially as you will disembark at Burano and admire the wonderful fisher-folk, whose good looks – and bad manners, I am sorry to say – can scarcely be exaggerated. Burano is celebrated for the beauty of its women and the rapacity of its children, and it is a fact that though some of the ladies are rather bold about it every one of them shows you a handsome face. The children assail you for coppers, and in their desire to be satisfied pursue your gondola into the sea. Chioggia is a larger Burano, and you carry away from either place a half-sad, half-cynical, but altogether pictorial impression; the impression of bright-coloured hovels, of bathing in stagnant canals, of young girls with faces of a delicate shape and a susceptible expression, with splendid

heads of hair and complexions smeared with powder, faded
yellow shawls that hang like old Greek draperies, and little
wooden shoes that click as they go up and down the steps of
the convex bridges; of brown-checked matrons with lustrous
tresses and high tempers, massive throats encased with gold
beads, and eyes that meet your own with a certain traditional
defiance. The men throughout the islands of Venice are almost
as handsome as the women; I have never seen so many good-
looking rascals. At Burano and Chioggia they sit mending
their nets, or lounge at the street corners, where conversation
is always high-pitched, or clamour to you to take a boat; and
everywhere they decorate the scene with their splendid colour
– cheeks and throats as richly brown as the sails of their
fishing-smacks – their sea-faded tatters which are always a
'costume,' their soft Venetian jargon, and the gallantry with
which they wear their hats, an article that nowhere sits so
well as on a mass of dense Venetian curls.

[137] A visit to Murano, already famous for glassmak-
ing, in 1608; from *Coryat's Crudities* by Thomas
Coryat.

I passed in a Gondola to pleasant Murano, distant about a
little mile from the citie, where they make their delicate Venice
glasses, so famous over al Christendome for the incomparable
finenes thereof, and in one of their working houses made a
glasse my selfe. Most of their principall matter whereof they
make their glasses is a kinde of earth which is brought thither
by Sea from Drepanum a goodly haven towne of Sicilie,
where Eneas buried his aged father Anchises. This Murano is
a very delectable and populous place, having many faire
buildings both publique and private. And divers very pleasant
gardens: the first that inhabited it were those of the towne
Altinum bordering upon the Sea coast, who in the time of the
Hunnes invasion of Italy, repaired hither with their wives and
children, for the more securitie of their lives, as other border-
ers also did at the same time to those Islands, where Venice
now standeth. Here did I eate the best Oysters that ever I did
in all my life. They were indeede but little, something lesse

then our Wainflete Oysters about London, but as green as a leeke, and gratissimi saporis & succi.

[138] A visit to the Murano glass foundries in 1621; from *Epistolae Ho-Elianae, or Familiar Letters* by James Howell.

(James Howell (1593–1666) was in Venice in 1621 as an agent for Admiral Sir Robert Mansell, a former Treasurer of the Navy who had established a glass factory in Broad Street. Howell's principal job was to find skilled Venetian glassblowers who might be persuaded to work in London – in which he was successful.)

Sir,

As soon as I came to Venice, I apply'd myself to dispatch your Business according to Instructions, and Mr Seymor was ready to contribute his best furtherance. These two Italians, who are the Bearers hereof, by report here, are the best Gentlemen-workmen that ever blew Crystal; one is ally'd to Antonio Miotti, the other is Cousin to Mazalao: for other things they shall be sent in the ship Lion, which rides here at Malamocco, as I shall send you account by conveyance of Mr Symns. Herewith I have sent a Letter to you from Sir Henry Wotton, the Lord Ambassador here, of whom I have receiv'd some Favours: He wish'd me to write, that you have now a double Interest in him; for whereas before he was only your Servant, he is now your Kinsman by your late marriage . . .

I was, since I came hither, in Murano, a little Island about the distance of Lambeth from London, where Crystal-Glass is made; and 'tis a rare sight to see a whole Street, where on the one side there are twenty Furnaces together at work. They say here, That altho' one should transplant a Glass-Furnace from Murano to Venice herself, or to any of the little Assembly of Islands about her, or to any other part of the Earth besides, and use the same Materials, the same Workmen, the same Fuel, the self-same Ingredients every way, yet they cannot make Crystal-Glass in that perfection, for beauty and lustre, as in Murano: Some impute it to the quality of the circumambient Air that hangs o'er the Place, which is purify'd

and attenuated by the concurrence of so many Fires that are
in those Furnaces Night and Day perpetually, for they are like
the Vestal-Fire, which never goes out. And it is well known,
that some Airs make more qualifying Impressions than others;
as a Greek told me in Sicily of the Air of Egypt, where there
be huge common Furnaces to hatch Eggs by the thousands in
Camel's Dung: for during the time of hatching, if the Air
happen to come to be overcast, and grow cloudy it spoils all;
if the Sky continue still, serene and clear, not one Egg in a
hundred will miscarry.

[139] On his first visit to Murano, in 1654, Richard
Lassels seems to have been quite unaware of the glass-
making; from *The Voyage of Italy.*

Having seen this triomph in the morneing and the preparations for the great dinner of the Duke who treated the Senate;
we went to dinner too, and towards the evening we went to
Muran to see the great curve of those fine Piottas which we
had scene in the morning.

Muran is an Iland half a mile from Venise but built like a
little Venise. In the midst of this Iland or little towne there is
a faire channel of water with houses on both sides: here they
mett this Evening and made the Curso, that is went hurrying
up and downe, and to and fro this channel in their Piottas,
their watermen being richly clad and the noblemen and gentry
being in their holyday lookes and clothes, with their trompe-
ters in each Piotta sounding several tunes and denounceing to
one an other an airy warre, as the brawny leggd watermen
striving to outrow one an other denounce a watery one.
Embassadours of Princes and all the nobility in the towne
appeare here, where having frighted the silly fish out of their
beads, are willing at last to lett their wearied watermen go to
their owne.

*(His account of his second visit is, however, rather more
predictable.)*

Againe we went to Muran where they make glasses called
Venise glasses, and there saw curious fashioned glasses with

covers. One sett of glasses we saw excelling the rest, to wit, being made for to be presented unto the Emperour, and having the Imperial Eagle in the topp of their covers. Each glasse was valewed at five crownes, and there were a dozen of them. Here allso they make those great looking glasses which are our Ladyes cheif housestuff, as well as the perfect symbol of their faire bricklenesse.

[140] Few visitors to Venice, even in the eighteenth century, got away without a visit to a glass foundry, and Président de Brosses was no exception; from *Selections from the Letters of de Brosses* translated by Lord Ronald Sutherland Gower.

I have just returned from Murano, where I went to see the manufacture of glass. The glass is not so large or so white as ours, but it is more transparent and less liable to have blemishes. The glass is not run in copper tubes, as with us, but blown like bottles. It requires powerful men to do this, particularly for balancing in the air the great globes of glass by a long rod of iron, through which they are blown. The workman takes a lump of melted matter from the crucible in the furnace at the end of his hollow rod; this matter has then the consistency of gum. He blows into it through the rod, forms it into a hollow globe, then balances it in the air, and, after turning it in the mouth of the furnace to keep it in a state of fusion, at length succeeds in forming it into a long oval shape. Then another workman, armed with a pair of shears, pierces the oval globe at the end. The first workman, still holding the rod, turns it with great rapidity, while the other gradually releases the hand which holds the shears. In this way the oval bowl gradually opens out at one end; it is then taken from the iron rod and placed on a second rod, and then opened at the other end in the same way by which the first opening was formed. A long cylindrical-shaped mass of glass of a large diameter is now obtained, which is again placed within the furnace to soften it, and when withdrawn is cut by a stroke of the scissors, length-ways, and stretched out flatly on a table covered with copper. It then has to be cooled in another furnace, then polished, and finally plated.

By the way, when I return home I shall expect at least the title of Excellency; here I am accustomed to that pleasant designation. As for that of *Illustrissimo*, I scorn anything so modest.

[141] The making of looking-glasses in 1780; from *A View of Society and Manners in Italy* by John Moore MD.

I had the honour of attending their Highnesses when they went to visit the island of Murano. This is about a mile from Venice, was formerly a very flourishing place, and still boasts some palaces which bear the marks of former magnificence, though now in a state of decay. The island is said to contain 20,000 inhabitants. The great manufactories of looking-glasses, are the only inducements which strangers have to visit this place. I saw one very fine plate, for a mirror, made in the presence of the Archduke in a few minutes: though not so large as some I have seen of the Paris manufactory, yet it was much larger than I could have thought it in the power of human lungs to blow. Instead of being cast, as in France and England, the Murano mirrors are all blown in the manner of bottles. It is astonishing to see with what dexterity the workman wields a long hollow cylinder of melted glass, at the end of an iron tube, which, when he has extended as much as possible, by blowing, and every other means his art suggests he slits with a sharp instrument, removing the two extremities from each other, and folding back the sides: the cylinder now appears a large sheet of glass, which being once more introduced into the furnace, is brought out a clear, finished plate.

This manufactory formerly served all Europe with looking-glasses; the quantity made here is still considerable; for although France and England, and some other countries, make their own mirrors, yet, by the natural progress of luxury, those countries which still get their mirrors and other things from Murano, use a much greater quantity now than formerly; so that on the supposition that the Murano manufacturers have lost three-fourths of their customers, they may still retain half as much trade as they ever had. It is surprising that, instead of blowing, they do not adopt the method of casting, which I should think a much easier process, and by which larger plates may be made. Besides mirrors, an infinite quantity of glass trinkets (margaritini, as they are called) of all shapes and colours are made here. Women of the inferior ranks wear them as ornaments, and as rosaries: they also mould this substance into many various whimsical forms, by way of ornamental furniture to houses and churches. In short, there are glass baubles enough made here, to bribe into slavery half the inhabitants of the coast of Guinea.

[142] The early settlements on the islands of the Lagoon by refugees from the mainland, and in particular the settlement of Torcello; from *Venice, an Historical Sketch of the Republic* by Horatio F. Brown.

The chronicles detail at length the legend of this last flight from the mainland, and chiefly how the people of Altino came to settle at Torcello. The Lombards, 'those cruellest of pagans,' were sweeping down upon Friuli, and the people of Altino resolved to fly. Some went to Ravenna, some to Istria, some to the Pentapolis; some, however, remained behind, in sore doubt whither they should turn to seek a home. These people made a three days' fast and prayer to God that He would show them where they might find a dwelling-place. Then a voice was heard, as though in thunder, saying to them, 'Climb ye up to the tower and look at the stare.' Then the Bishop Paul climbed the tower, and looking up to the heavens, he saw the stars arranged as it were like islands in the lagoon. Thus guided, the people of Altino moved to Torcello, leaving their home to be burned by the Lombards when they found it empty. The fugitives called their new abode Torcello, in memory of many-towered Altino, which they had left behind. Their first care was to build a church to the honour of Mary, the Virgin. It was beautiful in form, and very fair; its pavement was made in circles of precious marbles. Then to Mauro, the priest, who was also from Altino, were shown by miracle the places where other churches should be built. 'First,' he says, 'Saint Erasmus and Saint Hermes showed me the plan of a church to be raised to them. Then, as I was walking along another lido, I saw a wonderful sight: a large white cloud, and out of it issued two rays of the sun, of a glorious clarity, which fell upon me; and a liquid voice said to me, "I am the Saviour and Lord of all the earth. The ground whereon thou standest I give to thee, thereon to build a church in My name." Then came another most delicious voice which said, "I am Mary, mother of the Lord Jesus Christ; I bid you build another church to me." Then I came to a third lido, and I saw the whole place filled with a diverse multitude of people, and many bulls and cows, with calves. And when I drew near, lo! an old man sitting on the ground, and he spoke to me, while nigh unto him stood a younger man. The old man said unto me, "I am Peter, prince and apostle, the pastor of the flock. I charge you honour me, and build me a church that there, on my nativity, all the people of Torcello may gather together." Then the younger said unto me, "I am the servant of God, Antolinus. I suffered for the name of Christ; I bid you build a little church for me, hard by the Master's church. Be instant day and night in memory of me; and whatsoever you ask of me shall be given unto you. "Then I came to a fourth little lido, and I saw that it was all full of heavy-clustered vineyards; and the vines bore the whitest grapes. There came upon me the desire to eat, but I did not; and as I walked by the sea a white cloud appeared unto me; in the middle thereof was seated a little maid, fair of form, who spoke to me thus, "I am Giustina, who suffered in Padua city for Christ's sake, I beg you, priest of God, build me a little church in my honour." In the fifth place I came to, I met a girl of tender years. A great and splendid cloud, as though it were the sun, illumined her, and it drew nigh unto me. Then I looked within and saw a glorious man of noble mien, standing above the sphere of the sun, and he said unto me, "I am John the Baptist, the forerunner of our Lord; I beg thee in this place build me the church I now show thee." Then he showed me all the outside of the church, and gave me the blessing of God on my bishopric of Torcello, and encircled me with the ring, which he placed upon my finger.

Then I awoke from the great sleep. The writing was found in
my hand, the ring upon my finger.'

[143] A visit to the Lido in 1849; from *Effie in Venice*
by Mary Lutyens.

Charlotte [Ker] did not go out yesterday so John and the
Gondolier rowed me over to Lido, one of the outer Islands
between Venice and the Adriatic. I wished to see the open sea
and we walked across the Island over the Jews' burying
Ground, where they formerly were all obliged to be buried.
All the tombstones were well sculptured and with Hebrew
writing to them. On the other side we ran down to the sea.
The tide was coming and the green waves crested with white
foam were very splendid, and pretty shells striped in many
colours were lying on the sand. When we returned the wind
rose and it was quite stormy. A fleet of Venetian fishing boats
literally flew past us with their beautiful sails spread. They
are of a rich orange colour with a cross and the world in
black painted on them and when the sun shines on them you
cannot conceive anything more vivid in colour or more
elegant in form. John is very busy in the Doge's Palace all day
and as yet he has only drawn one capital of one Pillar and
there is something like hundreds on each side.

[144] Venetian funerals, and the cemetery church and
island of S. Michele; from James (now Jan) Morris's
Venice.

Marvellously evocative is a winter funeral in Venice. A kind
of trolley, like a hospital carriage, brings the coffin to the
quayside, the priest shivering in his wind-ruffled surplice, the
bereaved relatives desperately muffled; and presently the
ungainly death-boat lopes away through the mist down the
Grand Canal, high, crooked and solemn, with a glimpse of
flowers and a tumble of gilt, and a little train of mourning
gondolas. They keep close to the bank, in the shade of the tall
tottering palaces (themselves like grey symbols of the grave)

and thus disappear slowly into the distance, across the last canal.

The procession is not always so decorous when it arrives at San Michele, for this cemetery still serves the whole of Venice, and often there are two or three such cortèges arriving at the landing-stage simultaneously. Then there is a frightful conglomeration of brass impediments, a tangle of plumes, motor boats backing and roaring, gondoliers writhing at their rowlocks, hookers straining on the quay, mourners embarrassingly intermingled. It is a funeral jam. I once saw such a *mélange*, one bright summer morning, into which a funeral gondola of racy instincts was projected forcibly by an accomplice motor boat, slipping the tow neatly as it passed the San Michele landingstage: never were mourners more mute with astonishment than when this flower-decked bier came rocketing past their gondolas, to sweep beside the quay with a jovial flourish.

Once ashore, though, and there will be no such contretemps, for San Michele is run with professional efficiency, and the director stands as proudly in his great graveyard as any masterful cruiser captain, god-like on his bridge. The church at the corner of the island is beautifully cool, austere and pallid, and is tended by soft-footed Franciscans: Paolo Sarpi is buried at its entrance, and the Austrians used its convent as a political prison. The cemetery itself is wide and calm, a series of huge gardens, studded with cypress trees and awful monuments. Not so long ago it consisted of two separate islands, San Michele and San Cristoforo, but now they have been artificially joined, and the whole area is cluttered with hundreds of thousands of tombs – some lavishly monumental, with domes and sculptures and wrought-iron gates, some stacked in high modern terraces, like filing systems . . .

There is an annual pilgrimage of ballet-lovers to the modest tomb of Diaghilev; and an increasing trickle of visitors finds its way to the obscure burial-place, high in a tomb-terrace, of Frederick William Serafino Austin Lewis Henry Rolfe, 'Baron Corvo'. He died, according to British Consulate records, in October 1913, in the Palazzo Marcello, at the age of 53: his life in Venice had sunk from eccentricity to outrage to depravity, but he refused ever to leave the city, wrote some incomparable descriptions of it, died in poverty and obloquy, and was buried (characteristically) at his brother's expense. Silently this multitude of shades lies there beneath the dark trees of San Michele; and at night-time, I am told, a galaxy of little votive lamps flutters and twinkles on ten thousand tombstones, like so many small spirits.

At the eastern corner of San Michele is an old Protestant graveyard of very different temper. It is like a Carolina churchyard, lush, untended and overgrown, shaded by rich gnarled trees, with grassy walks and generations of dead leaves. Most of its graves are obscured by weeds, earth and foliage, and it is instructive to wander through all this seductive desolation, clearing a gravestone here and there, or peering through the thickets at a worn inscription. There are many Swiss and Germans in these graves; and many British seamen, who died on their ships in the days when the P. & O. liners used the port of Venice. There is an English lady, with her daughter, who perished in a ferry disaster off the Lido in the early 1900s; and several Americans with names such as Horace, Lucy or Harriet; and one or two diplomats, among whose flowery but almost illegible epitaphs you may discern a plethora of adjectives like 'noble-minded', 'lofty', 'much-respected', 'eminent'. There is a long-forgotten English novelist, G. P. R. James, whose merits as a writer, we are ironically assured, 'are known wherever the English language is spoken'; and there is an unfortunate Mr Frank Stanier, of Staffordshire, whose mourners wrote of him, in a phrase that might be kindlier put, that he 'Left Us In Peace, Febry 2nd, 1910'.

[145] The Armenian monastery on the island of S. Lazzaro is visited by Byron in 1816; from *Letters and Journals of Lord Byron, with Notices of his Life* by Thomas Moore.

By way of divertisement, I am studying daily, at an Armenian monastery, the Armenian language. I found that my mind wanted something craggy to break upon; and this – as the most difficult thing I could discover here for an amusement – I have chosen, to torture me into attention. It is a rich language, however, and would amply repay any one the trouble of learning it. I try, and shall go on; – but I answer for nothing, least of all for my intentions or my success. There are some very curious MSS in the monastery, as well as books; translations also from Greek originals, now lost, and from Persian and Syriac, etc.; besides works of their own people. Four years ago the French instituted an Armenian professorship. Twenty pupils presented themselves on Monday morning, full of noble ardour, ingenuous youth, and impregnable industry. They persevered, with a courage worthy of the nation and of universal conquest, till Thursday; when *fifteen* of the *twenty* succumbed to the six-and-twentieth letter of the alphabet. It is, to be sure, a Waterloo of an Alphabet – that must be said for them. But it is so like these fellows, to do by it as they did by their sovereigns – abandon both; to parody the old rhymes, 'Take a thing and give a thing' – 'Take a king and give a king.' They are the worst of animals, except their conquerors.

[146] Twelve years later, Byron's memory was still cherished at the monastery, as Lady Blessington discovered; from *An Idler in Italy* by the Countess of Blessington.

We enquired for, and conversed some time with, Father Pasquali, from whom poor Byron took lessons when at Venice, crossing the lagoon most mornings, and in all weather, to pursue his studies in the Armenian language, with this worthy man. Father Pasquali's countenance became animated when we named Byron, of whom he spoke in terms of warm regard, praising not only the extraordinary facility with which he acquired knowledge, but the unaffected kindness of his heart, and gentleness of his manners.

Here was another proof of the power possessed by Byron, of exciting regard in those with whom he came in contact, a power exercised without any effort on his part.

The grammar in which Byron studied the rudiments of the

Armenian language in this convent, is now in my possession, presented as a parting gift at Genoa. A few lines in his writing states the circumstance of his having used the book here with Father Pasquali, and his name is written in two or three places.

[147] William Beckford visits Torcello on 27 August 1780. The composition of his party and his description of the scene are both very much in the manner of the eighteenth-century dilettante; from his *Italy, with sketches of Spain and Portugal.*

Now we beheld vast wastes of purple flowers, and could distinguish the low hum of the insects which hover above them; such was the silence of the place. Coasting along these solitary fields, we wound amongst several serpentine canals, bordered by gardens of figs and pomegranates, with neat, Indian looking inclosures of cane and reed: an aromatic plant clothes the margine of the waters, which the people justly dignify with the title of marine incense. It proved very serviceable in subduing a musky odour, which attacked us the moment we landed; and which proceeds from serpents that lurk in the hedges. These animals, say the gondoliers, defend immense treasures, which lie buried under the ruins. Woe to those who attempt invading them or prying too curiously about. Not chusing to be devoured, we left many a mount of fragments unnoticed, and made the best of our way to a little green lane, free from weeds or adders; decorated with the name of the Podesta's residence; and on the other by a circular church. Some remains of tolerable antique sculpture are enchased in the walls, and the dome, supported by pillars of a smooth Grecian marble, though uncouth and ill-proportioned, impresses a sort of veneration and transports the fancy to the twilight-glimmering period when it was raised. Having surveyed what little was visible, and given as much career to our imaginations as the scene inspired, we walked over a soil, composed of crumbling bricks and cement, to the cathedral whose arches, turned on the antient Roman principle, convinced us that it dates as high as the sixth or seventh century.

Nothing can be well more fantastic than the ornament of this structure, formed from the ruins of the Pagan temples of Altina; and incrusted with a gold mosaic like that which covers our Edward the Confessor's tomb. The pavement, composed of various precious marbles, is richer and more beautiful than one could have expected, in a place where every object savours of the greatest barbarism. At the further end, beyond the altar, appears a semicircular niche, with seats like the gradines of a diminutive amphitheatre; above rise the quaint forms of the apostles in red, blue, green and black mosaic; and in the midst of the goodly group, a sort of marble chair, cool and penitential enough, where Saint Lorenzo Giustiniani sat to hold a provincial council, the Lord knows how long ago. The font for holy water, stands by the principal entrance fronting this curious recess, and seems to have belonged to some place of Gentile worship. The figures of nymphs cling around the sides; more devilish, more Egyptian than any I ever beheld. The dragons on old china are not more whimsical. I longed to have filled it with bats' blood, and to have sent it by way of present to the sabbath . . . The sculpture is most delicate; but I cannot say a great deal about it, as but little light reaches the spot where it is fixed. Indeed the whole church is far from luminous; its windows being narrow and near the roof, with shutters composed of blocks of marble, which nothing but the last whirlwind, one should think, could move from their hinges. By the time we had examined every nook and corner of this singular edifice, and caught perhaps some small portion of sanctity, by sitting in San Lorenzo's chair, dinner was prepared in a neighbouring convent; and the nuns, allured by the sound of our flutes and oboes, peeped out of their cells, and shewed themselves by dozens at the grate. Some few agreeable faces and interesting eyes enlivened the dark sisterhood: all seemed to catch a gleam of pleasure from the music: two or three of them, probably the last immured, let fall a tear, and suffered the recollection of the world and its prophane joys to interrupt, for a moment, their sacred tranquillity.

[148] But the most superb description of Torcello remains that of John Ruskin, in *The Stones of Venice.*

The inlet which runs nearest to the base of the campanile is not that by which Torcello is commonly approached. Another, somewhat broader, and overhung by alder copse, winds out of the main channel of the lagoon up to the very edge of the little meadow which was once the Piazza of the city, and there, stayed by a few grey stones which present some semblance of a quay, forms its boundary at one extremity. Hardly larger than an ordinary English farmyard, and roughly enclosed on each side by broken palings and hedges of honeysuckle and briar, the narrow field retires from the water's edge, traversed by a scarcely traceable footpath, for some forty or fifty paces, and then expanding into the form of a small square, with buildings on three sides of it, the fourth being that which opens to the water. Two of these, that on our left and that in front of us as we approach from the canal, are so small that they might well be taken for the outhouses of the farm, though the first is a conventual building, and the other aspires to the title of the 'Palazzo publico,' both dating as far back as the beginning of the fourteenth century; the third, the octagonal church of Santa Fosca, is far more ancient than either, yet hardly on a larger scale. Though the pillars of the portico which surrounds it are of pure Greek marble, and their capitals are enriched with delicate sculpture, they, and the arches they sustain, together only raise the roof to the height of a cattle-shed; and the first strong impression which the spectator receives from the whole scene is, that whatever sin it may have been which has on this spot been visited with so utter a desolation, it could not at least have been ambition. Nor will this impression be diminished as we approach, or enter, the larger church, to which the whole group of building is subordinate. It has evidently been built by men in flight and distress, who sought in the hurried erection of their island church such a shelter for their earnest and sorrowful worship as, on the one hand, could not attract the eyes of their enemies by its splendour, and yet, on the other, might not awaken too bitter feelings by its contrast with the churches which they had seen destroyed. The exterior is absolutely devoid of decoration, with the exception only of the western entrance and the lateral door, of which the former has carved side posts and architrave, and the latter, crosses of rich sculpture; while the messy stone shutters of the windows, turning on huge rings of stone, which answer the double purpose of stanchions and brackets, cause the whole building rather to resemble a refuge from Alpine storm than the cathedral of a populous city; and, internally, the two solemn mosaics of the eastern and western extremities, – one representing the Last Judgment, the other the Madonna, her tears falling as her hands are raised to bless, – and the noble range of pillars which enclose the space between, terminated by the high throne for the pastor and the semicircular raised seats for the superior clergy, are expressive at once of the deep sorrow and the sacred courage of men who had no home left them upon earth, but who looked for one to come, of men 'persecuted but not forsaken, cast down but not destroyed.' . . .

The severity which is so marked in the pulpit at Torcello is still more striking in the raised seats and episcopal throne which occupy the curve of the apse. The arrangement at first somewhat recalls to the mind that of the Roman amphitheatres; the flight of steps which lead up to the central throne divides the curve of the continuous steps or seats (it appears in the first three ranges questionable which were intended, for they seem too high for the one, and too low and close for the other), exactly as in an amphitheatre the stairs for access intersect the sweeping ranges of seats. But in the very rudeness of this arrangement, and especially in the want of all appliances of comfort (for the whole is of marble, and the arms of the central throne are not for convenience, but for distinction, and to separate it more conspicuously from the undivided seats), there is a dignity which no furniture of stalls nor carving of canopies ever could attain.

If the stranger would yet learn in what spirit it was that the dominion of Venice was begun, and in what strength she went forth conquering and to conquer, let him not seek to estimate the wealth of her arsenals or number of her armies, nor look upon the pageantry of her palaces, nor enter into the secrets of her councils; but let him ascend the highest tier of the stern ledges that sweep round the altar of Torcello, and then, looking as the pilot did of old along the marble ribs of the goodly temple-ship, let him repeople its veined deck with the shadows of its dead mariners, and strive to feel in himself the strength of heart that was kindled within them, when first, after the pillars of it had settled in the sand, and the roof of it had been closed against the angry sky that was still reddened by the fires of their homesteads, – first, within the shelter of its knitted walls, amidst the murmur of the waste of waves and the beating of the wings of the sea-birds round the rock that was strange to them, – rose that ancient hymn, in the power of their gathered voices:

> The sea is His, and He made it;
> And His hands prepared the dry land.

[149] In a letter to her mother dated 24 February 1850, Effie Ruskin describes a picnic on Torcello; from *Effie in Venice* by Mary Lutyens.

(On the picnic with the Ruskins were Karl Paulizza, First Lieutenant of Artillery in the Austrian army and Effie's closest friend in Venice; Charlotte Ker, a travelling companion of Effie's; and George Hobbs, Ruskin's servant.)

John excites the liveliest astonishment to all and sundry in Venice and I do not think they have made up their minds yet whether he is very mad or very wise. Nothing interrupts him and whether the Square is crowded or empty he is either seen with a black cloth over his head taking Daguerrotypes or climbing about the capitals covered with dust, or else with cobwebs exactly as if he had just arrived from taking a voyage with the old woman on her broomstick. Then when he comes down he stands very meekly to be brushed down by Domenico quite regardless of the scores of idlers who cannot understand him at all. Not withstanding the above against society in general he sometimes does enjoy himself. The other day he took Paulizza, Charlotte & I to Torcello. George, John and the two Gondoliers rowed us so that we went very fast. The day was cloudy but we were afraid to put off the day in case another opportunity should not occur again; the sun broke forth warmly and the afternoon was charming. Charlotte & I ran into the quiet churchyard to see if the violets were yet in flower but we were still a little too soon and only found a quantity of fresh leaves. At three o'clock we sat down in the same place as before, leaning against the old Monastery of the Brothers of Torcello now filled with slag; a black lizard roused by the sun's heat fell from above on my shoulder but was gone before I hardly saw it. George laid out the cloth upon which he spread cold fowls, Parmesan cheese, Italian bread, beef, cakes, Muscat & Champagne Wines – and a copper vessel full of cold water from the draw well completed our bill of fare John & Paulizza were in the greatest spirits and nothing could be merrier than the two. After dinner, to show us that the Champagne which they certainly did not take much of, had not gone into their heads, they ran races round the old buildings and so fast that one could hardly see them. Paulizza looked so funny with his sword jumping at every step and Blue spectacles on . . .

[150] The magical quality of the light on the Lagoon and at Torcello; from *Italian Hours* by Henry James.

The light here is in fact a mighty magician and, with all respect to Titian, Veronese and Tintoret, the greatest artist of them all. You should see in places the material with which it deals – slimy brick, marble battered and befouled, rags, dirt, decay. Sea and sky seem to meet half-way, to blend their tones into a soft iridescence, a lustrous compound of wave and cloud and a hundred nameless local reflections, and then to fling the clear tissue against every object of vision. You may see these elements at work everywhere, but to see them in their intensity you should choose the finest day in the month and have yourself rowed far away across the lagoon to Torcello. Without making this excursion you can hardly pretend to know Venice or to sympathise with that longing for pure radiance which animated her great colourists. It is a perfect bath of light, and I couldn't get rid of a fancy that we were cleaving the upper atmosphere on some hurrying cloud-skiff. At Torcello there is nothing but the light to see – nothing at least but a sort of blooming sand-bar intersected by a single narrow creek which does duty as a canal and occupied by a meagre cluster of huts the dwellings apparently of market-gardeners and fishermen, and by a ruinous church of the eleventh century. It is impossible to imagine a more penetrating case of unheeded collapse. Torcello was the mother-city of Venice, and she lies there now, a mere mouldering vestige, like a group of weather-bleached parental bones left impiously unburied. I stopped my gondola at the mouth of the shallow inlet and walked along the grass beside a hedge to the low-browed, crumbling cathedral. The charm of certain vacant grassy spaces, in Italy, overfrowned by masses of brickwork that are honeycombed by the suns of centuries, is something that I hereby renounce once for all the attempt to express; but you may be sure that whenever I mention such a spot enchantment lurks in it.

A delicious stillness covered the little campo at Torcello; I remember none so subtly audible save that of the Roman Campagna. There was no life but the visible tremor of the brilliant air and the cries of half-a-dozen young children who dogged our steps and clamoured for coppers. These children, by the way, were the handsomest little brats in the world, and each was furnished with a pair of eyes that could only have signified the protest of nature against the meanness of fortune . . .

The church, admirably primitive and curious, reminded me of the two or three oldest churches of Rome – St Clement and St Agnes. The interior is rich in grimly mystical mosaics of the twelfth century and the patchwork of precious fragments in the pavement not inferior to that of St Mark's. But the terribly distinct Apostles are ranged against their dead gold backgrounds as stiffly as grenadiers presenting arms – intensely personal sentinels of a personal Deity. Their stony stare seems to wait forever vainly for some visible revival of primitive orthodoxy, and one may well wonder whether it finds much beguilement in idly-gazing troops of Western heretics – passionless even in their heresy.

[151] Alexander Herzen, with his old friend Giuseppe Garibaldi, visits the island of Chioggia in February 1867; from Herzen's *My Past and Thoughts* translated by Constance Garnett.

(Alexander Ivanovich Herzen (1812–1870), the Russian writer, political thinker and journalist, was during the 1840s the leader of the Russian 'Westernizers', as opposed to the Slavophils, who believed in Mother Russia as represented by the old national traditions and the Orthodox Church. In 1847 he left Russia with his family, never to return. After living for five years in Italy and France, he moved in 1852 to London, where he spent the next thirteen years. He was a great admirer of Garibaldi.)

I left the Square and went to meet Garibaldi. On the water everything was still ... the noise of the carnival came in discordant snatches. The stern, frowning blocks of the houses pressed closer and closer upon the boat, peeped at it with their lanterns; at an entry the rudder splashes, the steel hook gleams, the gondolier shouts: '*Apri – sia stati*' ... and again the water flows quietly in a side-street, and all at once the houses move apart, we are in the Grand Canal ...

The city gave Garibaldi a brilliant reception. The Grand Canal was almost transformed into a single bridge; to get into our boat we had to step across dozens of others. The Government and its retainers did everything possible to show that they were sulky with Garibaldi. If Prince Amadeus had been commanded by his father to show all those petty indelicacies, all that vulgar resentment, how was it the Italian boy's heart did not speak, how was it that he did not for the moment reconcile the city with the king and the king's son with his conscience? Why, Garibaldi had bestowed the crowns of the two Sicilies upon them.

I found Garibaldi neither ill nor any older since our meeting in London in 1864. But he was depressed, worried, and not ready to talk with the Venetians who were presented to him next day. The masses of the common people were his real followers; he grew more lively in Chioggia, where boatmen and fishermen were waiting for him. Mingling with the

crowd, he said to those poor and simple people: 'How happy
and at home I am with you, how deeply I feel that I was born
a working man and have been a working man; the misfortunes of our country tore me away from peaceful work. I too
grew up on the sea-coast and know all about your work . . .'
A murmur of delight drowned the former boatman's words,
the people surged about him. 'Give a name to my new-born
child,' cried a woman. 'Bless mine.' 'And mine,' shouted the
others.

[152] When Frederick Rolfe first came to Venice in
1908, the Lagoon entranced him; from *The Quest for
Corvo* by A. J. A. Symons.

(F. Rolfe (1860–1913), who called himself 'Baron Corvo',
having vainly attempted to enter the Catholic priesthood,
published his most famous novel, *Hadrian the Seventh*, in
1904. In 1908 he moved to Venice, where his homosexuality,
his constant begging for money and his talent for biting any
hand that attempted to feed him lost him any friends he might
have had.)

I came to Venice in August for a six week's holiday; and lived
and worked and slept in my *barcheta* almost always. It
seemed that, by staying on, I could most virtuously and most
righteously cheat autumn and winter. Such was the effect of
this kind of Venetian life on me, that I felt no more than
twenty-five years old, in everything excepting valueless experience and valuable disillusion. The bounding joy of vigorous
health, the physical capacity for cheerful (nay, gay) endurance, the careless, untroubled mental activity, the perfectly
gorgeous appetite, the prompt, delicate dreamless nights of
sleep, which betoken healthy youth – all this (with indescribable happiness) I had triumphantly snatched from solitude
with the sun and the sea. I went swimming half a dozen times
a day, beginning at white dawn, and ending after sunsets
which set the whole lagoon ablaze with amethyst and topaz.
Between friends, I will confess that I am not guiltless of often
getting up in the night and popping silently overboard to
swim for an hour in the clear of a great gold moon –

plenilunio – or among the waving reflections of the stars. (O my goodness me, how heavenly a spot that is!) When I wanted change of scene and anchorage, I rowed with my two gondoglieri [sic]; and there is nothing known to physiculturalists (for giving you 'poise' and the organs and figure of a slim young Diadymenos) like rowing standing in the Mode Venetian. It is jolly hard work; but no other exercise bucks you up as does springing forward from your toe-tips and stretching forward to the full in pushing the oar, or produces such exquisite lassitude at night when your work is done. And I wrote quite easily for a good seven hours each day. Could anything be more felicitous?

And, one day, I replenished my stock of provisions at Burano; and at sunset we rowed away to find a station for the night. Imagine a twilight world of cloudless sky and smoothest sea, all made of warm, liquid, limpid heliotrope and violet and lavender, with bands of burnished copper set with emeralds, melting, on the other hand, into the fathomless blue of the eyes of the prides of peacocks, where the moon rose, rosy as mother-of-pearl. Into such glory we three advanced the black *barcheta*, solemnly, silently, when the last echo of *Ave Maria* died.

Slowly we came out north of Burano into the open lagoon; and rowed eastward to meet the night, as far as the point marked by five *pali*, where the wide canal curves to the south. Slowly we went. There was something so holy – so majestically holy – in that evening silence, that I would not have it broken even by the quiet plash of oars. I was lord of time and place. No engagements cried to be kept. I could go when and where I pleased, fast or slow, far or near. And I chose the near and the slow. I did more. So unspeakably gorgeous was the peace on the lagoon just then, that it inspired me with a lust for doing nothing at all but sitting and absorbing impressions motionlessly. That way come thoughts, new, generally noble.

The wide canal, in which we drifted, is a highway. I have never seen it unspeckled by the *sandali* of Buranelli fishers. Steam-boats and tank-barges of fresh water for Burano, and the ordinary barks of carriage, disturb it, not always, but often. My wish was to find a smaller canal, away – away. We

were (as I said) at the southern side, at the southward curve
marked by five *pali*. Opposite, on the other bank, begins the
long line of *pali* which shows the deep-water way right down
to the Ricevitorio of Treporti; and there, at the beginning of
the line, I spied the mouth of a canal which seemed likely to
suit me. We rowed across to it, and entered. It tended north-
eastward for two or three hundred metres, and then bended
like an elbow north-westward. It looked quite a decent canal,
perhaps forty metres in width, between sweet mud-banks
clothed with sea-lavender about two-foot lengths above high-
water mark in places. We pushed inshore, near to the inner
bank at the elbow, stuck a couple of oars into the mud fore
and aft, and moored there.

Baicolo and Caicio got out the draught board and ciga-
rettes, and played below their breath on the *puppa*; while I
sat still, bathing my soul in peace, till the night was dark and
Selene high in the limpid sapphire-blue. Then they lighted the
fanali, and put up the impermeable awning with wings and
curtains to cover the whole *barcheta*; and made a parmentier
soup to eat with our wine and *polenta*. And, when kapok-
cushions had been arranged on the floor, and summer sleeping
bags laid over them, we took our last dash overboard, said
our prayers, and went to bed, Baicolo at *prova* with his feet
towards mine amidships, and Caicio under the *puppa* with
his feet well clear of my pillowed head. So, we slept.

Soon after sunrise I awakened: it was a sunrise of opal and
fire: the boys were deep in slumber. I took down the awning,
and unmoored quietly, and mounted the *puppa* to row about
in the dewy freshness in search of a fit place for my morning
plunge. I am very particular about this. Deep water I must
have – as deep as possible – I being what the Venetians call
'appassionato per l'acqua'. Beside that, I have a vehement
dyspathy against getting entangled in weeds or mud, to make
my toe-nails dirtier than my finger-nails. And, being congeni-
tally myopic, I see more clearly in deep water than in shallow,
almost as clearly, in fact, as with a concave monocle on land.
So I left the *barcheta* to drift with the current, while I took
soundings with the long oar of the *puppa*, in several parts of
the canal, near both banks as well as in the middle. Nowhere
could I touch bottom; and this signified that my bathing place

was more than four metres in depth. Needless to say that I gave a joyful morning yell, which dragged from sleep the luxury-loving Baicolo to make coffee, and the faithful dog Caicio to take my oar and keep the *barcheta* near me; and then I plunged overboard to revel in the limpid green water. Lord, how lovely is Thy smooth salt water flowing on flesh!

(Five years later, desperate and penniless, having exhausted the patience of all his erstwhile benefactors, his disenchantment was complete.)

I'm in an awful state; and I firmly believe that I'm finished if I don't get relief *instanter*.

The last fortnight has been a chapter of misfortunes. I've been literally fighting for life through a series of storms. Do you realize what that means in a little boat, leaky and so coated with weed and barnacles by a summer's use, that it is almost too heavy to move with the oar, and behaves like an inebriate in winds or weather? I assure you it's no joke. And storms get up on this lagoon in ten minutes, leaving no time to make a port. I'm frequently struggling for 50–60 hours on end. Results: I've lost about 300 pages of my new MS of *Hubert's Arthur*. Parts were oiled by a lamp blown over them: winds and waves carried away the rest. At every possible minute I am rewriting them: but, horrible to say, grey mists float about my eyecorners just through sheer exhaustion. The last few days I have been anchored near an empty island, Sacca Fisola, not too far away from civilization to be out of reach of fresh water, but lonely enough for dying alone in the boat if need be. Well, to shew you how worn out I am, I frankly say that I have funked it. This is my dilemma. I'll be quite plain about it. If I stay out on the lagoon, the boat will sink, I shall swim perhaps for a few hours, and then I shall be eaten alive by crabs. At low water every mudbank swarms with them. If I stay anchored near an island, I must keep continually awake: for, the moment I cease moving, I am invaded by swarms of swimming rats, who in the winter are so voracious that they attack even a man who is motionless. I have tried it. And have been bitten. Oh my dear man you can't think how artful fearless ferocious they are. I rigged up two bits of chain, lying loose on my prow and poop with a string by which I could shake them when attacked. For two nights the dodge acted. The swarms came (up the anchor rope) and nuzzled me: I shook the chains: the beasts plopped overboard. Then they got used to the noise and sneered. Then they bit the strings. Then they bit my toes and woke me shrieking and shaking with fear.

Now this is what I have done. I am perfectly prepared to persevere to the end. So I have taken the boat to a 'squero' to be repaired. This will take a fortnight. When she is seaworthy again, I'll go out and face my fate in her. Meanwhile I'm running a tick at the Cavelletto, simply that I may eat and sleep to write hard at restoring the 300 old pages of *Hubert's Arthur*. When that is done, the boat will be ready. I will assign that MS to you and send it.

My dear man, I am so awfully lonely. And tired. Is there no chance of setting me straight?

(There was not. A few weeks later he was dead.)

LIFE, CUSTOMS AND MORALS IN VENICE

Illustration on previous page: A Venetian courtesan of the early seventeenth century, by Giacomo Franco. The hairstyle was characteristic of courtesans.

153] St Peter Damian, with ill-concealed satisfaction, attributes the death of Maria Argyra, niece of the Byzantine Emperor Basil II (the Bulgar-Slayer) and wife of the co-Doge Giovanni Orseolo, to divine retribution for her sybaritic Oriental ways; from his *Opuscula*. Translated by John Julius Norwich.

(In fact, it was an outbreak of plague early in 1006 AD which carried her off.)

Such was the luxury of her habits that she scorned even to wash herself in common water, obliging her servants instead to collect the dew that fell from the heavens for her to bathe in. Nor did she deign to touch her food with her fingers, but would command her eunuchs to cut it up into small pieces, which she would impale on a certain golden instrument with two prongs and thus carry to her mouth. Her rooms, too, were so heavy with incense and various perfumes that it is nauseating for me to speak of them, nor would my readers readily believe it. But this woman's vanity was hateful to Almighty God; and so, unmistakably, did He take his revenge.

For He raised over her the sword of His divine justice, so that her whole body did putrefy and all her limbs began to wither, filling her bedchamber with an unbearable odour such that no one – not a handmaiden, nor even a slave – could withstand this dreadful attack on the nostrils; except for one serving-girl who, with the help of aromatic concoctions, conscientiously remained to do her bidding. And even she could only approach her mistress hurriedly, and then immediately withdraw. So, after a slow decline and agonizing torments, to the joyful relief of her friends she breathed her last.

[154] Canon Pietro Casola, accompanied by an envoy of the King of France, discovers that a lying-in (in this case, of the wife of the Patrician Agnello Dolfin) is a great social occasion in fifteenth-century Venice; from *Canon Pietro Casola's Pilgrimage* by M. Margaret Newett.

Her room had a charming piece of Carrara marble picked out with gold, and chiselled so as Praxiteles and Pheidias could not have bettered; the ceiling was so finely decorated with gold and deep blue, and the walls so finely hung that I cannot describe the effect. There was so much gold everywhere that I am not sure whether Solomon in his golden glory would not have looked small. Among the ornaments was a dish of gold valued at about five hundred gold ducats. The bed was of cedar or some such sweet scented wood and gilded, but of the ornaments and dress of the noble lady I think it best to keep silence rather than speak for fear no one would believe me. My attention was called off perhaps by the five-and-twenty lovely young noble ladies, each one fairer than her neighbour, seated around the bed, their blonde hair elaborately puffed and their features touched up with colour. Their dresses were discreet *alla Venegiana*: they showed no more than six finger-breadths of bare breast below their shoulders, back and front. These damsels had so many jewels on their heads and around their throats, and wore so many costly rings, – precious stones, pearls, and gold, – that we, who talked the matter over afterwards, came to the conclusion that the total value

far exceeded one hundred thousand gold ducats. Their faces
were superbly painted and so was the rest of them that was
bare.

[155] Visitors to Venice from the fifteenth century
onwards were always impressed by the clothes of the
inhabitants – when they were not profoundly shocked
by them. This, once again, is from *Canon Pietro
Casola's Pilgrimage* by M. Margaret Newett.

The city of Venice preserves its ancient fashion of dress –
which never changes – that is, a long garment of any colour
that is preferred. No one would leave the house by day if he
were not dressed in this long garment, and for the most part
in black. They have so observed this custom, that the individ-
uals of every nation in the world – which has a settlement in
Venice – all adopt this style, from the greatest to the least,
beginning with the gentlemen, down to the sailors and *gal-
eotti*. Certainly it is a dress which inspires confidence, and is
very dignified. The wearers all seem to be doctors in law, and
if a man should appear out of the house without his toga, he
would be thought mad . . .

When the Venetian gentlemen take offfice or go on some
embassy, they wear very splendid garments; in truth, they
could not be more magnificent. They are of scarlet, of velvet,
of brocade, if the wearers hold high office; and all the linings
of every kind are very costly . . .

Their women appear to me to be small for the most part,
because if they were not, they would not wear their shoes –
otherwise called *pianelle* – as high as they do. For in truth I
saw some pairs of them sold, and also for sale, that were at
least half a Milanese braccio in height. They were so high
indeed that when they wear them, some women appear giants;
and certain also are not safe from falling as they walk, unless
they are well supported by their slaves. As to the adornment
of their heads, they wear their hair so much curled over their
eyes that, at first sight, they appear rather men than women.
The greater part is false hair; and this I know for certain
because I saw quantities of it on poles, sold by peasants in the

Piazza San Marco. Further, I inquired about it, pretending to wish to buy some, although I had a beard both long and white.

These Venetian women, especially the pretty ones, try as much as possible in public to show their chests – I mean the breasts and shoulders – so much so, that several times when I saw them I marvelled that their clothes did not fall off their backs. Those who can afford it, and also those who cannot, dress very splendidly, and have magnificent jewels and pearls in the trimming round their collars. They wear many rings on their fingers with great balass rubies, rubies and diamonds. I said also those who cannot afford it, because I was told that many of them hire these things. They paint their faces a great deal, and also the other parts they show, in order to appear more beautiful. The general run of the women who go out of the house, and who are not amongst the number of the pretty girls, go out well covered up and dressed for the most part in black even up to the head, especially in church. At first I thought they were all widows, and sometimes on entering a church at the service time I seemed to see so many nuns of the Benedictine Order. The marriageable girls dress in the same way, but one cannot see their faces for all the world. They go about so completely covered up, that I do not know how they can see to go along the streets. Above all – at least indoors – these Venetian women, both high and low, have pleasure in being seen and looked at; they are not afraid of the flies biting them, and therefore they are in no great hurry to cover themselves if a man comes upon them unexpectedly. I observed that they do not spend too much in shawls to cover their shoulders. Perhaps this custom pleases others; it does not please me.

[156] Thomas Coryat is impressed by the uniform dignity of the clothes of Venetian men in 1608; from *Coryat's Crudities*.

It is said there are of all the Gentlemen of Venice, which are there called Clarissimoes, no lesse then three thousand, all which when they goe abroad out of their houses, both they that beare office, and they that are private, doe weare gownes. Most of their gownes are made of blacke cloth, and over their left shoulder they have a flappe made of the same cloth, and edged with blacke Taffata: Also most of their gownes are faced before with blacke Taffata: There are others also that weare other gownes according to their distinct offices and degrees; as they that are of the Councell of tenne (which are as it were the maine body of the whole estate) doe most commonly weare blacke chamlet gownes, with marvielous long sleeves, that reach almost downe to the ground. Againe they that weare red chamlet gownes with long sleeves, are those that are called Savi, whereof some have authority onely by land, as being the principall Overseers of the Podestas and Praetors in their land cities, and some by Sea. There are others also that weare blew cloth gownes with blew flapps over their shoulders, edged with Taffata. These are the Secretaries of the Councell of tenne. Upon every great festivall day the Senators, and greatest Gentlemen that accompany the Duke to Church, or to any other place, doe weare crimson damaske gownes, with flappes of crimson velvet cast over their left shoulders. Likewise the Venetian Knights weare black damaske gownes with long sleeves: but thereby they are distinguished from the other Gentlemen. For they weare red apparell under their gownes, red silke stockings, and red pantafles. All these gowned men doe weare marvellous little blacke flat caps of felt, without any brimmes at all, and very diminutive falling bandes, no ruffes at all, which are so shallow, that I have seene many of them not above a little inch deepe. The colour that they most affect and use for their other apparel, I mean doublet, hose, and jerkin, is blacke: a colour of gravity and decency. Besides the forme and fashion of their attire is both very aunciant, even the same that hath beene used these thousand yeares amongst them, and also uniforme. For all of them use but one and the same forme of habite, even the slender doublet made close to the body, without much quilting or bombase, and long hose plaine, without those new fangled curiosities, and ridiculous superfluities of panes, plaites, and other light toyes used with us English men. Yet they make it of costly stuffe, well beseeming Gentlemen and eminent persons of their place.

[157] A traveller in 1714 observes an unusual use for the 'marvelous long sleeves' noted by Coryat; from *A New Voyage to Italy* by F. N. Misson.

I would not have you imagine, that I design'd only to break a Jest when I told you, that the *great Sleeve* does sometimes serve instead of a Basket, when a Nobleman goes to the market; for I once saw a large Sallad, and at another time a delicate Tail of a Cod thus honourably lodg'd.

[158] Fashions for men, it seems, did not change much between the time of Coryat and 1766; from *An Account of the Manners and Customs of Italy, with Observations on the Mistakes of Some Travellers with Regard to that Country* by Joseph Baretti.

(Joseph Baretti (1719–1789) came to London in 1751 as a teacher of Italian attached to the Italian Opera House. There he became a friend of Dr Johnson and the Thrales, and in 1760 published his *Italian and English Dictionary*. Later he broke with Mrs Thrale over her marriage to Piozzi. Johnson said of him: 'There are strong powers in his mind. He has not, indeed, many hooks, but with what hooks he has he grapples very forcibly.')

The winter-dress of a Venetian noble, consists of a logn woolen black gown bordered with ermine, which he ties about his middle with a silver clasp: this gown has large hanging sleeves. He wears likewise an enormous wig; but no hat or cap, though formerly a black cap was part of his dress. His summer-dress is likewise black, open, loose, and shorter than that of the winter, with a silk-coat under it made after an old fashion somewhat resembling what is called a Vandyke-dress. The peculiar dress of his lady is also old-fashioned, and made of black velvet . . .

   At Venice the inhabitants in general wear large grey cloaks, in summer of silk, and in winter of black silk lined with white plush, over their ordinary dress. The cloaks of the lower sort are stuffs of any colour. Such at least was the fashion of cloaks when I was there last: but the Venetians do not stick long to a fashion in point of cloaks. I remember the time when they were all of scarlet cloth, and afterwards of fine camblet . . .

[159] Thomas Coryat, in 1608, comments on Venetian ladies; *décolletages*, and their habit of bleaching their hair; from *Coryat's Crudities*.

Almost all the wives, widowes and mayds do walke abroad with their breasts all naked, and many of them have their backes also naked even almost to the middle, which some do cover with a slight linnen, as cobwebbe lawne, or such other thinne stuffe: a fashion me thinkes very uncivill and unseemely, especially if the beholder might plainly see them. For I beleeve unto many that have *prurientem libidinem*, they would minister a great incentive & formation of luxurious desires. Howbeit it is much used both in Venice and Padua. For very few of them do weare bands but only Gentlewomen, and those do weare little lawne or cambricke ruffes. There is one thing used of the Venetian women, and some others dwelling in the cities and towns subject to the Signiory of Venice, that is not to be observed (I thinke) amongst any other women in Christendome: which is so common in Venice, that no woman whatsoever goeth without it, either in her house or abroad; a thing made of wood, and covered with leather of sundry colors, some with white, some redde, some yellow. It is called a Chapiney, which they weare under their shoes. Many of them are curiously painted; some also I have scene fairely gilt: so uncomely a thing (in my opinion) that it is pitty this foolish custom is not cleane banished and exterminated out of the citie. There are many of these Chapineys of a great height, even half a yard high, which maketh many of their women that are very short, seeme much taller then the tallest women we have in England. Also I have heared that this is observed amongst them, that by how much the nobler a woman is, by so much the higher are her Chapineys. All their Gentlewomen, and most of their wives and widowes that are of any wealth, are assisted and supported eyther by men or women when they walke abroad, to the end they may not fall. They are borne up most commonly by the left arme, otherwise they might quickly take a fall. For I saw a woman fall a very dangerous fall, as she was going down the staires of one of the little stony bridges with her high Chapineys alone by her selfe: but I did nothing pitty her, because shee wore such frivolous and (as I may truely terme them) ridiculous instruments, which were the occasion of her fall. For both I myselfe, and many other strangers (as I have observed in Venice) have often laughed at them for their vaine Chapineys.

All the women of Venice every Saturday in the afternoone doe vie to annoint their haire with oyle, or some other drugs, to the end to make it looke faire, that is whitish. For that colour is most affected of the Venetian Dames and Lasses. And in this manner they do it: first they put on a readen hat, without any crowne at all, but brimmes of exceeding breadth and largeness: then they sit in some sun-shining place in a chamber or some other secret roome, where having a looking-glass before them they sophisticate and dye their haire with the foresaid drugs, and after cast it backe round upon the brimmes of the hat, till it be throughly dried with the heat of the sunne: and last of all they curle it up in curious locks with a frilling or crisping pinne of iron, which we cal in Latin *Calamistrum*, the toppe whereof on both sides aboue their forehead is acuminated in two peakes. That this is true, I know by mine owne experience. For it was my chaunce one day when I was in Venice, to stand by an Englishman's wife, who was a Venetian woman borne, while she was thus trimming of her haire: a favour not affoorded to every stranger.

[160] John Evelyn, in his more detailed description of the clothes of Venetian women in the 1640s, also finds their *cioppini* ridiculous; from *The Diary of John Evelyn* edited by William Bray.

It was now Ascension Weeke, and the greate Mart or Faire of the whole yeare was now kept, every body at liberty and jollie. The noblemen stalking with their ladys on *choppines*;

these are high-heeltd shoes, particularly affected by these proude dames, or, as some say, invented to keepe them at home, it being very difficult to walke with them; whence one being asked how he liked the Venetian dames, replied, that they were *mezzo carne, mezzo ligno,* half flesh, half wood, and he would have none of them. The truth is, their garb is very odd, as seeming allways in masquerade; their other habits also totaly different from all nations. They weare very long crisped haire, of severall strakes and colours, which they make so by a wash, dischevelling it on the brims of a broade hat that has no head, but an hole to put out their heads by; they drie them in the sunn, as one may see them at their windows. In their tire they set silk flowers and sparkling stones, their peticoates coming from their very armepits, so that they are neere three quarters and an half apron; their sleeves are made exceeding wide, under which their shift sleeves as wide, and commonly tucked up to the shoulder, strewing their naked armes, thro' false sleeves of tiffany, girt with a bracelet or two, with knots of points richly tagged about their shoulders and other places of their body, which they usually cover with a kind of yellow vaile of lawn very transparent. Thus attir'd they set their hands on the heads of two matron-like servants or old women, to support them, who are mumbling their beades. 'Tis ridiculous to see how these ladys crawle in and out of their *gondolas* by reason of their *choppines,* and what dwarfs they appeare when taken downe from their wooden scaffolds; of these I saw near thirty together, stalking half as high again as the rest of the world, for courtezans or the citizens may not weare *choppines,* but cover their bodies and faces with a vaile of a certaine glittering taffeta or lustreè, out of which they now and then dart a glaunce of their eye, the whole face being otherwise entirely hid with it; nor may the com'on misses take this habit, but go abroad bare-fac'd. To the corners of these virgin-vailes hang broad but flat tossells of curious Point de Venize; the married women go in black vailes. The nobility weare the same colour, but of fine cloth lin'd with taffeta in Summer, with fur of the bellies of squirrells in the Winter, which all put on at a certain day girt with a girdle emboss'd with silver; the vest not much different from what our bachelors of Arts weare in Oxford, and a hood of cloth made like a sack, cast over their left shoulder, and a round cloth black cap fring'd with wool which is not so comely; they also weare their collar open to shew the diamond button of the stock of their shirt. I have never seene pearle for colour and bignesse comparable to what the ladys wear, most of the noble families being very rich in jewells, especialy pearles, which are always left to the son or brother who is destined to marry, which the eldest seldome do. The Doge's vest is of crimson velvet, the Procurator's, &c. of damasc, very stately. Nor was I lesse surprised with the strange variety of the severall nations which were seen every day in the streetes and piazzas; Jews, Turks, Armenians, Persians, Moores, Greekes, Sclavonians, some with their targets and boucklers, and all in their native fashions, negotiating in this famous Emporium, which is allways crowded with strangers.

[161] But Richard Lassels, the English Catholic priest and travelling tutor, decides in 1654 that *cioppini* are, after all, no bad thing; from *The Voyage of Italy*.

As for the women here, they would glady get the same reputation that their husbands have, of being tall and hansome; but they overdo it with their horrible *cioppini*, or shooes a full half yard high I confesse, I wondered at first, to see women go upon stilts and appeare taller by the head, than myself, who am of the tallest size; and not be able to go any wither without resting their hands upon the showlders of two grave old women that usher them: but at last I perceived that it was good policy, and a pretty ingenious way either to clog women absolutely at home (as the Egyptians kept their wives at home by allowing them no shooes at all) by such heavy shooes; or at least to make them not able to go either farre, or alone, or invisibly.

[162] Hints for travellers to Venice in 1594; from *An Itinerary . . .* by Fynes Moryson, Gent.

Of the hiring of chambers, and the manner of diet in Venice, I have spoken jointly with that of Paduoa, in the discription of that City, onely I will adde, that this City aboundeth with good fish, which are twice each day to be sold in two markets of Saint Marke & Rialto, & that it spendeth weekly five hundred Oxen, & two hundred & fifty Calves, besides great numbers of young Goates, Hens, and many kinds of birds, besides that it aboundeth with sea birds, whereof the Venetian writers make two hundred kinds, and likewise aboundeth with savoury fruits, and many salted and dried dainties, and with all manner of victuals, in such sort as they impart them to other Cities. I will also adde that here is great concourse of all nations, as well for the pleasure the City yeeldeth, as for the free conversation; and especially for the commodity of trafficke. That in no place is to be found in one market place such variety of apparell, languages, and manners. That in the publike Innes a chamber may be hired for foure sols a day; but for the cheapenes and good dressing of meat, most men use to hire private chambers, and dresse their owne meat. That in the Dutch Inne each man paies two lires a meale. That no stranger may lie in the City more then a night, without leave of the Magistrates appointed for that purpose; but the next day telling them some pretended causes of your comming to the Towne, they will easily grant you leave to stay longer, and after that you shall be no more troubled, how long soever you stay, onely your Host after certaine daies giveth them account of you. To conclude this most noble City, as well for the situation, freeing them from enemies, as for the freedome of the Common-wealth, preserved from the first founding, and for the freedome which the Citizens and very strangers have, to injoy their goods, and dispose of them, and for manifold other causes, is worthily called in Latine Venetia, as it were Veni etiam, that is, come againe.

[163] Torture in Venice in 1608; from *Coryat's Crudities.*

On the fourth day of August being Thursday, I saw a very Tragicall and dolefull spectacle in Saint *Markes* place. Two men tormented with the strapado, which is done in this manner. The offender having his hands bound behind him, is conveighed into a rope that hangeth in a pully, and after hoysted up in the rope to a great height with two severall swinges, where he sustaineth so great torments that his joynts are for the time loosed and pulled asunder; besides such abundance of bloud is gathered into his hands and face, that for the time he is in the torture, his face and hands does looke as red as fire.

[164] An execution in 1741; from *The Letters of Horace Walpole*.

(Horace Walpole (1717–1797), dilettante and novelist, was the fourth son of Sir Robert Walpole. His house at Strawberry Hill, Twickenham became the paradigm of the 'Gothick' style. He travelled to France and Italy in 1739–41 with the poet Thomas Gray.)

We have had a poor man beheaded here this morning for stealing a cup out of a church. I was told it just at going to bed, and could not sleep for thinking of the unhappy creature, who was to suffer for so trivial a fault. Had he murdered or broke open a house he might have escaped; but to have taken from the church was death *without benefit of the clergy*, for they never pardon where they are concerned. And a poor man dies unpitied, with the vulgar and bigoted crying out, the sacrilegious wretch! To me, 'tis shocking, that what they have branded with this formidable title *sacrilege*, should be a capital crime. Only think, some dying usurer, or a superannuated old whore gives God a pair of silver candlesticks, and if a famished poor creature takes away one, he is to die for it. God gives us everything to use, and we think we make Him a fine present, by laying up some pounds of plate in an old sacristy, never to be used!

[165] The state of Venetian convents in 1685; from *Letters containing an Account of what seem'd most remarkable in travelling thro' Switzerland, Italy and some Parts of Germany* by G. Burnet, DD.

(Dr Gilbert Burnet (1643–1715), having refused four bishoprics before he was twenty-nine, was dismissed as King's Chaplain in 1674 for his criticisms of Charles II and travelled for some years on the Continent. He became Bishop of Salisbury in 1689, after the Glorious Revolution of the previous year.)

The Nuns of *Venice* have been under much Scandal for a great while; there are some Nunneries that are as famous for their Strictness and Exactness to their Rules, as others are for the Liberties they take; chiefly those of St *Zachary* and St *Laurence*, where none but Noble *Venetians* are admitted, and where it is not so much as pretended that they have retired for Devotion, but it is owned to be done merely that they might not be too great a Charge to their Family: They are not veiled; their Neck and Breast are bare, and they receive much Company; but that which I saw was in a publick Room, in which there were many Grills for several Parlours, so that the Conversation is very confused; for there being a different Company at every Grill, and the *Italians* speaking generally very loud, the Noise of so many loud Talkers is very disagreeable. The Nuns talk much, and very ungracefully, and allow themselves a Liberty in rallying, that other Places could not bear. About four Years ago the Patriarch intended to bring a Reform into those Houses; but the Nuns of St *Laurence*, with whom he began, told him plainly they were Noble *Venetians*, who had chosen that Way of Life as more convenient for them, but they would not subject themselves to his Regulations; yet he came and would have shut up their House, so they went to set fire to it; upon which the Senate interposed, and ordered the Patriarch to desist.

[166] Spectator sports in the Campo Santo Stefano in 1608, as described by Thomas Coryat; from *Coryat's Crudities*.

There are two very faire and spacious Piazzaes or maket places in the Citie, besides that of St *Marke* before mentioned, whereof the fairest is St *Stephens*, being indeed of a notable length, even two hundred eighty seven paces long, for I paced

it; but of a meane breadth, onely sixty one. Here every Sunday
and Holyday in the evening the young men of the citie doe
exercise themselves at a certaine play that they call Baloone,
which is thus: Sixe or seven yong men or thereabout weare
certaine round things upon their armes, made of timber,
which are full of sharpe pointed knobs cut out of the same
matter. In these exercises they put off their dublets, and
having put this round instrument upon one of their armes,
they tosse up and downe a great ball, as great as our football
in England: sometimes they will tosse the ball with this
instrument, as high as a common Church, and about one
hundred paces at the least from them. About them sit the
Clarissimoes of Venice, with many strangers that repair
thither to see their game. I have seene at the least a thousand
or fifteene hundred people there: If you will have a stoole it
will cost you a gazet; which is almost a penny.

[167] The battles on the bridges in the 1720s; from
*Travels through Germany, Bohemia, Hungary, Switzer-
land, Italy and Lorrain* by Johann Georg Keysler.

Formerly another diversion was exhibited at this season on a
bridge near St Barnabas's church; which was an engagement
betwixt the *Castellani* and *Nicoloti*. During this mock battle,
several persons on both sides are thrown over into the water.
This bridge is seven common paces broad, eighteen long, and
without any fence; and when such an engagement was going
to be exhibited, the water under it was made deeper than
usual. The combatants were not allowed to scratch or seize
one another, but only to shew their strength and address with
their arms and fists. But this diversion has been suppressed for
some time, having once occasioned a dangerous tumult, when
the populace assaulted with stones the houses where the nobles
were posted to view the battle and encourage the combatants.

[168] Another venerable piazza tradition, the *Forza
d'Ercole*, witnessed in 1739; from *Selections from the
Letters of de Brosses* translated by Lord Ronald Sutherland Gower.

I have not seen the combats between the gondoliers on the bridges, for to my great regret they have been abolished. Instead of that they have invented another sport, which they call the Force of Hercules. A certain number of naked men range themselves along both sides of the Piazzetta or in some other public place, facing each other in two lines equal in number. They then place little planks, whose ends are supported on their shoulders; others mount on these planks, another lot again above these, and thus continue until there is only one man on top, on whose head stands a child. All this climbing does not take place without the occasional shifting of the planks, and then this human house of cards comes toppling down into the water. This break-neck game often takes place near the Rialto. By the way, I do not understand the enthusiasm for that bridge; it is nothing so very wonderful, although undeniably handsome. It is entirely built of white marble, and has but a single span; but, as to size, it is nothing by the side of the Pont-Neuf.

[169] In the eighteenth century, Casanova finds himself a suitable *casinò* and makes sure it comes up to his standards; from *The Memoirs of Jacques Casanova de Seingalt* translated by Arthur Machen.

(A *casinò* – the accent falling firmly on the last syllable – was a small suite of rooms, possessed by nearly all well-to-do Venetian gentlemen, separate from the house in which they and their family lived; it was used for gambling, entertaining or dalliance.)

I had no time to lose, for I had no casino. I took a second rower so as to reach *St Mark's Square* more rapidly, and I immediately set to work looking for what I wanted. When a mortal is so lucky as to be in the good graces of the god *Plutus*, and is not crack-brained, he is pretty sure to succeed in everything; I had not to search very long before I found a casino suiting my purpose exactly. It was the finest in the neighbourhood of *Venice*, but, as a natural consequence, it was likewise the most expensive. It had belonged to the English ambassador, who had sold it cheap to his cook before leaving *Venice*. The owner let it to me until Easter for one hundred sequins, which I paid in advance on condition that he would himself cook the dinners and the suppers I might order.

I had five rooms furnished in the most elegant style, and everything seemed to be calculated for love, pleasure, and good cheer. The service of the dining-room was made through a sham window in the wall, provided with a dumb-waiter revolving upon itself, and fitting the window so exactly that masters and servants could not see each other. The drawing-room was decorated with magnificent looking-glasses, crystal chandeliers, girandoles in gilt, bronze, and with a splendid pier-glass placed on a chimney of white marble; the walls were covered with small squares of real china, representing little *Cupids* and naked amorous couples in all sorts of positions, well calculated to excite the imagination; elegant and very comfortable sofas were placed on every side. Next to it was an octagonal room, the walls, the ceiling, and the floor of which were entirely covered with splendid Venetian glass, arranged in such a manner as to reflect on all sides every position of the amorous couple enjoying the pleasures of love. Close by was a beautiful alcove with two secret outlets; on the right, an elegant dressing-room; on the left, a boudoir which seemed to have been arranged by the mother of Love, with a bath in *Carrara* marble. Everywhere the wainscots were embossed in ormolu or painted with flowers and arabesques.

After I had given my orders for all the chandeliers to be filled with wax candles, and the finest linen to be provided wherever necessary, I ordered a most delicate and sumptuous supper for two, without regard to expense, and especially the most exquisite wines. I then took possession of the key of the principal entrance, and warned the master that I did not want to be seen by anyone when I came in or went out.

I observed with pleasure that the clock in the alcove had an alarum, for I was beginning, in spite of love, to be easily influenced by the power of sleep.

Everything being arranged according to my wishes, I went, as a careful and delicate lover, to purchase the finest slippers I could find, and a cap in *Alençon* point.

I trust my reader does not think me too particular; let him recollect that I was to receive the most accomplished of the sultanas of the master of the universe, and I told that fourth *Grace* that I had a casino. Was I to begin by giving her a bad idea of my truthfulness?

At the appointed time, that is two hours after sunset, I repaired to my palace; and it would be difficult to imagine the surprise of his honour the French cook, when he saw me arrive alone. Not finding all the chandeliers lighted up as I had ordered, I scolded him well, giving him notice that I did not like to repeat an order.

'I shall not fail, sir, another time, to execute your commands.'

'Let the supper be served.'

'Your honour ordered it for two.'

'Yes, for two; and this time be present during my supper, so that I can tell you which dishes I find good or bad.'

The supper came through the revolving dumb-waiter in very good order, two dishes at a time. I passed some remarks upon everything; but, to tell the truth, everything was excellent: game, fish, oysters, truffles, wine, dessert, and the whole served in very fine *Dresden* china and silver-gilt plate.

I told him that he had forgotten hard eggs, anchovies, and prepared vinegar to dress a salad. He lifted his eyes towards heaven, as if to plead guilty to a very heinous crime.

After a supper which lasted two hours, and during which I must certainly have won the admiration of my host, I asked him to bring me the bill. He presented it to me shortly afterwards, and I found it reasonable. I then dismissed him, and lay down in the splendid bed in the alcove; my excellent supper brought on very soon the most delicious sleep which, without the burgundy and the champagne, might very likely not have visited me, if I had thought that the following night would see me in the same place, and in possession of a lovely divinity.

[170] Eighteenth-century social life in Venice tended to revolve around the *casinò*, but William Beckford was

unimpressed; from *Italy, with sketches of Spain and Portugal.*

Many of the noble Venetians have a little suite of apartments in some out-of-the-way corner, near the grand piazza, of which their families are totally ignorant. To these they skulk in the dusk, and revel undisturbed with the companions of their pleasures. Jealousy itself cannot discover the alleys, the winding passages, the unsuspected doors, by which these retreats are accessible. Many an unhappy lover, whose mistress disappears on a sudden with some fortunate rival, has searched for her haunts in vain. The gondoliers themselves, though the prime managers of intrigue, are often unacquainted with these interior cabinets. When a gallant has a mind to pursue his adventures with mystery, he rows to the piazza, orders his bark to wait, meets his goddess in the crowd, and vanishes from all beholders. Surely, Venice is the city in the universe best calculated for giving scope to the observations of a devil upon two sticks. What a variety of lurking-places would one stroke of his crutch uncover! . . .

Madame de Rosenberg arrived, to whom I had the happiness of being recommended. She presented me to some of the most distinguished of the Venetian families at their great casino which looks into the piazza, and consists of five or six rooms, fitted up in a gay flimsy taste, neither rich nor elegant, where were a great many lights, and a great many ladies negligently dressed, their hair falling very freely about them, and innumerable adventures written in their eyes. The gentlemen were lolling upon the sofas, or lounging about the apartments.

The whole assembly seemed upon the verge of gaping, till coffee was carried round. This magic beverage diffused a temporary animation; and, for a moment or two, conversation moved on with a degree of pleasing extravagance; but the flash was soon dissipated, and nothing remained save cards and stupidity.

In the intervals of shuffling and dealing, some talked over the affairs of the grand council with less reserve than I expected; and two or three of them asked some feeble questions about the late tumults in London. It was one o'clock before all the company were assembled, and I left them at three, still dreaming over their coffee and card-tables. Trieze is their favourite game: *uno, due, tre, quatro, cinque, fante, cavallo re*, are eternally repeated; the apartments echoed no other sound.

I wonder a lively people can endure such monotony, for I have been told the Venetians are remarkably spirited; and so eager in the pursuit of amusement as hardly to allow themselves any sleep. Some, for instance, after declaiming in the Senate, walking an hour in the square, and fidgeting about from one casino to another till morning dawns, will get into a gondola, row across the Lagunes, take the post to Mestre or Fusina, and jumble over craggy pavements to Treviso, breakfast in haste, and rattle back again as if the Devil were charioteer: by eleven the party is restored to Venice, resumes robe and perriwig, and goes to council.

[171] Laws affecting women in eighteenth-century Venice; from *Letters from Italy . . . in the Years 1770 and 1771* by Anna, Lady Miller.

A new regulation in the coffee-houses had just taken place before our arrival: the partitions, which formed kind of cells in the interior of them, into which two or three people might retire and fasten the door, are now taken away, and the rooms quite open and public. At first the senate had determined to exclude the women entirely from entering the coffee-houses, but they remonstrated so violently and effectually against this measure, that they were allowed the liberty of appearing publickly, but absolutely forbid to retire in private into any room, and the little rooms were without exception ordered to be thrown into the large ones. Another law has just been promulgated, which is, that if any *fille de joie* is found walking the streets about the *Place St Mark, &c.* for the first offence she is to have her head completely shaved, and suffer imprisonment for a time specified; and for the second offence, her eye-brows are also to be shaved, she is to be branded between the eyes, and banished the Republic.

[172] The theatre in Venice does not greatly appeal to an eighteenth-century English traveller; from *A View of Society and Manners in Italy* by John Moore MD.

The number of playhouses in Venice is very extraordinary, considering the size of the town, which is not thought to contain above one hundred and fifty thousand inhabitants; yet there are eight or nine theatres here, including the opera-houses. You pay a trifle at the door for admittance; this entitles you to go into the pit, where you may look about, and determine what part of the house you will sit in. There are rows of chairs placed in the front of the pit, next the orchestra; the seats of these chairs are folded to their backs, and fastened by a lock. Those who choose to take them, pay a little more money to the door-keeper, who immediately unlocks the seat. Very decent-looking people occupy these chairs; but the back part of the pit is filled with footmen and gondoleers, in their common working clothes. The nobility, and better sort of citizens, have boxes retained for the year; but there are always a sufficient number to be let to strangers: the price of those varies every night, according to the season of the year, and the piece acted.

A Venetian playhouse has a dismal appearance in the eyes of people accustomed to the brilliancy of those of London. Many of the boxes are so dark, that the faces of the company in them can hardly be distinguished at a little distance, even when they do not wear masks. The stage, however, is well illuminated, so that the people in the boxes can see, perfectly well, every thing that is transacted there; and when they choose to be seen themselves, they order lights into their boxes.

Between the acts you sometimes see ladies walking about, with their Cavalieri Serventés, in the back part of the pit, when it is not crowded. As they are masked, they do not scruple to reconnoitre the company, with their spying-glasses, from this place: when the play begins, they return to their boxes. This continual moving about from box to box, and between the boxes and the pit, must create some confusion, and, no doubt, is disagreeable to those who attend merely on account of the piece. There must, however, be found some *douceur* in the midst of all this obscurity and confusion, which, in the opinion of the majority of the audience, over-balances these obvious inconveniences.

The music of the opera here is reckoned as fine as in any town in Italy; and, at any rate, is far superior to the praise of so very poor a judge as I am. The dramatic and poetical parts of those pieces are little regarded: the poet is allowed to indulge himself in as many anachronisms, and other inconsist-encies, as he pleases. Provided the music receives the appro-bation of the critic's ear, his judgment is not offended with any absurdities in the other parts of the composition. The celebrated Metastasio has disdained to avail himself of this indulgence in his operas, which are fine dramatic composi-tions. He has preserved the alliance which ought always to subsist between sense and music.

But as for the music of the serious operas, it is, in general, infinitely too fine for my ear; to my shame I must confess, that it requires a considerable effort for me to sit till the end.

[173] A French ambassador to Venice in the 1750s finds visits to the theatre a diplomatic necessity, and criticizes a production to considerable effect; from *Memoirs and Letters of the Cardinal de Bernis* translated by Katharine Prescott Wormeley.

Before my embassy to Venice, the nobility in the theatre and other places of meeting never bowed to the ambassadors, nor did the ambassadors bow to them. I changed that savage custom; I accustomed the nobles and the ladies to be bowed to by me, and to return my bow; gradually they became so accustomed to it that they ended by bowing first. I alone enjoyed that civility which the other foreign ministers had tried in vain to obtain.

The embassy to Venice is usually considered as a post of little importance. This is why the Courts have not, for a long time, sent men of much ability to fill it. It is true that it does not seem very necessary to do so in view of the little influence the Republic of Venice now has in the affairs of Europe. And yet I do not know a better school in which to train ambassadors. Nothing is of indifference in that country; every word, every action produces its effect; thus an observing and reflecting minister accustoms himself to reason out all his actions, and to consider nothing as of no consequence. Moreover, in Venice he treats with an invisible government, and always by writing; which forces him to great circumspection in order to send nothing to the Senate that is not well-digested and maturely reflected. He must, moreover, if he hopes to make the affairs with which he is charged succeed, employ an industry all the greater because it must be employed with prudence . . .

One portion of the nobility protected the Abbé Chiai, a rival, very inferior, to the celebrated Goldoni, who is the Molière of the Italians. This abbé gave to the public a comedy entitled 'The Venetian Lady in Paris.' The play had a great success on its first representation, but I was warned that it spoke indecently of French valour. The Austrian ambassador (Rosemberg) urged me, no doubt maliciously, to go and see the play. I promised him to go the next day, – which I did; and I saw throughout the performance that all eyes were turned to me to examine the expression of my face, on which no displeasure appeared. The next day the government sent questioners to ask what I thought of the comedy; I said simply that I thought it pretty, except the part of a Frenchman, for the first rule of the stage was to give to each nation the character that belonged to it. I said no more; and that night as the play was about to begin before an audience more numerous than before, a messenger from the State inquisitors arrived with an order not to play the piece, which, in spite of cabals, has never been returned to the stage. The next day an amusing notice was posted up which said: *La Veneziana in Parigi morta improvisamente del morbo gallico* [Sudden death of the Venetian lady in Paris by the French disease – i.e. syphilis].

It must not be supposed that, although the Venetian nobles are forbidden to hold any intercourse with ambassadors (a very wise severity; if the Republic ever renounces it, she will lose her morals, and soon she will change her laws; the one follows the other), it must not be thought, I say, that in spite of this rigour foreign ministers do not have any sort of intercourse with the magistrates; they speak to one another by third parties; they communicate many things by signs at the Opera, a circumstance which renders the frequenting of theatres and the use of the mask necessary to the foreign ministers.

[174] A visiting singer is warned by the manager of the theatres about the danger of political indiscretion; from *Reminiscences* by Michael Kelly.

(Michael Kelly (1762–1826) was a celebrated Irish singer and actor, who studied singing in Naples in 1779, and then sang in several Italian cities. He was in Venice in 1782. He went on to become principal tenor in Vienna, where he was a friend and admirer of Mozart and sang the role of Don Basilio in the first production of *The Marriage of Figaro*.)

'In this city,' said [the manager], 'you will find innumerable pleasures; your youth and good spirits will lay you open to many temptations; but against one thing, and one thing only, I particularly caution you: – never utter one word against the laws or customs of Venice, – do not suffer yourself to be betrayed even into a jest on this subject. You never know to whom you speak; in every corner spies are lurking, numbers of whom are employed at a high price to ensnare the unwary, and report the language of strangers; but with no other protection than a *silent tongue*, you may do what you like, and enjoy every thing without molestation. I will relate an anecdote,' added he, 'which will give you some idea of our police.

'A countryman of yours came to this city, accompanied by a Swiss valet; he took up residence at the Scuda di Francia. On his return home one evening, he found his writing-desk broken open, and a large sum of money taken from it. After making peaceable inquiries, without effect, he flew into a violent rage, charged the landlord and waiters, &c. with being thieves; but above all, he called them Venetian thieves, and cursed himself for having come into a country where the property of a traveller was not safe even in his own hotel. In the height of his wrath he dismissed his valet for going out and leaving the door of his apartment unlocked; and having vented his displeasure, thought the matter ended; but not so. On the third morning after this event, he was roused out of his sleep by the officers of the Inquisition, who informed him, that he must go immediately before the three grand inquisitors. His feelings were not to be envied when, hoodwinked, he was led on board a gondola, and thence into a room hung with black, where sat his judges. After due preparation and solemnity, and a severe lecture on the enormity of the abuse which he had uttered against the Venetian state, its laws, and subjects, he received a peremptory order to quit its territories in twenty-four hours; this he of course tremblingly promised to obey; but just as he turned to leave the tribunal, a curtain was suddenly drawn aside, behind which lay the strangled corpse of his Swiss valet, and the stolen bag of money by his side.' I confess this instance of the summary mode of administering justice in Venice, made a deeper impression upon me than all the good Signor's advice.

[175] Venetian social customs in 1739; from *Selections from the letters of de Brosses* translated by Lord Ronald Sutherland Gower.

. . . in no other place in the world does so much liberty and licence exist so entirely as here. Do not meddle with the government, and you can do just as you please. Whatever is known by the name of a bad action in the high moral sense is allowed with impunity. However, in spite of the warm blood, and in spite of the liberty given by wearing of masks, the allurements of the night, the narrow streets, and especially the bridges without any parapets, from which one can push a man into the sea without his being aware of it – in spite of all this, there are not more than four accidents a year, and these only among the visitors. From this you can judge how mistaken are the ideas people have regarding Venetian stilettoes. This is also the case respecting their jealousy of their wives; however, this requires qualification. As soon as a young lady of the nobility is engaged she puts on a mask, and no one ever sees her face again except those who are allowed to do so by her betrothed or relatives, but this is very uncommon. When she marries she becomes the common property of all the family, which is a good idea, as no more precautions are necessary, and one is sure to have children of the same blood. The youngest son often bears the name of husband, but besides that it is the custom to have a lover; it would indeed be a disgrace were a lady known to be without one. But in all this politics play an important part. The family make use of their privileges as does the King of France in the election of the abbot of Cîteaux; the lady is allowed to make her choice, only one or two men being included. She must choose a nobleman, and he must have been in the Senate and in the Councils, and of a family powerful enough to favour intrigues, and to whom one is able to say, 'Dear sir, to-morrow I shall require so many votes for my brother-in-law or for my husband.' This being arranged, a lady has complete liberty to do as she pleases. Let us, however, be just. Our Ambassador told me the other day that he did not know more than fifty ladies who lived matrimonially with their lovers; the others are restrained by religious scruples.

The visitors are somewhat at a disadvantage under these circumstances, for the patricians are not accustomed to ask them to their houses or to their parties. They prefer living amongst themselves with elbow room, so that they discuss their plots and intrigues with their friends before their wives, which would be impossible if strangers were present. Much, however, can be done, if precautions are used, by the help of the gondola, for that is the lady's sanctum. It has never been known that the signora's gondolier has revealed things to the signora's husband; were it known, he would be drowned the next day by his fellows. Formerly it was the convents which had the reputation of favouring assignations; there are still several that have the credit of this commerce, and at this moment there are three of these establishments all by the ears as to which of them shall have the honour of bestowing a mistress on the Papal Nuncio, who has just arrived. Indeed, these nuns are the most attractive among all the women in Venice, and if I had to remain a long while here it is to them that I would pay my attentions. All those that I have seen at the celebration of the Mass behind the grating, talking and laughing among themselves all the time the service lasted, seemed extremely attractive, and their costume enhanced their good looks. They wear a charming little cap, a simple dress, nearly always white, which shows as much of the neck and shoulders as our actresses display on the stage when dressed *à la romaine*.

I believe the first families of the Venetian nobility to be the most ancient in Europe, for there are many descendants of those who elected the first Doge, more than thirteen hundred years ago. There are, both in the ancient as well as in the modern nobility – between whom, by the way, there is not that gulf fixed as is the case in Genoa – many very wealthy families, although the Republic takes good care that they shall not become too wealthy. For instance, quite recently a daughter of the house of Pisani, who has 50,000 ducats a year, wanted to marry a man of her name almost as rich as herself. Not only did the State forbid her doing so, but it compelled her to marry a man who had no fortune whatever. The nobility here prove their descent by the 'Golden Book,' where the name of every noble is inscribed when he is born; those who have neglected to enter their names in that book are not regarded as of noble birth, and it thus happens that among the lower classes some of the oldest families are to be found. Once the 'Golden Book' was suddenly closed, and since then only those whose names appear in the book and their descendants are regarded as belonging to the nobility of Venice . . .

It is only in this place that such a thing as I saw the other day *can* be seen, namely a minister of State and a priest, for this individual is both, in a public theatre, in the presence of four thousand persons, chaffing one of the most notorious improprieties of the town, and receiving taps on his nose from her fan. Do you know that I found one day a dagger in the dress of the above lady! She said that in her profession one had the right of carrying a dagger for the management of her domestic affairs. I am less surprised at this since I find the nuns and abbesses also carry weapons on them, and I heard that one of the latter ladies, who is still living, had had a duel with poniards with another lady about the Abbé de Pomponne. This affair made rather a scandal, for the combat did not take place in a convent.

[176] The *Cavaliere Servente*, or *Cicisbeo*; from *Letters from Italy ... in the Years 1770 and 1771* by Anna, Lady Miller.

I think I have not yet mentioned the manners of the Venetians, at least not entered into any detail on that subject, nor will my time now allow me, were I much better qualified for the task than I really am. However, not wholly to disappoint you, take this account of some of their women at least, particularly the nobility. The custom of *Cavalieri Serventi* prevails universally here: this usage would appear in a proper light, and take off a great part of the odium thrown upon the Italians, if the Cavalieri Serventi were called husbands; for the real husband, or beloved friend, of a Venetian lady (often for life), is the *Cicisbeo*. The husband married in church is the choice of her friends, not by any means of the lady. It is from such absurd tyranny of the relations and friends of young girls, not suffering them to chuse for themselves, that this chusing of Cicisbeos, or Cavalieri Serventis, has taken its rise, and will never be relinquished in Italy, whilst the same incongruous combinations subsist: this surely lessens the criminality, at least in some degree. The Venetian ladies have a gay manner of dressing their heads, which becomes them extremely when young, but appears very absurd when age has furrowed over their fine skins, and brought them almost to the ground. I felt a shock at first sight of a tottering old pair I saw enter a coffee-house the other evening; they were both shaking with the palsy, leant upon each other, and supported themselves by a crutch-stick; they were bent almost double by the weight of years and infirmities, yet the lady's head was dressed with great care; a little rose-coloured hat, nicely trimmed with blond, was stuck just above her right ear, and over her left was a small matt of artificial flowers; her few grey hairs behind were tied with ribbon, but so thinly scattered over her forehead, that large patches of her shrivelled skin appeared between the parting curls: the *Cavaliere* was not dressed in the same stile, all his elegance consisted in an abundance of wig which flowed upon his shoulders. I inquired who this *venerable* couple were, and learnt, that the gentleman had been the faithful *Cavaliere* of the same lady above forty years;

that they had regularly frequented the *Place St Mark* and the coffee-houses, and with the most steady constancy had loved each other, till age and disease were conducting them hand in hand together to the grave. However, a forty years constancy is far from *universal* at Venice; *coquettes* are to be found there, as well as elsewhere: I have seen some instances of coquetry at fourscore; a *Donna Nobile*, whom a catarrh and Satan had bound, 'lo, these eighteen years!' was sustaining herself on the arm of a brisk Cicisbeo about twenty-five, in the *Place St Mark*; she had often changed *Cavalieres*, as you may suppose. Several instances of the most fatal effects from jealousy are to be found in the annals of modern Venetian gallantry.

[177] On Venetian morals in the early nineteenth century, few people were better qualified to report than Byron; from *Letters and Journals of Lord Byron, with Notices of his Life* by Thomas Moore.

The general state of morals here is much the same as in the Doges' time; a woman is virtuous (according to the code) who limits herself to her husband and one lover; those who have two, three, or more, are a little *wild*; but it is only those who are indiscriminately diffuse, and form a low connection, such as the Princess of Wales with her courier,[1] (who, by the way, is made a knight of Malta,) who are considered as overstepping the modesty of marriage. In Venice, the Nobility have a trick of marrying with dancers or singers: and, truth to say, the women of their own order are by no means handsome; but the general race – the women of the 2^d and other orders, the wives of the Advocates, merchants, and proprietors, and untitled gentry, are mostly *bel' sangue*, and it is with these that the more amatory connections are usually formed: there are also instances of stupendous constancy. I

---

[1] The Princess of Wales, afterwards Queen Caroline, left England in 1814. At Milan, in October of that year, Bartolommeo Bergami was engaged as her courier. In the Queen's trial before the House of Lords (August–November 1820), evidence was offered in support of the charge of her having committed adultery with Bergami, who was undoubtedly treated by her with great favour.

know a woman of fifty who never had but one lover, who dying early, she became devout, renouncing all but her husband: she piques herself, as may be presumed, upon this miraculous fidelity, talking of it occasionally with a species of misplaced morality, which is rather amusing. There is no convincing a woman here, that she is in the smallest degree deviating from the rule of right or the fitness of things, in having an *Amoroso*: the great sin seems to lie in concealing it, or in having more than one; that is, unless such an extension of the prerogative is understood and approved of by the prior claimant.

In my case, I do not know that I had any predecessor, and am pretty sure that there is no participator; and am inclined to think, from the youth of the party, and from the frank undisguised way in which every body avows everything in this part of the world, when there is anything to avow, as well as from some other circumstances, such as the marriage being recent, etc., etc., etc., that this is the *premier pas*: it does not much signify.

[178] Festive window-dressing has always been something of a speciality in Venice: it certainly impressed Mrs Piozzi in 1785; from her *Glimpses of Italian Society*.

It was upon the day appointed for making a new chancellor, however, that one ought to have looked at this lovely city, when every shop, adorned with its own peculiar produce, was disposed to hail the passage of its favourite in a manner so lively, so luxuriant, and at the same time so tasteful – there's no telling. Milliners crowned the new dignitary's picture with flowers, while columns of gauze, twisted round with ribbon in the most elegant style, supported the figure on each side, and made the prettiest appearance possible. The furrier formed his skins into representations of the animal they had once belonged to; so the lion was seen candling the kid at one door, while the fox stood courting a badger out of his hole at the other. The poulterers and fruiterers' were by many thought the most beautiful shops in town, from the variety of fancies displayed in the disposal of their goods; and I admired at the truly Italian ingenuity of a gunsmith, who had found the art of turning his instruments of terror into objects of delight by his judicious manner of placing and arranging them. Every shop was illuminated with a large glass chandelier before it, besides the wax candles and coloured lamps interspersed among the ornaments within. The senators have much the appearance of our lawyers going robed to Westminster Hall, but the gentiluomini, as they are called, wear red dresses, and remind me of the doctors of the ecclesiastical courts in Doctors' Commons.

[179] The economics of living in Venice in the late eighteenth century; from *Travels in France and Italy* by Arthur Young.

November 1. The cheapness of Italy is remarkable, and puzzles me not a little to account for; yet it is a point of too much importance to be neglected. I have, at Petrillo's, a clean good room, that looks on the grand canal and to the Rialto, which, by the way, is a fine arch, but an ugly bridge; an excellent bed, with neat furniture, very rare in Italian inns, for the bedstead is usually four forms like trussers set together; fine sheets, which I have not met with before in this country; and my dinner and supper provided at the old price of 8 *pauls* a day, or 3s. 4d. including the chamber. I am very well served at dinner with many and good dishes, and some of them *solids*; two bottles of wine, neither good nor bad, but certainly cheap; for though they see I drink scarcely half of it in my negus at supper, yet a bottle is brought every night. I have been assured, by two or three persons, that the price at Venice, *à la mercantile*, is only 4 to 6 *pauls*; but I suppose they serve a foreigner better. To these 8 *pauls* I add 6 more for a *gondola*; – breakfast 10 *soldi*; if I go to the opera it adds 3 *pauls*; – thus, for about 7s. 3d. a day, a man lives at Venice, keeps his servant, his coach, and goes every night to a public entertainment. To dine well at a London coffee-house, with a pint of bad port, and a very poor dessert, costs as much as the whole day here. There is no question but a man may live

better at Venice for £100 a year than at London for £500;
and yet the difference of the price of the common necessaries
of life, such as bread, meat, etc., is trifling. Several causes
contribute to this effect at Venice; its situation on the Adriatic,
at the very extremity of civilized Europe, in the vicinity of
many poor countries; the use of gondolas, instead of horses,
is an article perhaps of equal importance. But the manners of
the inhabitants, the modes of living, and the very moderate
incomes of the mass of the people, have perhaps more weight
than either of those causes. Luxury here takes a turn much
more towards enjoyment than consumption; the sobriety of
the people does much, the nature of their food more; pastes,
macaroni, and vegetables are much easier provided than beef
and mutton. Cookery, as in France, enables them to spread a
table for half the expense of an English one. If cheapness of
living, *spectacles*, and pretty women are a man's objects in
fixing his residence, let him live at Venice: for myself I think I
would not be an inhabitant to be Doge, with the power of
the Grand Turk. Brick and stone, and sky and water, and not
a field nor a bush even for fancy to pluck a rose from! My
heart cannot expand in such a place: an admirable monument
of human industry, but not a theatre for the feelings of a
farmer! – Give me the fields, and let others take the tide of
human life at Charing Cross and Fleet Ditch.

[180] The economics of living in Venice in the early
nineteenth century; Lord Byron writes, on September 8
1818, to his friend James Wedderburn Webster; from
'The Flesh is Frail', Byron's Letters and Journals edited
by Leslie A. Marchand.

You ask about Venice; I tell you, as before, that I do not
think *you* would like it, at least few English do, and still fewer
remain there. Florence and Naples are the Lazarettoes where
they carry the infection of their Society; indeed, if there were
as many of them in Venice as residents as Lot begged might
be permitted to be the salvation of Sodom, it would not be
my abode a week longer; for the reverse of the proposition, I
should be sure that they would be the damnation of all

pleasant or sensible society. I never see any of them when I can avoid it, and when, *occasionally*, they arrive with letters of recommendation, I do what I can for them, if they are sick, – and, if they are well, I return my card for theirs, but little more.

Venice is not an expensive residence (unless a man chooses it). It has theatres, society, and profligacy rather more than enough. I keep four horses on one of the islands, where there is a beach of some miles along the Adriatic, so that I have daily exercise. I have my gondola, and about fourteen servants, including the nurse for a little girl (a natural daughter of mine), and I reside in one of the Mocenigo palaces on the Grand Canal; the rent of the whole house, which is very large and furnished with linen, etc., etc., inclusive, is two hundred a year (and I gave more than I need have done). In the two years I have been at Venice I have spent about *five* thousand pounds, and I need not have spent a *third* of this, had it not been that I have a passion for women which is expensive in its variety every where, but less so in Venice than in other cities. You may suppose that in *two years*, with a large establishment, horses, house, box at the opera, gondola, journeys, women, and Charity (for I have not laid out all upon my pleasures, but have bought occasionally a shilling's worth of salvation), villas in the country, another carriage and horses purchased for the country, books bought, etc., etc., – in short everything I wanted, and *more* than I ought to have wanted, that the sum of five thousand pounds sterling is no great deal, particularly when I tell you that more than half was laid out in the Sex; – to be sure I have had plenty for the money, that's certain . . .

If you are disposed to come this way, you might live very comfortably, and even splendidly, for less than a thousand a year, and find a palace for the rent of one hundred, that is to say, an Italian palace; you know that all houses with a particular front are called so – in short an enormous house. But, as I said, I do not think you would like it, or rather that Lady Frances would not; it is not so gay as it has been, and there is a monotony to many people in its Canals and the comparative silence of its streets. To me who have been always passionate for Venice, and delight in the dialect and

The Grand Canal: detail from the view of Venice drawn by Jacopo
de' Barbari in 1500

A Venetian theatre – S.Samuele

Santa Fosca on the island of Torcello

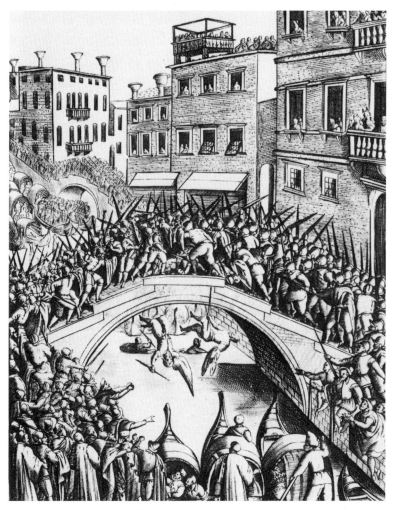

The battle on the bridges

A ridotto in eighteenth-century Venice

A Carnival procession in Venice, c. 1700

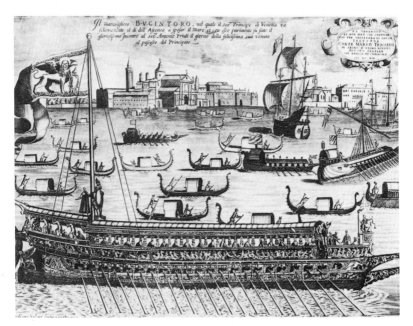

The Bucintoro on Ascension Day, 1619: engraved
by Jan Sedeler after Stefano Scolari

Carnival in Venice: 'downright madness... St Mark's Place is like a
throng of fools,' wrote James Drummond, Earl of Perth in 1695

naïveté of the people, and the romance of its old history and institutions and appearance, all its disadvantages are more than compensated by the sight of a single gondola. The view of the Rialto, of the Piazza, and the Chaunt of Tasso (though less frequent than of old), are to me worth all the cities on earth, save Rome and Athens.

[181] The dream-like charm of Venice in 1872; from *The Letters of John Addington Symonds* edited by H. M. Schneller and R. L. Peters.

... When you are at Venice it is like being in a dream, and when you dream about Venice it is like being awake. I do not know how this should be, but Venice seems made to prove that La vita è un sogno. What the Venice dream is all the world knows. Motion that is almost imperceptible, colour too deep and gorgeous to strike the eye, gilding so massive and ancient as to wear a mist of amber brown upon its brightness, white cupolas that time has turned to pearls, marble that no longer looks like stone, but blocks cut from summer clouds, a smooth sea that is brighter and more infinite than the sky it reflects – these are some of the ingredients of the dream which are too familiar for description. Nothing can describe the elemental warmth of the days, the sea-kisses of the wind at evening, the atmosphere of breathless tepid moonlight in the night. Some people dislike this part of the dream. It just suits me – only I dream of myself in it dressed in almost nothing and very lazy.

Music in Venice

[182] Thomas Coryat describes an obviously memorable concert given in 1608 at the Scuola di S. Rocco. Oddly enough, he makes no mention of the astonishing collection of Tintorettos, which had been in place since the end of the previous century; from *Coryat's Crudities*.

The third feast was upon Saint *Roches* day being Saturday and the sixth day of August, where I heard the best musicke that ever I did in all my life both in the morning and the afternoone, so good that I would willingly goe an hundred miles a foote at any time to heare the like. The place where it was, is neare to Saint *Roches* Church, a very sumptuous and magnificent building that belongeth to one of the sixe Companies of the citie. This building hath a marvailous rich and stately frontispice, being built with passing faire white stone, and adorned with many goodly pillars of marble. There are three most beautifull roomes in this building; the first is the lowest, which hath two rowes of goodly pillars in it opposite to each other which upon this day of Saint *Roch* were adorned with many faire pictures of great personages that hanged round about them, as of Emperours, Kings, Queenes,

Dukes, Duchesses, Popes, &c. In this roome are two or three faire Altars: For this roome is not appointed for merriments and banquetings as the halles belonging to the Companies of London, but altogether for devotion and religion, therein to laud and prayse God and his Saints with Psalmes, Hymnes, spirituall songs and melodious musicke upon certain daies dedicated unto Saints. The second is very spacious and large, having two or three faire Altars more: the roofe of this roome which is of a stately height, is richly gilt and decked with many sumptuous embossings of gold, and the walles are beautified with sundry delicate pictures, as also many parts of the roofe; unto this room you must ascend by two or three very goodly paire of staires. The third room which is made at one corner of this spacious roome, is very beautifull, having both roofe and wals something correspondent to the other; but the floore much more exquisite and curious, being excellently distinguished with checker worke made of several kinds of marble, which are put in by the rarest cunning that the wit of man can devise. The second roome is the place where this festivitie was solemnized to the honour of St *Roch*, at one end whereof was an Altar garnished with many singular ornaments, but especially with a great multitude of silver Candlesticks, in number sixty, and Candles in them of Virgin waxe. This feast consisted principally of Musicke, which was both vocall and instrumental, so good, so delectable, so rare, so admirable, so superexcellent, that it did even ravish and stupifie all those strangers that never heard the like. But how others were affected with it I know not; for mine owne part I can say this, that I was for the time even rapt up with St *Paul* into the third heaven. Sometimes there sung sixteene or twenty men together, having their master or moderator to keepe them in order; and when they sung, the instrumentall musitians played also. Sometimes sixteene played together upon their instruments, ten Sagbuts, foure Cornets, and two Violdegambaes of an extraordinary greatness; sometimes tenne, sixe Sagbuts and foure Cornets; sometimes two, a Cornet and a treble violl. Of those treble viols I heard three severall there, whereof each was so good, especially one that I observed above the rest, that I never heard the like before. Those that played upon the treble viols, sung and played together, and sometimes two singular fellowes played together upon Theorboes, to which they sung also, who yeelded admirable sweet musicke, but so still that they could scarce be heard but by those that were very neare them. These two Theorbists concluded that nights musicke, which continued three whole howers at the least. For they beganne about five of the clocke, and ended not before eight. Also it continued as long in the morning: at every time that every severall musicke played, the Organs, whereof there are seven faire paire in that room, standing al in a rowe together, plated with them. Of the singers there were three or foure so excellent that I thinke few or none in Christendome do exell them, especially one, who had such a peerelesse and (as I may in a maner say) such a supernaturall voice for sweetnesse, that I think there was never a better singer in all the world, insomuch that he did not onely give the most pleasant contentment that could be imagined, to all the hearers, but also did as it were astonish and amaze them. I alwaies thought that he was an Eunuch, which if he had beene, it had taken away some part of my admiration, because they do most commonly sing passing wel; but he was not, therefore it was much the more admirable. Againe it was the more worthy of admiration, because he was a middle-aged man, as about forty yeares old. For nature doth more commonly bestowe such a singularitie of voice upon boyes and striplings, then upon men of such yeares. Besides it was farre the more excellent, because it was nothing forced, strained, or affected, but came from him with the greatest facilitie that ever I heard. Truely I think that had a Nightingale beene in the same roome, and contended with him for the superioritie, something perhaps he might excell him, because God hath granted that little birde such a priviledge for the sweetnesse of his voice, as to none other: but I think he could not much. To conclude, I attribute so much to this rare fellow for his singing, that I thinke the country where he was borne, may be as proude for breeding so singular a person as Smyrna was of her *Homer*, *Verona* of her *Catullus*, or *Mantua* of *Virgil*: But exceeding happy may that Citie, or towne, or person bee that possesseth this miracle of nature.

[183] A night at the Venice opera in 1645; from *The Diary of John Evelyn* edited by William Bray.

This night, having with my Lord Bruce taken our places before, we went to the Opera where comedies and other plays are represented in recitative musiq by the most excellent musicians vocal and instrumental, with variety of sceanes painted and contrived with no lesse art of perspective, and machines for flying in the aire, and other wonderfull motions; taken together it is one of the most magnificent and expansive diversions the wit of man can invent. The history was, Hercules in Lydia; the sceanes changed thirteen times. The famous voices, Anna Rencia, a Roman, and reputed the best treble of women; but there was an eunuch who in my opinion surpass'd her; also a Genoeze that sung an incomparable base. This held us by the eyes and eares till two in the morning, when we went to the Chetto de san Felice, to see the noblemen and their ladies at *Basset*, a game at cards which is much used, but they play not in public, and all that have inclination to it are in masquerade, without speaking one word, and so they come in, play, loose or gaine, and go away as they please. This time of licence is onely in Carnival and this Ascension Weeke; neither are their Theaters open for that other magnificence or for ordinary comedians save on these solemnities, they being a frugal and wise people and exact observers of all sumptuarie laws.

[184] One of the first foreign travellers to mention the four great Venetian orphanages as centres of music was the German Johann Georg Keysler, who was in Venice in 1730; from his *Travels through Germany, Bohemia, Hungary, Switzerland, Italy and Lorrain.*

The four principal hospitals in Venice, are, 1. *SS. Giovanni e Paolo*; 2. *Spedale de gl' Incurabili*; 3. *S. Lazaro de Mendicanti*; and 4. *Spedale della Pietà*; where not only foundlings, but other poor children, and even grown-up persons are taken in. Some of the girls are instructed in music, and attain to great skill not only in singing, but also in playing on the violin, organ, hautboy, theorbo, and other instruments. Every

Saturday and Sunday, very fine pieces of music are performed in the churches of these hospitals, which begin about two hours before sun-set. A person gives two or three pence at such times for a chair or convenient seat. The young women, who are the only performers in these concerts, appear in public but twice a year, when they walk abroad with their instructors. They are not permitted to quit the hospital, except it be to be married: and even then it is with difficulty they obtain leave of the hospital, because it is not an easy matter to fill their places; besides, the care and expence of their education is very considerable. Bologna is the finest voice at present in the *Pietà* hospital, and Teresia in that of the *Mendicanti*. The republic allows a salary for a music-master to every one of these four hospitals. And the most celebrated musicians do not think the office beneath their acceptance.

[185] The music of Vivaldi, and the singing at the orphanages, in 1739; from *Selections from the Letters of de Brosses* translated by Lord Ronald Sutherland Gower.

Not that I am in want of music here, for there is scarcely an evening on which there is not a concert; but all the world rushes during the Carnival to the opera with as much ardour as if they never had heard music before. The passion of the natives for the art is extraordinary. Vivaldi has made himself one of my intimate friends, probably in order that he may sell me his concertos expensively.

Four of his compositions are good, and I have gained my wish, which was to hear him play and listen to good music; he is a *vecchio*, and is full of prodigious enthusiasm for his work. I have heard him compose a concerto with all its different parts more rapidly than a copyist could note it down. I am much surprised to discover that he is not much appreciated here, where everything depends upon the fashion of the day, and where his work has been so long known, and where last year's music is no longer the vogue. The famous Saxon composer[1] is the man of the hour. I have heard him at

[1] J. A. Hasse, who had spent four years in Venice from 1727 to 1731 and was to spend the last twelve years of his life there, dying in the city in 1783.

his house, and also the famous Faustina Bordoni, his wife, who sings with much taste, and in a light and charming way, but her voice is no longer a young one. She is certainly a most delightful person, but that does not make her the greatest of songstresses.

The best music here is that of the charitable establishments. Of these there are four, all containing natural daughters, female orphans, or those girls whom their parents are unable to educate. They are maintained at the expense of the State, and their principal education is that of music. They can sing like angels, and play the violin, the flute, the organ, the hautboy, the violoncello, and the bassoon; the largest instrument of music has no terror for them. They are treated like nuns. They alone perform at these concerts; and at each of these, forty of the students play. I can assure you there can be nothing more charming than to see a young and pretty nun, dressed in white, with a bunch of pomegranate flowers in her hair, conducting the orchestra and beating time with the greatest skill and precision. Their voices are excellent, light, and well trained. The Zabetta, of the Hospital for Incurables, is remarkable for the extent of her voice and the high notes she commands. She has all the suffrages of the people here, and one would run the risk of being maltreated by the populace did one venture to compare her to any of the other musicians. But between ourselves, my dear friends, I think that Margarita of the Mendicanti is equal to the Zabetta, and she pleases me more.

Of these four charities the one to which I go the most often is that of the Pietà; it is there where the symphonies are the best given; and it is there that alone we hear that famous violinist so much vaunted at the Opera in Paris, namely, the Chiaretta. She would be the greatest player of the violin in Italy were it not that l'Anna Maria surpasses even her. I have had the good fortune to hear the latter, who is so fantastical that she often does not play more than once in a year. They have here a kind of music unknown to us, and which seems to be especially adapted for outdoor playing: these are the great concertos in which there is no *violino principale*.

[186] Going behind the scenes at the Mendicanti in
1743, Jean Jacques Rousseau got a nasty shock; from
The Confessions of Jean Jacques Rousseau.

(Jean Jacques Rousseau (1712–1778) was in Venice in
1743–4, serving as secretary to the French Ambassador, the
Comte de Montaigu.)

A kind of music far superior, in my opinion, to that of operas,
and which in all Italy has not its equal, nor perhaps in the
whole world, is that of the *scuole*. The *scuole* are houses of
charity, established for the education of young girls without
fortune, to whom the republic afterwards gives a portion
either in marriage or for the cloister. Amongst talents cultivated in these young girls, music is in the first rank. Every
Sunday at the church of each of the four *scuole*, during
vespers, motettos or anthems with full chorusses, accompanied by a great orchestra, and composed and directed by
the best masters in Italy, are sung in the galleries by girls only;
not one of whom is more than twenty years of age. I have not
an idea of anything so voluptuous and affecting as this music;
the richness of the art, the exquisite taste of the vocal part,
the excellence of the voices, the justness of the execution,
everything in these delightful concerts concurs to produce an
impression which certainly is not the mode, but from which I
am of opinion no heart is secure. Carrio and I never failed
being present at these vespers of the *Mendicanti*, and we were
not alone. The church was always full of the lovers of the art,
and even the actors of the opera came there to form their
tastes after these excellent models. What vexed me was the
iron grate, which suffered nothing to escape but sounds, and
concealed from me the angels of which they were worthy. I
talked of nothing else. One day I spoke of it at le Blond's: if
you are so desirous, said he, to see those little girls, it will be
an easy matter to satisfy your wishes. I am one of the
administrators of the house, I will give you a collation with
them. I did not let him rest until he had fulfilled his promise.
In entering the saloon, which contained these beauties I so
much sighed to see, I felt a trembling of love which I had
never before experienced. M. le Blond presented to me one

after the other, these celebrated female singers, of whom the names and voices were all with which I was acquainted. Come, Sophia, – she was horrid. Come, Cattina, – she had but one eye. Come, Bettina, – the small pox had entirely disfigured her. Scarcely one of them was without some striking defect. Le Blond laughed at my surprise; however, two or three of them appeared tolerable; these never sung but in the chorusses; I was almost in despair. During the collation, we endeavoured to excite them, and they soon became enlivened; ugliness does not exclude the graces, and I found they possessed them. I said to myself, they cannot sing in this manner without intelligence and sensibility, they must have both; in fine, my manner of seeing them changed to such a degree, that I left the house almost in love with each of these ugly faces. I had scarcely courage enough to return to vespers. But after having seen the girls, the danger was lessened. I still found their singing delightful; and their voices so much embellished their persons, that, in spite of my eyes, I obstinately continued to think them beautiful.

[187] Of all surviving travellers' reports, however, perhaps the most authoritative is that of Dr Burney, who was in Venice in 1770; from *The Present State of Music in France and Italy* by Charles Burney, Mus. D.

(Dr Charles Burney (1726–1814), musician and travel writer, was father of the novelist Fanny Burney.)

I went to [the performance] of the *Pietà*, the evening after my arrival, Saturday, August 4. The present *Maestro di Capella* [sic] is Signor Furlanetti, a priest, and the performers, both vocal and instrumental, are all girls; the organ, violins, flutes, violoncellos, and even french-horns, are supplied by these females. It is a kind of Foundling Hospital of natural children, under the protection of several nobles, citizens, and merchants, who, though the revenue is very great, yet, contribute annually to its support. These girls are maintained here till they are married, and all those who have talents for music are taught by the best masters of Italy. The composition and performance which I heard to-night did not exceed mediocrity; among the singers I could discover no remarkable fine voice, nor performer possessed of great taste. However, the instruments finished with a symphony, the first movement of which, in point of spirit, was well written and well executed . . .

In the afternoon I went to the hospital *de' Mendicanti*, for orphan girls, who are taught to sing and play, and on Sundays and festivals they sing divine service in chorus. Signor Bertoni is the present *Maestro di Capella*. There was a hymn performed with solos and chorusses, and a *mottetto a voce sola*, which last was very well performed, particularly an accompanied recitative, which was pronounced with great force and energy. Upon the whole, the compositions had some pretty passages, mixed with others that were not very new. The subjects of the fugues and chorusses were trite, and but slightly put together. The girls here I thought accompanied the voices better than at the *Pietà*: as the chorusses are wholly made up of female voices, they are never in more than three parts, often only in two; but these, when reinforced by the instruments, have such an effect, that the full complement to the chords is not missed, and the melody is much more sensible and marked, by being less charged with harmony. In these hospitals many of the girls sing in the counter-tenor as low as A and G, which enables them always to keep below the *soprano* and *mezzo soprano*, to which they sing the base; and this seems to have been long practised in Italy, as may be seen in the examples of composition given in the old writers, such as Zarlino, Glariano, Kircher, and others, where the lowest part of three is often written in the counter-tenor clef. From hence I went to the *Ospedaletto*, of which Signor Sacchini is the master, and was indeed very much pleased by the composition of part of the famous hymn *Salve Regina*, which was singing when I entered the church; it was new, spirited, and full of ingenious contrivances for the instruments, which always *said* something interesting without disturbing the voice. Upon the whole, there seemed to be as much genius in this composition as in any that I had heard since my arrival in Italy. The performers here too are all orphan girls; one of them, *la Ferrarese*, sung very well, and had a very extraordinary compass of voice, as she was able to reach the highest E of our harpsichords, upon which she could dwell a considerable time, in a fair, natural voice . . .

(During his stay in Venice, Burney met the Neapolitan composer Gaetano Latilla, to whom he took an immediate liking.)

I admired his candour in advising me to go to the *Incurabili*, to hear the girls perform there, with whom he said I should be much pleased. They are scholars of Signor Galuppi, who is *Maestro di Capella* of this Conservatorio.

Unluckily when I arrived there, the performance was begun; however, I had only lost the overture and part of the first air. The words are taken from three or four of the Psalms in Latin, from the hymn *Salve Regina*, and one of the Canticles put into Latin verse, and in dialogue. I knew not whether I was most delighted with the composition, or with the execution; both were admirable.

Signor Buranello[1] has preserved all his fire and imagination from the chill blasts of Russia, whence he is lately returned. This ingenious, entertaining, and elegant composer abounds in novelty, in spirit, and in delicacy, and his scholars did his music great justice. Several of them had uncommon talents for singing, particularly *Rota*, *Pasqua Rossi*, and the *Ortolana*; the two last sung the Canticle in dialogue. The overture, and the whole of this last performance were for two orchestras. In the overture, which was full of pretty passages, the two bands echoed each other. There were two organs, and two pair of french-horns. In short, I was extremely entertained by this performance, and the whole company, which was very numerous, seemed equally delighted.

The young singers, just mentioned, are absolute nightingales; they have a facility of executing difficult divisions equal to that of birds. They did such things in that way, especially the *Rota*, as I do not remember to have heard attempted before. The able master was discoverable in all the cadences of these young performers. The instrumental parts were very well executed, and the whole indicated a superior genius in the composer and conductor of the performance.

---

[1] The popular nickname of Galuppi, who was born on the lagoon island of Burano.

This music, which was of the higher sort of theatric stile, though it was performed in a church, was not mixed with the church service, and the audience sat the whole time, as at a concert; and, indeed, this might be called a *concerto spirituale*, with great propriety . . .

It seems as if the genius of Signor Galuppi, like that of Titian, became more animated by age. He cannot now be less than seventy years old, and yet it is generally allowed here that his last operas, and his last compositions for the church, abound with more spirit, taste, and fancy, than those of any other period of his life . . .

At the Hospitals and in Churches, where it is not allowed to applaud in the same manner as at the Opera, they cough, hem, and blow their noses, to express admiration.

[188] Mention of Galuppi (1706–1785) inevitably brings to mind Browning's poem, 'A Toccata of Galuppi's'. So far as we know, 'Il Buranello' never wrote a toccata in his life; but – at least after the death of Vivaldi in 1741 – he was the leading figure of the Venetian musical scene, and he was to inspire, seventy years after his death, the loveliest poem on Venice ever written in English; from Robert Browning's *Men and Women*, 1855.

A TOCCATA OF GALUPPI'S

1

Oh Galuppi, Baldassaro, this is very sad to find!
I can hardly misconceive you; it would prove me deaf and
    blind;
But although I take your meaning, 'tis with such a heavy
    mind!

2

Here you come with your old music, and here's all the
    good it brings.
What, they lived once thus at Venice, where the merchants
    were the kings,

Where St Mark's is, where the Doges used to wed the sea
    with rings?

                              3

Ay, because the sea's the street there; and 'tis arched by
    . . . what you call
. . . Shylock's bridge with houses on it, where they kept
    the carnival!
I was never out of England – it's as if I saw it all.

                              4

Did young people take their pleasure when the sea was
    warm in May?
Balls and masks begun at midnight, burning ever to
    midday,
When they made up fresh adventures for the morrow, do
    you say?

                              5

Was a lady such a lady, cheeks so round and lips so red, –
On her neck the small face buoyant, like a bell-flower on
    its bed,
O'er the breast's superb abundance where a man might
    base his head?

                              6

Well, and it was graceful of them – they'd break talk
    offend afford
– She, to bite her mask's black velvet – he to finger on his
    sword,
While you sat and played Toccatas, stately at the
    clavichord?

                              7

What? Those lesser thirds so plaintive, sixths diminished,
    sigh on sigh,

Told them something? Those suspensions, those solutions
  – 'Must we die?'
Those commiserating sevenths – 'Life might last! we can
  but try!'

8

'Were you happy?' – 'Yes.' – 'And are you still as happy?'
  – 'Yes – And you?'
– 'Then more kisses' – 'Did *I* stop them, when a million
  seemed so few?'
Hark – the dominant's persistence, till it must be answered
  to!

9

So an octave struck the answer. Oh, they praised you, I
  dare say!
'Brave Galuppi! that was music! good alike at grave and
  gay!
I can always leave off talking when I hear a master play.'

10

Then they left you for their pleasure: till in due time, one
  by one,
Some with lives that came to nothing, some with deeds as
  well undone,
Death stepped tacitly and took them where they never see
  the sun.

11

But when I sit down to reason, think to take my stand nor
  swerve,
While I triumph o'er a secret wrung from nature's close
  reserve,
In you come with your cold music till I creep thro' every
  nerve.

12

Yes, you, like a ghostly cricket, creaking where a house
    was burned:
'Dust and ashes, dead and done with, Venice spent what
    Venice earned.
'The soul, doubtless, is immortal – where a soul can be
    discerned.

13

'Yours for instance you know physics, something of
    geology,
Mathematics are your pastime; souls shall rise in their
    degree;
Butterflies may dread extinction, – you'll not die, it cannot
    be!

14

'As for Venice and its people, merely born to bloom and
    drop,
Here on earth they bore their fruitage, mirth and folly
    were the crop.
What of soul was left, I wonder, when the kissing had to
    stop?

15

'Dust and ashes!' So you creak it, and I want the heart to
    scold.
Dear dead women, with such hair, too – what's become of
    all the gold
Used to hang and brush their bosoms? I feel chilly and
    grown old.

[189] An English visitor to the Mendicanti in 1780
finds the all-female orchestra entertaining; from *Italy,
with sketches of Spain and Portugal* by William
Beckford.

The sight of the orchestra still makes me smile. You know, I suppose, it is entirely of the female gender; and that nothing is more common than to see a delicate white hand journeying across an enormous double bass, or a pair of roseate cheeks puffing with all their efforts at a french-horn. Some of them are grown old and Amazonian, who have abandoned their fiddles and their lovers, take vigorously to the kittle-drum; and one poor limping lady, who had been crossed in love, now makes an admirable figure on the bassoon.

[190] A German visitor of about the same time, however, responds with a mixture of admiration and tetchiness; from Goethe's *Italian Journey*.

Map in hand, I tried to find my way through the labyrinth to the Church of the Mendicants. Here is the Conservatorio, which at the present time enjoys the highest reputation. The women were singing an oratorio behind the choir screen; the church was filled with listeners, the music beautiful and the voices superb. An alto sang the part of King Saul, the protagonist in the work. I have never heard such a voice. Some passages in the music were of infinite beauty and the text was perfectly singable – a kind of Italian Latin which made one smile at times but which gave the music wide scope.

The performance would have been even more enjoyable if the damned conductor had not beaten time against the screen with a rolled sheet of music as insolently as if he were teaching schoolboys. The girls had so often rehearsed the piece that his vehement slapping was as unnecessary as if, in order to make us appreciate a beautiful statue, someone were to stick little patches of red cloth on the joints.

This man was a musician, yet he did not, apparently, hear the discordant sound he was making which ruined the harmony of the whole. Maybe he wanted to attract our attention to himself by this extraordinary behaviour; he would have convinced us better of his merits by giving a perfect performance. I know this thumping out the beat is customary with the French; but I had not expected it from the Italians. The public, though, seemed to be used to it. It was not the only

occasion on which I have seen the public under the delusion
that something which spoils the enjoyment is part of it.

[191] Mrs Piozzi, married as she was to an Italian
musician of real talent, seems to have been accorded
privileged treatment in 1784; from her *Glimpses of
Italian Society*.

Apropos to singing, we were this evening carried to a well-
known conservatory called the Mendicanti, who performed
an oratorio in the church with great, and I dare say deserved,
applause. It was difficult for me to persuade myself that all
the performers were women, till, watching carefully, our eyes
convinced us, as they were but slightly grated. The sight of
girls, however, handling the double bass and blowing into the
bassoon did not much please me; and the deep-toned voice of
her who sung the part of Saul, seemed an odd, unnatural
thing enough. What I found most curious and pretty was to
hear Latin verses of the old leonine race broken into eight
and six, and sung in rhyme by these women, as if they were
airs of Metastasio – all in their dulcified pronunciation, too,
for the patois runs equally through every language when
spoken by a Venetian.

Well, these pretty sirens were delighted to seize upon us,
and pressed our visit to their parlour with a sweetness that I
know not who would have resisted. We had no such intent,
and amply did their performance repay my curiosity for
visiting Venetian beauties so justly celebrated for their seducing manners and soft address. They accompanied their voices
with the fortepiano, and sung a thousand buffo songs with all
that gay voluptuousness for which their country is renowned.

[192] Byron at the opera at the Fenice on the first day
of Carnival – St Stephen's Day – in 1816; from *The
Letters and Journals of Lord Byron, with Notices of his
Life* by Thomas Moore.

Yesterday being the feast of St Stephen, every mouth was put
in motion. There was nothing but fiddling and playing on the

virginals, and all kinds of conceits and divertissements, on every canal of this aquatic city. I dined with the Countess Albrizzi and a Paduan and Venetian party, and afterwards went to the opera, at the Fenice theatre (which opens for the Carnival on that day), – the finest, by the way, I have ever seen: it beats our theatres hollow in beauty and scenery, and those of Milan and Brescia bow before it. The opera and its sirens were much like other operas and women, but the subject of the said opera was something edifying; it turned – the plot and the conduct thereof – upon a fact narrated by Livy of a hundred and fifty married ladies having poisoned a hundred and fifty husbands in good old times. The bachelors of Rome believed this extraordinary mortality to be merely the common effect of matrimony or a pestilence; but the surviving Benedicts, being all seized with the cholic, examined into the matter, and found that 'their possess had been drugged;' the consequence of which was, much scandal and several suits at law. This is really and truly the subject of the musical piece at the Fenice; and you can't conceive what pretty things are sung and recitativoed about the *horrenda strage*. The conclusion was a lady's head about to be chopped off by a lictor, but (I am sorry to say) he left it on, and she got up and sung a trio with the two Consuls, the Senate in the back-ground being chorus. The ballet was distinguished by nothing remarkable, except that the principal she-dancer went into convulsions because she was not applauded on her first appearance; and the manager came forward to ask if there was 'ever a physician in the theatre.' There was a Greek one in my box, whom I wished very much to volunteer his services, being sure that in this case these would have been the last convulsions which would have troubled the ballerina; but he would not. The crowd was enormous, and in coming out, having a lady under my arm, I was obliged, in making way, almost to 'beat a Venetian and traduce the state,' being compelled to regale a person with an English punch in the guts, which sent him as far back as the squeeze and the passage would admit. He did not ask for another, but with great signs of disapprobation and dismay, appealed to his compatriots, who laughed at him.

[193] Thirty-five years later to the day, Effie Ruskin also goes to the first night of the opera at the Fenice, as she writes to her mother; from *Effie in Venice* by Mary Lutyens.

Last night was the St Stefano day when the Carnival commences and the Fenice opens. I had not intended going as John likes attending to the music and does not like the box filled with people talking so I did not intend to ask him – but Ct Wrbna, thinking it a pity I should not go, asked if I would like to go. I said, 'Oh! yes, but I could not go alone.' He said, 'Oh? I'll manage all that in five minutes,' and in a very short time Princess Jablonowska sent me a note saying that Falkenhayn had sent her one of the Emperor's boxes which are at the disposal of the Suite of the G. Duke and would I accompany her. I went with her. Nugent & General Duodo, whom we met, took care of us and I was very glad that Wrbna's kindness has enabled me to go for I never saw anything so brilliant in Italy, every place was filled and the crowd in the Parterre innumerable. I was next box to the Governor [General Gorzkowski], and in the middle of the House the Emperor's box was brilliantly lighted with the Grand Duke in Austrian uniform [he was Colonel of an Austrian infantry regiment] and the Duchess, who looked very handsome in Pink glacé with low body & short sleeves and most splendid pearls almost covering her neck, her hair with two large plaits on each side. Behind her sat Wrbna and on the other side of the box the other ladies and gentlemen of the suite. The Opera was Semiramide [by Rossini] and the Music very fine . . .

We came away before the end as it was so long. I wish they did not talk so much in the Theatre for it is impossible to pay any attention to the Opera, for first came Nugent talking English as fast as he could, at the same time the Princess talking her Venetian and General Duodo replying – then came Falkenhayn with his German & Wrbna with his French making your box a sort of Babel, and as it would be considered quite contrary to etiquette that Ladies should ever be left alone in their box, whenever one gentleman has paid his visit of a quarter of an hour or so another arrives to take his place and you never have a chance of being alone a minute. I complained of it last night to Mdme Pal. and they were all against me; they said that the Theatre was public property and every body had a right to call upon any body that they knew, and as most people went every night for an hour it was economical as it saved them lighting their rooms at home, and that having a box at the Opera was the cheapest way for all to see people & society. I thought the system quite wrong as people who cannot see their friends at home ought not to have a box &c. but it is useless arguing with people who have been brought up to a different set of rules & who are happy in their mode of Life, such as it is, and I never saw better behaved people – but for my part I think their visiting in the Theatre quite superfluous; for instance if, as in London, you did not see your acquaintances often it might be allowed, but here I see Jane or Nugent or Wrbna or Falkenhayn or Mde Jablonowska every day, and some of them always walk at three on the Square where I can join them if I choose, but I prefer walking along with Beppo and when the Band plays I go up to the Gallery [of] the Ducal Palace and walk up and down in the sun where I hear the music delightfully without being near the crowd.

Courtesans

[194] Venetian courtesans in the sixteenth century; from *Lives of the Courtesans: Portraits of the Renaissance* by Lynne Lawner.

From the 'Novelle' of Matteo Bandello:

There is a custom in Venice . . . namely that a courtesan take six or seven lovers, assigning to each a certain night of the week when she dines and sleeps with him. During the day she is free to entertain whomever she wishes so that her mill never lies idle and does not rust from lack of the opportunity to grind grain. Once in a while, a wealthy foreigner insists on having one of her nights, warning her that otherwise she will not get a cent from him. In this case, it is her duty to request permission from the lover whose evening that would ordinarily be and to arrange to see him during the day instead. Each lover pays a monthly salary, and their agreement includes the provision that the courtesan is allowed to have foreigners as overnight guests.

From a Venetian State ordinance of 1562:

Prostitutes of this city are forbidden to wear gold, silver, or silk, except for caps made of pure silk. They are not to

wear chains, rings set with precious stones, or any other kind
of ring or earring. In addition, they are not to wear any
jewels, real or false, and this applies both inside and outside
their houses, even when they are outside the city. Furnishings
must conform in every way to the law. There should not be
anything of silk in the house. Forbidden are tapestries, fancy
materials on the walls, elaborate headboards [*spalliere*], decorated chests, gilded leathers [*cuori d'oro*). Instead, prostitutes
are to use only Bergamasque or Brescian materials [rough
materials manufactured on the mainland, mainly for export],
fifty percent wool, plainly striped or colored as they are
nowadays. They are not allowed to slash these materials [in
order to insert, ribbon-style, more precious ones]; if they do,
they will be fined 10 ducats the first time and banished the
next time.

*From 'Habiti antichi e moderni di tutto il mondo', 1590, by
Cesare Vecellio:*
  Public prostitutes operating in infamous places do not dress
all alike. They may be all of a kind in another sense, but their
various economic levels determine wide differences in the
quality of their clothes. Nevertheless, most of them wear a
somewhat masculine outfit: silk or cloth waistcoats adorned
with conspicuous fringes and padded like young men's vests,
especially those of Frenchmen. Next to their bodies they wear
a man's shirt, more or less delicate according to what they
can spend, that arrives below the knees, and over it they wrap
an overskirt or a silk or cloth apron reaching to their feet, but
in the winter season a gown lined in cotton or silk. Their
clogs are ten inches high, decorated with fringes, their stockings embroidered silk or cotton, Roman slippers placed inside
the clogs. Many of them wear men's breeches, often of
ormesin [a kind of silk manufactured in Venice similar to that
made in Ormuz in the Persian Gulf], and one instantly
recognizes them for what they are because of these trousers
and certain little round pieces of silver they use as ornaments.
It is difficult to describe their hairdos, especially since one
seldom sees them at the window; usually they stand in
doorways and on the streets in order to draw passersby into
their web. They try to be entertaining by singing little love

songs, but most of them sound hoarse and off-key, as women of that low condition well might.

Courtesans who wish to get ahead in the world by feigning respectability go around dressed as widows or married women. Most courtesans dress as young virgins anyway. In fact, they button themselves up even more than virgins do. But a compromise must eventually be reached between the wearing of a mantle that hides their bodies and their need to be seen, at least to some extent. Finally, courtesans are forced to open up at the neck, and one recognizes at once who they are, for the lack of pearls speaks loud and clear. Courtesans are prohibited from wearing pearls. Indeed, in order to remedy this situation, some arrange to be accompanied by a lover-protector, borrowing his name as if the two of them were married. In this way courtesans feel free to wear things forbidden to them by law.

Aside from this limitation, however, they dress in the most lavish manner, their underwear including embroidered hosiery, petticoats, and undershirts, and garments of silk brocade. Inside their high clogs they wear Roman-style shoes. I am speaking, of course, of the high-class courtesans. Those, on the other hand who exercise their wicked profession in public places wear waistcoats of silk with gold braid or embroidery and skirts covered with overskirts or silk aprons. Light scarves on their heads, they go around the city flirting, their gestures and speech easily giving away their identity.

Courtesans especially favor these head veils fastened with buttons and bows. They also wear more elaborate skirts than other women. And even though they are forbidden to wear pearls at home, they wear them as well as other jewelry, including valuable earrings. Courtesans stand at their windows making amorous signs to whoever interests them, displaying an astute haughtiness. After frequenting a Venetian patrician, they grab onto his family name, using it as their own and thus fooling many foreign men who come to the city and mistake them for Venetian ladies. Procuresses lend a helping hand. When a foreigner expresses the desire to enjoy the favors of a highborn lady, a procuress dolls up some common prostitute, then leads her and him to a secret meeting-place with so much ceremony that he is taken in and believes she's a noblewoman. Not knowing what Venetian noblewomen are like – namely, that they are deeply about their respectability, the foreigners go around bragging that they have slept with them when this is as far from the truth as one could get!

[195] Thomas Coryat speaks of the Venetian courtesans with first-hand knowledge – though arguably protesting his innocence just a little too much; from *Coryat's Crudities*.

But since I have taken occasion to mention some notable particulars of their women, I will insist farther upon that matter, and make relation of their Cortezans also, as being a thing incident and very proper to this discourse, especially because the name of a Cortezan of Venice is famoused over all Christendome. I hope it will not be ungratefull to the Reader to reade that of these notable persons, which no Author whatsoever doth impart unto him but my selfe. Only I feare least I shall expose my selfe to the severe censure and scandalous imputations of many carping Critics, who I thinke will taxe me for luxury and wantonnesse to insert so lascivious a matter into this Treatise of Venice. Wherefore at the end of this discourse of the Cortezans I will add some Apologie for my self, which I hope will in some sort satisfie them, if they are not too captious . . .

As for the number of these Venetian Cortezans it is very great. For it is thought there are of them in the whole City and other adjacent places, as Murano, Malamocco, &c. at the least twenty thousand, whereof many are esteemed so loose, that they are said to open their quivers to every arrow . . . And indeede such is the variety of the delicious objects they minister to their lovers, that they want nothing tending to delight. For when you come into one of their Palaces (as indeed some few of the principallest of them live in very magnificent and portly buildings fit for the entertainment of a great Prince) you seeme to enter into a Paradise of *Venus*. For their fairest roomes are most glorious and glittering to behold. The walles round about being adorned with most sumptuous

tapistry and gilt leather, such as I have spoken of in my
Treatise of Padua . . .

As for her selfe shee comes to thee decked like the Queene
and Goddesse of love, in so much that thou wilt thinke she
made a late transmigration from Paphos, Cnidos, or Cythera,
the auncient habitations of Dame *Venus*. For her face is
adorned with the quintessence of beauty. In her cheekes thou
shalt see the Lilly and the Rose strive for the supremacy, and
the silver tramels of her haire displayed in that curious
manner besides her two frisled peakes standing up like prety
Pyramides, that they give thee the true *Cos amoris* . . . Also
the ornaments of her body are so rich, that except thou cost
even geld thy affections (a thing hardly to be done) or carry
with thee *Ulysses* hearbe called Moly which is mentioned by
Homer, that is, some antidote against those Venereous titilla-
tions, shee wil very neare be numme and captivate thy senses,
and make reason vale bonnet to affection. For thou shalt see
her decked with many chaines of gold and orient pearle like a
second *Cleopatra*, (but they are very litle) divers gold rings
beautified with diamonds and other costly stones, jewels in
both her eares of great worth. A gowne of damaske (I speake
this of the nobler Cortizans) either decked with a deep gold
fringe (according as I have expressed it in the picture of the
Cortizan that I haue placed about the beginning of this
discourse) or laced with five or sixe gold laces each two inches
broade. Her petticoate of red chamlet edged with rich gold
fringe, stockings of carnation silke, her breath and her whole
body, the more to enamour thee, most fragrantly perfumed.
Though these things will at the first sight seeme unto thee
most delectable allurements, yet if thou shalt rightly weigh
them in the scales of a mature judgement, thou wilt say with
the wise man, and that very truely, that they are like a golden
ring in a swines snowst . . .

But beware notwithstanding all these *illecebræ & lenocinia
amoris*, that thou enter not into termes of private conversation with her. For then thou shalt finde her such a one as
Lipsius truly cals her, *callidam & caldam Solis filiam*, that is,
the crafty and hot daughter of the Sunne. Moreover I will tell
thee this newes which is most true, that if thou shouldest
wantonly converse with her, and not give her that *salarium*

iniquitatis, which thou hast promised her, but perhaps cunningly escape from her company, she will either cause thy throate to be cut by her Ruffiano, if he can after catch thee in the City, or procure thee to be arrested (if thou art to be found) and clapped up in the prison, where thou shalt remaine till thou hast paid her all thou didst promise her . . .

Thus have I described unto thee the Venetian Cortezans; but because I have related so many particulars of them, as few Englishmen that have lived many yeares in Venice, can do the like, or at the least if they can, they will not upon their returne into England, I beleeve thou wilt cast an aspersion of wantonnesse upon me, and say that I could not know all these matters without mine owne experience. I answere thee, that although I might have knowne them without my experience, yet for my better satisfaction, I went to one of their noble houses (I wil confesse) to see the manner of their life, and observe their behaviour, but not with such an intent as we reade *Demosthenes* went to *Lais*, to the end to pay something for repentance; but rather as *Panutius* did to *Thais*, of whom we read that when he came to her, and craved a secret roome for his pastime, she should answere him that the same roome where they were together, was secret enough, because no body could see them but onely God; upon which speech the godly man tooke occasion to persuade her to the fear of God and religion, and to the reformation of her licentious life, since God was able to prie into the secretest corners of the world. And so at last converted her by this meanes from a wanton Cortezan to a holy and religious woman. In like manner I both wished the conversion of the Cortezan that I saw, and did my endevour by perswasive termes to convert her, though my speeches could not take the like effect that those of *Panutius* did. Withall I went thither partly to the end to see whether those things were true that I often heard before both in England, France, Savoy, Italy, and also in Venice it selfe concerning these famous women . . .

Therefore I instantly request thee (most candid reader) to be as charitably conceited of me, though I have at large deciphered and as it were anatomized a Venetian Cortezan unto thee, as thou wouldest have me of thy selfe upon the like request.

[196] Coryat also makes an interesting discovery about what was, to any young courtesan, one of the primary occupational hazards; from *Coryat's Crudities*.

There is one most notable thing more to be mentioned concerning these Venetian Cortezans, with the relation whereof I will end this discourse of them. If any of them happen to have any children (as indeede they have but few, for according to the old proverbe the best carpenters make the fewest chips) they are brought up either at their own charge, or in a certaine house of the citie appointed for no other use but onely for the bringing up of the Cortezans bastards, which I saw Eastward above Saint *Markes* streete neare to the sea side. In the south wall of which building that looketh towards the sea, I observed a certaine yron grate inserted into a hollow peece of the wall, betwixt which grate and a plaine stone beneath it, there is a convenient little space to put in an infant. Hither doth the mother or some body for her bring the child shortly after it is borne into the world; and if the body of it be no greater, but that it may conveniently without any hurt to the infant bee conveighed in at the foresaid space, they put it in there without speaking at all to any body that is in the house to take charge thereof. And from thenceforth the mother is absolutely discharged of her child. But if the child be growne to that bignesse that they cannot conveigh it through that space, it is carryed backe againe to the mother, who taketh charge of it herselfe, and bringeth it up as well as she can. Those that are brought up in this foresaid house, are removed therehence when they come to yeares of discretion, and many of the male children are employed in the warres, or to serve in the Arsenall, or Galleys at sea, or some other publique service for the Common weale. And many of the females if they bee faire doe matrizare, that is, imitate their mothers in their gainfull facultie, and get their living by prostituting their bodies to their favourites.

[197] Venetian prostitutes in 1687; from *A New Voyage to Italy* by F. N. Misson.

There are whole Streets of that Sort of Ladies of Pleasure, who receive all Comers; and whereas the Habits of other Persons are Black and Melancholy, these are drest in Red and Yellow, like Tulips; with their Breasts open, their Faces painted a Foot deep, and always a Nosegay on the Ear: You may see them standing by Dozens at the Doors or Windows; and the Passers by seldom 'scape without torn Sleeves.

[198] Rousseau has, in 1744, what he was always to consider a lucky escape; from *The Confessions of Jean Jacques Rousseau*.

I always had a disinclination to girls of pleasure, but at Venice those were all I had within my reach; most of the houses being shut against me on account of my place. The daughters of M. Le Blond were very amiable, but difficult of access; and I had too much respect for the father and mother ever once to have the least desire for them . . . I lived upwards of a year in that city as chastely as I had done in Paris: and at the end of eighteen months, I quitted it without having approached the sex, except twice by means of the singular opportunities of which I am going to speak.

The first was procured me by that honest gentleman, Vitali, sometime after the formal apology I obliged him to make me. The conversation at table turned on the amusements of Venice. These gentlemen reproached me with my indifference with regard to the most delightful of them all; at the same time extolling the gracefulness and elegant manners of the women of easy virtue of Venice; and adding that they were superior to all others of the same description in any other part of the world. Dominic said I must make an acquaintance with the most amiable of them all; he offered to take me to her apartments, and assured me I should be pleased with her. I laughed at this obliging offer: and Count Piati, a man in years and venerable, observed to me, with more candour than I should have expected from an Italian, that he thought me too prudent to suffer myself to be taken to such a place by my enemy. In fact I had no inclination to do it: but notwith-standing this, by an incoherence, I cannot myself comprehend,

I at length was prevailed upon to go, contrary to my inclination, the sentiment of my heart, my reason, and even my will; solely from weakness, and being ashamed to show an appearance to the least mistrust; and besides, as the expression of the country is, *per non parer troppo cogliono* [not to seem too foolish]. *The Padoana* whom we went to visit was pretty, she was even handsome, but her beauty was not of that kind which pleased me. Dominic left me with her, I sent for *Sorbetti*, and asked her to sing. In about half an hour I wished to take my leave after having put a ducat on the table, but this by a singular scruple she refused until she had deserved it, and I from as singular a folly consented to remove her doubts. I returned to the palace, so fully persuaded that I should feel the consequences of this step that the first thing I did was to send for the king's surgeon to ask him for Ptisans. Nothing can equal the uneasiness of mind I suffered for three weeks, without its being justified by any real inconvenience or apparent sign. I could not believe it was possible to withdraw with impunity from the arms of the Padoana. The surgeon himself had the greatest difficulty in removing my apprehensions; nor could he do this by any other means than by persuading me I was formed in such a manner as not to be easily infected: and although in the experiment I exposed myself less than any other man would have done, my health in that respect never having suffered the least inconvenience, is in my opinion a proof the surgeon was right. However, this has never made me imprudent, and if in fact, I have received such an advantage from nature I can safely assert I have never abused it.

[199] Byron's *amours* in Venice are legendary. A few days after his arrival in 1816 he is already writing of the effect his young landlady has upon him; from 'The Flesh is Frail', Byron's Letters and Journals edited by Leslie A. Marchand.

I have fallen in love, which, next to falling into the canal, (which would be of no use, as I can swim) is the best or the worst thing I could do. I have got some extremely good apartments in the house of a 'Merchant of Venice,' who is a good deal occupied with business, and has a wife in her twenty-second year. Marianna (that is her name)[1] is in her appearance altogether like an antelope. She has the large, black, oriental eyes, with that peculiar expression in them which is seen rarely among *Europeans* – even the Italians – and which many of the Turkish women give themselves by tinging the eyelid, – an art not known out of that country, I believe. This expression she has *naturally*, – and something more than this. In short, I cannot describe the effect of this kind of eye, – at least upon me. Her features are regular, and rather aquilinemouth small – skin clear and soft, with a kind of hectic colour – forehead remarkably good: her hair is of the dark gloss, curl, and colour of Lady J * * 's [Jersey's]: her figure is light and pretty, and she is a famous songstress – scientifically so; her natural voice (in conversation, I mean) is very sweet; and the naiveté of the Venetian dialect is always pleasing in the mouth of a woman.

(Some ten weeks later, he wrote again.)

Venice is in the *estro* of her carnival, and I have been up these last two nights at the ridotto and the opera, and all that kind of thing. Now for an adventure. A few days ago a gondolier brought me a billet without a subscription, intimating a wish on the part of the writer to meet me either in gondola or at the island of San Lazaro, or at a third rendezvous, indicated in the note. 'I know the country's disposition well' – in Venice 'they do let Heaven see those tricks they dare not show,' &c. &c.; so, for all response, I said that neither of the three places suited me; but that I would either be at home at ten at night *alone*, or at the ridotto at midnight, where the writer might meet me masked. At ten o'clock I was at home and alone (Marianne was gone with her husband to a conversazione), when the door of my apartment opened, and in walked a well-looking and (for an Italian) *bionda* girl of about nineteen, who informed me that she was married to the brother of my *amorosa*, and wished to have some conversation with

[1] Marianna Segati who with her husband, a draper, lived in the Frezzeria, a narrow street just off the Piazza San Marco.

me. I made a decent reply, and we had some talk in Italian
and Romaic (her mother being a Greek of Corfu), when lo!
in a very few minutes, in marches, to my very great astonishment, Marianna S[egati], *in propria persona*, and after making polite courtesy to her sister-in-law and to me, without a
single word seizes her said sister-in-law by the hair, and
bestows upon her some sixteen slaps, which would have made
your ear ache only to hear their echo. I need not describe the
screaming which ensued. The luckless visitor took flight. I
seized Marianna, who, after several vain efforts to get away
in pursuit of the enemy, fairly went into fits in my arms; and,
in spite of reasoning, eau de Cologne, vinegar, half a pint of
water, and God knows what other waters beside, continued
so till past midnight.

After damning my servants for letting people in without
apprizing me, I found that Marianna in the morning had seen
her sister-in-law's gondolier on the stairs, and, suspecting that
his apparition boded her no good, had either returned of her
own accord, or been followed by her maids or some other
spy of her people to the conversazione, from whence she
returned to perpetrate this piece of pugilism. I had seen fits
before, and also some small scenery of the same genus in and
out of our island: but this was not all. After about an hour,
in comes – who? why, Signor S[egati], her lord and husband,
and finds me with his wife fainting upon the sofa, and all the
apparatus of confusion, dishevelled hair, hats, handkerchiefs,
salts, smelling-bottles – and the lady as pale as ashes without
sense or motion. His first question was, 'What is all this?' The
lady could not reply – so I did. I told him the explanation
was the easiest thing in the world; but in the mean time it
would be as well to recover his wife – at least, her senses.
This came about in due time of suspiration and respiration.

You need not be alarmed – jealousy is not the order of the
day in Venice, and daggers are out of fashion; while duels, on
love matters, are unknown – at least, with the husbands. But,
for all this, it was an awkward affair; and though he must
have known that I made love to Marianna, yet I believe he
was not, till that evening, aware of the extent to which it had
gone. It is very well known that almost all the married women
have a lover; but it is usual to keep up the forms, as in other

nations. I did not, therefore, know what the devil to say. I
could not out with the truth, out of regard to her, and I did
not choose to lie for my sake; – besides, the thing told itself. I
thought the best way would be to let her explain it as she
chose (a woman being never at a loss – the devil always sticks
by them) – only determining to protect and carry her off, in
case of any ferocity on the part of the Signor. I saw that he
was quite calm. She went to bed, and next day – how they
settled it, I know not, but settle it they did. Well – then I had
to explain to Marianna about this never to be sufficiently
confounded sister-in-law; which I did by swearing innocence,
eternal constancy, &c. &c. But the sister-in-law, very much
discomposed with being treated in such wise, has (not having
her own shame before her eyes) told the affair to half Venice,
and the servants (who were summoned by the fight and the
fainting) to the other half. But, here, nobody minds such
trifles, except to be amused by them. I don't know whether
you will be so, but I have scrawled a long letter out of these
follies.

[200] The story of Byron's stormy affair with Margarita Cogni, better known as La Fornarina; from *Letters
and Journals of Lord Byron, with Notices of his Life* by
Thomas Moore.

In short, in a few evenings, we arranged our affairs, and for a
long space of time she was the only one who preserved over
me an ascendancy which was often disputed, and never
impaired.

The reasons of this were, firstly, her person; – very dark,
tall, the Venetian face, very fine black eyes. She was two-
and-twenty years old ... She was, besides, a thorough Venetian in her dialect, in her thoughts, in her countenance, in
every thing, with all their *naïveté* and pantaloon humour.
Besides, she could neither read nor write, and could not
plague me with letters, – except twice that she paid sixpence
to a public scribe, under the piazza, to make a letter for her,
upon some occasion when I was ill and could not see her. In
other respects, she was somewhat fierce and 'prepotente,'

that is, overbearing, and used to walk in whenever it suited her, with no very great regard to time, place, nor persons; and if she found any women in her way, she knocked them down . . .

When I came to Venice for the winter, she followed; and as she found herself out to be a favourite, she came to me pretty often. But she had inordinate self-love, and was not tolerant of other women. At the 'Cavalchina,' the masked ball on the last night of the carnival, where all the world goes, she snatched off the mask of Madame Contarini, a lady noble by birth, and decent in conduct, for no other reason, but because she happened to be leaning on my arm. You may suppose what a cursed noise this made; but this is only one of her pranks.

At last she quarrelled with her husband, and one evening ran away to my house. I told her this would not do: she said she would lie in the street, but not go back to him; that he beat her, (the gentle tigress!) spent her money, and scandalously neglected her. As it was midnight I let her stay, and next day there was no moving her at all. Her husband came, roaring and crying, and entreating her to come back: – *not* she! He then applied to the police, and they applied to me: I told them and her husband to *take* her; I did not want her; she had come, and I could not fling her out of the window; but they might conduct her through that or the door if they chose it. She went before the commissary, but was obliged to return with that 'becco ettico,' as she called the poor man, who had a phthisic. In a few days she ran away again. After a precious piece of work, she fixed herself in my house, really and truly without my consent; but, owing to my indolence, and not being able to keep my countenance, for if I began in a rage, she always finished by making me laugh with some Venetian pantaloonery or another; and the gipsy knew this well enough, as well as her other powers of persuasion, and exerted them with the usual tact and success of all she-things; high and low, they are all alike for that . . .

In the mean time, she beat the women and stopped my letters. I found her one day pondering over one. She used to try to find out by their shape whether they were feminine or no; and she used to lament her ignorance, and actually studied her alphabet, on purpose (as she declared) to open all letters addressed to me and read their contents . . .

That she had a sufficient regard for me in her wild way, I had many reasons to believe. I will mention one. In the autumn, one day, going to the Lido with my gondoliers, we were overtaken by a heavy squall, and the gondola put in peril – hats blown away, boat filling, oar lost, tumbling sea, thunder, rain in torrents, night coming, and wind unceasing. On our return, after a tight struggle, I found her on the open steps of the Mocenigo palace, on the Grand Canal, with her great black eyes flashing through her tears, and the long dark hair, which was streaming, drenched with rain, over her brows and breast. She was perfectly exposed to the storm; and the wind blowing her hair and dress about her thin tall figure, and the lightning flashing round her, and the waves rolling at her feet, made her look like Medea alighted from her chariot, or the Sybil of the tempest that was rolling around her, the only living thing within hail at that moment except ourselves. On seeing me safe, she did not wait to greet me, as might have been expected, but calling out to me – 'Ah! can' della Madonna, xe esto il tempo per andar' al' Lido?' (Ah! dog of the Virgin, is this a time to go to Lido?) ran into the house, and solaced herself with scolding the boatmen for not foreseeing the 'temporale.' I am told by the servants that she had only been prevented from coming in a boat to look after me, by the refusal of all the gondoliers of the canal to put out into the harbour in such a moment; and that then she sat down on the steps in all the thickest of the squall, and would neither be removed nor comforted. Her joy at seeing me again was moderately mixed with ferocity, and gave me the idea of a tigress over her recovered cubs.

But her reign drew near a close. She became quite ungovernable some months after, and a concurrence of complaints, some true, and many false – 'a favourite has no friends' – determined me to part with her. I told her quietly that she must return home (she had acquired a sufficient provision for herself and mother &c. in my service), and she refused to quit the house. I was firm, and she went threatening knives and revenge. I told her that I had seen knives drawn before her time, and that if she chose to begin, there was a knife and fork also, at her service on the table, and that intimidation would not do. The next day, while I was at dinner, she walked in (having broken open a glass door that led from the hall below to the staircase, by way of prologue), and advancing straight up to the table, snatched the knife from my hand, cutting me slightly in the thumb in the operation. Whether she meant to use this against herself or me I know not – probably against neither – but Fletcher seized her by the arms, and disarmed her. I then called my boatmen, and desired them to get the gondola ready, and conduct her to her own house again, seeing carefully that she did herself no mischief by the way. She seemed quite quiet, and walked down stairs. I resumed my dinner.

We heard a great noise, and went out, and met them on the staircase, carrying her up stairs. She had thrown heself into the canal. That she intended to destroy herself, I do not believe; but when we consider the fear women and men who can't swim have of deep or even of shallow water (and the Venetians in particular, though they live on the waves), and that it was also night, and dark, and very cold, it shows that she had a devilish spirit of some sort within her. They had got her out without much difficulty or damage, excepting the salt water she had swallowed, and the wetting she had undergone.

I foresaw her intention to refix herself, and sent for a surgeon, enquiring how many hours it would require to restore her from her agitation; and he named the time. I then said, 'I give you that time, and more if you require it; but at the expiration of this prescribed period, if *she* does not leave the house, *I* will.'

All my people were consternated. They had always been frightened at her, and were now paralysed: they wanted me to apply to the police, to guard myself, &c. like a pack of snivelling servile boobies as they were. I did nothing of the kind, thinking that I might as well end that way as another; besides, I had been used to savage women, and knew their ways.

Eating and drinking

[201] Francis Misson was, in 1687/8, one of the many for whom eating and drinking in Venice were something of a nightmare; from his *A New Voyage to Italy*.

The Water is almost all very bad too. Of a great Number of Wells which are in this City, there are but very few good for any thing. The best Water is the Rain-Water, which some private Persons preserve in Cisterns; that they fetch from the *Brenta*.

The common Wines are also very unpleasant; that which they call (*dolce*) *sweet*, is to the *French* Palates of a disgustful Taste; and the (*Garbo* or *Brusco*) *sour*, on the contrary is extreamly sharp. After they have drawn off the pure Liquor, they mix Water with the Stalks and Skins of Grapes, that they may squeeze some sharpness from them. 'Tis also sometimes mixt with Lime, Allum, &c. which gives it some piquant Briskness, but makes it very harsh; besides, this Mixture palls and weakens the Wine, which was not very strong before. They have also a very ill Way of making their Bread; let it be as fresh as you will, the Dough has been Bruis'd so much and is so hard, that you must break it as they do Bisket, with a

Hammer. In other respects the Entertainment is pretty good, in the *French* Inns, which are the only Places where you may be tolerably accommodated in.

[202] Despite the number of wells, both the quality and, at times, the available quantity of water gave cause for anxiety, as Samuel Sharp wrote in 1766; from his *Letters from Italy . . . in the Years 1765 and 1766.*

Living in the midst of salt water, all the water they drink, except what is brought from the *Brenta*, is collected from the rain which falls on their houses: To this end they dig a well, which at a certain depth, they surround with a wall of terras, made very compact, that the salt water in the canals may not transude into the well: Then they lay a bed of sand, thro' which the rain water filters into the well, as they imagine, in the most perfect state of purity: However, as every house-keeper thinks his well better finished than that of his neigh-bour, one may conclude that some of them are porous, and do admit more or less salt water into them. The frequency of diarrhœas in this city, is another argument, that the water they drink is purgative; but perhaps one of the greatest inconveniences of these wells, is, that they do not contain water enough for a family in long droughts, which frequently happen in Italy.

[203] Venetian food seldom found favour with foreign-ers, as Lady Miller wrote on 6 June 1771; from her *Letters from Italy . . . in the Years 1770 and 1771.*

The provisions here are tolerable, but the Venetians are wretched cooks: they told me, that almost all the meat comes from Dalmatia; it is coarse and lean; their poultry is good, as is the fish; the scuttle-fish disgusts at first sight, for when dressed it fills the dish with a black juice like ink, but tastes agreeably when you have conquered your prejudice to its colour. They have an odious custom here, of using the blood of animals in their soups and ragouts; not liking the soup they served up yesterday, I desired our host to have it made better

to-day; when it came upon the table I thought it of an odd
colour, and the taste was extremely disagreeable; upon
inquiry I was told, it was made after the Venetian manner,
and particularly delicate and elegant, even *eccellentisimo*,
there being a greater quantity than ordinary of fowls and
pigeons blood in it: guess if I had any further appetite for
Venetian soup. – We do not propose making any long stay
here. As soon as our curiosity is gratified we shall depart, but
our day is not yet fixed.

(This letter was later followed by another.)

The very day after I wrote last I was attacked by an indispo-
sition, occasioned by the water we drink having a brackish
taste, which I did not perceive for some time, having always
mixed it with wine. The common English remedies had not
the desired effect, I believe I should have been extremely ill,
(and would not hear of a Venetian physician) had not M——
mentioned my disorder to Mr U—— who was not at all
surprised at it, the water of Venice having frequently a like
effect upon strangers: he advised my drinking a mineral water
of *Nocera*; I took his prescription, the first glass relieved me
much, and half the bottle completed the cure.

[204] Venetian specialities in 1817; from *William
Rose's Letters from the North of Italy*, quoted in George
Bull's *Venice, the Most Triumphant City*.

(William Rose (1775–1843) was in 1800 made Clerk to the
House of Lords – an appointment which did not prevent him
from spending several years abroad after the peace of 1814.
In 1817 he lived a year in the Veneto and married a Venetian
wife. After his return to England his principal achievement
was a translation of Ariosto.)

For the Venetian holidays I have mentioned there are set
dishes, as there are with us, and some of them of as strange
composition: witness, one of fruits, preserved with sugar,
spices, and mustard, which is the Venetian equivalent for a
minced-pie. For the rest, the fare of Christmas even, though
meagre, is, as I have said, magnificent, always bating a sort of

pye-pottage, called 'torte de lasagne', which might, I suppose, pair off with plum-porridge itself.

There is indeed one circumstance very favourable to the meagre department of the kitchen. The Mediterranean and Adriatic, in addition to most of those of our own coasts, have various delicate fish which are not to be found in the British seas. Of the tunny, sword-fish, and many others of the larger classes, you have of course read. Some others, which are rare with us, as the red mullet, swarm in these latitudes; and some tribes which are known to us, here break into varieties which are infinitely better flavoured than the parent stock. Amongst such may be reckoned a sort of lobster, a crab of gentler kind, and various shell fish, entitled sea fruit in Italy, all which might well merit the eloquence of an Athenaeus.

But not to pass by the 'torte de lasagne', of which I had nearly lost sight, though its taste is fresh in my recollection: it is composed of oil, onions, paste, parsley, pine-nuts, raisins, currants, and candied orange peel, a dish which, you will recollect, is to serve as a prologue to fish or flesh!

It ought, however, to be stated that the ordinary pottage of this country, and which is, generally speaking, that of all ranks in Venice, requires no prejudices of education or habit to make it go down, but may be considered as a dish to be eat at sight. It consists in rice boiled in beef broth, not sodden, and 'rari nantes', as in England and France, but firm, and in such quantity as to nearly, or quite, absorb the 'bouillon' in which they are cooked: To this is added grated Parmesan cheese. And the mess admits other additions, as tomatos, onions, celery, parsley, etc. Rice thus dressed, which have drunk up the broth, are termed 'risi destirai', as capable of being spread, right or left, with the spoon. There is also a vulgar variety of the dish, termed 'risi a la bechera', or rice dressed butcher fashion. In this the principal auxiliary is marrow, which, if it is entirely incorporated in the grain, makes a pottage that (speaking after a friend) would almost justify the sacrifice of an Esau.

Ceremonies

[205] The Byzantine Emperor, John VIII Palaeologus, arrives in Venice in 1438 on his way to attend a Council at Ferrara, and is escorted from the Lido by the Doge and a fleet of ships; from *Chronicon* by George Phrantzes, edited by E. Bekken. Translated by John Julius Norwich.

(Phrantzes – or, more properly, Sphranzes – (1401–1478) was a Byzantine historian: he was not himself an eye-witness of this event, but claimed as his authority the Emperor's brother Demetrius, Despot of the Morea.)

I shall not describe the journey from Constantinople to Italy, as that would be superfluous and tedious. But how the Emperor made his entrance into Venice with those others that were with him, that shall I tell, because it was a glorious and festive scene and a story worthy of the telling . . .

On 7 February the triremes sailed all together from Parenzo into the open sea. But the Emperor's trireme, being faster than the rest, reached Venice before the others and on the 8th of the month, at seven o'clock in the morning, dropped anchor by the church of St Nicholas on the Lido. And a whole convoy of ships came out from the city of Venice to meet the Emperor, in such numbers that the sea was scarcely visible for the mass of vessels. The Senate, that is to say the Venetian signory, sent a representative with the message that the Emperor should not leave his trireme till the day following, since the Doge wished to call on him with the entire Senate, to bid him welcome; and so it came about. Then the Doge arrived with the great men of the city and all his Council, and made his reverence to the Emperor, who remained seated; and the Senators followed him, all bareheaded. To the right of the Emperor, and a little below him, sat his brother the Despot Demetrios; to his right the Doge. They spoke a few words of greeting to each other and then talked quietly among themselves; then the Doge said to the Emperor: 'Tomorrow I shall return with all these gentlemen, to do due honour to Your Majesty according to the will of God, and to lead Your Majesty formally into the city.'

And so the Doge and his Council withdrew. On the next day – it was Sunday, 9 February – the Doge returned at eleven in the morning, attended by his principal dignitaries, the members of the Senate and many noblemen from the Great Council, on a vessel which the Senate uses on such occasions and is called the Bucintoro. It was beautifully decorated and adorned with scarlet hangings, and had at its prow golden lions and cloth of gold, and was painted all over with brightly coloured pictures of every kind; one could see at a glance that it was the ship of a great chief of state. With him there came yet other ships, which the Latins call four-oared barges, some twelve in number, also decorated and painted inside and out, just like the vessel of the Doge himself. In them sat the Lords of the Great Council; and they carried golden banners and trumpets and musical instruments of all kinds.

There was one barge which sailed in front of all the rest and had been very specially decorated; this was called the Emperor's barge. And the crew of this vessel wore long robes embroidered with gold, and carried on their hats a badge with the symbol of St Mark the Evangelist (the lion) and beneath it the emblem of the Emperor (the double eagle)

while the military escort wore different robes and bore banners of various kinds. All around the ship there flew imperial
standards in great numbers, with golden ones in front, and
four men stood in the prow, wearing golden robes and red
wigs threaded with golden threads. In the middle of these
four there was another man, beautiful to look upon, who
sometimes sat, sometimes stood, his robes glistening with
gold, and holding in his hand a sceptre so that one could
easily see that he was captain of the ship. Around him stood
other men representing the princes of foreign lands, all glori-
ously robed in their different ways, who waited on him with
great reverence. And in the prow of the ship a sort of column
had been erected, on which was a square platform, each side
of it measuring scarcely an ell; and on this platform there
stood a man clad from head to foot in armour that shone like
the sun, holding a most fearsome sword in his two hands; to
his right and left sat two children, dressed as angels and with
angels' wings. And these were not simply illusions, but real
people who moved about. On the prow of the ship were
golden lions, and between them a double-headed eagle, and
other figures which I simply cannot describe. And the ship
moved fast, being sometimes ahead of the Emperor's trireme,
sometimes alongside it, while the sound of the trumpets rang
round about it. And so many other ships joined it, that there
was no counting them. Just as one cannot count the stars in
the heavens, or the leaves in the forest, or the grains of sand
in the sea, or the drops of rain, so was it with these vessels.

And – for I must delay no longer – the Doge now
approached the Emperor's barge with his retinue, came on
board and prostrated himself before the Emperor, who sat on
his throne while his brother, who was as I have said on his
right, occupied a seat a little below the imperial throne. Then
the Doge seated himself on the Emperor's left, on a chair
similar to the Despot's, and they clasped each other by the
hand and spoke amicably together. Then the two of them
sailed in great state, to the sound of trumpets and other kinds
of music, into the rich and lordly city of Venice, that most
wondrous of cities, so rich in colour and in accoutrements of
gold, exquisite as a perfectly carved sculpture, deserving of all
praises, that city of all wisdom, which might justly be

described as a second Promised Land. For it was of this place,
I believe, that the prophet spoke when he said, in the 23rd
Psalm, 'On the waters has God laid its corner stone'. For
what can one seek in Venice and not find? Truly is she worthy
of the highest praise.

It was about noon when they began their entry into the
city, and they continued their journey until sunset, when they
entered the palace of the Count of Ferrara. And the whole
city was agog in its eagerness to greet the Emperor, and there
was much noise and many cries of jubilation. Then could we
gaze with astonishment on that wonder, which we now saw
for the first time, the famous Temple of St Mark, the august
Palace of the Doges, and the other sumptuous palaces of the
nobles, embellished with reddish marble and gold, as beautiful
as beautiful can be. He who has not seen it will never believe
it and he who has seen it is unable to describe it, such is its
magnificence, so perfectly is it situated and so superbly built,
so intelligent are its men and women, and so vast the number
of its inhabitants, all of whom stood and rejoiced at the
arrival of the Emperor. Their souls were torn from their
bodies at the sight of such glory; indeed, they were quite
beside themselves and could well say: 'Earth and sea are
today become Heaven.'

For just as man cannot comprehend the works and wonders that God has created in heaven, but can only stand
amazed before them, so were they also filled with astonishment at what they saw that day. And as they reached the
great bridge that is called the Rialto, then was the bridge
raised, and the triremes passed beneath it. And there was a
great multitude present, and once again the golden standards,
the trumpets, the acclamations and the applause: in a word, a
most festive sight. Who could describe the honour that they
showed, the praises that they lavished on the Emperor? And
so, as I have said, they entered the palace of the Count, and
the trireme anchored there. It was the time of sunset: the
Doge and his councillors took leave of the Emperor and
returned to their homes.

[206] The festivities held in 1495 to celebrate the Venetian Republic's signature of a new international alliance; from *The Memoirs of Philip de Commines*.

After this I retired to my lodgings, and they sent for the rest of the ambassadors one after another. At my coming out of the council I met the Neapolitan ambassador in a fine new gown, and very gay; and indeed he had reason to be so, for this was a lucky turn of affairs for him. After dinner all the ambassadors of the league met together in boats upon the water (which in Venice is their chief recreation); the whole number of their boats (which are provided at the charge of the Signory, and proportioned to every man's retinue) was about forty, every one of them adorned with the arms of their respective masters; and in this pomp they passed under my windows with their trumpets and other instruments of music. The ambassadors of Milan (at least one of them), who had kept me company for many months, would take no manner of notice of me now. For three days together I and my domestics kept within doors; though indeed I cannot say either they or I were affronted all the while. At night there were extraordinary fire-works upon the turrets, steeples, and tops of the ambassadors' houses, multitudes of bonfires were lighted, and the cannon all round the city were fired. I was in a covered boat, rowing by the wharves to see this triumphal sight, about ten o'clock at night, especially before the ambassadors' houses, where there was great banqueting.

But this was not the day on which the league was proclaimed; for the Pope had sent to them to defer it for some days, till Palm-Sunday, at which time he had ordered that every prince in whose dominions it was published, and all the ambassadors then with him, should carry an olive-branch in their hand, in token of their alliance and peace; and that upon the same day it should be published both in Germany and Spain. At Venice they made a gallery of wood a good height above the ground (as they are wont to do at the inauguration of their Doges), which reached from the palace to the end of the piazza of St Mark; upon which (after mass had been sung by the Pope's nuncio, who absolved all people who were present at the solemnity) they marched in procession; the

Signory and the ambassadors all very splendidly dressed,
several of them in crimson velvet gowns which the Signory
had presented to them, at least to the Germans; and all their
retinue in new gowns, but these were a little of the shortest.
After the procession was ended, a great many pageants and
mysteries were exhibited to the people: first of all, Italy, and
then the allied kings and princes, and the Queen of Spain. At
their return, at a porphyry stone, where such things are
usually done, proclamation was made, and the alliance published. There was at that time a Turkish ambassador, who
looked privately through a window and saw this solemnity.
He had taken leave, but was asked to stay to see this festival;
and at night, by the assistance of a Greek, he paid me a visit,
and stayed four hours in my chamber; and his great desire
was to cultivate a friendship betwixt his master and mine. I
was twice invited to this feast, but desired to be excused; yet
I stayed nearly a month after in the town, and was all the
while as civilly entertained as before the publication of this
alliance. At length I was recalled; and, having had an audience
of leave, they gave me a passport, and conducted me safely to
Ferrara at their own expense. The Duke of Ferrara came in
person to meet me, and entertained me two days very handsomely at his own charge. The same civility I received at
Bologna from Prince John Bentivoglio; and, being sent for to
Florence, I continued there in expectation of my master's
coming, with the relation of whose affairs I shall now
proceed.

[207] In 1782, the Venetians welcome the future Tsar
Paul I, travelling with his wife under the romantic aliases
of 'Count and Countess of the North'; from *Venice, its
individual growth from the earliest beginnings to the fall
of the Republic* by Pompeo Molmenti, translated by
Horatio F. Brown.

But of all foreign princes the Grand Duke of Russia, Paul
Petrovitch, and his wife, Maria Teodorovna, were the most
splendidly entertained. It was the first time that a Russian
prince had come to the lagoons. The novelty of the visit

naturally added to the popular joy; moreover at that moment, Venice, for political reasons, desired to stand well with Russia. As the illustrious guests wished their visit to be private in character, the Doge did not take part in the reception, though nothing was neglected to amuse and delight the noble and unwonted visitors. The Procurator Pesaro and the Savio de Terraferma, Grimani, were charged to go as far as Conegliano to meet the royal guests, who were travelling under the title of Counts of the North. On their way from Mestre to Venice they were followed by a train of sumptuously decorated boats; the Rialto and the fondamenta were swarming with the populace, who applauded their passage. The evening of their arrival at the *Leon bianco* there was a reception given by the nobles at the Casino dei Filarmonici, where the prince and princess were received by about two hundred lacqucys dressed in velvet and gold. They were delighted with the masquerade, and were fascinated by the *brio* of the Venetian ladies presented to them by the Chevalieress Andriana Foscarini. The princess danced the minuet with Pesaro, who represented the Doge, at the ball given in the Teatro San Benedetto. The boxes assigned to the princess were transformed into so many elegant boudoirs decorated in papier-maché, with volutes, and carved and gilded stucco-work. The hall where dancing went on was adorned with festoons of blue silk with silver fringes, the stage with silver teas reliefs and great mirrors from Murano. At a huge table sat eighty ladies, with as many cavaliers behind their chairs. They also gave a concert of a hundred voices chosen from the various conservatories of the city; the entertainments closed with a regatta and a grand display on the Piazza di San Marco. In the middle was an amphitheatre of one thousand five hundred feet in circumference, with several tiers of steps, above which came the boxes, reaching to the height of the columns of the Procuratie. On one side of San Geminiano was a huge pavilion; at the other extremity, towards San Marco, rose a triumphal arch eighty feet high. The people were excluded from the show, and yet every box was full, and the tiers of steps swarmed with spectators. The subject of the procession was the 'Triumph of Peace'; the goddess entered seated on a great car, while Abundance crowned her head with olive and

Mars and Bellona lay at rest below her throne. She had sixteen musicians, and her car was preceded by four others, each drawn by eight pure white oxen. Presently some stout and brawny athletes, dressed to represent various nations, led in a bull tied by the horns with two long ropes; the baiting began, and when the show was over the barriers were removed and the mob poured into the midst of the arena, with cries of *Viva San Marco!*

[208] Ruskin, in light-hearted mood, describes in a letter to his father the welcome accorded to the Emperor Franz Josef in 1851, in St Mark's Square; from his *Letters from Venice 1851–52* edited by J. L. Bradley.

Sunday morning. [14 September 1851]
My dearest Father,

I hardly know whether it is Sunday or not – for last night everybody living on the Grand canal received a request from the Podesta that they would hang out carpets at ½ past six to do honour to the emperor who was to pass through Venice at seven – and accordingly we were waked at six by a cannonade which lasted with little intermission till ½ past 7; heavy firing from all the batteries and pontoons off the ducal palace – very pretty to look at – and shaking every pillar of the palace to its foundation – I doubt not more mischief has been done to it by this morning's work than by any five years of 'winter and rough weather' it has had to endure – But everybody thought it very fine of course – and the upper balconies of St Mark's were filled with people – (I never saw *one* there to look at the church – or at the bronze horses) and Effie and I went up to the top of the little red marble loggia of the campanile: where we saw all we wanted. The emperor is a well made youth, with rather a thin – ugly – not unpleasant face – he and Radetsky went about together looking just like a great white baboon and a small brown monkey; a barrel organ would have made the thing complete: St Mark's place had a file of soldiers all round it – a large body of men – I imagine about 3000 altogether: and at the door of the church there was a cushion – and the priests came out with the emperor and made him kneel down on it – and all the soldiers kneeled down too – and the chief priest held up his fingers after the manner of Wall in *Midsummer Night* – and then they all got up again – much edified: and a brown dog trotted right into the middle of the Emperor's staff and twice round his cushion – after the manner of Lance's dog – and I thought he was going to proceed to extremities – but he thought better of it, and went into the square and looked all round at the soldiers, and then cocked his tail, and went away home leaving two or three sentries in helmets in a state of indignation impossible to be described. So the soldiers defiled before the emperor, and the mob ran after them – the emperor and Radetsky letting anybody come near them who liked – at last he went away down the grand canal – which was all hung with carpets and tapestries, and looked like a street of old clothes warehouses from one end to another – and there was a great crowd of gondolas, and much splashing and swearing – and now everybody is gone home to breakfast – highly satisfied – and I am going to church. Dearest love to my mother. Ever my dearest Father,

Your most affect^e Son J. Ruskin.

[209] The entry of King Victor Emanuel into Venice on 10 September 1864; from *The Fourth Generation, Reminiscences* by Janet Ross.

(Janet Ross (1842–1927) settled in Tuscany in 1867 and wrote several books about Italian life and history. Earlier, she had spent six years in Egypt as correspondent for *The Times*.)

The entry of the King was a splendid spectacle. Victor Emanuel, ugly as he was, looked every inch a king as he stood on the prow of the *Bucentoro*, hailed with the wildest enthusiasm from the fleet of gondolas on the Grand Canal and by the crowd on shore. All the palaces had magnificent sheets of damask or embroideries hanging from their windows, even in the poorest quarters of the town something had been suspended, a counterpane, a shawl, or a small flag. The tri-colour waved everywhere, and patriotic songs resounded on all sides. The review on St Mark's Square roused the Venetians almost

to frenzy. When the agile little Bersaglieri tore round the
Piazza the people positively danced with excitement and
shouted themselves hoarse. Malet, who appeared in his red
Guard's uniform, was followed and cheered all the way to
our hotel – rather a trial for a shy Englishman. Suddenly I
heard my name, Janet, called from the crowd, and turning
round saw to my infinite joy my Poet. He was at Venice as
correspondent of the *Morning Post*, and as most of the party
I was with were bent upon bric-à-brac hunting, we made
several excursions together.

[210] An eye-witness account of the *Sposalizio del Mar*
in 1654; from Richard Lassels' *Voyage of Italy*.

We cast to be at Venise at the feast of the Ascension, and saw
the stately Sea triomph which they yearly celebrate upon this
day when the Duke is commonly sayd to marry the Sea, in
memory of the grant of Pope Alexander the Third, who
granted unto the Duke of Venise the Dominion over the
Adriatick Sea, as a husband hath dominion over his wife.

This Ceremony is performed thus: About our eight in the
morning the Senators in their scarlet gownes, come to the
Dukes pallace, and their taking him up, they walke in procession wise to the Shoare where the Bucentaure lyes at anker.
Then ascending into it by a hansome and said bridge the
Duke being accompanied by the Popes Nuncio and the
Patriarke of Venise, who sitt on either hand of him, and the
Senate round about the deck of the Bucentauro; the anker is
furthwith weighed and the Bucentauro beginns to move
gravely and slowly to the tune of trumpets and the musick of
the voyces which sing chearfull Hymeneal tunes. Round about
the Bucentauro are a thousand *Piottas* (or barges) and gondolas richly covered overhead with the richest canopies they
can make of velvets, silkes, satins, and broad gold laces; and
their watermen, that row them richly clad in livreys of taffetas
as allso their trumpeters in the same Livrye. Thus Embassadours of fforein Princes, and the noble men of the country
and strangers of quality waite upon the Duke's Galley for the
space of a good English mile, where the duke stopping and

throwing a ring into the Sea, is sayd to marry the Sea, and so
returning to a monastery in a Little Iland hard by, he heares
high Masse sung with excellent musick, and so returnes home
againe in the same triomphal manner he went out. I confesse,
of all the sights that ever I saw, nothing ever appeared to me
more maiesticall, then (standing upon the walls of the Castle
in the halfway) to see the Sea covered with such rich boates
(a thousand in number) all waiting upon the Bucentauro, as
if Neptune himself had been going to be marryed; and all
echoing with the fanfarres of trumpets.

[211] The Ascension Day celebrations in 1730; from
*Travels through Germany, Bohemia, Hungary, Switzer-
land, Italy and Lorrain* by Johann Georg Keysler.

The Ascension-festival affords all the diversions of the carnaval, as masquerades, opera's, *&c.* excepting the ridotto's and
the dissolute revels about the close of the latter. But to a
person of any taste the loss of those extravagant festivities is
sufficiently compensated by the delightfulness of the season,
the annual fair, and the solemnity of the *doge's* marriage with
the sea. The annual fair begins on the Sunday before Ascension-day, and lasts till Whitsunday. During this fair, St Mark's
Place is taken up with booths so arranged as to form several
streets; and all sorts of goods are exposed to sale at the shops
in the little streets called *Le Mercerie*, near the *Piazza di S.
Marco*. On Ascension-eve, vespers are performed with great
pomp and splendor, and the pretended miraculous blood of
Christ, with other remarkable relics kept in St Mark's treasury, are exposed to public view in the great church, which is
dedicated to that saint.

On Ascension-day, about ten o'clock in the morning, the
signal being given by a discharge of great guns and ringing of
bells, the *doge*, or, if he happens to be indisposed, the *vice-
doge* (who is always one of the six *consiglieri*) goes on board
the *bucentoro* or bucentaur, and, accompanied by several
thousand barques and gondola's, a great number of gallies
finely ornamented on that occasion, and the splendid yachts
of foreign ambassadors, is rowed out to sea about two

hundred paces, between the islands of St Erasmo and il Lido di Malamocco. The patriarch, (who on this day, according to an ancient custom, in commemoration of the simple diet of the primitive clergy, is entertained in the Olivetan convent, on the island of St Helena, with chesnuts and water) and several of the dignified clergy come on board the *bucentoro*, and present the *doge* and *signoria*, as they pass, with artificial flowers or nosegays, which, at their return, they make presents of to their acquaintance. The *doge*, at his putting off and return, is saluted by the cannon of a fort on the Lido, of the castle on the island Rasmo, or Erasmo, and with the small arms of the soldiers, who are drawn up along the Lido shore. These islands lie about two Italian miles from the city; and an eminence on the island of Lido affords a distinct view of this pompous processor, and of the vast number of boats, &c. which cover the surface of the water, and make a beautiful appearance. In the mean time several hymns are performed on board the *bucentoro*, by the band of music belonging to St Mark's church, and several prayers appointed for the occasion are read or sung, till the *doge* has passed the two forts of Lido and St Erasmo; and then he proceeds a little farther towards the Lido shore, the stern of his barge being turned towards the main sea. Here the patriarch pours into the sea some water, which has been consecrated with particular prayers, and is said to have the virtue of allaying storms and the fury of the waves. After this the *doge* drops a gold ring into the sea, through a hole near his seat, at the same time repeating these words, *Desponsamus te, mare, in signum veri perpetuique dominii; i.e.* 'We espouse thee, O sea, in sign of our real and perpetual dominion over thee.' The ring indeed is of gold, but is plain, and without any stones; so that it cannot be of any great value. This ceremony is said to have been first instituted by pope Alexander III in gratitude for the good offices which the Venetians had done him. For under the *doge*, Sebastiano Ziani, they defeated and took prisoner Otho, son of the emperor Frederic I. The truth of the whole story is dubious; but the circumstance of the emperor's purchasing the pope's pardon, with the scandalous submission of lying down and suffering the pope to tread on his neck, is without any foundation. However, on this day prints representing this extraordinary transaction, and paltry poems on the same subject, are publicly carried about and sold at Venice . . .

The *doge* in his return goes ashore at the island of Lido, where he hears mass performed by the patriarch in St Nicholas's church. In the evening the principal members of the council, and all who attended the *doge* in the *bucentaur*, are entertained at the *doge*'s palace; where the desert, which represents *gondola*'s, forts, *&c.* is exposed the whole day to the admiration of the populace . . .

[212] The Regatta in Venice; from *Venice, its individual growth from the earliest beginnings to the fall of the Republic* by Pompeo Molmenti, translated by Horatio F. Brown.

The regatta was the most peculiarly Venetian of spectacles, and therefore the most popular with strangers who visited the lagoon. The race started from the point of Sant' Antonio di Castello, followed the Grand Canal, and on reaching its end opposite the Ponte della Croce, turned round a pole (*paletto*) and retraced its course down the canal to the *macchina*, or pavilion erected on boats at the *volta di canal*, between the Foscari and Balbi palaces, where the prizes were delivered. There were four races and four prizes for each race. The first prize was a purse of money attached to a red flag, the second a green flag, the third a blue flag, the fourth a yellow flag with a porker painted on it, and a live porker as a jibe at the competitor's slowness. All the winners received money. Sometimes women took part in the races. The course was kept along the canal by the *bissone*, *peote*, *margarote*, *balotine*, boats of eight and more oars, sumptuously or fantastically adorned at the expense of wealthy patricians, or art guilds, while at the palace windows, hung with tapestries, carpets, and flags, stood the ladies of Venice, and the mob crowded the landing-places, the traghettos, and the innumerable boats of every build that followed the fortunes of the race.

For the regatta which the Duke of Brunswick arranged [in 1685] at his own expense he employed enormous mythological and symbolical figures decorated with a sumptuousness which was almost grotesque. At the winning post near the Palazzo Foscari a huge whale opened his jaws, whence issued a man dressed as a marine monster, who delivered the prizes.

[213] The regatta of 1740; from a letter of Lady Mary Wortley Montagu in *The Letters and Works of Lady Mary Wortley Montagu* edited by Lord Wharncliffe.

(Lady Mary Wortley Montagu (1689–1762) was the daughter of the first Duke of Kingston, and the wife of Edward Wortley Montagu, ambassador to Constantinople in 1716, with whom she had eloped at the age of twenty-three. She was well known for her letters, which give lively pictures of contemporary life and of the places she visited.)

You seem to mention the regatta in a manner as if you would be pleased with a description of it. It is a race of boats: they are accompanied by vessels which they call Piotes, and Bichones, that are built at the expense of the nobles and strangers that have a mind to display their magnificence; they are a sort of machines adorned with all that sculpture and gilding can do to make a shining appearance. Several of them cost one thousand pounds sterling, and I believe none less than five hundred; they are rowed by gondoliers dressed in rich habits, suitable to what they represent. There was enough of them to look like a little fleet, and I own I never saw a finer sight. It would be too long to describe every one in particular; I shall only name the principal: – the Signora Pisani Mocenigo's represented the Chariot of the Night, drawn by four sea-horses, and showing the rising of the moon, accompanied with stars, the statues on each side representing the hours to the number of twenty-four, rowed by gondoliers in rich liveries, which were changed three times, all of equal richness, and the decorations changed also to the dawn of Aurora and the mid-day sun, the statues being new dressed every time, the first in green, the second time red, and the last blue, all equally laced with silver, there being three races. Signor Soranzo represented the Kingdom of Poland, with all the provinces and rivers in that dominion, with a concert of the best instrumental music in rich Polish habits; the painting and gilding were exquisite in their kinds. Signor Contarini's piote showed the Liberal Arts; Apollo was seated on the stern upon Mount Parnassus, Pegasus behind, and the Muses seated round him: opposite was a figure representing Painting, with Fame blowing her trumpet; and on each side Sculpture and Music in their proper dresses. The Procurator Foscarini's was the Chariot of Flora guided by Cupids, and adorned with all sorts of flowers, rose-trees, &c. Signor Julio Contarini['s] represented the Triumphs of Valour; Victory was on the stern, and all the ornaments warlike trophies of every kind. Signor Correri's was the Adriatic Sea receiving into her arms the Hope of Saxony. Signor Alvisio Mocenigo's was the Garden of Hesperides; the whole fable was represented by different statues. Signor Querini had the Chariot of Venus drawn by doves, so well done, they seemed ready to fly upon the water; the Loves and Graces attended her. Signor Paul Doria had the Chariot of Diana, who appeared hunting in a large wood: the trees, hounds, stag, and nymphs, all done naturally: the gondoliers dressed like peasants attending the chase: and Endymion, lying under a large tree, gazing on the goddess. Signor Angelo Labbia represented Poland crowning Saxony, waited on by the Virtues and subject Provinces. Signor Angelo Molino was Neptune waited on by the Rivers. Signor Vicenzo Morosini's piote showed the Triumphs of Peace: Discord being chained at her feet, and she surrounded with the Pleasures, &c.

I believe you are already weary of this description, which can give you but a very imperfect idea of the show; but I must say one word of the bichonis, which are less vessels, quite open, some representing gardens, others apartments, all the oars being gilt either with gold or silver, and the gondoliers' liveries either velvet or rich silk, with a profusion of lace, fringe, and embroidery. I saw this show at the Procurator Grimani's house, which was near the place where the prizes were delivered: there was a great assembly invited on the same occasion, which were all nobly entertained.

I can get no better ink here, though I have tried several times, and it is a great vexation to me to want it.

[214] Mark Twain succumbs to a moonlight festival on the water; from *The Innocents Abroad*.

There was a fête – a grand fête in honor of some saint who had been instrumental in checking the cholera three hundred years ago, and all Venice was abroad on the water. It was no common affair, for the Venetians did not know how soon they might need the saint's services again, now that the cholera was spreading every where. So in one vast space – say a third of a mile wide and two miles long – were collected two thousand gondolas, and every one of them had from two to ten, twenty and even thirty colored lanterns suspended about it, and from four to a dozen occupants. Just as far as the eye could reach, these painted lights were massed together – like a vast garden of many-colored flowers, except that these blossoms were never still; they were ceaselessly gliding in and out, and mingling together, and seducing you into bewildering attempts to follow their mazy evolutions. Here and there a strong red, green, or blue glare from a rocket that was struggling to get away, splendidly illuminated all the boats around it. Every gondola that swam by us, with its crescents and pyramids and circles of colored lamps hung aloft, and lighting up the faces of the young and the sweet-scented and lovely below, was a picture; and the reflections of those lights, so long, so slender, so numberless, so many-colored and so distorted and wrinkled by the waves, was a picture likewise, and one that was enchantingly beautiful. Many and many a party of young ladies and gentlemen had their state gondolas handsomely decorated, and ate supper on board, bringing their swallow-tailed, white-cravatted varlets to wait upon them, and having their tables tricked out as if for a bridal supper. They had brought along the costly globe lamps from their drawing-rooms, and the lace and silken curtains from the same places, I suppose. And they had also brought pianos and guitars, and they played and sang operas, while the plebeian paper-lanterned gondolas from the suburbs and the back alleys crowded around to stare and listen.

There was music every where – chorusses, string bands, brass bands, flutes, every thing. I was so surrounded, walled in, with music, magnificence and loveliness, that I became inspired with the spirit of the scene, and sang one tune myself. However, when I observed that the other gondolas had sailed away, and my gondolier was preparing to go overboard, I stopped.

The fête was magnificent. They kept it up the whole night long, and I never enjoyed myself better than I did while it lasted.

[215] The celebrations in connection with the marriage of Jacopo, son of Doge Francesco Foscari, to Lucrezia Contarini in 1441; from *Venetian Life* by William Dean Howells.

A splendor so exceptional, even in the most splendid age of the most splendid city, as that which marked the nuptial feasts of the unhappy Jacopo Foscari, could not be left unnoticed in this place. He espoused Lucrezia, daughter of Lionardo Contarini, a noble as rich and magnificent as Jacopo's own father, the Doge; and, on the 29th of January, 1441, the noble Eustachio Balbi being chosen lord of the feasts, the bridegroom, the bride's brother, and eighteen other patrician youths, assembled in the Palazzo Balbi, whence they went on horseback to conduct Lucrezia to the Ducal Palace. They were all sumptuously dressed in crimson velvet and silver brocade of Alexandria, and rode chargers superbly caparisoned. Other noble friends attended them; musicians went before; a troop of soldiers brought up the rear. They thus proceeded to the court-yard of the Ducal Palace, and then, returning, traversed the Piazza, and threading the devious little streets to the Campo San Samuele, there crossed the Grand Canal upon a bridge of boats, to San Barnaba opposite, where the Contarini lived. On their arrival at this place the bride, supported by two Procuratori di San Marco, and attended by sixty ladies, descended to the church and heard mass, after which an oration was delivered in Campo San Barnaba before the Doge, the ambassadors, and a multitude of nobles and people, in praise of the spouses and their families. The bride then returned to her father's house, and jousts took place in the campos of Santa Maria Formosa and

San Polo (the largest in the city), and in the Piazza San Marco. The Doge gave a great banquet, and at its close one hundred and fifty ladies proceeded to the bride's palace in the Bucintoro, where one hundred other ladies joined them, together with Lucrezia, who, seated between Francesco Sforza (then General-in-chief of the Republic's armies) and the Florentine ambassador, was conducted, amid the shouts of the people and the sound of trumpets, to the Ducal Palace. The Doge received her at the rive of the Piazzetta, and, with Sforza and Balbi led her to the foot of the palace stairs, where the Dogaressa, with sixty ladies, welcomed her. A state supper ended this day's rejoicings, and on the following day a tournament took place in the Piazza, for a prize of cloth of gold, which was offered by Sforza. Forty knights contested the prize and supped afterward with the Doge. On the next day there were processions of boats with music on the Grand Canal; on the fourth and last day there were other jousts for prizes offered by the jewelers and Florentine merchants; and every night there were dancing and feasting in the Ducal Palace. The Doge was himself the giver of the last tournament, and with this the festivities came to an end.

[216] A grand Venetian wedding in 1771; from *Letters from Italy . . . in the years 1770 and 1771* by Anna, Lady Miller.

I could not comply with the obliging invitations we received to two wedding balls and suppers: one was the marriage of the Doge's son *Alvise Mocenigo, e la novil Donna Polissena Contarini*; the other was of *Alessandro Barziza, e Adriana Berlenda Berlandis*: though I could not partake of the amusements in the evenings, I thought I might possibly venture to see the ceremony in the church; we were accordingly present at the first of these, that of *Mocenigo*. I was extremely well pleased that I had not permitted so fine a show to escape me, though afflicted with a tormenting pain in my stomach the whole time. The procession of the gondolas to the church was very fine; the gondoliers, dressed in gold and silver stuffs, made a most brilliant contrast with the blackness of their boats. We got into the church before the bride and bride-groom with their *suite* arrived, where the pillars and walls were covered with crimson damask, fringed with gold; the altar richly adorned with lace and flowers, and the steps up to it spread over with Persian carpets; the whole church was illuminated with large wax tapers, though at noon-day.

As soon as the company were disembarked from their gondolas, they formed themselves into a regular procession; the ladies walked two and two: they were all dressed in thin black silk gowns (excepting the bride), with large hoops; the gowns are strait-bodied, with very long trains, like the *robes de cour* at Versailles; their trains tucked up on one side of the hoop, with a prodigious large tassel of diamonds. Their sleeves were covered up to the shoulders with falls of the finest Brussels lace, a drawn tucker of the same round the bosom, adorned with rows of the finest pearl, each as large as a moderate gooseberry, till the rows descended below the top of the stomacher; then two ropes of pearl, which came from the back of the neck, were caught up at the left side of the stomacher, and finished in two fine tassels. Their heads were dressed prodigiously high in a vast number of buckles, and two long drop curls on the neck. A great number of diamond pins and strings of pearl adorned their heads, with large *sultanes* or feathers on one side, and magnificent diamond ear-rings.

The bride was dressed in cloth of silver, made in the same fashion and decorated in the same manner with the other ladies; but her bosom was quite bare, and she had a fine diamond necklace and an enormous *bouquet* of natural flowers. Her hair was dressed as high as the others, with this difference, that it was in curls behind as well as before; and had three curls which fell down her back from her poll, the two side ones reaching half way down her back, and the middle curl not quite so far: these three curls had a singular appearance, but not near so good an effect as the heads of the other ladies, whose hair was plaited in large folds, and appeared much more graceful: her diamonds were very fine, and in great profusion. She is but seventeen years old; is of a comely sort of beauty, and very full grown of her age. All the ladies that walked, about sixty in number, were relations or intimate friends to the young couple; many of them extremely handsome. The men appeared to me to be all alike; they were dressed in black gowns like lawyers, with immense periwigs. The bridegroom is a slender fair little man, seemed to be much charmed with his new wife; he very politely sent us the *epithalamiums* and other poems made on the occasion, elegantly covered and adorned with engravings. I was extremely sorry at not being well enough to go to the ball and supper; however I persuaded M – to comply with their very polite invitation: he danced English country-dances, but did not stay to supper. I was not well enough to go to the other wedding; but he went, and it passed much in the same manner with the first. Is it not singular, that the Doge's dignity should forbid his being present at his own son's wedding?

[217] Carnival, from Boxing Day till Shrove Tuesday, has always been the most famous of Venice's festivities. In the mid-seventeenth century, however, it seems that Venice during the Carnival was not an altogether agreeable place to be; from *The Diary of John Evelyn* edited by William Bray.

1646. In January Sign. Molino was chosen Doge of Venice, but the extreame snow that fell, and the cold, hindered my going to see the solemnity, so as I stirred not from Padoa till Shrovetide, when all the world repaire to Venice to see the folly and madnesse of the Carnevall; the women, men, and persons of all conditions disguising themselves in antiq dresses, with extravagant musiq and a thousand gambols, traversing the streetes from house to house, all places being then accessible and free to enter. Abroad, they fling eggs fill'd with sweete water, but sometimes not over sweete. They also have a barbarous costome of hunting bulls about the streets and piazzas, which is very dangerous, the passages being generally narrow. The youth of the severall wards and parishes contend on other masteries and pastimes, so that 'tis impossible to recount the universal madnesse of this place during this time of licence. The greate banks are set up for those who will play at bassett; the comedians have liberty, and the operas are open; witty pasquils are thrown about, and the mountebanks have their stages at every corner. The diversion which cheifely tooke me up was three noble operas, where were excellent voices and musiq, the most celebrated of which was the famous Anna Rencha, whom we invited to a fish dinner after foure daies in Lent, when they had given over at the theater. Accompanied with an eunuch whom she brought with her, she entertain'd us with rare musiq, both of them singing to an harpsichord. It growing late, a gentleman of Venice came for her to shew her the gallys, now ready to sayle for Candia. This entertainment produced a second, given us by the English Consul of the merchants, inviting us to his house, where he had the Genoeze, the most celobrated base in Italy, who was one of the late opera band. This diversion held us so late at night, that conveying a gentle-woman who had supped with us to her gondola at the usual place of landing, we were shot at by two carbines from out another gondola in which was a noble Venetian and his courtezan unwilling to be disturb'd, which made us run in and fetch other weapons, not knowing what the matter was, till we were informed of the danger we might incur by pursuing it farther.

[218] Masks have always been a feature of Carnival, as they were in 1688 when Francis Misson described their uses; from his *A New Voyage to Italy*.

The Carnaval begins always the second Holiday after *Christmas*; that is, from that Time People are permitted to wear Masks, and to open the Play-Houses, and the Gaming-Houses. Then they are not satisfied with the ordinary Libertinism, they improve and refine all their Pleasures, and plunge into them up to the Neck. The whole City is disguis'd. Vice and Vertue are never so well counterfeited, and both the Names and Use of 'em is absolutely chang'd. The Place of St *Mark* is fill'd with a Thousand sorts of Jack-Puddings. Strangers and Courtesans come in Shoals from all parts of *Europe*: There is every where a general Motion and Confusion, as if the World were turn'd Fools all in an Instant. It is true, that the Fury of these Bacchanals does not rise suddenly to the height; there is some moderation in the beginning; but when they begin to be sensible of the dreaded approach of the fatal *Wednesday*, which imposes an universal Silence, then they celebrate their great Feasts, and all without reserve. Since it is true, that every thing must be ascrib'd to the Policy in *Venice*, you must suppose there are particular Reasons for the permitting of this Licentiousness during the Carnaval; but perhaps too we need not look for any Mystery. Two Things come into my Mind on this Occasion. The common People always love Sports and other Divertisements. As abominable as that Monster *Nero* was, he was lamented by the Rabble because of his Shows. I'm apt to think then, that the Nobility, who otherwise are not much beloved, are glad to find some cunning ways to please and amuse the People. At the last Carnaval, there were seven Sovereign Princes, and many Thousand other Foreigners: How much Money all this Multitude must bring to *Venice*? 'Tis the other Thing that seems to me of some Moment . . .

The Places which they call *Ridotti* are properly Academies of *Basset*: They are open'd at the same time with the Theatres; and there are none but *Noble-men* who keep the Bank. They dismiss the Gamesters when they please; and they have so much good Fortune joyn'd to their Privileges and Skill, that the Bank is always the Winner. There are Ten or Twelve Chambers on a Floor, with Gaming-Tables in all of them. You can scarcely turn your self in them; but tho' the Throng is so great, yet there is always a profound Silence. None are permitted to enter into these Places without Masks: at least a Postiche Nose, or a *Mustachio*. The Courtesans come thither in Shoals; and other Ladies also, who under the Shelter of their Masks may enjoy all the publick Pleasures of the Carnaval; but they are still follow'd by Spies, or by their Husbands. Besides the Chambers for Gaming, there are some Rooms for Conversation, where they also sell Liquors, Sweetmeats, and such-like Things. Nobody puts off his Mask, or Nose; and by the Privilege of this Disguise, provided a Man be pretty well dress'd, he may speak to the Ladies, and even to those whom he may suppose to be of the highest Quality: but must carefully avoid either the Saying or Doing of any thing that may give Offence, for the Mask is Sacred; and one will seem to take no notice of what is said to his Wife, that has many *Bravo*'s at his Devotion at the Doors: You know by that Name they call their Hectors and profess'd Murderers. Not that it is absolutely impossible to act a successful Piece of Gallantry with the best guarded Lady of 'em all, when they are not over severe. As the Difficulty augments Desire, so this Desire invents the Means; and those who understand the Practice of this Country, will do more with an Ogling Glance, than in other Countries by the longest assiduities: But all these things are out of my Sphere, and therefore I must beg Leave to go no further . . .

The greatest Masquerading is in the Place of St *Mark*; where the Croud is sometimes so great, that one cannot turn himself. You may put your self in what Equipage you please, but to do it well, you must be able to maintain the Character of the Person whose Dress you have taken. Thus, for Example, when the *Harlequins* meet, they jeer one another, and act a thousand Fooleries. The Doctors dispute; the Bullies vapour and swagger; and so of the Rest. Those who are not willing to be Actors on this great Theatre, take the Habit of *Noblemen*; some *Polonian* Dress, or the like, which obliges them to nothing. The Maskers are not permitted to wear Swords. The Women are also habited as they please, and some of 'em appear in most magnificent Dresses. At the same time the Place is filled with Puppet-shows, Rope-Dancers, and all such Sorts of People as you see in *London* at *Bartholomew-Fair*. But those which in my Opinion are the pleasantest of all, are a Kind of Almanack-makers and Fortune-tellers, who have their little Stages environ'd with Spheres, Globes, Astronomical Figures, Characters, and conjuring Books of all Sorts. These Pronouncers of Oracles have a long Tin Pipe, thro' which they speak in the Ear of the Curious, who stand below the Scaffold. They say more or less, according to the various Characters of the Consulters, and without seeming to take any notice, observe their Countenance. When they perceive they smile, or by some other Gesture denote their Approbation, they give over speaking a little, and ring a little Bell with wonderful Gravity, to intimate, that by virtue of their Art, they have dived into a very secret Affair, and succeeded very happily in their Divining. When they swear only *per Dio*, it signifies nothing; that is only a common Phrase, which no body regards. But when they would be believed, they call to witness the Saint of *Padua*, or the most blessed Lady of *Loretto*, and then all the Spectators put on a serious Face, and pull off their Hats as devoutly as if they were singing a Psalm at the Gallows. It is pleasant to see Priests and Monks of all Orders, so busie about that Pipe, that one wou'd think they fansie no body has Business to enquire after but themselves.

I will say nothing of the Bull-baitings, Goose-catching, Combats at *Coups de poing*, Balls, Races in *Gondola's*, or of their Feasting on *Shrove-Thursday*, on which Day they cut off a Bull's-Head, before the whole Senate, in memory of a Victory obtain'd in the *Friul*. These Stories are too long to be related; and may be found in several Books.

The Carnaval is not the only Time in which they wear Masks at *Venice*. They use 'em in all Feasts of Pleasure: With the Mask they run to the Audiences of Ambassadors: And on *Ascension-Day* all are masked from the Noblemen in the *Bucentauro*, to the Mob in the Streets.

[219] An expatriate Scot at the end of the seventeenth century condemns the Carnival as 'madness'; from *Letters from James Drummond, Earl of Perth* . . .

We arrived here about three weeks ago. The Carnevall took up ten days of it, where we saw what in Scotland would be thought downright madness; everybody is in a mask, a thing of tafeta, called a bahul, is put on the head, which covers one's face to the nose. The upper part is covered by people of quality with a white mask like what the ladys used to tye on with a chin-cloak long ago. The bahul hangs down about the shoulders a hand-breadth below the top of the shoulder. A Venetian nobleman's gown, an Armenian long garment furred, a vest called a Hongrois, which reaches to the knee, furred, or a plain scarlet, is what grave people wear; others are cloathed as they please, some like doctors of law, others with peacocks' trains and hatts as broad as six hatts, others as harlequins, ladys as country girls, and some as oddly as one's wildest dreams could represent them; *en fin*, no extravagant conceipt can outdo what one sees on St Mark's Place. Sometimes a company of noblemen and ladys dress themselves up like country people and dance torlanos in the open place, which is the frolick I saw that I like the best, for they dance scurvily when they pretend to French or English dances (for here they dance country dances at all their balls). A torlano is somewhat like the way our Highlanders dance, but the women do it much more prettily than the men. Sometimes you shall see a young pair of eyes with a huge nose and a vast beard playing on a guitar and acting like a mountebank. On one hand you shall hear a dispute in physick, turning all into ridiculous; on the other one, on a subject of law; some dialogues of mere wits, and things said that are surprizing enough. But on the whole matter St Mark's Place is like a throng of foolls. On Shrove Thursday a bull is beheaded by a butcher chosen by his fellows for that feat, and if he does it well in the presence of the Doge and all the Senate is treated *in serenissimo*, feasted, and has the best musick at supper that can be. He I saw do it did it cleverly at one blow, and did not seem to strain neither. The Doge's guards conducted him to and from the place, and a firework is sett on fire in fair daylight. A fellow is drawn upon a flying rope, such as mountebanks use, in a ship about the bigness of a gondola (which is a very long small boat), and all the way he fires gunns and throws grenade amongst the people, but they are only paper ones. Then he flyes down from the top of St Mark's steeple, where he had left his gondola. This steeple is disjointed from the church 70 or 80 paces. And thus they divert the people here to amuse them and keep them from frameing conceits of government and religion, such as our giddy people frame to themselves and make themselves the scorn and reproach of mankind; for now all goes under the name of English, and we are said to be so changeable and foolish that nothing from our parts seems strange. Beheading, dethroneing and banishing of kings being but children's play with us.

[220] The irresistible frivolity of Carnival in 1867 – the first Carnival after Venice was freed from Austrian domination; from Alexander Herzen's *My Past and Thoughts* translated by Constance Garnett.

There is no more magnificent absurdity than Venice. To build a city where it is impossible to build a city is madness in itself; but to build there one of the most elegant and grandest of cities is the madness of genius. The water, the sea, their sparkle and glimmer, call for a peculiar sumptuousness. Molluscs adorn their shells with mother-of-pearl and pearls.

A single superficial glance at Venice will show one that it is a city of strong character, of vigorous mind, republican, trading, oligarchical; that it is the knot tying something together over the waters – a warehouse for merchandise under a military flag, a city of noisy popular assemblies and a silent city of secret councils and measures; in its squares the whole population is jostling from morning till night, while the rivers of its streets flow silently to the sea. While the crowd surges and clamours in Saint Mark's Square, the boat glides by and vanishes unobserved. Who knows what is under its black awning? The very place to drown people, within hail of lovers' trysts.

The men who felt at home in the Palazzo Ducale must have been of a special caste of their own. They did not stick at anything. There is no earth, there are no trees, what does it matter? Give us more carved stones, more ornaments, gold, mosaics, sculptures, pictures, frescoes. Here there is an empty corner left: put a thin, wet sea-god with a beard in the corner! Here is a porch: get in another lion with wings, and a gospel of Saint Mark! There it is bare and empty: put a carpet of marble and mosaic! and here, lacework of porphyry! Is there a victory over the Turks or over Genoa? does the Pope seek the friendship of the city? Then more marble. A whole wall is covered with a curtain of carving, and above all, more pictures. Paul Veronese, Tintoretto, Titian must mount the scaffold with their brushes: every step of the triumphal progress of the Beauty of the Sea must be depicted for posterity in paint or sculpture. And so full of life was the spirit that dwelt in these stones that new routes and new seaports,

Columbus and Vasco da Gama, were not enough to crush it. For its destruction the 'One and Indivisible' republic had to rise up on the ruins of the French throne, and on the ruins of that republic the soldier who in Corsican fashion stabbed the lion with a stiletto poisoned by Austria. But Venice survived the poison and is alive again after half a century.

But is she alive? It is hard to say what has survived except the grand shell, and whether there is another future for Venice . . . And, indeed, what future can there be for Italy at all? For Venice, perhaps, it lies in Constantinople, in the free federation of the rising Slav-Hellenic nationalities, which begins to stand out in vague outlines from the mists of the East.

And Italy? . . . Of that later. Just now there is the carnival in Venice, the first carnival in freedom after twenty years' captivity. The Square has been transformed into the hall of the Parisian Opera. Old Saint Mark gladly takes his part in the fête with his pictures of saints and his gilt, with his patriotic flags and his pagan horses. Only the doves who come at two o'clock every day to the Square to be fed are shy and flutter from cornice to cornice to convince themselves that this really is their dining-room in such disorder.

The crowd keeps growing, *le peuple s'amuse*, plays the fool heartily with all its might, with great comic talent in declamation and language, in action and gesticulation, without the spiciness of the Parisian pierrots, without the vulgar jokes of the German, without our native filth. The absence of everything indecent surprises one, though the significance of it is clear. This is the recreation, the diversion, the playfulness of a whole people, and not the dress-parade of the brothels, of their *succursales*, whose inmates, while they strip off so much else, put on a mask, like Bismarck's needle on a gun, to intensify and make sure their aim. Here they would be out of place; here their sister, wife and daughter are diverting themselves, and woe to him who insults a mask. For the time of carnival the mask is for the woman what the Stainislay ribbon in his buttonhole used to be for a stationmaster.[1]

___

[1] A year ago I saw the carnival in Nice. There is a fearful difference; to say nothing of soldiers fully armed and the gendarmes and the commissaires of police with their scarves . . . the conduct of the people themselves, not of

At first the carnival left me in peace, but it kept growing, and with its elemental force was bound to draw everyone in.

Nothing is too nonsensical to happen when Saint Vitus' Dance takes hold of a whole population in fancy dress. Hundreds, perhaps more, of mauve dominoes were sitting in the big hall of a restaurant; they had sailed across the Square in a gilt ship drawn by bulls (everything that walks on dry land and with four legs is a luxury and rarity in Venice), now they were eating and drinking. One of the guests suggested a curiosity to entertain them, and undertook to obtain it; that curiosity was myself.

The gentleman, who scarcely knew me, ran to me at the Albergo Danieli, and begged and besought me to go with him for a minute to the masqueraders. It was silly to go, it was silly to make a fuss. I went, I was greeted with '*Evviva!*' and full glasses. I bowed in all directions and talked nonsense, the '*Evvivas*' were more hearty than ever; some shouted: '*Evviva el amico de'Garibaldi*', others drank to the *poeta Russo!* Afraid that the mauve masks would drink to me as the *pittore Slavo scultore i maestro*, I beat a retreat to the Piazza San Marco.

In the square there was a thick wall of people. I leaned against a pilaster, proud of the title of poet; beside me stood my conductor who had carried out the dominoes' *mandat d'amener*. 'My God, how lovely she is!' broke from my lips as a very young lady made her way through the crowd. My guide without a word seized me and at once set me before her. 'This is that Russian,' my Polish count began. 'Will you give me your hand after that word?' I interrupted. Smiling, she held out her hand and said in Russian that she had long wanted to see me, and glanced at me so sympathetically that I pressed her hand once more and followed her with my eyes so long as she was in sight:

'A blossom, torn by the hurricane, carried by the tide of blood from her Lithuanian fields!' I thought, looking after her. 'Your beauty shines for strangers now.'

---

the tourists, amazed me. Drunken masqueraders were swearing and fighting with people standing at their gates, while pierrots were violently knocked down into the mud – (Herzen's Note.)

[221] The last of the really great balls to be given in Venice was the so-called Beistegui Ball of September 1951. The preparations and the ball itself are here described by Susan Mary Alsop; from her *To Marietta from Paris.*

We are going to Italy again and I am a little worried about it. The first part of the trip will be heavenly, picture us bowling down the straight roads of France in a couple of weeks' time, guidebooks in hand, Sens, Auxerre, Avallon, Tonnere, Tanlay, Ancy-le-Franc (the last three are châteaux in Burgundy), eventually to arrive in Venice, for the ball given by Charlie de Bestegui which has been talked about in the papers as the most elaborate party given anywhere since before the war. Already when we were in Rome some of the principessas and comtessas were already worrying about their costumes, and I asked about the reaction of the mayor of Venice, who is a Communist, and of the poverty-stricken Venetian populace, only to be told that the Venetians will be simply delighted, being pleased by the publicity as well as the money the ball will bring to Venice, indirectly. But Bill and I are uncomfortable, torn between our Puritan consciences and our great curiosity to see the party. Curiosity wins, for we aren't likely to see anything like it again. Most great Venetian palaces are museums, or shuttered and quiet; for one night at least we shall be in eighteenth-century Venice.

Charlie de Bestegui is a very rich Spanish-Mexican whose genius is in decoration. Before the war he was famous in Paris as a bachelor whose taste ran to beautiful women and beautiful houses, but he outdid himself during the war which he spent, as a neutral with diplomatic status, restoring a large eighteenth-century château outside Paris, called Groussay . . .

8 September 1951

Well, I feel like Stendhal's young hussar in *Le Rouge et le Noir* trying to describe the Battle of Waterloo . . . We arrived at the Europa Hotel to find a huge crowd all down the Grand Canal waiting for a regatta which was about to take place. As my things were taken out of the motor launch (I was carrying all of Odette's as well as my own), a cry of 'Bestegui, Bestegui' went up from the crowd and everyone laughed. You can imagine we trembled with shame and horror, but most surprisingly, the tone was friendly then and the next night . . .

The next morning broke grey with black clouds – no one dared to call up the Palazzo Labia, but word came that Charlie was taking his tapestries in and out of the courtyard as the clouds got blacker or lightened, and that he was *très courageux* . . .

The day was a kaleidoscope of strange and wonderful sights – Diana [Cooper] being dressed by both Oliver Messel and Cecil Beaton and at the same time stitching away at a sack for Duff to tie around his waist to hold a flask, as he discovered that he had no pocket in his domino and was taking no chances at a Bestegui party. Harry's Bar at lunch filled with people saying to each other triumphantly, 'they say they have some spirit gum left at a shop near the Rialto.' David Herbert in the piazza carrying a broken drum, looking as if he was going to cry, saying, 'Does anyone know where one can get a skin for a red Indian drum?' Monsieur Antonio and Monsieur Alexander and all the other good Paris hairdressers running through the streets like Paul Reveres, carrying gold lacquer and white powder from hotel to hotel. Three men from Time-Life leaving our hotel in masques and dominos cunningly concealed their camera. Oh, so many funny sights and, of course, every dressmaker and pansy in the world, but they somehow seemed submerged, and this is true of the whole week, by the genial friends who were there too, and we all had such fun laughing, and everyone was in such a good humor, that it wasn't a bit like the horrible atmosphere the newspapers have described . . .

All the way to the Palazzo Labia, and you remember how far it is, the bridges and the sides of the canals were jammed with people, clapping each gondola as it went by and shouting how beautiful and have a good time! At the piazza by the palace, there were grandstands and four thousand people standing. We arrived just as Diana did, and it was an unforgettable sight, fifty or more gondolas circling for the landing stage, filled with people in beautiful costumes – Diana's gondola coming through them, and she stepping out assisted by her Negro pages. She turned on the landing wharf to look down at the scene, and I don't think I ever saw anything more beautiful than that – the light from the palace windows falling on her face and the pearls and the blonde hair (a wig just the color of her own hair but done like the Tiepolo picture [of Cleopatra, which hung in the Labia palace]). Her dress was blue brocade, very decolletée and in shape just like the picture, which you will remember is roughly Queen Elizabeth shape or a bit later, very becoming to her. We then went upstairs and watched the entrées come in – you have seen the palace, so I won't describe it, and you will see pictures of the clothes. I was most impressed by the Italian women – the French clothes were perhaps better, but the Italians more beautiful; the four seasons done by four very young Italian princesses was a sensational entrée.

The only bad costumes were Marie Laure de Noailles' – monstrous as the Lion of St Mark – and the Jacques Faths, all glittering gold, white, and like an oversweet dessert. Barbara Hutton, referred to in the papers as having spent fifteen thousand on her costume, was identical with Tony Pawson – in fact, everyone got them mixed up all evening . . . Funniest entree was the Chachavadze – Elizabeth as Catherine the Great, stupendous in black velvet, preceded by what was said to be her lovers, but looked a motley group to me. Besides Potemkin, there were Chips Channon and P. Coats as Bonnie Prince Charlie and the British Ambassador, and there was old Baroness Lomonaco as the Irish patriarch and lots of unidentifiable figures. There had been a placement row about Elizabeth's dinner, as someone said that Bonnie Prince Charlie and the British Ambassador couldn't sit together at the Empress of Russia's table or couldn't sit ahead of each other, or something. This had been referred to Duff, who said that the Empress would never have asked them together anyway and to leave him alone with the *Times* crossword, for God's sake . . .

Because of Charlie's beastliness about invitations, the house was not crowded nor hot – in fact, it was a splendid party entirely apart from the spectacles. Lots of the best kind of supper and lots of anything one wanted to drink – everyone in a good humor, two good jazz orchestras. I had never expected to enjoy myself but really did. Every time one went to a balcony, the crowd roared applause, and I never saw one policeman or heard one hiss – on the contrary, cries for Don Carlos, which is what the Venetians call Charlie!

Envoi

Once did she hold the gorgeous East in fee,
And was the safeguard of the West: the worth
Of Venice did not fall below her birth,
Venice, the eldest child of liberty.
She was a maiden city, bright and free;
No guile seduced, no force could violate;
And when she took unto herself a mate,
She must espouse the everlasting sea.
And what if she had seen those glories fade,
Those titles vanish, and that strength decay,
Yet shall some tribute of regret be paid
When her long life hath reached its final day:
Men are we, and must grieve when even the shade
Of that which once was great has passed away.

Wordsworth

O Venice! Venice! when thy marble walls
 Are level with the waters, there shall be
A cry of nations o'er thy sunken halls,
 A loud lament along the sweeping sea!
 If I, a northern wanderer, weep for thee,
What should thy sons do? – anything but weep:
And yet they only murmur in their sleep.
In contrast with their fathers – as the slime,
The dull green ooze of the receding deep,
Is with the dashing of the spring-tide foam
That drives the sailor shipless to his home,
Are they to those that were; and thus they creep,
Crouching and crab-like, through their sapping streets.
Oh! agony – that centuries should reap
No mellower harvest! Thirteen hundred years
Of wealth and glory turn'd to dust and tears
And every monument the stranger meets,
Church, palace, pillar, as a mourner greets;
And even the Lion all subdued appears,
And the harsh sound of the barbarian drum,
With dull and daily dissonance, repeats
The echo of thy tyrant's voice along
The soft waves, once all musical to song,
That heaved beneath the moonlight with the throng
Of gondolas – and to the busy hum
Of cheerful creatures, whose most sinful deeds
Were but the overbeating of the heart,
And flow of too much happiness, which needs
The aid of age to turn its course apart
From the luxuriant and voluptuous flood
Of sweet sensations, battling with the blood.

Byron

Bibliography

ALSOP, SUSAN MARY, *To Marietta from Paris 1945–1960*, New York, 1975

ARETINO, PIETRO, *Aretino, Selected Letters*, transl. and with an introduction by George Bull, London, 1976

BARETTI, JOSEPH, *An Account of the Manners and Customs of Italy; with Observations on the Mistakes of some Travellers with Regard to that Country*, London, 1768

BECKFORD, WILLIAM, *Italy, with Sketches of Spain and Portugal*, London, 1834

BERNIS, CARDINAL DE, *Memoirs and Letters of Cardinal de Bernis*, transl. by Katharine Prescott Wormeley, London, 1902

BLESSINGTON, COUNTESS OF, *The Idler in Italy*, London, 1840

BROOKE, RUPERT, *Letters*, chosen and edited by G. Keynes, London, 1968

BROSSES, PRÉSIDENT CHARLES DE, *Selections from the Letters of de Brosses*, transl. by Lord Ronald Sutherland Gower, London, 1897

BROWN, HORATIO F., *Venice, an Historical Sketch of the Republic*, London, 1893

——, *Life on the Lagoons*, London, 1884

BROWNING, ELIZABETH BARRETT, *Elizabeth Barrett Browning's Letters to Mrs David Ogilvy 1849–1861*, edited by Peter N. Heydon and Philip Kelley, New York, 1973

BROWNING, ELIZABETH BARRETT and ROBERT, *Letters of the Brownings to George Barrett*, edited by Paul Landis with the assistance of Ronald E. Freeman, Illinois, 1958

BROWNING, ROBERT, *More than Friend, the Letters of Robert Browning to Katharine de Kay Bronson*, edited, with an Introduction, by Michael Meredith 1985

BULL, GEORGE, *Venice, the Most Triumphant City*, London, 1980

BURNET, G., DD, *Letters containing an Account of what seem'd most remarkable in travelling thro' Switzerland, Italy and some Parts of Germany, in the Years 1685 and 1686*, London, 1724

BURNEY, DR CHARLES, *The Present State of Music in France and Italy*, London, 1773

BRYON, LORD, *'The Flesh is Frail', Byron's Letters and Journals*, edited by Leslie A. Marchand, London, 1973–82

——, *Letters and Journals of Lord Byron, with Notices of his Life*, by Thomas Moore, London, 1833

CASANOVA DE SEINGALT, JACQUES, *The Memoirs of Jacques Casanova de Seingalt*, transl. by Arthur Machen, 6 vols, London, 1958–60

CASOLA, CANON PIETRO, *Canon Pietro Casola's Pilgrimage to Jerusalem in the Year 1494*, by M. Margaret Newett, Manchester, 1907

COMMINES, PHILIP DE, *The Memoirs of Philip de Commines, Lord of Argenton*, edited with Life and Notes by Andrew R. Scoble, 2 vols, London, 1901

CORYAT, THOMAS, *Coryat's Crudities, Reprinted from the Edition of 1611 ... being a more particular Account of the Travels (mostly on Foot) in Different Parts of the Globe, than any hitherto published*, 3 vols, London, 1776

DANTI, ALIGHIERI, *Inferno*, translated by Dorothy L. Sayers, London, 1949

DAVID, ELIZABETH, *Italian Food*, London, 1954

CHARLES DICKENS, *The Letters of Charles Dickens*, edited by Kathleen Tillotson, Oxford, 1977

——, *The Letters of Charles Dickens*, edited by his sister-in-law and his eldest daughter, London, 1880

DISRAELI, BENJAMIN, *The Letters of Benjamin Disraeli, Earl of Beaconsfield*, London, 1887

DOBSON, MRS, *The Life of Petrarch*, 2 vols, London, 1805

DRUMMOND, JAMES, *Letters from James Drummond, Earl of Perth, to his sister the Countess of Errol and other members of his family*, edited by W. Jerdan, London, 1845

EASTLAKE, ELIZABETH, LADY, *The Journals and Correspondence of Lady Eastlake*, edited by Charles Eastlake Smith, 2 vols, London, 1895

EVELYN JOHN, *The Diary of John Evelyn*, edited by William Bray, London, 1890

FELIX FABRI, *Felix Fabri*, transl. by Aubrey Stewart, London, 1892

GIBBON, EDWARD, *The Letters of Edward Gibbon*, 3 vols, edited by J. E. Norton, London, 1956

GOETHE, J.W., *Italian Journey, 1786–1788*, transl. by W. H. Auden and Elizabeth Mayer, London, 1962

HAZLITT, WILLIAM, *Notes of a Journey Through France and Italy*, London, 1826

HERZEN, ALEXANDER, *My Past and Thoughts*, transl. by Constance Garnett, 6 vols, London, 1924–7

HOWELL, JAMES, *Epistolae Ho-Elianae, or Familiar Letters*, 2 vols, edited by J. Jacobs, 1890

HOWELL, WILLIAM DEAN, *Venetian Life*, Boston, 1881

JAMES HENRY, *Italian Hours*, London, 1909

——, *The Letters of Henry James*, edited by Leon Edel, 4 vols, London, 1974–84

——, *The Wings of the Dove*, London, 1902

KELLY MICHAEL, *Reminiscences*, London, 1826

KEYSER, JOHANN GEORG, *Travels through Germany, Bohemia, Hungary, Switzerland, Italy and Lorrain*, 4 vols, London, 1760

LASSELS, RICHARD, *The Voyage of Italy*, Paris, 1670

LAWNER, LYNNE, *Lives of the Courtesans: Portraits of the Renaissance*, New York, 1987

LITHGOW, WILLIAM, *The Totall Discourse of The Rare Adventures and Painefull Peregrinations of long Nineteene Yeares Travoyles from Scotland to the most famous Kingdomes in Europe, Asia and Affrica*, Glasgow, 1906

LUYTENS, MARY, *Effie in Venice: her picture of society life with John Ruskin, 1849–52*, London, 1965

MALIPIERO, DOMENICO, *Annali Veneti dall'anno 1457 al 1500*, edited by T. Gar and A. Sagredo, Florence, 1843

MANN, THOMAS, *Death in Venice*, translated by H. T. Lowe-Porter, London, 1928

MENDELSSOHN-BARTHOLDY, FELIX, *Letters from Italy and Switzerland*, transl. from the German by Lady Wallace, London, 1860

MILLER, ANNA, LADY, *Letters from Italy, describing the Manners, Customs, Antiquities, Paintings, Etc. of that Country, in the Years 1770 and 1771*, London, 1776

MISSON, F.N., *A New Voyage to Italy, with Curious Observations on several Other Countries*, London, 1714

MOLMENTI, POMPEO, *Venice, its individual growth from the earliest beginnings to the fall of the Republic*, transl. by Horatio F. Brown, London, 1908

MOORE, JOIIN, MD, *A View of Society and Manners in Italy, with Anecdotes relating to some Eminent Characters*, London, 1787

MOORE, THOMAS, *see* Byron

MORRIS, JAMES (now JAN), *Venice*, London, 1960

MORYSON, FYNES, *An Itinerary written by Fynes Moryson, Gent., first in the Latin tongue and then translated by him in to English: containing his Ten Yeers Travell through the Twelve Dominions of Germany, Behmerland, Sweitzerland, Netherland, Denmarke, Poland, Italy, Turky, France, England, Scotland and Ireland. Divided into III Parts*, London, 1617

NEWETT, M. MARGARET *see* Casola

NORWICH, JOHN JULIUS, *Venice: The Rise to Empire*, London, 1977

——, *Venice: The Greatness and the Fall*, London, 1981

——, *A History of Venice* (the above volumes published in one volume) London, 1982

PETRARCH, FRANCESCO, *Epistolae de rerum familiaribus et variae*, edited by G. Fracassetti, 3 vols, Florence, 1859–63

PHRANTZES, G., *Chronicon*, edited by E. Bekker, Corpus Scriptorum Historiae Byzantinae, Bonn, 1829–97

PIOZZI, MRS HESTER, *Glimpses of Italian Society in the Eighteenth Century*, London, 1892

RAY, DR JOHN, FRS, *Observatzons ... made on his journey*

through Part of the Low Countries, Germany, Italy and France, London, 1673

ROSS JANET, *The Fourth Generation, Reminiscences*, London, 1912

ROTH, CECIL, *Personalities and Events in Jewish History*, Philadelphia, 1961

ROUSSEAU, JEAN JACQUES, *The Confessions of Jean Jacques Rousseau*, London, 1874

RUSKIN, JOHN, *The Stones of Venice* (5th edition), London, 1893

——, *Letters from Venice 1851–52*, edited by J. L. Bradley, Yale, 1978

SANUDO, MARIN, *Diarii*, 58 vols, Venice, 1879–1903

SAYERS, DOROTHY L., *see* Dante

SHARP, SAMUEL, *Letters from Italy, describing the Customs and Manners of that County, In the years 1765 and 1766*, London, 1767

STENDHAL (MARIE HENRI BEYLE), *Rome, Naples and Florence*, transl. by Richard N. Coe, London, 1959

SYMONDS, JOHN ADDINGTON, *Letters*, edited by H. M. Schneller and R. L. Peters, Detroit, 1967–69

SYMONDS, A. J. A., The Quest for Corvo, London, 1966

TAFUR, PERO, *Travels and Adventures 1435–1439*, transl. and edited with an Introduction by Malcolm Letts, London, 1926

THOMAS, WILLIAM, *The History of Italy (1549)*, edited by H. B. Parks, Ithaca, New York, 1963

TWAIN, MARK, *The Innocents Abroad*, Connecticut, 1869

——, *A Tramp Abroad*, London, 1880

VASARI, GIORGIO, *Lives of the Artists, a selection*, transl. by George Bull, London, 1965

——, *Lives of the Most Eminent Painters, Sculptors and Architects*, 10 vols, transl. by Gaston du C. de Vere, London, 1912–14

VILLEHARDOUIN, GEOFFREY DE, *La Conquête de Constantinople*, Paris, 1939

WAGNER RICHARD, *My Life*, transl. by Andrew Gray, edited by Mary Whittall, Cambridge, 1983

——, *Richard to Minna Wagner, letters to his first wife*, transl. by William Ashton Ellis, London, 1909

WALPOLE, HORACE, *The Letters of Horace Walpole*, 42 vols, edited by W. S. Lewis *et al.*, London, 1937–81

WORTLEY MONTAGU, LADY MARY, *The Letters and Works of Lady Mary Wortley Montagu*, edited by Lord Wharncliffe, in 2 vols, London, 1861

WOTTON, SIR HENRY, *Letters and Dispatches from Sir Henry Wotton to James the First and his Ministers in the Years 1617–20*, London, 1850

—, *Reliquiae Wottonianae* ... by the Curious Pencil of the Ever Memorable Sir Henry Wotton Kt, Late Provost of Eton College.

YOUNG, ARTHUR, *Travels in France and Italy in the Years 1787, 1788 and 1789*, London, 1915

Index

INDEX OF PLACES

GENERAL INDEX